AI and Digital Nomads Shaping Global Industrial Technology Transitions

Patricia Ordóñez de Pablos
Universidad de Oviedo, Spain

Xi Zhang
Tianjin University, China

Muhammad Anshari
Universiti Brunei Darussalam, Brunei

Mohammad Nabil Almunawar
Universiti Brunei Darussalam, Brunei

IGI Global
Scientific Publishing
Publishing Tomorrow's Research Today

Vice President of Editorial Melissa Wagner
Director of Acquisitions Mikaela Felty
Director of Book Development Jocelynn Hessler
Production Manager Mike Brehm
Cover Design Jose Rosado

Published in the United States of America by
IGI Global Scientific Publishing
701 East Chocolate Avenue
Hershey, PA, 17033, USA
Tel: 717-533-8845
Fax: 717-533-7115
Website: https://www.igi-global.com E-mail: cust@igi-global.com

Library of Congress Cataloging-in-Publication Data

Names: Ordóñez de Pablos, Patricia, 1975- editor | Zhang, Xi, 1982- editor | Anshari Ali, Muhammad, 1977- editor | Almunawar, Mohammad Nabil, 1960- editor
Title: AI and digital nomads shaping global industrial technology transitions / edited by Patricia Ordóñez de Pablos, Xi Zhang, Muhammad Ali, Mohammad Nabil Almunawar.
Description: Hershey, PA : IGI Global Scientific Publishing, [2026] | Includes bibliographical references and index. | Summary: "Advanced digital technologies are crucial to build sustained competitive advantages for companies and countries in the digital age. Innovative ideas, products and services can have a positive impact on economies and societies and prepare us for a more resilient future"-- Provided by publisher.
Identifiers: LCCN 2024055582 (print) | LCCN 2024055583 (ebook) | ISBN 9798337301594 h/c | ISBN 9798337301600 s/c | ISBN 9798337301617 ebook
Subjects: LCSH: Artificial intelligence--Industrial applications | Telecommuting--Technological innovations | Artificial intelligence--Economic aspects | Globalization
Classification: LCC TA347.A78 A3874 2025 (print) | LCC TA347.A78 (ebook)
LC record available at https://lccn.loc.gov/2024055582
LC ebook record available at https://lccn.loc.gov/2024055583

British Cataloguing in Publication Data
A Cataloguing in Publication record for this book is available from the British Library.

Table of Contents

Detailed Table of Contents

The fusion of Industry 5.0 and Society 5.0 is driving sustainable transformations and human-centric innovations that enhance smart manufacturing and resilient communities. This chapter explores how AI, IoT, blockchain, and digital twins boost human-machine collaboration, leading to improved efficiency and industrial resilience. Innovations also introduce challenges, such as ethical AI and workforce adaptation. Society 5.0 aims to create smart ecosystems that foster economic progress, while Industry 5.0 emphasizes human-driven decision-making and circular economy practices to minimize environmental impact. The chapter analyzes challenges and opportunities, providing strategies to bridge gaps and accelerate sustainable innovations for an intelligent future.

The rise of Industry 5.0 observes a major shift toward the integration of cutting-edge technologies such as Artificial intelligence with the global economic landscape. The purpose of this chapter is to explore the importance of AI adoption in promoting digital economies, illuminating the connectivity of technology, firm strategies, and human resources. Besides, it also highlights transformative potential and the challenges associated with organizational change by addressing the complexities and implications of AI adoption. Essential components of this research are the Technology, Organization and People (TOP) framework, in which an organizational perspective is a comprehensive approach to understanding and improving AI adoption. The findings of this study will contribute to bridging gaps in present knowledge by

Preface

INTRODUCTION

Advanced digital technologies are crucial to build sustained competitive advantages for companies and countries in the digital age. Innovative ideas, products and services can have a positive impact on economies and societies and prepare us for a more resilient future.

The convergence of artificial intelligence (AI) and the digital nomad phenomenon has become a transformative force in contemporary industrial technology transitions. A digital nomad is someone who earns a living by working remotely and independently through digital means. As remote working capabilities expand and AI systems grow increasingly sophisticated, we are witnessing the emergence of a globally distributed workforce that operates beyond traditional geographical constraints. This shift is fundamentally reshaping the dynamics of industrial innovation, transitioning from centralised corporate research hubs to a decentralised network of knowledge workers contributing to technological advancement from virtually anywhere in the world. Digital nomads, equipped with AI-powered tools and platforms, are emerging as pivotal agents in accelerating technology transfer and the exchange of ideas across diverse industrial sectors.

The symbiotic relationship between AI and digital nomadism is redefining the nature of industrial expertise and knowledge creation. Machine learning algorithms empower mobile professionals to access, analyse, and synthesise vast quantities of industrial data in real time, while their geographic mobility enables them to observe and engage with technological challenges across varied markets and cultural contexts. This distinctive combination fosters the development of more adaptive and contextually responsive solutions to industrial problems. Furthermore, AI-enabled communication and collaboration platforms are dismantling conventional disciplinary boundaries, facilitating the formation of interdisciplinary teams of digital nomads equipped to address complex industrial challenges that necessitate diverse perspectives and skill sets.

The implications for global industrial technology transitions are both profound and impactful. Nations and regions that embrace this distributed innovation model stand to benefit from enhanced access to global talent and accelerated knowledge exchange, whereas those adhering to rigid, location-dependent paradigms risk marginalisation within an increasingly competitive global landscape. Moreover, the integration of AI and digital nomadism is contributing to the democratisation of innovation by lowering the capital thresholds required for technological development, thereby enabling smaller enterprises and emerging actors to compete alongside established industrial incumbents.

OBJECTIVES OF THE BOOK

The book provides innovative knowledge and insights into crucial issues for competitiveness of countries and nations today. In particular this book:

- Explores challenges and opportunities of AI in the digital age
- Discusses experience of AI in different industries (healthcare, manufacturing, etc)
- Analyses digital nomads, labor mobility and digital tools
- Addresses emerging topics in the field of technology policy
- Provides recommendations for AI policies and industry policies
- Wide coverage of different sectors and industries

IMPACT

The expected impact of the book has several dimensions:

- Scientific dimension: contributes to the advance of 3 main key fields: artificial intelligence, digital transformation and the future of industry.
- Economic dimension: offers valuable knowledge to different stakeholders about opportunities offered by the application of AI in different fields and the creation of new jobs. Discover how AI can boost the transition towards greener and digital economies. Explore the role of AI in the green and blue economy. Analyze inclusive economic growth in the digital age.
- Societal dimension: it highlights the key role of AI in the creation of more inclusive societies.

CONTENTS OF THE BOOK

The book is formed by a collection of 8 chapters that address key issues to understand digital transformation and digital nomads today. From artificial, digital transformation and intelligence and organizational learning to digital nomads, e-commerce and sustainability, the book will provide valuable knowledge and insights to understand better the opportunities and challenges of the green transition in the digital age.

Chapter 1, titled "The Learning Loop - Mastering and Enabling AI in Organizations" (by Teresa Aires and Jeff Schatten) analyses "the recursive relationship between artificial intelligence and organizational learning, which manifests as organizations develop AI competencies while deploying AI to strengthen their learning capabilities. The AI Learning Loop framework illuminates how these processes create cycles of advancement, where each improvement in AI mastery enhances an organization's capacity to learn. As organizations progress through the Loop's eight phases, they build capabilities through structured training programs, experiential learning, and AI-enhanced systems that impact employee retention, financial performance, and adaptability. This chapter examines key implementation challenges, presents organizational readiness frameworks, develops comprehensive learning strategies, and explores emerging trends in AI-enabled learning. The comprehensive examination offers theoretical understanding of AI's role in organizational learning and actionable guidance for strategic planning and implementation in diverse organizational contexts".

Chapter 2, titled "Leveraging AI and Digital Solutions to Enhance Sustainability in Green and Blue Economies" (by Pinnika Yadav, PB Kiran, Rajesh Vemula, Vikas Kumar, Preeti Kumari and Ruben Michael), provides discussion on "how digital solutions, including artificial intelligence (AI), drive sustainability in terrestrial (green) and aquatic (blue) economies. By examining case studies and technological implementations, it highlights the potential and challenges of digital innovations, particularly AI, in promoting environmental sustainability, economic growth, and social well-being. The study covers the current state of green and blue economies, digital interventions like smart agriculture, renewable energy, marine monitoring, and sustainable fisheries, and their impacts. The research uses both qualitative and quantitative methods, gathering data through interviews, surveys, and literature. Results will provide success stories, challenges, and best practices, offering recommendations for policymakers and stakeholders. The study aims to contribute to the theoretical and practical understanding of how digital technologies, especially AI, can advance sustainability in these economies, with future research directions identified".

Chapter 3, titled "Digital Nomadism and AI Pioneering the Future of Global Industry Transitions" (by Tiago Cardoso), affirms that "the digital age, driven by artificial intelligence (AI) and digital nomadism, is reshaping global industries and societies. AI enhances productivity, optimizes processes, and enables real-time decision-making, fostering innovation and economic growth. Simultaneously, digital nomadism challenges traditional work models by promoting a mobile, borderless workforce that drives creativity and technological adoption. Despite these opportunities, disparities in digital access and ethical concerns demand inclusive policies to ensure equitable growth and societal cohesion. Addressing job displacement, skills development, and ethical AI implementation is crucial for a sustainable future. This chapter highlights the transformative potential of AI and digital nomadism while emphasizing the need for strategies that align technological progress with human-centric values and sustainability".

Chapter 4, titled "AI-Driven Digital Nomads-Transforming Labor Markets and Industrial Growth in the Digital Economy" (by Muhammad Usman Tariq), explores "the transformative effect of AI-driven digital nomadism on global labor markets and industrial development in the digital economy. AI technologies empower digital nomads by aiding flexible, location-independent work and breaking down terrestrial and socioeconomic barriers. This change is driving a revolution across technology, healthcare, and creative sectors, as digital nomads control AI to access global prospects, work together remotely, and contribute to particular fields. The chapter studies how AI simplifies the growth of freelance economies, supports cross-border mobility, and nurtures inclusivity, allowing marginalized groups to participate in the digital economy. Moreover, it addresses issues relevant to labor laws, taxation, and healthcare accessibility, supporting AI-driven policy reforms to defend digital nomads' rights".

Chapter 5, titled "The Rise of Digital Nomad Visas: Transforming Global Work, Travel, and Local Economies" (by Thandayuthapani S and Thirumoorthi P), states that "the coming of computerized Wanderer Visas denotes an extraordinary change in worldwide work and travel elements, reshaping both nearby economies and labor force versatility. These visas enable telecommuters to thrive in new environments and contribute financially, free from traditional business constrain. This paper examines the evolution and impact of advanced migrant visas, focusing on their role in promoting financial flexibility in developed nations, enhancing local labor markets, and promoting sustainable travel industry models. ls. Through examination of contextual investigations and strategy structures, it surveys what these visas mean for social and financial scenes, upholding versatile approaches that upgrade shared benefits for advanced travelers and host networks".

Chapter 6, titled "Digital Leadership in Education AI and Digital Nomadism Transforming Global Learning Landscapes" (by Ahmed Alkaabi, Ahmad Qablan, Hesham Badawy, Hosam Badawy, Khawla Hassan Almaazmi, Sumayya Andi and Asma Yousaf Khan), states that "the educational sector has witnessed a paradigm shift with the advent of Artificial Intelligence (AI) and digital leadership. In this chapter, we explore how AI technologies are reshaping leadership practices, curriculum delivery, and workforce management in the educational sphere. Special emphasis is placed on digital nomadism and its implications for leadership in globally interconnected institutions. By analyzing case studies from the UAE, KSA, and Qatar, the chapter examines how educational systems in these countries integrate AI and digital strategies to address localized and global challenges. Policy recommendations are provided to guide effective AI adoption and inclusive educational practices globally".

Chapter 7, titled "Human-Centric Innovations and Sustainable Transformations-Bridging Industry 5.0 and Society 5.0 for Smart Manufacturing and Resilient Communities" (by Raffi Mohammed, Prasad Babu Bayrisetti, Chiranjeevi Aggala, Subramanya Sarma S, Kiran Kumar Bunga, Subhani Mohammed, Ranga Jarabala and Jagan Mohan Rao Saride), notes that "the fusion of Industry 5.0 and Society 5.0 is driving sustainable transformations and human-centric innovations that enhance smart manufacturing and resilient communities. This chapter explores how AI, IoT, blockchain, and digital twins boost human-machine collaboration, leading to improved efficiency and industrial resilience. Innovations also introduce challenges, such as ethical AI and workforce adaptation. Society 5.0 aims to create smart ecosystems that foster economic progress, while Industry 5.0 emphasizes human-driven decision-making and circular economy practices to minimize environmental impact. The chapter analyzes challenges and opportunities, providing strategies to bridge gaps and accelerate sustainable innovations for an intelligent future".

Finally, Chapter 8, titled "Transformation to Digital Economy in The Era of Industry 5.0: AI Adoption with Technology, Organization and People (TOP) Framework" (by Syed Mudasser Abbas and Muhammad Irshad) affirms that "the rise of Industry 5.0 observes a major shift toward the integration of cutting-edge technologies such as Artificial intelligence with the global economic landscape. The purpose of this chapter is to explore the importance of AI adoption in promoting digital economies, illuminating the connectivity of technology, firm strategies, and human resources. Besides, it also highlights transformative potential and the challenges associated with organizational change by addressing the complexities and implications of AI adoption. Essential components of this research are the Technology, Organization and People (TOP) framework, in which an organizational perspective is a comprehensive approach to understanding and improving AI adoption. The findings of this study will contribute to bridging gaps in present knowledge by clarifying key factors in influencing AI integration and providing visions to lead strategies in the transforming digital economy".

Patricia Ordóñez de Pablos
The University of Oviedo, Spain

Muhammad Anshari
Universiti Brunei Darussalam, Brunei

Mohammad Nabil Almunawar
Universiti Brunei Darussalam, Brunei

Chapter 1

The Learning Loop: Mastering and Enabling AI in Organizations

Teresa Aires
https://orcid.org/0009-0002-2865-6194
Nova School of Business and Economics, Portugal

Jeff Schatten
Washington and Lee University, USA

ABSTRACT

The Learning Loop: Mastering and Enabling AI in Organizations focuses on the recursive relationship between artificial intelligence and organizational learning, which manifests as organizations develop AI competencies while deploying AI to strengthen their learning capabilities. The AI Learning Loop framework illuminates how these processes create cycles of advancement, where each improvement in AI mastery enhances an organization's capacity to learn. As organizations progress through the Loop's eight phases, they build capabilities through structured training programs, experiential learning, and AI-enhanced systems that impact employee retention, financial performance, and adaptability. This chapter examines key implementation challenges, presents organizational readiness frameworks, develops comprehensive learning strategies, and explores emerging trends in AI-enabled learning. The comprehensive examination offers theoretical understanding of AI's role in organizational learning and actionable guidance for strategic planning and implementation in diverse organizational contexts.

DOI: 10.4018/979-8-3373-0159-4.ch001

INTRODUCTION: THE DUAL NATURE OF AI AND ORGANIZATIONAL LEARNING

"We now accept the fact that learning is a lifelong process of keeping abreast of change. And the most pressing task is to teach people how to learn." – Peter Drucke

Peter Drucke's observation gains renewed significance as organizations navigate not only the challenge of understanding AI but also the complexities of learning through it. The interplay between artificial intelligence and organizational learning reveals a compelling duality. Organizations must both master AI technologies and leverage these same technologies to enhance their learning capabilities. This dual process highlights the importance of comprehending two interconnected concepts found in the AI Learning Loop: organizational learning and the learning organization.

Organizational learning is defined as "a process in which an organization's members actively use data to guide behavior in such a way as to promote the ongoing adaptation of the organization" (Edmondson & Moingeon, 1998, p. 28). In the AI Learning Loop, organizations engage in a deliberate process of developing AI competencies through both constant learning and practical application. Conversely, the learning organization embodies the structural framework that systematically facilitates this learning. As Örtenblad (2018) explains, it represents an organizational form designed to support continuous transformation and adaptation. While organizational learning describes how companies evolve through experience and develop AI skills, the learning organization outlines the architectural elements (AI systems) that sustain such learning effectively.

This duality fosters an intriguing recursive relationship termed as the AI Learning Loop: as organizations learn to implement AI systems, these systems, in turn, enhance the organization's capacity to learn. Grasping this relationship is essential as companies strive to thrive in an increasingly AI-driven business environment. Not only that, but recent research shows organizations with integrated AI and organizational learning capabilities are 1.6 times more likely to manage various environmental uncertainties than organizations with limited learning capabilities (Ransbotham et al., 2024). The following sections examine each phase of the AI Learning Loop, delving into how organizations harness AI technologies and, reciprocally, how these technologies facilitate more effective organizational learning. Each chapter provides practical insights with application tips.

The Learning Loop: Theoretical Foundations

The relationship between artificial intelligence and organizational learning represents a unique evolution of established organizational theory. This chapter introduces the AI Learning Loop (Figure 1) to conceptualize the recursive relationship between AI implementation and organizational learning capabilities. Drawing from Edmondson and Moingeon's (1998) distinction between organizational learning processes and learning organization structures, this framework illustrates how AI both requires learning processes to implement effectively and enhances structural learning capabilities once deployed. This dual relationship creates a virtuous cycle where improvements in one area accelerate developments in the other, leading to continuous organizational evolution. The AI Learning Loop also draws upon and extends other established theoretical perspectives.

A. Senge's Mental Models and Systems Thinking

Building on Senge's (1990) mental models and systems thinking—his third and fifth disciplines—, the AI Learning Loop represents a contemporary application of his foundational concepts. Senge's (1990) concept of mental models refers to assumptions that influence how humans view the world and consequently act. These mental pictures matter to organizations because they enable and prevent ideas to be implemented depending on how much these ideas conflict with existing mental models (Senge, 1990). In Phase 2 (Knowledge Acquisition Through Experience) of the AI Learning Loop, organizations acquire knowledge through daily experiences with AI and must challenge their implicit assumptions about AI capabilities and limitations to move to Phase 3 (AI Enhancement of Individual Capabilities), where they enhance individual capabilities. As teams document lessons about AI implementation and share insights across the organization in Phase 2, they engage in what Senge described as "surfacing and testing mental models" (p. 18). This process allows organizations to move beyond merely adapting to AI technologies and toward using AI to fundamentally enhance their learning capabilities.

Senge (1990) also distinguished between adaptive learning - where organizations simply respond to environmental changes - and generative learning - where organizations expand their capabilities. This distinction helps explain how organizations evolve from adapting to AI technologies to leveraging these technologies for deeper organizational transformation. The feedback loop between implementing AI and enhancing organizational learning capability creates what Senge (1990) described as "creative tension" - that productive gap between current organizational reality and aspirational vision (p. 9). Organizations experiencing this tension have two paths forward: either elevate current capabilities toward the vision, or adjust expectations to match present realities (Senge, 1990, p. 9). This tension drives progress as organizations strive to close the gap between their AI aspirations and current implementation levels.

Senge's (1990) creative tension is present in the AI Learning Loop as organizations work to close the gap between their current AI capabilities and their vision of becoming more effective learning organizations. Systems thinking, another cornerstone of Senge's (1990) work, offers organizations a framework for navigating this tension by focusing on "interrelationships, not things, and processes, not snapshots" (p. 14). Such a holistic perspective becomes particularly relevant during Phase 5 of the AI Learning Loop (Creating Integrated Learning Systems) when organizations develop integrated learning ecosystems. In this mature phase, organizations transcend the limited view of AI as merely another technological tool. Instead, they recognize the intricate connections between technological implementation and broader organizational learning processes. The systems perspective enables organizations to create environments where human capabilities and artificial intelligence mutually reinforce each other. And as with Senge's learning laboratories, which provide "practice fields for management teams" (p. 21), Phase 5 creates environments where technology and human learning processes reinforce each other, enabling what Senge characterized as the shift from adaptive to truly generative learning.

B. Davis's Technology Acceptance Model

For organizations just beginning their AI journey, Davis's (1989) Technology Acceptance Model provides key insights into the initial adoption phase. When examining Davis's (1989) model, two critical factors emerge that shape technology adoption. Perceived usefulness represents the degree to which individuals believe implementing a particular system will enhance their job performance - essentially the anticipated benefits or advantages the technology offers (Davis, 1989). Perceived ease of use, in contrast, concerns the degree to which potential users expect the system will require minimal effort to learn and integrate into their workflow (Davis, 1989). These constructs help explain why technically superior solutions sometimes fail to gain traction when users perceive them as either offering insufficient benefit or demanding excessive effort to master. They should thus guide early AI implementation approaches, as organizations must deliberately address both the practical value proposition (perceived usefulness) and accessibility concerns (perceived ease of use) to encourage widespread adoption. Neglecting either dimension typically results in resistance or superficial implementation that fails to deliver substantive organizational benefits.

TAM's emphasis on cognitive mechanisms underlying acceptance decisions also informs Phase 2 of the model. Davis's (1989) research demonstrates that users' early perceptions significantly influence their willingness to engage with technologies in ways that produce experiential knowledge. These insights illuminate how organizations progress through the Learning Loop, as positive perceptions established in Phase 1 (Initial AI Learning & Implementation) create the foundation for deeper experiential engagement and knowledge acquisition in subsequent phases.

C. Venkatesh et al.'s (2003) Unified Theory of Acceptance and Use of Technology (UTAUT)

With the Unified Theory of Acceptance and Use of Technology, Venkatesh and colleagues (2003) added moderating factors and additional determinants to earlier models. These factors help explain how organizations surpass basic implementation and enter sustainable learning systems. Through the identification of four factors driving user adoption - performance expectancy, effort expectancy, social influence, and facilitating conditions - Venkatesh et al. (2003) extend Davis's (1989) Technology Acceptance Model. What makes their framework particularly valuable for understanding AI adoption is how it recognizes that these factors do not operate uniformly across all contexts. Their research showed that variables like gender, age, previous tech experience, and whether people have a choice in using the technology significantly reshape how the main factors play out in practice (Venkatesh et al., 2003). This approach helps explain why AI implementations that succeed in one context might struggle in another, despite similar technical merits.

D. The Recursive Relationship in the Learning Loop

While TAM and UTAUT primarily focus on technology acceptance, the AI Learning Loop extends these frameworks by recognizing the recursive relationship between AI implementation and learning capabilities. Venkatesh et al. (2003) acknowledged this potential recursivity when they noted that prior experience with technology influences future adoption decisions. The AI Learning Loop goes further by demonstrating how this experience actively transforms organizational learning capabilities. This dual relationship creates a virtuous cycle where improvements in one area accelerate developments in the other, leading to continuous organizational evolution.

The back-and-forth relationship present in the AI Learning Loop connects well with how Rai, Constantinides, and Sarker (2019) think about human-AI partnerships in digital settings. They describe different levels of how people and AI work together—from basic replacement (where AI takes over human tasks) to enhancement (where people and AI make each other better) to integration (where humans and AI blend together as an integrated system) (Rai, Constantinides, & Sarker, 2019). These patterns of collaboration offer additional insight into how the recursive relationship manifests in practice. For example, organizations may begin with AI substituting for basic learning tasks, move toward augmentation as they gain experience, and eventually develop assemblages where the boundaries between human and AI contributions to organizational learning become less distinct. The type of hybrid relationship an organization develops will influence how it moves through the Learning Loop phases and how it experiences the virtuous cycle of organizational evolution described above.

The AI Learning Loop (see figure 1) consists of eight interconnected phases that organizations typically progress through as they develop AI learning relationships. While presented sequentially for clarity, these phases often overlap, and organizations may move through them at different rates for different applications. The following sections explore each phase in detail, drawing upon both theoretical insights and practical implementation experiences from diverse organizational contexts.

Figure 1.

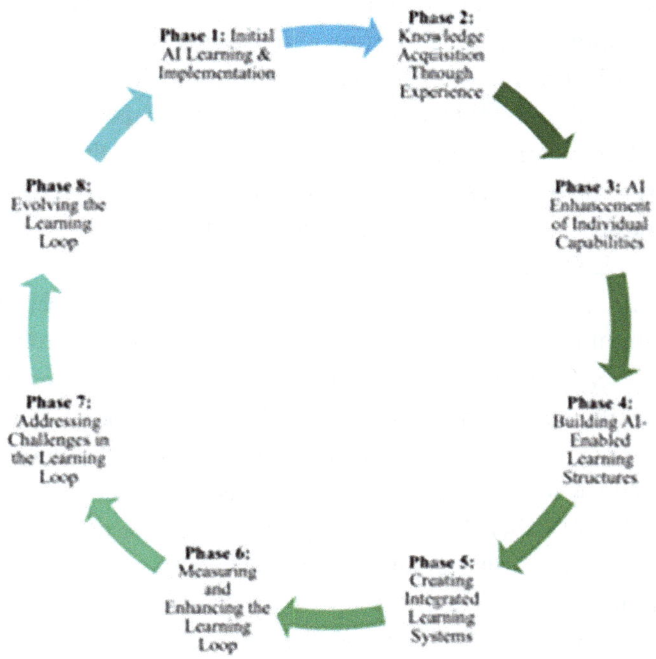

Application Tips

- Challenge implicit assumptions about AI capabilities to accelerate learning progress
- Use systems thinking to identify interconnections between AI implementation and learning outcomes
- Address both perceived usefulness and perceived ease of use in early implementation phases
- Consider moderating factors like experience and social influence when planning adoption strategies
- Document how your organization progresses through different phases of AI maturity

Phase 1: Initial AI Learning & Implementation

Large organizations have figured out organized ways to build AI skills across their teams. Microsoft shows this well with their Microsoft Learn platform—an online training center that creates custom, flexible learning journeys for different Microsoft tools and services, including AI and cloud computing. It integrates AI-driven skill assessments and certification processes, enabling learners to showcase expertise in areas crucial to today's fast-evolving job market (Graceffo, 2024).

Beyond education, Microsoft Learn also emphasizes assessment and certification. Microsoft's certifications are increasingly valued credentials as employers seek AI-ready talent (Graceffo, 2024; Deloitte Insights, 2020). Initiatives like the Azure AI Fundamentals Certification address the rising demand for AI literacy in the business realm. This program provides a thorough introduction to AI concepts, making them accessible to professionals from diverse backgrounds (Danfernandezmsft, Saldana, Supernova-eng, & Dend, 2020).

The curriculum covers essential AI topics such as machine learning, computer vision, and natural language processing. It is designed to offer a robust foundation in AI principles, catering to both newcomers and seasoned professionals aiming to broaden their skill sets (Microsoft Certified: Azure AI Fundamentals, 2024). The certification serves as a valuable credential, indicating a baseline understanding of AI technologies and their business applications. For instance, Microsoft Learn Expert Tiago Costa (2024) shares the story of a long-time help desk professional who transitioned to an Azure architect role after moving into cloud computing as an Azure administrator.

Microsoft Learn exemplifies the learning loop concept in action and stands as a potent tool for learning organizations. As AI keeps changing rapidly, training materials are constantly refreshed to keep up with industry shifts and new tech developments. This ongoing updating helps people learn information that's useful right now, creating a workplace where continuous learning becomes second nature. Not only that but Azure specifically targets Davis's (1989) dimensions of perceived usefulness and perceived ease of use by demonstrating the business value of AI while making complex concepts accessible to professionals from diverse backgrounds. As Microsoft showcases a structured digital learning approach, other organizations have developed comprehensive workplace-based programs that seamlessly integrate AI training into their operational frameworks.

IKEA's extensive AI literacy initiative illustrates how large organizations can embed technical learning within their existing workflows. Announced in early 2024, IKEA Retail set ambitious goals to provide AI training to around 30,000 workers and 500 leaders across the organization (Crist, 2024a; Ingka Group, 2024). IKEA's approach is distinctive in its focus on practical application over purely theoretical knowledge. The company has crafted a multi-tiered training ecosystem, ranging from basic AI fundamentals accessible to all employees to specialized courses in responsible AI and algorithmic ethics (Crist, 2024a).

What distinguishes IKEA's approach is how thoroughly they customize training programs based on organizational roles. The company designs specific learning pathways matched to various levels and job responsibilities throughout their hierarchy.

While providing foundational AI courses as a common baseline for all employees, they strategically offer specialized training in critical areas such as responsible AI implementation and generative AI capabilities (Crist, 2024a). Leadership development is specifically addressed through programs like AI Exploration Days, which assist leaders in connecting AI capabilities with strategic business objectives (Crist, 2024a). This structured yet flexible approach reflects Francesco Marzoni, Global Data and Analytics Officer at IKEA Retail, commitment to futureproofing their workforce while maintaining innovation leadership (Crist, 2024a).

The practical essence of IKEA's learning approach is demonstrated through tools like Hej Copilot, developed in partnership with Microsoft. This AI tool is seamlessly integrated into employees' daily workflows, aiding tasks such as image creation, idea generation, and presentation design (Ingka Group, 2024). According to Francesco Marzoni, this approach offers “a blended experience for learning,” merging theoretical knowledge with practical application to ensure workforce readiness for future innovations (Ingka Group, 2024).

IKEA's approach mirrors wider workforce developments, responding to increasing staff interest in AI skill development. The human-centered implementation philosophy becomes evident in their Digital Ethics Stance & Policy, which explicitly places employees “at the forefront of all technological adoption” (Ingka Group, 2024). This thoughtful equilibrium demonstrates how organizations can advance technologically while building employee capabilities, making AI knowledge development central to organizational growth rather than treating it as a separate technical project.

PricewaterhouseCoopers (PwC) offers another compelling example of building AI capabilities systematically across a professional services organization. PwC has established itself among the leading AI consulting firms through a substantial $1 billion investment over three years to modernize technology infrastructure, develop personnel skills, and establish partnerships with Microsoft and OpenAI (McGregor, 2024). Their approach spans their entire workforce of 75,000 professionals worldwide (McGregor, 2024).

PwC developed a unique learning model centered on peer education. Instead of solely depending on external trainers or centralized learning programs, they identified and trained experienced staff members to mentor their colleagues within each department (Joffe, 2024). PwC’s approach ensures that AI training is directly relevant to specific team needs and challenges. The firm's strategy evolved from early lessons on effective AI implementation. Their experience revealed that technical training alone was insufficient for meaningful adoption (Joffe, 2024). This understanding shaped their certification framework, which integrates technical education with practical applications customized to specific employee responsibilities (Joffe, 2024).

Organizations build AI competence most effectively by blending structured educational programs with practical application opportunities, while simultaneously using these technologies to enhance their learning methodologies. This reciprocal relationship positions AI beyond merely another capability to develop—it becomes a catalyst fundamentally transforming how organizations evolve and generate knowledge.

Application Tips

- Create role-specific AI training pathways rather than one-size-fits-all programs
- Balance theoretical knowledge with hands-on application opportunities
- Implement peer education models where experienced staff mentor colleagues
- Demonstrate business value early to address perceived usefulness concerns
- Integrate AI learning into existing workflows rather than treating it as separate

Phase 2: Knowledge Acquisition Through Experience

NTT DATA, a Japanese global IT company that focuses on digital transformation, consulting, and managed services in various industries, has around 200,000 employees and shows a thorough approach to organizational learning in today's AI landscape. They have created a structured GenAI Talent Development Framework with four expertise levels, from basic knowledge to advanced leadership skills (NTT DATA Establishes Generative AI Talent Development Framework, 2024). Their framework is tailored to specific roles, meeting the different learning needs of consultants, developers, and sales teams (Stokes, 2024). This approach works particularly well in places like India, where NTT DATA has its biggest overseas workforce of 40,000 people, showing the framework can scale across different cultural settings (Ghai, 2024). Davis's (1989) Technology Acceptance Model helps explain why NTT DATA's approach works so well - it addresses both how useful employees perceive the technology to be (through role-specific customization) and how easy they think it is to use (through graduated skill levels), which encourages people to engage with AI tools.

Their strategy emphasizes four key areas critical to organizational AI learning:

- **Data Literacy:** Using AI effectively requires a basic understanding of data concepts throughout the organization. This goes beyond just technical skills - people need to think critically about data quality, recognize potential biases, and understand limitations.

- **AI Tool Familiarity:** Regular hands-on use of AI tools builds practical understanding and comfort with what AI can and cannot do. Using the tools teaches far more than just reading about them.
- **Ethical AI Usage:** Daily practice helps organizations work through the ethical aspects of using AI. This includes creating practical guidelines for responsible use and helping people recognize potential biases and risks.

The current skills landscape across industries reveals a blend of formal instruction and practical application. Successful AI adoption requires both structured learning programs and opportunities for experiential learning through daily work activities.

The Estée Lauder Companies (ELC) illustrates this blend of structured and experiential learning through their market-responsive AI applications (Ransbotham et al., 2024). The global beauty leader employs sophisticated "fuzzy matching" algorithms to identify existing products that rapidly meet emerging consumer trends in the volatile cosmetics industry (Ransbotham et al., 2024). This AI-driven approach enables ELC to quickly repackage and reposition items in their extensive product portfolio when sudden demand shifts occur, turning potential market disruptions into strategic advantages (Ransbotham et al., 2024). Their day-to-day application of AI for trend detection creates valuable organizational knowledge that transcends formal training programs (Ransbotham et al., 2024). As teams repeatedly use these tools to respond to market fluctuations, they develop nuanced understanding of both AI capabilities and implementation constraints that would be impossible to acquire through theoretical instruction alone.

ELC's incremental approach to building AI capabilities is supported by Davenport and Ronanki's (2018) research, which found that organizations achieve greater success with focused, practical AI applications than with highly ambitious transformational projects. Their analysis shows that organizations benefit most from starting with 'low-hanging fruit' that enhance specific business processes rather than attempting comprehensive organizational transformation (Davenport & Ronanki, 2018).

Learning Through Failure

While successful AI deployments provide valuable examples, implementation failures often deliver equally important organizational lessons. Unsuccessful AI projects can often reveal critical gaps in organizational readiness, implementation approaches, and technology-business alignment that might otherwise remain undetected. Organizations that systematically analyze these outcomes accelerate their AI learning trajectories.

To extract value from implementation challenges, organizations should establish formal processes that examine both technical and organizational factors. Psychological safety—defined as "a climate of mutual respect and caring" where employees feel confident taking risks without jeopardizing their jobs (Edmondson, 1999, p. 375)—is particularly critical when learning from AI failures. When organizations create psychologically safe environments, team members can openly talk about failed implementations without worrying about being blamed or punished, which turns potential failures into valuable learning experiences for everyone. Organizations should care as research has consistently shown that psychological safety leads to better employee engagement, improved performance, more creativity (Frazier et al., 2017), and more knowledge sharing (Zhang, Fang, Wei, & Chen, 2010). When teams feel safe discussing AI project problems—whether technical issues, process misalignments, or unrealistic expectations—they feed into a continuous improvement loop that makes future implementations better. Without this safety, important insights often stay hidden because employees don't want to report problems with AI systems, which ultimately slows down how quickly the organization can learn and adapt.

The dual approach to learning AI reflects the iterative nature of organizational learning, where reflection and action form an ongoing cycle. Effective AI adoption requires more than technical training; it demands a holistic strategy that integrates both capability development and deeper understanding. As organizations build AI proficiency through structured programs and everyday applications, they simultaneously leverage these technologies to enhance their own learning processes. This creates a recursive dynamic: greater AI understanding enables more advanced learning systems, which in turn accelerate AI adoption. NTT DATA's framework demonstrates how mastering AI fundamentals creates the foundation needed to implement the more sophisticated learning technologies we'll explore next.

This approach aligns with research by Davenport and Ronanki (2018), who categorize AI applications into three types: process automation, cognitive insights, and cognitive engagement. Their study of 152 projects found that organizations typically begin with process automation (47% of projects), followed by developing cognitive insights (38%), with more complex cognitive engagement applications appearing later (16%). Understanding this progression helps organizations plan their AI learning journey strategically.

Application Tips

- Develop systematic ways to capture lessons from daily AI interactions
- Foster psychological safety so teams openly discuss implementation challenges

- Encourage regular reflection on both successful and unsuccessful AI initiatives
- Create knowledge repositories that make experiential insights accessible across the organization
- Use fuzzy matching and other AI techniques to identify patterns across different implementation experiences

Phase 3: AI Enhancement of Individual Capabilities

AI-powered learning systems are changing how organizations develop their workforce's capabilities. Synthesia, a company that uses AI to create professional videos with virtual presenters, simplifying video production, demonstrates how AI can tailor educational content to individual learning styles and needs through a multifaceted approach to personalization that yields measurable results. The platform transforms traditional one-size-fits-all training into customized learning experiences by enabling content delivery that aligns with individual comprehension patterns and preferences (Lukan, 2024). Teleperformance's implementation of Synthesia showcases this adaptability, training 380,000 people across 170 markets, with content delivered in over 40 languages while achieving significant cost and time efficiencies—saving $5,000 and five days per video (Lukan, 2024).

The effectiveness of this personalized approach is further validated by empirical outcomes across multiple organizations: by using Synthesia, BSH achieved a 70% improvement in training efficiency, Cohesity reported a 200% increase in video view retention, and Persado documented a 95%-time savings in video creation (Lukan, 2024). These metrics are particularly significant as Fauscette (2024) highlights how AI-enabled personalization can address accessibility needs while maintaining learning effectiveness. The consistent achievement of such substantial improvements across diverse organizational contexts suggests that AI-driven adaptability in learning delivery can meaningfully enhance the educational experience when properly leveraged through platforms like Synthesia.

The metrics from Synthesia's implementation reveal a multilayered business impact that extends beyond simple cost reduction. What makes these results particularly significant is how they address fundamental challenges in corporate learning environments: scale, consistency, and engagement. AI-powered video creation enables rapid deployment across linguistic and geographic boundaries and thus fundamentally transforms the economics of global training initiatives. Companies that once had to sacrifice either quality, consistency, or cost can now achieve all three at once. This change allows learning and development teams to shift from simply creating content to becoming strategic designers of learning experiences. They can focus on how people learn rather than getting caught in production details.

The consistent performance improvements across different organizational contexts suggest that personalized, AI-driven learning approaches offer structural advantages over traditional methodologies regardless of industry or company size. These advantages stem from addressing a fundamental limitation of conventional training: the inability to scale personalization cost-effectively. Through the analysis of how different learners interact with content and automatically adapting to individual needs, these systems create learning experiences that respond to cognitive and preference patterns in ways that static content cannot. Organizations implementing similar technologies should establish comprehensive measurement frameworks that capture not just efficiency metrics but also effectiveness indicators such as knowledge retention, skill application, and time-to-competency. Such holistic evaluation provides a more complete understanding of how AI-enhanced learning transforms organizational capability development beyond simple cost reduction.

While Synthesia showcases the power of personalized content delivery, other platforms focus on making organizational knowledge more accessible and actionable in real-time. EveryAnswer's system for instant knowledge access illustrates how AI can provide employees with contextually relevant information precisely when needed (Newsfile Corp., 2024). The platform empowers businesses to customize AI systems by leveraging their own materials, such as documents, knowledge repositories, websites, and common queries (Newsfile Corp., 2024).

The real-time knowledge access capabilities exemplified by platforms like Every-Answer represent a fundamental shift in learning paradigms—moving from episodic training to continuous performance support. This evolution addresses a persistent challenge in traditional learning models: the gap between knowledge acquisition and application. By providing contextually relevant information precisely when needed, these systems significantly reduce cognitive load while simultaneously reinforcing learning through immediate application. The integration of such capabilities into workflow systems creates "learning in the flow of work" environments where skill development occurs naturally through daily activities rather than as separate educational initiatives, effectively transforming everyday work into continuous learning opportunities.

Application Tips

- Implement AI tools that adapt to individual learning styles and preferences
- Provide contextually relevant information precisely when employees need it
- Measure improvements in training efficiency, content retention, and time savings
- Integrate learning directly into workflows rather than as separate activities
- Focus on accessibility and inclusion when personalizing learning experiences

Phase 4: Building AI-Enabled Learning Structures

Organizations are increasingly utilizing AI to construct robust learning infrastructures that support continuous development. Amazon's comprehensive approach through its Technical Academy and Machine Learning University exemplifies how AI can be integrated into organizational learning structures. In 2021, the company committed to investing $1.2 billion through 2025 in an upskilling initiative aimed at hundreds of thousands of Amazon employees (Segal, 2021). The Amazon Technical Academy is a free program designed to encourage Amazon employees to transition into software engineering roles (Coyle, 2021). Additionally, through its Machine Learning University, Amazon offers a six-week training course covering essential topics in coding and machine learning (Amazon Staff, 2024). According to Amazon, employees who participated in these programs received an average salary increase of up to 8.6%, and about 75% experienced career advancement (Amazon, 2021).

IBM's continuous adaptation practices demonstrate how AI can help organizations swiftly respond to changing skill requirements. IBM prioritizes regular retraining with fresh data to ensure that their AI models prevent performance degradation and maintain cutting-edge accuracy (Stryker, 2024). Rigorous monitoring protocols systematically evaluate model outputs, detecting potential biases or inconsistencies that might emerge over time (Stryker, 2024). Feedback from users and stakeholders is carefully integrated, allowing AI systems to be refined and improved based on real-world usage and practical insights (Stryker, 2024). UTAUT's finding that the effect of effort expectancy diminishes with experience (Venkatesh et al., 2003) explains why organizations like Amazon's Technical Academy and IBM's continuous adaptation practices evolve their support structures as users gain proficiency. The initial barriers to learning are highest at the outset but decrease as users gain experience—precisely the pattern we observed in our case studies.

Similarly, the Marriott Development Academy, an initiative by Marriott International for employee development, offers self-paced, blended learning options for aspiring managers to acquire essential soft skills for leadership roles (Global Opportunity Forum, 2022; Dagli, 2022). In the Australian market, this program has helped fill over 55% of leadership vacancies with internal candidates (Global Opportunity Forum, 2022; Dagli, 2022). Marriott also developed the Global Voyage Leadership Development program, a 12–18-month initiative featuring hands-on and virtual training in subjects such as engineering, revenue management, rooms operations, and accounting and finance to support university graduates (Global Opportunity Forum, 2022; Dagli, 2022). UTAUT's identification of social influence as a key determinant moderated by experience and voluntariness (Venkatesh et al., 2003) illuminates why Marriott Development Academy incorporates peer learning and mentorship components in its learning structures. These social mechanisms are particularly important in mandatory usage contexts and during early implementation phases, aligning with our observations of organizational learning practices.

These implementations reflect key aspects of Davenport and Ronanki's (2018) four-step framework for AI integration: understanding technologies, creating a portfolio of projects, launching pilots, and scaling successful implementations. Their framework emphasizes the importance of technological literacy, strategic project selection, and systematic testing before broader deployment (Davenport & Ronanki, 2018)—principles evident in the learning structures developed by organizations like Amazon, IBM, and Marriott. Such structured approaches provide the foundation for more comprehensive learning management systems across the enterprise.

As organizations like Amazon, IBM, and Marriott showcase the effectiveness of AI-enabled learning structures, many have begun implementing comprehensive learning management systems (LMS) that systematize and scale these approaches across their entire operations. These LMS platforms represent a natural evolution that combines the personalized education exemplified by Synthesia, the knowledge access capabilities of EveryAnswer, and the structured learning pathways of Amazon's Technical Academy into integrated, enterprise-wide solutions.

Enablers of AI Adoption

Policy-level support and governance plays a foundational role in establishing the guardrails within which AI-enabled learning can flourish. Organizations that demonstrate implementation success typically develop comprehensive policy frameworks that clarify priorities, allocation of resources, and decision rights. IKEA exemplifies this approach when placing employees at the center of technological adoption, balancing technological advancement with employee empowerment. Similarly, NTT DATA's GenAI Talent Development Framework demonstrates how governance can be structured to set global standards while allowing flexibility for local implementation. These policy frameworks provide essential clarity in complex implementation environments, supporting learning initiatives while maintaining appropriate controls.

AI talent acquisition strategies have emerged as essential complements to internal training initiatives. While the chapter has demonstrated the importance of upskilling existing employees, many organizations recognize the need for specialized expertise that may not be developable internally within required timeframes. PwC's approach illustrates how organizations can combine internal development with strategic talent management. Their strategy evolved from early implementation lessons that revealed technical training alone was insufficient for meaningful adoption. Their peer education approach ensures that AI training remains relevant to specific team needs while leveraging existing domain expertise. The Marriott

Development Academy shows a related approach by focusing on filling leadership vacancies internally. These strategic talent approaches directly enable the learning loop by creating knowledge transfer mechanisms between specialists and general staff, establishing the human infrastructure necessary for sustained AI learning while accelerating the organization's progression through subsequent stages of AI maturity.

External partnerships increasingly function as structural accelerators for AI-enabled learning. Organizations demonstrating implementation maturity typically cultivate diverse partnership ecosystems rather than relying exclusively on internal capabilities. IKEA's collaboration with Microsoft to develop their Hej Copilot tool exemplifies how strategic partnerships can provide both technical capabilities and knowledge transfer. Likewise, Scale AI's work on machine unlearning demonstrates how specialized external expertise can address complex AI implementation challenges that would be difficult to solve internally. These partnerships create knowledge flows that enhance organizational capabilities while providing specialized expertise that would be impractical to develop internally.

Application Tips

- Develop clear governance frameworks that provide guardrails without stifling innovation
- Combine internal development with strategic external talent acquisition
- Form partnerships with specialized providers to accelerate capability development
- Create continuous adaptation practices that systematically refine AI systems
- Design upskilling initiatives with concrete metrics for career advancement

Phase 5: Creating Integrated Learning Systems

The convergence of organizational learning processes and learning organization structures generates potent feedback loops that enhance overall organizational effectiveness. When organizations adeptly combine their AI learning processes with AI-enabled learning structures, they experience tangible improvements across various dimensions including employee retention and satisfaction (Winstead, 2023).

The virtuous cycle functions as follows: as organizations enhance their AI implementation (organizational learning), these systems bolster the organization's capacity to learn (learning organization). This increased learning capacity then elevates the organization's ability to adopt and adapt to new AI capabilities, creating a continuous improvement loop.

A. Systematic Learning Integration

Learning management systems are advanced digital platforms that have transformed how organizations approach education and training (Hashemi-Pour, Kirvan, & Brush, 2024). At their core, these software platforms provide a comprehensive structure for designing, executing, and evaluating learning activities across diverse settings from corporate environments to government agencies (Hashemi-Pour, Kirvan, & Brush, 2024). Most learning management systems feature two primary components: a backend server handling essential functions and a user-facing interface enabling interaction with the system.

These platforms fulfill several essential functions:

1. **Content Development and Distribution:** These platforms enable instructors to create educational materials and deliver them consistently across various devices and locations.
2. **Learning Assessment:** LMS technology tracks participation metrics, measures achievement levels, and produces comprehensive analytics that showcase learning progress throughout the educational journey.
3. **Collaborative Learning Spaces:** Contemporary systems feature engagement mechanisms including discussion boards, video conferencing tools, and collaborative workspaces that transform passive information reception into dynamic knowledge creation.

The incorporation of artificial intelligence into learning management systems represents a significant evolution in organizational learning approaches. Docebo exemplifies this transformation through its cloud-based platform that streamlines employee training and e-learning program delivery. The system demonstrates how AI enhances organizational learning by applying sophisticated analytics to track and optimize educational outcomes throughout the enterprise (Davey, 2024). By swiftly processing vast amounts of data, the platform identifies patterns and trends that traditional methods might overlook, generating metrics that offer deep insights into learner performance (Davey, 2024). AI-powered analytics transcend simple tracking, transforming raw data into actionable intelligence that aids organizations in continuously enhancing their learning experiences (Tremblay, 2024). Through powerful visualization tools and intelligent reporting, Docebo enables learning and development professionals to precisely understand how their training programs are performing and identify areas for strategic improvement (Tremblay, 2024).

When implementing such AI-powered learning systems, organizations face a critical strategic choice between a platform approach and a foundation model approach. Many organizations, particularly small and mid-sized companies with limited technical resources, adopt a platform approach by utilizing existing AI solutions like Docebo. This approach offers faster implementation, reduced technical complexity, and lower initial costs, making it accessible for organizations beginning their AI journey. In Uruguay, this platform strategy allowed the Agency for Electronic Government and Information and Knowledge Society (AGESIC) to dramatically improve help desk ticket classification accuracy from 50% to 92%, demonstrating how third-party solutions can yield significant benefits without extensive AI expertise (Red Hat, 2024).

Another AI training company, Sana Labs' automated adaptation capabilities showcase how AI can perpetually refine learning pathways by transforming educational experiences (Nordell Westling, n.d.). Intelligent learning technologies facilitate personalization, creating adaptive systems that dynamically respond to individual learner capabilities and knowledge gaps. These AI-powered platforms can significantly accelerate skill acquisition, allowing learners to master complex content more efficiently and retain knowledge for longer periods (Nordell Westling, n.d.). In reimagining learning as a fluid, responsive process, such technologies address critical challenges in workforce development, particularly for individuals seeking to upskill or transition between careers in a rapidly evolving job market (Nordell Westling, n.d.).

Organizations with substantial data science capabilities and specific learning requirements may pursue a foundation model approach instead, developing custom AI solutions tailored to their unique needs. Scale AI's work on machine unlearning demonstrates this approach. Valued at $7 billion, Scale AI provides high-quality training data for AI applications and has pioneered machine unlearning in the context of large language models (LLMs) (Balnojan, 2024). They employ the Weighted Model Distance Penalty as a benchmark to remove harmful knowledge from LLMs, ensuring models do not retain harmful information (Yue & Berrios, 2024). This methodology systematically eliminates problematic data points and biases, advancing research in machine unlearning and setting a standard for safer, more reliable AI applications (Yue & Berrios, 2024; Balnojan, 2024).

The strategic choice between these approaches is influenced by several factors beyond technical considerations. Data sensitivity and governance requirements often play a crucial role, particularly for organizations handling personal or proprietary information (Red Hat, 2024). Resource availability, existing technical expertise, and long-term strategic goals also shape this decision (Red Hat, 2024). Increasingly, forward-thinking organizations are adopting hybrid approaches, selectively building custom AI capabilities for critical learning functions while leveraging established platforms for more standard learning management needs.

Regardless of the implementation approach, these examples illustrate how AI transcends being merely a tool for learning; it becomes a fundamental component of modern learning organization structures. The technology enables organizations to create more responsive, personalized, and effective learning environments while maintaining the systematic approach necessary for organizational-level learning.

B. Learning Centered Talent Assessment

Traditional credentials are increasingly being supplanted by skills-based assessment approaches, reflecting both shifting market demands and a deeper understanding of learning dynamics in AI-enabled environments. The rise of microcredentials—which doubled from 2021 to 2022—signals a fundamental shift in how organizations assess and develop talent (Welding, 2024). A 2022 survey of over 510 professionals, including 350 hiring and training managers, revealed two crucial insights with distinct implications: 74% of respondents believe that alternative credentials effectively address specific skill gaps in their organizations, while an even more telling 76% of leaders value these credentials primarily because they demonstrate a candidate's fundamental learning agility (Fong, Etter, & Sullberg, 2023). This distinction is essential - organizations increasingly recognize that beyond technical proficiency in current tools, the capacity to continuously learn has become the more valuable long-term competency in the AI era.

This pivotal shift toward valuing learning agility represents a strategic adaptation to technological acceleration. In fields like AI where technology evolves rapidly, technical knowledge becomes outdated with increasing speed. Forward-thinking organizations recognize this and are reshaping their talent development approaches—shifting from credential-based requirements to models that value demonstrated capabilities and potential for growth. This transformation reflects a deeper understanding that the capacity to continuously acquire new skills often proves more valuable than static knowledge repositories. Progressive organizations are now designing career frameworks that explicitly value and reward learning velocity alongside traditional performance metrics, creating cultures where continuous skill acquisition becomes a core element of professional identity rather than an occasional requirement.

The complementary relationship between traditional degrees and microcredentials reveals an emerging model that balances depth with adaptability. Rather than representing competing approaches, these credential types increasingly function as complementary components of a comprehensive learning portfolio. Traditional degrees provide the conceptual foundations and critical thinking capabilities essential for navigating complexity, while microcredentials deliver the specific, timely skills required for immediate application. Organizations adopting similar principles in their talent development strategies are creating structured learning pathways that combine foundational knowledge development with rapid skill acquisition modules. These pathways help employees develop comprehensive capabilities while remaining adaptable to technological changes.

Tech companies are leading this transformation with innovative certification programs that transform talent assessment and development. Google's Career Certificates and Microsoft's learning platforms show the shift toward skills-based hiring by providing practical training applied to the job market; an approach which is faster and cheaper than traditional degrees. Participation in these progressive learning programs enables staff members to cultivate comprehensive skill portfolios while navigating ongoing technological shifts. The structured yet flexible learning pathways help personnel develop integrated capabilities while preserving adaptability as technologies transform.

Such a balanced approach fosters workforce resilience amid persistent technological upheaval, creating teams capable of maintaining effectiveness despite continuous marketplace disruption. In the tech industry, where traditional credentials are increasingly giving way to demonstrated capabilities, the ability to quickly learn and apply new skills often proves more valuable than static knowledge (Vargas, 2022).

This shift is evidenced by a comprehensive survey of 1,010 executives and hiring managers—employers overwhelmingly prefer candidates who combine traditional degrees with microcredentials, with 68% favoring entry-level candidates possessing both qualifications over those with only a college degree (13%) or only a microcredential (14%) (Finley, 2023). Traditional institutions are responding to this pressure—approximately 60% of surveyed deans, chairs, and administrators are considering revising their MBA programs to emphasize analytical and soft skills development (Wiley, 2023).

The impact on career advancement has been substantial. Career advancement now increasingly depends on continuous skill acquisition. Professionals must regularly pursue new certifications and credentials to remain competitive and grow professionally (Gallagher, 2019). This shift represents a fundamental change in talent strategy—moving away from reliance on fixed qualifications toward valuing an employee's proven ability to learn and adapt.

Application Tips

- Start with platform approaches if your organization has limited technical resources
- Consider foundation model approaches for unique learning requirements or sensitive data
- Use AI-powered analytics to identify patterns and optimize learning experiences

- Implement automated adaptation capabilities that refine learning pathways based on performance
- Consider hybrid approaches that combine established platforms with custom capabilities

Phase 6: Measuring and Enhancing the Learning Loop

Integrating AI into organizational learning requires balancing technical capabilities with human considerations. Based on implementations across various industries, several key frameworks have emerged to guide organizations through this transformation.

A. Tools and Methodologies for Tracking and Enhancing Learning Cycles

As companies work to establish productive learning cycles, they need effective tools to measure progress and identify areas for improvement. These systems go beyond traditional learning metrics to capture the recursive relationship between AI implementation and organizational learning capacity.

Comprehensive Learning Analytics Platforms

Learning analytics platforms have become essential for tracking AI-enabled learning effectiveness. These systems collect and analyze data from numerous sources, creating comprehensive insights into learning processes and outcomes. Watershed LRS (Learning Record Store), for example, brings together information from various learning experiences—formal training programs, workplace applications, and AI interactions—to build complete learning profiles. This unified approach reveals meaningful patterns that might otherwise go unnoticed, especially in complex AI implementations.

These platforms' value lies mostly in connecting learning activities to business results. Organizations such as Visa and Danone have relied on Watershed LRS to align learning initiatives with organizational goals by integrating learning analytics which aggregated, cleaned, and sorted the organizations' data (*Learning Ecosystem Case Study: Danone | Watershed*, n.d.; *Learning Ecosystem Case Study: Visa University | Watershed*, n.d.).

Platforms such as Visier help organizations correlate learning metrics with performance indicators, allowing them to measure the actual business impact of AI learning initiatives. A major retailer with 11,000 employees saw significant improvements using this analytics approach (A Retail Group Drove Sales Performance With Visier - Customer Story | Global Retailer, n.d.). The company gained immediate visibility into sales performance metrics, enabling prompt data-driven decision making (A Retail Group Drove Sales Performance With Visier - Customer Story | Global Retailer, n.d.). Their system successfully combined sales performance data with workforce information, creating a unified view that revealed important operational patterns and trends (*A Retail Group Drove Sales Performance With Visier - Customer Story | Global Retailer*, n.d.). Additionally, the retailer leveraged AI-based forecasting tools to identify potential workforce issues before they could negatively affect sales performance, allowing for proactive rather than reactive management (*A Retail Group Drove Sales Performance With Visier - Customer Story | Global Retailer*, n.d.).

Skillscape Mapping and Gap Analysis Tools

Organizations increasingly employ skillscape mapping tools to visualize their current AI capabilities against future requirements. Tools like Degreed help organizations build comprehensive learning ecosystems that bring together scattered learning resources while spotting skill gaps. When Ericsson implemented Degreed, it solved the problem of learning resources spread across multiple platforms by creating a single access point that cut content search time in half for 74% of surveyed employees (Ericsson Transforms Workforce Learning With Degreed, n.d.). Similarly, Citigroup leveraged Degreed to transform learning for its 200,000 employees across 160 countries, consolidating multiple learning systems and content libraries into a cohesive platform (*We Built this Citi on Learning & Skills (n.d.))*. Within eight weeks of implementation, Citi saw content engagement increase, as employees accessed learning through mobile devices (*We Built this Citi on Learning & Skills (n.d.))*. Both companies demonstrate how AI-enabled learning platforms can systematically track skill development while aligning learning with strategic priorities. Ericsson specifically used the platform to build critical capabilities in seven skill areas essential for growth, particularly focusing on 5G, AI, and machine learning – directly supporting their transformation into a 5G industry leader (*Ericsson Transforms Workforce Learning With Degreed, n.d.*). These implementations reflect how organizations can use sophisticated learning analytics to create virtuous learning cycles that connect individual capability development with organizational strategic objectives.

AI Readiness Scorecards and Maturity Models

Structured assessment frameworks help organizations track their progress in creating effective learning cycles. Assessment tools like Deloitte's AI Readiness & Management Framework evaluate organizations across several dimensions, including data infrastructure, talent capabilities, and governance structures (Deloitte Development LLC, 2024). These assessments offer clear benchmarks for measuring progress and identifying improvement areas, providing structured approaches to evaluate AI implementation.

Comprehensive assessment frameworks provide organizations with structured approaches to evaluate their AI implementation progress. Deloitte's AI Readiness & Management Framework (aiRMF) exemplifies this approach by integrating ten distinct capability areas that span the entire AI implementation lifecycle (Deloitte Development LLC, 2024). The framework evaluates organizational readiness across three core functions: setting direction, core essential capabilities, and managing AI holistically throughout the enterprise (Deloitte Development LLC, 2024). This multidimensional assessment examines critical areas including data readiness, AI infrastructure, workforce preparation, and governance structures, providing clear benchmarks for measuring progress (Deloitte Development LLC, 2024).

The aiRMF goes beyond simple assessment by offering organizations a navigational roadmap for their AI journey (Deloitte Development LLC, 2024). It helps define target outcomes while charting practical implementation paths that align with specific business and mission needs. The need for such frameworks is underscored by sobering industry research from McKinsey & Company which showed that though employees feel ready to scale AI capabilities, business leaders are struggling to adopt it (Mayer et al., 2025). AI Readiness Scorecards can address both technical foundations and human factors and thus enable organizations to advance their AI capabilities systematically.

Beyond Deloitte's approach, several major consulting firms have developed AI maturity models that provide organizations with roadmaps for progression. Gartner's AI maturity model outlines five levels—from initial awareness through transformational—each with specific capabilities across dimensions including data, skills, and governance (Panetta, 2019). These thorough assessments examine the full implementation process, enabling organizations to recognize capability gaps, direct investments strategically, and speed up their advancement toward enterprise-wide AI maturity.

B. Assessing Organizational AI Learning Readiness

Organizational readiness for AI-enabled learning extends far beyond technical infrastructure. A comprehensive readiness assessment must examine the interplay between technical capabilities, human capital, and organizational culture. The technical foundation includes not only the quality and management of existing datasets but also the organization's ability to integrate new AI systems with existing learning platforms while maintaining robust security protocols.

Workforce preparedness represents another crucial dimension of readiness (Miake-Lye, Delevan, Ganz, Mittman, & Finley, 2020; Baggio, Digentiki, & Varma, 2019). Organizations must understand current digital literacy levels and AI competencies across all organizational strata. This understanding goes beyond simple skills assessment to encompass cultural attitudes toward AI adoption and the organization's collective capacity for change. Organizations may benefit from viewing readiness assessment as an iterative process that evolves with the implementation effort (Madsen, Miller, & John, 2005).

Leadership alignment proves particularly critical in determining readiness (Miake-Lye et al., 2020). Executive understanding and support must extend beyond superficial endorsement to include meaningful resource allocation and strategic alignment (Cinite, Duxbury, & Higgins, 2009). Effective organizations demonstrate this alignment through clear governance frameworks that balance innovation with risk management, ensuring that AI learning initiatives advance core organizational objectives while maintaining appropriate controls.

C. Developing Comprehensive Learning Strategies

Successful AI learning strategies begin with a clear articulation of learning objectives that directly support business goals. These objectives should define not only what the organization hopes to achieve but also how success will be measured. Organizations must develop specific performance indicators that capture both immediate learning outcomes and longer-term business impact. Recent industry research reinforces this approach, with data showing that organizations taking a structured approach to AI implementation are seeing substantial returns, with nearly three-quarters reporting clear value from their projects (Mitchell, 2022).

Implementation planning requires a sophisticated approach that balances ambition with pragmatism. To increase effectiveness, organizations should roll out AI in phases, starting with carefully chosen pilot programs that enable quick learning and refinement. Healthcare organizations have proven this approach works, successfully scaling AI by beginning with focused departmental pilots before wider implementation (Mitchell, 2022). Atlantic Health System, a nonprofit health network, found success by starting in their neurology department before expanding to cardiology and other areas (Mitchell, 2022). Similarly, Mayo Clinic started by implementing AI in radiology due to its abundance of digital data (Stiepan, 2022). This focused departmental approach allowed them to develop implementation expertise with clearly defined use cases and measurable outcomes. After establishing success protocols and organizational learning patterns in this initial domain, they methodically expanded to broader clinical applications, applying the lessons learned from radiology to help doctors with patient diagnosis and treatment planning across multiple specialties (Fox, 2024). This phased expansion exemplifies how iterative learning about AI implementation in one department can be systematically translated into broader organizational learning structures.

The design of content and delivery must address the specific characteristics of AI-enabled learning. Organizations need to create learning pathways that blend theory with practical application, so people can use new skills immediately in their work. For best results, programs should offer both structured learning and hands-on experimentation, helping learners develop real competence rather than surface-level understanding.

D. Guidelines for Balancing Human and AI-Enabled Learning

Integrating AI into organizational learning requires careful consideration of how human and artificial intelligence complement each other. Many organizations understand that AI should enhance rather than replace human learning capabilities. The US Patent & Trademark Office uses AI projects to speed up patent classification, identify fraud, and help examiners search more patents in less time (Mitchell, 2022). This perspective guides how organizations implement AI tools, ensuring they amplify human insight rather than try to replace it.

Ethical considerations are fundamental to AI-enabled learning. Organizations must establish clear principles for AI use in learning settings, promoting transparency in AI-driven decisions while safeguarding learner privacy and tackling potential biases. At Salesforce, employees have free access to upskilling programs with AI courses and AI certifications which include prompting, AI basics, and AI ethics (Crist, 2024b). These principles should evolve through ongoing dialogue between technical experts, learning professionals, and organizational stakeholders.

Organizations should carefully consider how they explain AI-driven decisions across different contexts. Intriguingly, research by Binns et al. (2018) reveals that explanation approaches become more significant when people can compare different styles side by side. However, when users interact repeatedly with just one explanation format, they tend to focus more on the specifics of each case rather than how it's explained (Binns et al., 2018). This insight has practical implications for how companies might approach transparency differently depending on whether users will encounter multiple AI systems or develop an ongoing relationship with a single platform.

Quality assurance in AI-enabled learning requires continuous attention to both technical performance and learning outcomes. Organizations should develop sophisticated monitoring systems that track not only immediate learning results but also longer-term impacts on organizational performance. This monitoring should inform continuous improvement of both AI systems and learning design.

E. Ensuring Implementation Sustainability

Sustainable implementation of AI-enabled learning demands attention to multiple dimensions of organizational capacity. Technical sustainability faces significant integration challenges as organizations scale AI implementations. As Davenport and Ronanki (2018) observed in their research, one of the greatest obstacles organizations encounter is connecting AI components with existing systems and processes. Unlike comprehensive enterprise applications, AI technologies often address specific tasks within larger workflows, creating complex integration requirements when deploying beyond pilot projects (Davenport & Ronanki, 2018). This fragmented nature of AI implementation demands close collaboration between technical teams and business process owners throughout the scaling process.

Scaling also requires code streamlining, new technologies, distributed data approaches, additional teams, and data labeling capabilities according to Ernst & Young's (EY) Dan Diasio (Mitchell, 2022). Organizational sustainability necessitates ongoing alignment between learning initiatives and business objectives. A recent EY industry survey indicates that over half of CIOs and IT leaders consider data and analytics, including AI implementations, as a top investment priority for the coming years (Mitchell, 2022). To maximize success, organizations should regularly review and update learning content while ensuring learning facilitators maintain current knowledge of AI capabilities and limitations.

Cultural sustainability emerges from the organization's ability to foster genuine acceptance and adoption of AI-enabled learning. This requires creating an environment that encourages experimentation while maintaining a focus on human-centric learning approaches. Organizations bear responsibility to balance innovation with stability, ensuring that learning systems evolve without disrupting essential organizational functions. For instance, Atlantic Health System ensures stakeholder involvement from the beginning of AI implementations, with cross-functional team participation being crucial to successful integration into workflows (Mitchell, 2022).

Financial sustainability demands sophisticated approaches to resource allocation and return measurement. Organizations must create clear frameworks for assessing both direct and indirect returns on AI learning investments. While pilot projects often demonstrate technical success, achieving economic viability at scale presents additional hurdles related to timing and resource requirements (Mitchell, 2022). These frameworks should consider not only immediate cost savings but also longer-term impacts on organizational capability and performance.

Beyond financial considerations, knowledge sustainability represents another critical dimension for long-term implementation success. As AI systems and organizational needs continuously evolve, mechanisms for preserving and updating institutional knowledge become essential. Organizations demonstrating implementation longevity typically establish robust knowledge management practices: documenting not only technical processes but also implementation decisions, lessons learned, and contextual factors that influenced system design. This comprehensive knowledge capture proves particularly valuable during team transitions, as new personnel can understand not just what was done but why specific approaches were chosen. Leading organizations further strengthen knowledge sustainability by implementing structured knowledge transfer protocols, creating overlap periods when team changes occur, and establishing ongoing communities of practice where implementation insights are regularly shared. These practices ensure that critical understanding doesn't reside exclusively with individual experts but becomes embedded in organizational memory. By treating knowledge as a strategic asset requiring active management, organizations maintain implementation momentum even as personnel changes occur and create foundations for continuous improvement that build upon rather than repeat previous learning cycles.

This comprehensive framework gives organizations valuable guidance for implementing AI-enabled learning while focusing on both technical excellence and human development. Success stems from consistently applying these principles while remaining flexible enough to adapt to changing organizational requirements and technological progress.

F. Iterative Learning Models and AI Governance Structures

While technical capabilities and implementation strategies receive significant attention, governance frameworks specifically designed for AI learning cycles remain underdeveloped in many organizations. Effective AI governance differs fundamentally from traditional IT governance by emphasizing continuous adaptation rather than static compliance.

AI governance structures should actively facilitate organizational learning by creating protected spaces for experimentation. They should also establish clear distinctions between experimental and production AI systems, with corresponding differences in oversight requirements. The relationship between governance and learning becomes particularly crucial when addressing ethical considerations that extend beyond traditional risk frameworks. Rather than treating governance as separate from the learning process, forward-thinking organizations create explicit feedback mechanisms between implementation experiences and governance evolution. This integrated approach transforms governance from a static compliance function into a dynamic capability that both guides and learns from AI implementation experiences.

Application Tips

- Implement analytics that connect learning activities directly to business outcomes
- Use AI readiness scorecards to identify and address capability gaps
- Start with focused departmental pilots before expanding to broader applications
- Create learning objectives that define not just what to achieve but how success will be measured
- Design quality assurance systems that monitor both technical performance and learning outcomes

Phase 7: Addressing Challenges in the Learning Loop

Companies trying to build effective learning cycles with AI run into numerous roadblocks. Phase 7 highlights eight main barriers: strategy problems, technical limitations, workforce challenges, industry differences, regulatory hurdles, data silos and infrastructure constraints, budget restrictions, and organizational resistance to change. These challenges they overlap and influence each other in ways that demand comprehensive solutions; they do not exist in isolation.

A. Strategic Challenges

Many organizations rush into AI adoption without sufficient research or clear implementation strategies (K. Martin, 2024). This hasty approach often leads to misaligned initiatives and inefficient resource allocation. The challenge is compounded by difficulties in measuring success—traditional metrics for learning effectiveness often prove inadequate for AI-enabled environments. Conventional methods like course completion rates and survey feedback fail to capture the complexity of AI-powered learning systems (Lake, 2024).

B. Technical Barriers

This strategic challenge is exacerbated by technical hurdles, particularly when attempting to integrate AI with legacy infrastructure (K. Martin, 2024). Technical problems compound these strategic issues, especially when companies try fitting AI into outdated systems. Organizations grapple with integrating data from diverse sources, preparing and cleaning data, and ensuring proper governance, with nearly one-third of executives citing data-related issues among their top three AI implementation concerns (Tello & Subramanian, 2022). Even when these foundational elements are in place, AI integration requires careful identification of use cases, model fine-tuning, and seamless system integration, demanding close collaboration between AI experts and domain specialists (Kumar, 2024). Recent empirical research supports the significance of these technical barriers. Bérubé, Giannelia, and Vial (2021) conducted a Delphi study with AI experts who consistently ranked data-related issues among the most significant implementation barriers. These challenges are further intensified by outdated infrastructure, as many businesses still operate with systems, tools, and applications that cannot support advanced AI implementations (YEC, 2023).

C. Workforce Challenges

C. 1. Human Factors

The human dimension of AI adoption proves as significant as technical challenges in determining implementation success. Employee resistance stems from more than simple technology aversion—it represents deeper organizational tensions around change, role definition, and professional identity. Booyse and Scheepers' (2024) interviews with senior managers revealed lingering trust concerns even among leadership, with specific worries about AI transparency affecting adoption decisions. This resistance materializes through daily operational choices: avoidance of new AI tools, skepticism toward AI-generated insights, and reluctance to incorporate AI recommendations into workflows.

Beyond the technical skills gap, organizations face significant psychological barriers to AI adoption. Resistance to AI implementation often stems from deeper concerns about job security, technological efficacy, and identity threats. The research shows something often seen in practice - people's attitudes toward AI largely depend on whether they see it as useful, easy to use, and valuable to their work (Amin et al., 2024). When they do not see these benefits, resistance naturally follows. This makes organization's messaging and support crucial to successful adoption (Hamilton, 2025). When employees perceive AI as threatening their professional identity or lack confidence in their ability to adapt, resistance naturally follows. Particularly instructive is Golgeci et al.'s (2025) framework conceptualizing AI resistance as manifesting through employee fears, inefficacies, and antipathies—emotional responses that require thoughtful organizational intervention. Addressing this resistance demands more than technical training; it requires transparent communication about AI's purpose, collaborative implementation approaches that engage affected employees, and deliberate positioning of AI as augmenting rather than replacing human capabilities (Hamilton, 2025). Organizations that successfully navigate these psychological barriers typically create environments where experimentation and curiosity are encouraged and where employees can maintain a sense of agency in how AI transforms their work.

A critical factor in AI adoption is securing genuine leadership buy-in across organizational hierarchies. The success of AI initiatives often hinges on executive support that goes beyond mere approval to active championing (Ariganello, 2024). When leaders model enthusiasm for AI and clearly articulate its strategic benefits—focusing on ROI, risk mitigation, or asset protection depending on executive priorities (Ariganello, 2024)—it creates cascading acceptance throughout the organization. However, this leadership support must be authentic; employees consistently demonstrate greater receptivity to AI technologies when they trust both the technology itself and their leaders' intentions for implementing it (De Cremer, 2025). No matter how sophisticated the technology, its acceptance fundamentally depends on leaders who can demonstrate genuine "concern for employee well-being and fairness" (De Cremer, 2025) while making clear that AI will enhance (rather than replace) human contributions.

Strich, Mayer, and Fiedler (2021) highlight another critical challenge in AI implementation: the impact on employees' professional role identity. They found that AI systems that substitute human decision-making can lead to identity concerns among employees, manifesting in uncertainty about their future roles and value (Strich, Mayer, & Fiedler; 2021). Despite considerable effort being invested in creating more transparent AI systems, Binns et al. (2018) challenge the notion that there's a single optimal approach to explaining algorithmic decisions as different explanation styles show variable effects across contexts. Such findings underscore the importance of considering the human element in AI implementation and the need for organizations to proactively address potential identity concerns.

C. 2. Skills Gap

Another significant challenge lies in the substantial skills gap between current organizational capabilities and the competencies required for effective AI utilization (Pallardy, 2024). For instance, in a 2024 survey, while a substantial majority of information technology workers (81%) believe they are prepared to incorporate artificial intelligence into their current job responsibilities, only a small fraction (12%) has accumulated meaningful hands-on experience working directly with AI technologies (AI Skills Report, 2024).

There is a complicated gap between how ready people think they are for AI and their actual preparedness. This disconnect creates real problems - teams miscalculate project scope, allocate too few resources, and set unrealistic deadlines because they don't understand what they're getting into. When teams overstate their readiness, they usually underestimate how complicated AI integration truly is. This leads to missed deadlines, quality problems, or sometimes completely abandoning otherwise promising AI projects. Therefore, organizations should tackle this head-on with practical reality checks: use hands-on skill assessments rather than simply asking people how comfortable they feel with AI and create controlled test environments where teams can experience AI's complexity before launching major initiatives.

Bérubé et al. (2021) identified a particular skills gap that has received insufficient attention: the lack of skills for 'industrialization' of AI, which they define as 'the ability to insert AI into everyday organizational processes' (p. 6709). Their research highlights that beyond data science and engineering skills, organizations require specialized capabilities to operationalize AI within existing business processes. The contextual nature of effective AI implementation further complicates this skills challenge. Technical knowledge alone proves insufficient without the practical judgment developed through hands-on experience with specific organizational data, processes, and decision environments. Organizations addressing this challenge most effectively are implementing "learning-by-doing" approaches: creating supervised practice opportunities with real organizational data, developing cross-functional projects where technical and domain experts collaborate closely, and establishing communities of practice where emerging insights can be shared across organizational boundaries. These approaches recognize that AI proficiency develops most effectively through structured experiential learning rather than passive knowledge acquisition, accelerating the development of contextually relevant capabilities while reducing the risks associated with the perception-reality gap.

Research by Pinski, Haas, and Benlian (2023) complements these findings by emphasizing the concept of 'metaknowledge' in AI contexts—accurate understanding of what one knows and doesn't know about AI. According to Fügener et al. (2021), when interactions between humans and AI involve ambiguous task allocation, metaknowledge becomes particularly crucial. Pinski, Haas, and Benlian (2023) suggest that organizations must go beyond developing basic AI literacy to fostering accurate self-assessment of AI knowledge. Their empirical study demonstrates that interactive, gamified learning experiences significantly improve both AI literacy and AI literacy metaknowledge compared to traditional text-based approaches, which may help organizations address the barriers related to understanding both technical aspects and business applications of AI technologies (Pinski, Haas, & Benlian; 2023).

These workforce challenges are further complicated by natural resistance to new learning methodologies, especially when they represent significant departures from established practices (Pallardy, 2024). Moreover, performance metrics that were effective in traditional learning environments prove insufficient for measuring key AI learning components, such as system adaptability, learning speed, and decision-making effectiveness (Bronsdon, 2024).

D. Industry-Specific Variations

These challenges manifest differently across industries, creating unique contexts for the dual relationship between AI learning and learning through AI. Manufacturing sectors face unique obstacles in integrating AI learning with physical operations, including cultural resistance, high initial costs, blended technology, and stringent regulations and compliance requirements (Pourak, 2024). In contrast, service industries must balance AI capabilities with maintaining human touchpoints to preserve customer relationships and service quality (Ambrozi, 2023). Knowledge-intensive industries encounter difficulties in capturing and transferring specialized expertise through AI systems while safeguarding intellectual property (Kim, 2024). Understanding these industry-specific variations is essential for adapting the theoretical frameworks of organizational learning and learning organizations to practical implementation contexts.

E. Regulatory and Ethical Challenges

Beyond technical and organizational hurdles, AI-enabled learning initiatives face a complex landscape of regulatory requirements and ethical considerations. These challenges are particularly significant as they involve not only compliance issues but fundamental questions about how AI systems should function in learning contexts. Mikalef et al. (2022) suggest implementing both technical safeguards and organizational processes to detect and mitigate potential harms. Their work shows how responsible AI goes beyond avoiding harm and should ensure AI systems are aligned with organizational values and societal expectations (Mikalef et al., 2022).

Evolving Regulatory Frameworks

Organizations implementing AI-enabled learning must navigate diverse global regulatory approaches, each presenting different implications for innovation and compliance. As Schatten and Aires (2025) observe in their book *AI Will Take Your Job, and It's for the Best,* regions have adopted markedly different regulatory philosophies—from the European Union's stringent, preemptive framework to the United States' more permissive environment that prioritizes innovation with targeted interventions for specific problems. This regulatory spectrum directly impacts how organizations can implement and scale their AI learning initiatives.

Global companies face a real challenge navigating different regulatory approaches, especially when the same learning system must meet contradictory requirements across countries. They are constantly balancing innovation against responsible implementation - being too cautious can sacrifice competitive edge, while weak governance creates ethical and legal vulnerabilities. Smart organizations build governance approaches that can bend with evolving regulations without breaking their ethical backbone. They tap into AI's potential for transforming learning while still taking seriously the real concerns about privacy protection, fair treatment, and keeping humans meaningfully involved in decisions that matter.

These regulations may seem like boxes to check, yet they reshape how systems are designed and implemented. As AI becomes more embedded in everyday business, the growing demand for human oversight in high-risk applications is changing how organizations build learning platforms. For instance, when an AI system suggests personalized learning paths that might significantly affect someone's career trajectory, organizations should add human review steps where managers evaluate these suggestions before sharing them with employees. These approaches not only help with potential regulatory compliance but also enhance system effectiveness through complementary human judgment.

Data Privacy and Security

Organizations face a genuine dilemma when implementing AI in learning environments. These systems need extensive data on how employees interact with content, where they struggle, and performance metrics to provide tailored solutions. Yet collecting this information creates significant privacy and security concerns. The data in question often contains sensitive details about employee capabilities and limitations. An AI system tracking which staff members struggle with concepts creates detailed performance profiles that could affect promotion decisions or job security. For multinational companies, the challenge multiplies across different jurisdictional boundaries with varying protection standards.

Forward-thinking companies do not wait for regulations to catch up. Many implement governance frameworks that exceed minimum requirements. Their approach includes building privacy protections into system architecture from day one, gathering only essential information, and creating strict access controls to keep sensitive data compartmentalized. These sophisticated approaches require substantial financial investment and specialized expertise. Smaller organizations or those with limited technical resources struggle to implement these protections, potentially widening the capability gap between companies with mature AI systems and those still developing basic data management practices.

Algorithmic Bias and Fairness

Despite appearances of objectivity, AI systems often mirror—and sometimes magnify—human biases embedded in their training data. When these systems guide learning opportunities, the consequences ripple through organizations in troubling ways. A learning recommendation system trained primarily on historical data might consistently steer certain demographic groups toward limited career paths, simply because historical patterns show these distributions. As Ferrara (2023) notes, these biases can silently preserve inequality while appearing more objective than human decisions.

The stakes rise as learning increasingly determines career trajectories. When AI systems influence skill development access, they shape advancement opportunities and ultimately affect organizational diversity at leadership levels. Consider an AI-powered learning system that analyzes performance history to recommend development paths. Such systems might consistently suggest technical certification to employees from certain backgrounds while routing others toward non-technical training, regardless of individual aptitude or interest.

Companies addressing these challenges deploy both technical and governance solutions. Leading organizations implement specialized tools to detect bias patterns—examining whether recommendations consistently disadvantage specific groups. They apply sophisticated algorithms that adjust models to reduce these disparities. IBM's AI Fairness 360 toolkit exemplifies this approach, offering metrics to measure fairness across demographic groups, providing interpretable explanations, and offering algorithms to correct detected biases (Bellamy et al., 2019).

Transparency and Explainability

The "black box" nature of many AI systems presents challenges in learning contexts, where understanding how recommendations or assessments are generated is often crucial for learner trust and development. In qualitative interviews with South African senior managers, Booyse and Scheepers (2024) found lack of trust and transparency in AI to be one of the barriers to AI adoption in decision making. Organizations ought to know how and why AI proposes a solution to confidently present it to employees and regulators (Marr, 2024).

Organizations are addressing this challenge through both technical and communication strategies. Large Language Models (LLMs) are increasingly developing reasoning capabilities so users can understand how they arrived at a response (Mckenzie, 2025). As Sharma (2025) explains, AI transparency requires honesty about what the AI was trained to do and how it relates to the organization's goals.

Increasing transparency requirements should drive the implementation of explainability features in learning management systems, allowing users to understand how and why certain learning recommendations are made. These modifications can satisfy transparency requirements while potentially increasing user trust and adoption rates, demonstrating how thoughtful implementation of regulatory considerations can align with business objectives.

F. Data Silos and Legacy Infrastructure Constraints

Structural barriers create significant obstacles in organizational AI adoption journeys. Outdated systems and disconnected data repositories form fundamental challenges requiring resolution before meaningful AI implementation becomes possible. The scope of these obstacles appears nearly universal, with research indicating 98% of IT organizations encounter difficulties with digital transformation initiatives (Salesforce, 2024). Data silos represent a particularly troublesome impediment, with 80% of organizations citing them as major concerns, while 72% grapple with systems characterized by problematic interdependencies (Salesforce, 2024).

These architectural limitations impose substantial financial demands. Companies face considerable expenses when upgrading technical infrastructure to accommodate AI initiatives. Analysis from a comprehensive survey involving 750 IT decision-makers demonstrated that legacy technology modernization cost businesses an average of $2.9 million during 2023 alone (Wilkinson, 2024). This sizeable investment typically competes against other essential organizational priorities, forcing difficult resource allocation decisions that potentially delay or undermine AI adoption efforts.

The intricacies of these challenges redirect leadership focus away from strategic AI initiatives toward risk management considerations. Research reveals 69% of CIOs designate cybersecurity and technology risk management as their primary personal working time allocation for the upcoming year (Howard, 2025). This protective stance, though necessary, frequently occurs at the expense of innovative AI implementations. To address this imbalance, CIOs must establish stronger collaborative relationships with security leaders to develop cybersecurity frameworks that enable rather than restrict business-driven IT initiatives, including AI adoption programs.

The practical consequences of these structural impediments extend well beyond technical complications. When valuable information remains trapped within isolated systems, AI applications cannot access the comprehensive data required for effective learning and pattern identification. This fragmentation diminishes the potential for AI to generate meaningful organizational insights while simultaneously creating additional integration expenses often overlooked during initial implementation planning. Organizations achieving success typically implement phased approaches, systematically addressing data standardization and infrastructure modernization before attempting sophisticated AI deployments.

G. Financial Constraints

The financial dimension of AI implementation presents organizations with significant resource allocation challenges that can substantially impact adoption timelines and success rates. Large enterprises are making considerable investments in this space, with 65% of major companies allocating $50 million or more to AI and big data technologies (C. Martin, 2020). Yet despite these substantial financial commitments, business adoption remains challenging, suggesting that monetary investment alone doesn't guarantee successful implementation.

Talent acquisition represents a particularly expensive aspect of AI adoption. The specialized skills required for AI implementation command substantial salary premiums that organizations must be prepared to accommodate. Recent labor market analysis reveals striking compensation differentials: professionals transitioning from non-AI to AI-focused roles can expect average salary increases of £ 35.8% in annual compensation (Pardo, 2024). This creates substantial financial barriers, particularly for small and mid-sized organizations that must compete with larger enterprises for limited AI expertise.

Despite these significant upfront costs, emerging evidence suggests promising financial returns for organizations that successfully implement AI technologies. Agentic AI deployments yield approximately $3.50 for every $1 invested, with typical breakeven periods of 14 months (Masood, 2025). Organizations like UPS have quietly trimmed $300 million in logistics costs, while financial institutions have added $34 million to their topline revenue through strategic AI implementations (Masood, 2025). The financial impact manifests across both cost reduction and revenue enhancement, with 42% of organizations reporting operational expense savings and 59% experiencing revenue increases (Masood, 2025).

These financial dynamics create complex decision-making environments for organizational leaders. While the potential returns appear substantial, the significant upfront investment and uncertain implementation timelines generate risk that must be carefully managed. Organizations must rectify capital expenditure forecasts, evaluate net present value implications, and prioritize use cases with clear EBITDA impact potential (Masood, 2025). Those that successfully navigate these financial constraints typically adopt phased implementation approaches that allow for gradual investment scaling based on demonstrated returns, rather than committing to comprehensive funding without validation of organizational value.

H. Organizational Inertia

Beyond technology and resource challenges, organizations face a fundamental obstacle when implementing AI—human resistance to change. This organizational friction often presents a greater barrier than any technical limitation, manifesting in various ways throughout company hierarchies.

Slack's Workforce Lab provides compelling evidence of this resistance dynamic. Their research uncovered distinct response patterns to AI, including a significant portion of employees (19%) who not only avoid AI tools but actively disapprove of colleagues using them (Maurer, 2024). This open resistance exists alongside a substantial group (20%) who use AI tools secretly, revealing the complex social tensions surrounding adoption (Maurer, 2024).

Most striking is the disconnect between intellectual acknowledgment and practical implementation. While corporate decision-makers overwhelmingly acknowledge AI's strategic importance, their personal usage rates remain strikingly low (De Freitas, 2025). Such a disparity suggests that logical arguments for AI adoption fail to address deeper psychological concerns about the technology's perceived limitations in understanding human contexts and needs.

Organizations typically underestimate how deeply entrenched work practices become in organizational identity. Change management research has identified key failure patterns that directly affect AI initiatives: embedded opposition to new ways of working, cookie-cutter approaches that ignore organizational uniqueness, and treating transformational initiatives as temporary projects (Dempsey et al., 2021). When organizations treat AI primarily as a technical installation rather than a cultural shift, they inadvertently strengthen resistance rather than fostering acceptance.

The cultural dimension becomes even more critical when we consider its impact on organizational performance. Recent research demonstrates that companies achieving alignment between purpose, strategy, and culture experience substantially stronger revenue growth, with adaptability emerging as the critical success factor (Bradford, 2025). Addressing cultural barriers to AI becomes essential for organizational performance.

Comprehensive analyses of AI implementation success factors underscore this reality. When researchers systematically evaluated nineteen implementation variables, ethical considerations emerged as the most significant determinant of success—outranking purely technical factors (Merhi, 2023). Despite this evidence, many organizations continue emphasizing technological aspects while underinvesting in the human and ethical dimensions that ultimately determine whether AI becomes integrated into everyday work or remains an underutilized investment.

Application Tips

- Proactively address professional identity concerns when implementing AI learning systems
- Create structured opportunities for hands-on AI experience to bridge the perception-reality gap
- Secure genuine leadership buy-in that goes beyond approval to active championing
- Address data siloes before attempting sophisticated AI learning implementations
- Implement phased approaches that systematically address infrastructure modernization

Phase 8: Evolving the Learning Loop

The evolution of AI-enabled organizational learning points toward significant transformations in how organizations develop and maintain their learning capabilities. This future landscape emerges at the intersection of technological advancement and organizational adaptation, shaped by both the processes of organizational learning and the structures of learning organizations.

Organizational learning processes are moving toward a more sophisticated integration of AI capabilities. Organizations will likely develop increasingly nuanced approaches to learning about AI systems, moving beyond basic implementation to a deep understanding of AI's role in organizational processes. As organizations evolve, learning about AI becomes more embedded in organizational routines, rather than existing as a separate educational initiative.

Learning organization structures are similarly poised for transformation. The rigid walls separating formal training from everyday work continue dissolving as AI makes contextual learning possible in the flow of work. Companies now develop frameworks capable of adapting instantaneously to evolving learning requirements, powered by AI systems that anticipate and address emerging skill needs before traditional training cycles could respond. Such a structural evolution indicates a shift toward more fluid, responsive learning architectures that can scale and adapt as organizational needs change.

The relationship between AI and organizational learning suggests a deepening integration where AI systems become not just tools for learning but active participants in the learning process. Building upon the foundations described in Serrat's (2017) framework, the evolving landscape extends the concept of organizational learning to include AI as both a subject of learning and an enabler of learning processes. Organizations will likely need to develop new competencies in managing this dual role of AI, ensuring that both human and artificial intelligence contribute effectively to organizational learning.

This evolution requires organizations to develop comprehensive readiness across multiple dimensions. Jöhnk, Weißert, and Wyrtki (2021) provide a list of AI-readiness factors from expert interviews and scientific and practitioner literature. First, strategic alignment includes business pontetial, customer readiness, management support, process fit, and data-driven decision making (Jöhnk, Weißert, & Wyrtki; 2021). Resources encompass financial budget, personnel, and IT infrastructure while knowledge includes AI awareness, upskilling, and ethics (Jöhnk, Weißert, & Wyrtki; 2021). Finally, culture comprises innovativeness, collaborative work, and change management and data involves data availability, quality, accessibility, and flow (Jöhnk, Weißert, & Wyrtki; 2021). Organizations that lag in these areas might struggle to progress beyond initial AI implementation stages, regardless of their strategic vision.

These theoretical developments in AI-enabled organizational learning manifest in concrete trends that organizations must prepare to address:

- **Hybrid learning ecosystems** emerge where human and machine capabilities enhance one another. These environments integrate AI-enabled learning tools with human expertise in increasingly sophisticated ways, creating multidimensional learning spaces that capitalize on the distinct advantages each brings to knowledge development.
- **Adaptive learning architectures** respond organically to shifting organizational requirements. These systems incorporate forward-looking capabilities that enable companies to prepare for future skill needs rather than merely reacting to current gaps.

- **Organizational learning processes** mature beyond basic tool implementation toward nuanced integration approaches. This evolution moves past simple adoption toward profound understanding of how AI transforms fundamental learning dynamics across the organization.

As these developments accelerate, organizations must balance adaptability in learning methodologies with maintaining core learning capabilities that support sustainable growth. The evolution toward human-AI symbiosis in learning environments represents perhaps the most significant emerging trend among those discussed above. Unlike earlier approaches that positioned AI primarily as a delivery mechanism for predetermined content, emerging systems establish collaborative relationships where both human and artificial intelligence actively contribute to knowledge development. This symbiotic trend represents the most advanced expression of the dual relationship introduced at the beginning of this chapter—where AI is simultaneously the subject of learning and the enabler of learning processes. The future success of organizational learning will likely depend on finding the right balance between embracing AI-enabled innovation and maintaining the human elements that make learning meaningful and effective.

Application Tips

- Design hybrid learning experiences that leverage the complementary strengths of humans and AI
- Develop predictive capabilities to anticipate future skill requirements
- Create knowledge sustainability practices to preserve insights during team transitions
- Establish communities of practice where implementation insights are regularly shared
- Focus on the human-AI symbiosis rather than viewing AI as merely a delivery mechanism

VIII. CONCLUSION: THE SYMBIOTIC RELATIONSHIP BETWEEN AI AND ORGANIZATIONAL LEARNING

The relationship between artificial intelligence and organizational learning reveals a fundamental transformation in how organizations develop and maintain their capabilities. The transformation demands a dual mastery from organizations—simultaneously developing expertise in AI systems while harnessing AI's capacity to enhance organizational learning. This duality creates a distinctive dynamic where process and structure continuously reinforce each other.

From an organizational learning perspective, companies systematically develop AI competencies through both structured programs and daily experiences. This process perspective reveals organizations continuously refining strategies based on real-world evidence and practical implementation experiences. Successful enterprises approach AI not merely as technical implementation but as transformative learning journey encompassing both technological expertise and organizational understanding.

The AI Learning Loop framework illustrates how AI systems themselves transform into essential components of organizational architecture, amplifying both individual development capabilities and collective institutional learning capacity. This structural transformation goes beyond simple tool adoption to fundamentally reshape how organizations capture, share, and apply knowledge. AI-enabled learning structures create more responsive, personalized, and effective learning environments while maintaining the systematic approach necessary for organizational-level learning. The integration of these approaches—process dynamics and structural elements—generates powerful amplification loops that elevate organizational effectiveness. As organizations develop increasingly sophisticated AI implementations, these systems simultaneously strengthen learning capabilities throughout the enterprise, creating self-reinforcing cycles of continuous advancement.

This virtuous pattern transforms not only learning processes but fundamentally reshapes talent assessment approaches, work structures, and innovation methodologies. Moving forward, AI integration into organizational learning will demand sustained attention to both process evolution and structural adaptation. Lasting success requires more than deploying technical systems—it necessitates creating environments where human and artificial intelligence mutually enhance capabilities. Organizations mastering this equilibrium—cultivating robust learning processes while developing adaptable learning architectures—position themselves advantageously within increasingly AI-driven competitive landscapes.

The synthesis of process and structure in AI-enabled organizational learning encompasses both technical implementation and human dynamics. Organizations thriving in this environment recognize that human factors—resistance patterns, leadership engagement, and cultural readiness—significantly influence implementation outcomes. The most effective learning organizations transform implementation failures into valuable assets through structured analysis, creating knowledge repositories that accelerate future initiatives. Their governance structures balance innovation with appropriate controls while enabling the iterative learning essential for AI mastery. This comprehensive approach—addressing technical and human dimensions through structured yet flexible processes—creates the foundation for sustained AI learning success.

REFERENCES

A retail group drove sales performance with Visier - Customer Story | global retailer. (n.d.). https://explore.visier.com/global-luxury-retailer/

Amazon. (2021). Amazon Upskilling Report 2021. Retrieved from https://assets.aboutamazon.com/80/a2/7e01e544475aaf15b4f8d5067cc6/amazon-upskilling-report-final.pdf

Ambrozi, A. (2023). 11 Challenges Of Adopting AI In Business (And How To Address Them Head-On). Forbes. Retrieved from https://www.forbes.com/councils/forbesbusinesscouncil/2023/10/24/11-challenges-of-adopting-ai-in-business-and-how-to-address-them-head-on/

Amin, S. M., El-Gazar, H. E., Zoromba, M. A., El-Sayed, M. M., & Atta, M. H. R. (2025). Sentiment of nurses towards artificial intelligence and resistance to change in healthcare organisations: A mixed-method study. *Journal of Advanced Nursing*, *81*(4), 2087–2098. PMID: 39235193

Ariganello, J. (2024). *Council Post: AI and the C-Suite: Crafting Compelling Narratives for Executive Buy-In*. Forbes. https://www.forbes.com/councils/forbescommunicationscouncil/2024/10/29/ai-and-the-c-suite-crafting-compelling-narratives-for-executive-buy-in/

Baggio, A., Digentiki, E., & Varma, R. (2019). Organizations do not change. People change! McKinsey & Company. Retrieved from from https://www.mckinsey.com/capabilities/people-and-organizational-performance/our-insights/the-organization-blog/organizations-do-not-change-people-change

Balnojan, S. (2024). How Unlearning Helps To Build $7B Data & AI Companies. There Data Point Thrusday. Retrieved from https://www.thdpth.com/p/how-unlearning-helps-to-build-7b

Bellamy, R. K. E., Dey, K., Hind, M., Hoffman, S. C., Houde, S., Kannan, K., Lohia, P., Martino, J., Mehta, S., Mojsilovic, A., Nagar, S., Ramamurthy, K. N., Richards, J., Saha, D., Sattigeri, P., Singh, M., Varshney, K. R., & Zhang, Y. (2019). AI Fairness 360: An extensible toolkit for detecting and mitigating algorithmic bias. *IBM Journal of Research and Development, 63*(4/5), 4:1-4:15. https://doi.org/DOI: 10.1147/jrd.2019.2942287

Bérubé, M., Giannelia, T., & Vial, G. (2021). Barriers to the Implementation of AI in Organizations: Findings from a Delphi Study. *Proceedings of the 54th Hawaii International Conference on System Sciences*, 6702-6711.

Binns, R., Van Kleek, M., Veale, M., Lyngs, U., Zhao, J., & Shadbolt, N. (2018). 'It's Reducing a Human Being to a Percentage' Perceptions of Justice in Algorithmic Decisions. In *Proceedings of the 2018 Chi conference on human factors in computing systems* (pp. 1-14).

Booyse, D., & Scheepers, C. B. (2024). Barriers to adopting automated organisational decision-making through the use of artificial intelligence. *Management Research Review*, *47*(1), 64–85.

Bradford, N. (2025). How Organizational Culture Shapes AI Adoption and Success: Q&A with Jessica Kriegel of Culture Partners. *SHRM*. https://www.shrm.org/topics-tools/flagships/ai-hi/how-organizational-culture-shapes-ai-adoption-success

Bronsdon, C. (2024). Metrics for Measuring and Improving AI Agent Performance. Galileo. Retrieved from https://www.galileo.ai/blog/ai-agent-metrics

Certified, M. Azure AI Fundamentals. (2024). Microsoft Learn. Retrieved from https://learn.microsoft.com/en-us/credentials/certifications/azure-ai-fundamentals/?practice-assessment-type=certification

Cinite, I., Duxbury, L. E., & Higgins, C. (2009). Measurement of perceived organizational readiness for change in the public sector. *British Journal of Management*, *20*(2), 265–277.

Costa, T. (2024). Discover the power of Microsoft Certifications for your career. TechCommunity, Microsoft. Retrieved from https://techcommunity.microsoft.com/t5/microsoft-learn-blog/discover-the-power-of-microsoft-certifications-for-your-career/ba-p/4090763

Coyle, M. (2021). Skills today for tomorrow's jobs. Amazon. Retrieved from https://www.aboutamazon.com/news/workplace/skills-today-for-tomorrows-jobs

Crist, C. (2024a). Ikea embarks on companywide AI literacy initiative. Retail Dive. Retrieved from https://www.retaildive.com/news/ikea-companywide-ai-literacy-initiative/713863/

Crist, C. (2024b). Salesforce offers free hands-on AI courses for everyone through 2025. HR Dive. Retrieved from https://www.hrdive.com

Dagli, K. (2022). 10 companies with Exceptional Employee Development Programs: Together mentoring software. RSS. Retrieved from https://www.togetherplatform.com/blog/best-training-and-development-programs

Danfernandezmsft, S. Supernova-eng, & Dend. (2020). Microsoft Learn Overview and tour. Microsoft Learn. Retrieved from https://learn.microsoft.com/en-us/teamblog/microsoft-learn-tour

Davenport, T. H., & Ronanki, R. (2018). Artificial intelligence for the real world. *HBR'S 10 MUST*, 67.

Davey, K. (2024). AI-Powered LMS Platform: How to Improve Learning with AI. Docebo. Retrieved from https://www.docebo.com/learning-network/blog/ai-lms/

Davis, F. D. (1987). User acceptance of information systems: the technology acceptance model (TAM). Working Paper. https://deepblue.lib.umich.edu/handle/2027.42/35547

De Cremer, D. (2025, March). *Employees Won't Trust AI If They Don't Trust Their Leaders*. Harvard Business Review. https://hbr.org/2025/03/employees-wont-trust-ai-if-they-dont-trust-their-leaders#

De Freitas, J. (2025). *Why people resist embracing AI*. Harvard Business Review. https://hbr.org/2025/01/why-people-resist-embracing-ai

Deloitte Development LLC. (2024). *AI Readiness & Management Framework (AIRMF)*. https://www2.deloitte.com/content/dam/Deloitte/us/Documents/public-sector/ai-readiness-and-management-framework.pdf

Dempsey, M., Geitner, L., Brennan, A., & McAvoy, J. (2021). A review of the success and failure factors for change management. *IEEE Engineering Management Review*, *50*(1), 85–93.

Edmondson, A. (1999). Psychological safety and learning behavior in work teams. *Administrative Science Quarterly*, *44*(2), 350–383.

Edmondson, A., & Moingeon, B. (1998). From organizational learning to the learning organization. *Management Learning*, *29*(1), 5–20.

Ericsson Transforms Workforce Learning with Degreed (n.d.) Degreed. https://explore.degreed.com/success-stories/ericsson/

Fauscette, M. (2024). Generative AI and Personalized Education: Adapting Learning Materials to Individual Needs. Arion Research LLC. Retrieved from https://www.arionresearch.com/blog/generative-ai-and-personalized-education-adapting-learning-materials-to-individual-needs

Ferrara, E. (2023). Fairness and bias in artificial intelligence: A brief survey of sources, impacts, and mitigation strategies. *Sci*, *6*(1), 3.

Finley, A. P. (2023). The Career-Ready Graduate: What Employers Say about the Difference College Makes. American Association of Colleges and Universities. Retrieved from https://dgmg81phhvh63.cloudfront.net/content/user-photos/Research/PDFs/AACU-2023-Employer-Report.pdf

Fong, J., Etter, B., & Sullberg, D. (2023). The Effect of Employer Understanding and Engagement on Non-Degree Credentials. University Professional and Continuing Education Association, Collegis Education. Retrieved from https://collegiseducation.com/wp-content/uploads/2023/02/UPCEA-Collegis-Employers-and-Microcredentials-Report.pdf

Fox, A. (2024). Mayo Clinic taps AI start-up to unlock data. Healthcare IT News. Retrieved from https://www.healthcareitnews.com/news/mayo-clinic-taps-ai-start-unlock-data

Frazier, M. L., Fainshmidt, S., Klinger, R. L., Pezeshkan, A., & Vracheva, V. (2017). Psychological safety: A meta-analytic review and extension. *Personnel Psychology*, *70*(1), 113–165.

Fügener, A., Grahl, J., Gupta, A., & Ketter, W. (2021). Cognitive Challenges in Human–Artificial Intelligence Collaboration: Investigating the Path Toward Productive Delegation. *Information Systems Research*, *33*(2), 678–696.

Gallagher, S. (2019). How the value of educational credentials is and isn't changing. *Harvard Business Review*. Retrieved from https://hbr.org/2019/09/how-the-value-of-educational-credentials-is-and-isnt-changing

Ghai, N. (2024). NTT DATA launches AI upskilling programme for all employees. The Economic Times. Retrieved from https://economictimes.indiatimes.com/news/company/corporate-trends/ntt-data-launches-ai-upskilling-programme-for-all-employees/articleshow/114547254.cms?from=mdr

Global Opportunity Forum. (2022). Five companies investing in upskilling the workforce. Retrieved from https://goi.mit.edu/2022/04/21/five-companies-investing-in-upskilling-the-workforce/

Golgeci, I., Ritala, P., Arslan, A., McKenna, B., & Ali, I. (2025). Confronting and alleviating AI resistance in the workplace: An integrative review and a process framework. *Human Resource Management Review*, *35*(2), 101075.

Graceffo, E. (2024). Live at build: Microsoft Learn releases new AI skill-building resources. TechCommunity, Microsoft. Retrieved from https://techcommunity.microsoft.com/t5/microsoft-learn-blog/live-at-build-microsoft-learn-releases-new-ai-skill-building/ba-p/4137354

Hamilton, D. (2025). *The rise of AI resentment at work: Why employees are pushing back*. Forbes. https://www.forbes.com/sites/dianehamilton/2025/02/03/the-rise-of-ai-resentment-at-work-why-employees-are-pushing-back/

Hashemi-Pour, C., Kirvan, P., & Brush, K. (2024). What is a learning management system (LMS)? TechTargetNetwork. Retrieved from https://www.techtarget.com/searchcio/definition/learning-management-system

Hat, R. (2024). *Evaluating frameworks to define an AI corporate strategy*. Harvard Business Review. https://hbr.org/sponsored/2024/03/evaluating-frameworks-to-define-an-ai-corporate-strategy

Howard, C. (2025). The Top CIO Challenges, According to 12k+ of Your CIO Peers. *Gartner*. https://www.gartner.com/en/articles/cio-challenges#:~:text=Sixty%2Dnine%20percent%20of%20CIOs,evolve%20the%20cybersecurity%20operating%20model

Ingka Group. (2024). Ikea retail unleashes AI Revolution: Empowering Thousands to master the future of tech. Retrieved from https://www.ingka.com/newsroom/ikea-retail-unleashes-ai-revolution-empowering-thousands-to-master-the-future-of-tech/

Insights, D. (2020). Talent and workforce effects in the age of AI. Retrieved from https://www2.deloitte.com/content/dam/insights/us/articles/6546_talent-and-workforce-effects-in-the-age-of-ai/DI_Talent-and-workforce-effects-in-the-age-of-AI.pdf

Joffe, J. (2024). Training the AI muscle: PwC's approach to bridging AI theory and everyday use. Ragan Communications. Retrieved from https://www.ragan.com/pwc-bridging-ai-theory-and-everyday-use/

Jöhnk, J., Weißert, M., & Wyrtki, K. (2021). Ready or not, AI comes—An interview study of organizational AI readiness factors. *Business & Information Systems Engineering*, *63*(1), 5–20.

Kim, S. (2024). How AI Supports Knowledge Transfer in A&D Manufacturing. iBase-t. Retrieved from https://www.ibaset.com/how-ai-is-solving-knowledge-transfer-challenges/

Kumar, A. (2024). Top 15 Challenges of Artificial Intelligence in 2025. Simplilearn.com. Retrieved from https://www.simplilearn.com/challenges-of-artificial-intelligence-article

Lake, K. (2024). Leveraging AI For Effective L&D Measurement. eLearning Industry. Retrieved from https://elearningindustry.com/leveraging-ai-for-effective-ld-measurement

Learning Ecosystem Case Study | Visa University | Watershed. (n.d.). https://www.watershedlrs.com/case-studies/financial-services/visa/?utm_source=chatgpt.com

Learning Ecosystem Case Study: Danone | Watershed. (n.d.). https://www.watershedlrs.com/case-studies/food-and-beverage/danone/

Lukan, E. (2024). 9 Impactful Uses of AI in Learning and Development in 2024. Synthesia. Retrieved from https://www.synthesia.io/learn/ai-applications/learning-and-development

Madsen, S. R., Miller, D., & John, C. R. (2005). Readiness for organizational change: Do organizational commitment and social relationships in the workplace make a difference? *Human Resource Development Quarterly*, *16*(2), 213–234.

Marr, B. (2024). *Examples that illustrate why transparency is crucial in AI.* Forbes. https://www.forbes.com/sites/bernardmarr/2024/05/17/examples-that-illustrate-why-transparency-is-crucial-in-ai/

Martin, C. (2024). *Research: More than half of large businesses are increasing investments in AI, big data.* AI Business. https://aibusiness.com/data/research-more-than-half-of-large-businesses-are-increasing-investments-in-ai-big-data

Martin, K. (2024). 9 Common Challenges to AI Adoption and How to Avoid Them. Naviant. Retrieved from https://naviant.com/blog/ai-challenges-solved/

Masood, A. (2025). The Agentic Imperative Series Part 5— Return on Investment of Agentic AI: A business leader's Perspective. *Medium.* https://medium.com/@adnanmasood/the-agentic-imperative-series-part-5-return-on-investment-of-agentic-ai-a-business-leaders-8e4f9784c4b0#:~:text=Recent%20studies%20indicate%20that%20this,Opportunity%20Value%20of%20Agentic%20AI)

Maurer, R. (2024). Study highlights worker attitudes toward AI adoption. *SHRM.* https://www.shrm.org/topics-tools/news/technology/study-highlights-worker-attitudes-toward-ai-adoption

Mayer, H., Yee, L., Chui, M., & Roberts, R. (2025). *Superagency in the workplace: Empowering people to unlock AI's full potential.* McKinsey & Company. https://www.mckinsey.com/capabilities/mckinsey-digital/our-insights/superagency-in-the-workplace-empowering-people-to-unlock-ais-full-potential-at-work#/

McGregor, J. (2023). The Future Of Work 50 2023. *Forbes.* Retrieved from https://www.forbes.com/sites/jenamcgregor/2023/11/08/the-future-of-work-50-2023/?

Mckenzie, S. (2025). *Transparent AI: How Advanced Reasoning is Reshaping Trust in Machine Intelligence.* World Certification Institute. https://www.worldcertification.org/how-advanced-reasoning-is-reshaping-trust-in-machine-intelligence/

Merhi, M. I. (2023). An evaluation of the critical success factors impacting artificial intelligence implementation. *International Journal of Information Management, 69*, 102545.

Miake-Lye, I. M., Delevan, D. M., Ganz, D. A., Mittman, B. S., & Finley, E. P. (2020). Unpacking organizational readiness for change: An updated systematic review and content analysis of assessments. *BMC Health Services Research, 20*, 1–13. PMID: 32046708

Mikalef, P., Conboy, K., Lundström, J. E., & Popovič, A. (2022). Thinking responsibly about responsible AI and 'the dark side'of AI. *European Journal of Information Systems, 31*(3), 257–268.

Mitchell, R. (2022). How to launch—and scale—a successful AI pilot project. CIO. Retrieved from https://www.cio.com/article/410642/how-to-launch-and-scale-a-successful-ai-pilot-project.html

Newsfile Corp. (2024). EveryAnswer Launches AI Expert Platform for Enterprise Knowledge Management and customer Service. Retrieved from https://finance.yahoo.com/news/everyanswer-launches-ai-expert-platform-152200456.html?guccounter=1&guce_referrer=aHR0cHM6Ly93d3cucGVycGxleGl0eS5haS8&guce_referrer_sig=AQAAANMCO-LGmukIJzoIml2Ij9r-qw-bBxK3W7sOjcarQq4FZIwZeX2Cq6JZXExEJT28wZOigbfZ74TrL41AeMAgVenfqQkI9jKSRip0liY_bIpqMPf8sh4xrp1ZUXx7pZRBV7Qll_lC2CflKFcjIO1mnb8BVQXDB9Y3hb-O-qEvBque

Nordell Westling, A. (n.d.). Sana Learning Platform. MIT SOLVE. Retrieved from https://solve.mit.edu/challenges/good-jobs-and-inclusive-entrepreneurship/solutions/30709

NTT DATA Establishes Generative AI Talent Development Framework. (2024). NTT DATA. Retrieved from https://us.nttdata.com/en/news/press-release/2024/october/ntt-data-establishes-generative-ai-talent-development-framework

Örtenblad, A. (2018). What does "learning organization" mean? *The Learning Organization, 25*(3), 150–158. DOI: 10.1108/TLO-02-2018-0016

Pallardy, R. (2024). The AI Skills Gap and How to Address It. Information Week. Retrieved from https://www.informationweek.com/it-leadership/the-ai-skills-gap-and-how-to-address-it

Panetta, K. (2019). The CIO's Guide to Artificial Intelligence. *Gartner*. https://www.gartner.com/smarterwithgartner/the-cios-guide-to-artificial-intelligence

Pardo, S. B. (2024). Tech workers could earn up to 35% more by switching to an AI / ML role, data reveals. *The Accountant*. https://www.theaccountant-online.com/news/tech-workers-could-earn-up-to-35-more-by-switching-to-an-ai-ml-role-data-reveals/?cf-view

Pinski, M., Haas, M. J., & Benlian, A. (2024). Building metaknowledge in ai literacy–the effect of gamified vs. text-based learning on ai literacy metaknowledge.

Pourak, K. (2024). Navigating AI Integration In Manufacturing: Challenges, Benefits And Strategies. Forbes. Retrieved from https://www.forbes.com/councils/forbestechcouncil/2024/05/31/navigating-ai-integration-in-manufacturing-challenges-benefits-and-strategies/

Rai, A., Constantinides, P., & Sarker, S. (2019). Next Generation Digital Platforms: Toward Human-AI Hybrids. *Management Information Systems Quarterly*, *43*(1), iii–ix.

Ransbotham, S., Kiron, D., Khodabandeh, S., Chu, M., & Zhukhov, L. (2024). *Learning to Manage Uncertainty, With AI*. MIT Sloan Management Review and Boston Consulting Group.

Salesforce. (2024). *85% of IT leaders see AI boosting productivity, but data integration and overwhelmed teams hinder success*. https://www.salesforce.com/news/stories/connectivity-report-announcement-2024/#:~:text=Adding%20to%20these%20concerns%2C%2098,overly%20dependent%20on%20one%20another

Schatten, J., & Aires, T. (2025). *AI Will Take Your Job, and It's for the Best*. Emerald Publishing.

Segal, M. (2021). Amazon Commits $1.2 Billion to Provide Access to Education and Skills Training for Workforce. ESG Today. Retrieved from https://www.esgtoday.com/amazon-commits-1-2-billion-to-provide-access-to-education-and-skills-training-for-workforce/

Senge, P. (1990). The Leader's New Work: Building Learning Organizations. Sloan Management Review reprint series; reprint 3211.

Serrat, O. (2017). *Knowledge solutions: Tools, methods, and approaches to drive organizational performance*. Springer Nature.

Sharma, R. (2025). *Why transparency is key to unlocking AI's full potential.* World Economic Forum. https://www.weforum.org/stories/2025/01/why-transparency-key-to-unlocking-ai-full-potential/

Skills Report, A. I. (2024). Pluralsight. Retrieved from https://www.pluralsight.com/resource-center/ai-skills-report-2024

Staff, A. (2024). 9 free skills training programs for Amazon employees. Amazon. Retrieved from https://www.aboutamazon.com/news/workplace/our-upskilling-2025-programs

Stiepan, D. (2022). Using AI in radiology clinical practice. Mayo Clinic. Retrieved from https://newsnetwork.mayoclinic.org/discussion/using-ai-in-radiology-clinical-practice/

Stokes, E. (2024). NTT DATA introduces Generative AI Talent Development Framework for global workforce — EdTech Innovation Hub. EdTech Innovation Hub. Retrieved from https://www.edtechinnovationhub.com/news/ntt-data-gen-ai-talent-development-framework

Strich, F., Mayer, A. S., & Fiedler, M. (2021). What do I do in a world of artificial intelligence? Investigating the impact of substitutive decision-making AI systems on employees' professional role identity. *Journal of the Association for Information Systems*, *22*(2), 9.

Stryker, C. (2024). Artificial Intelligence Implementation: 8 Steps for Success. IBM. Retrieved from https://www.ibm.com/think/insights/artificial-intelligence-implementation

Tello, J., & Subramanian, L. (2022). The magic behind turning data into profit. Deloitte Development LLC. Retrieved from https://www2.deloitte.com/content/dam/Deloitte/us/Documents/deloitte-analytics/us-ai-institute-challenges-of-using-artificial-intelligence-final.pdf

Tremblay, R. (2024). What is Learning Analytics & How It's Used in L&D. Docebo. Retrieved from https://www.docebo.com/learning-network/blog/learning-analytics/

Vargas, J. (2022). What employers want: The battle between skills and degrees. The EvoLLLution. Retrieved from https://evolllution.com/programming/credentials/what-employers-want-the-battle-between-skills-and-degrees

Venkatesh, N., Morris, N., Davis, N., & Davis, N. (2003). User acceptance of information Technology: Toward a unified view. *Management Information Systems Quarterly*, *27*(3), 425. DOI: 10.2307/30036540

We Built this Citi on Learning & Skills (n.d.). https://explore.degreed.com/wp-content/uploads/2024/01/Citi-Degreed-Success-Story-1.pdf

Welding, L. (2024). The Rise and Future of Microcredentials in Higher Education. BestColleges.com. Retrieved from https://www.bestcolleges.com/research/microcredentials-rise-in-higher-education/#fn-4

Wiley. (2023). How MBA programs are changing with the market. AACSB. Retrieved from https://www.aacsb.edu/insights/articles/2023/03/how-mba-programs-are-changing-with-the-market

Wilkinson, L. (2024). Legacy tech upgrades cost the average business nearly $3M last year. *CIO Dive.* https://www.ciodive.com/news/legacy-technology-technical-debt-costs-enterprise-data-AI/721885/#:~:text=Dive%20Brief:%20*%20Legacy%20tech%20upgrades%20cost,systems%2C%20according%20to%20the%20report%20published%20Thursday

Winstead, A. (2023). Fostering a Culture of Continuous Learning in the Workplace. Intellum. Retrieved from https://www.intellum.com/resources/blog/continuous-learning-in-the-workplace

YEC. (2023). 10 Hurdles Companies Are Facing When Implementing AI (And How To Overcome Them). Forbes. Retrieved from https://www.forbes.com/councils/theyec/2023/10/25/10-hurdles-companies-are-facing-when-implementing-ai-and-how-to-overcome-them/

Yue, S., & Berrios, D. (2024). Introducing WMDP: Measuring and Mitigating Catastrophic Risk Potential from LLMs. Scale. Retrieved from https://scale.com/blog/measuring-mitigating-risk-wmdp

Zhang, Y., Fang, Y., Wei, K. K., & Chen, H. (2010). Exploring the role of psychological safety in promoting the intention to continue sharing knowledge in virtual communities. *International Journal of Information Management, 30*(5), 425–436.

Chapter 2

Leveraging AI and Digital Solutions to Enhance Sustainability in Green and Blue Economies

Pinnika Syam Yadav
https://orcid.org/0000-0003-4954-1273
Christ University, India

P. B. Narendra Kiran
https://orcid.org/0000-0002-9883-3240
Christ University, India

Rajesh Vemula
https://orcid.org/0009-0004-3282-6453
Christ University, India

Vikas Kumar
https://orcid.org/0000-0003-3455-9227
Mittal School of Business, India

Preeti Kumari
Mittal School of Business, India

Ruben Anto Michael
https://orcid.org/0000-0002-1481-3067
Christ University, India

ABSTRACT

This research explores how digital solutions, including artificial intelligence (AI), drive sustainability in terrestrial (green) and aquatic (blue) economies. By examining case studies and technological implementations, it highlights the potential and challenges of digital innovations, particularly AI, in promoting environmental sustainability, economic growth, and social well-being. The study covers the current state of green and blue economies, digital interventions like smart agriculture, renewable energy, marine monitoring, and sustainable fisheries, and their impacts. The research uses both qualitative and quantitative methods, gathering data through interviews, surveys, and literature. Results will provide success stories, challenges, and best practices, offering recommendations for policymakers and stakeholders.

DOI: 10.4018/979-8-3373-0159-4.ch002

The study aims to contribute to the theoretical and practical understanding of how digital technologies, especially AI, can advance sustainability in these economies, with future research directions identified.

1. INTRODUCTION

The concepts of the blue economy and green economy represent modern and innovative approaches to sustainable development that focus on responsible and efficient resource use. The blue economy specifically emphasizes the sustainable and responsible utilization of marine resources with the aim to significantly enhance economic growth, improve livelihoods, create employment opportunities, and promote the health of marine ecosystems (Van Hoof, 2019). It encompasses a wide range of sectors including, but not limited to, fishing, maritime transport, tourism, and renewable energy. All these sectors are grounded in fundamental principles that prioritize not only resource sustainability but also marine conservation and inclusive economic growth, ensuring that communities benefit from their natural resources (Spalding, 2016). Sustainable practices under the blue economy include sustainable fisheries management, marine conservation efforts, the development of sea-based renewable energy sources, and eco-friendly marine transportation systems. These practices aim to achieve a delicate balance between economic gains and ecosystem protection, ensuring that the resources and health of our oceans are preserved for future generations to enjoy and utilize responsibly. This holistic approach integrates environmental stewardship and economic development, paving the way for a more sustainable and prosperous future for coastal and marine communities worldwide.

Conversely, the green economy seeks to minimize various environmental hazards and the ongoing issue of resource scarcity while fostering a form of sustainable growth that does not cause harm to the environment (Chen et al., 2019). With the increasing prevalence of environmental concerns in society, "green" products have gained significant public attention and awareness (Haque et al., 2023). The green economy encompasses a wide range of sectors such as clean energy production, sustainable agricultural practices, effective waste management, and eco-friendly industrial practices that aim to reduce carbon footprints (Azam & Ponnam, 2023). It places a strong emphasis on sustainable development through the reduction of ecological risks, addressing the limitations of resources, driving economic expansion, and improving social equity among varying demographics. This comprehensive approach reflects a holistic view of economic development, one that values not only environmental health but also social well-being, integrating the needs of both the planet and its inhabitants for a sustainable future.

Currently, both economies are gaining substantial momentum as various countries and industries increasingly recognize the urgent need for sustainable development practices. In response to these demands, governments around the world are actively implementing supportive policies and establishing comprehensive frameworks aimed at fostering sustainability. Simultaneously, the private sector is stepping up its efforts by investing heavily in innovative green technologies as well as sustainable practices that aim to minimize environmental impact. Nevertheless, challenges remain; regulatory barriers, technological gaps, and financial constraints continue to hinder progress. The integration of digital strategies is gradually transforming these sectors, but achieving comprehensive sustainability still appears to be a distant goal. Digital strategies, which incorporate advanced technologies such as the Internet of Things (IoT), Artificial Intelligence (AI), big data analytics, and blockchain, are proving to be crucial for the optimization of resource management, the monitoring of environmental impacts, and the enhancement of operational efficiency (Li & Wang, 2022; Yi et al., 2022). These technological tools facilitate real-time data collection and analysis, which fosters better decision-making processes and promotes proactive measures toward the mitigation of environmental damage (Fang et al., 2024). Furthermore, the implementation of digital technologies enhances communication and cooperation among various stakeholders, thereby promoting integrated environmental management efforts. Technologies such as IoT, AI, and big data analytics not only drive the advancement of environmental sustainability but also enable precise monitoring and management of resources, predictive maintenance of infrastructure, along with real-time assessments of environmental impacts. Meanwhile, blockchain technology plays a pivotal role in ensuring transparency and accountability within supply chains, thus working to reduce illegal practices that can harm the environment. In the evolving green economy, digital strategies encompass intelligent grids, precision agriculture methodologies, and innovative digital waste management platforms.

2. LITERATURE REVIEW

The green economy, a paradigm for sustainable development, is defined by its commitment to reducing environmental risks, enhancing resource efficiency, and fostering low-carbon growth while ensuring social equity (Chen et al., 2019; Singh et al., 2025). This model seeks to harmonize economic progress with ecological sustainability, contrasting with traditional approaches that often prioritize immediate economic gains at the expense of the environment (Chen et al., 2019). Its foundational principles encompass sustainability, decarbonization, and circularity, with the primary objectives of diminishing greenhouse gas emissions, minimizing ecological degradation, and guaranteeing equitable access to resources, thereby emphasizing enduring environmental and social well-being (Chen et al., 2019; Shuja et al., 2017; Singh et al., 2025). Key sectors propelling this transition include renewable energy, such as solar, wind, and bioenergy, supported by advancements like smart grids and energy management systems (Khalid, 2024; Yadav et al., 2025); sustainable agriculture, employing precision farming and IoT for resource conservation (Shuja et al., 2017); waste management, enhanced by digital platforms and AI for improved recycling (Singh et al., 2025); and green manufacturing, adopting energy-efficient processes through automation and AI (Li et al., 2014; Yadav et al., 2025).

Complementing the green economy is the blue economy, which, as outlined by Van Hoof (2019) and Spalding (2016), focuses on the sustainable utilization of marine resources to stimulate economic growth while preserving ocean health (Spalding, 2016; Van Hoof, 2019). Guided by the principles of marine ecosystem protection and sustainable practices (Van Hoof, 2019), its goals include economic diversification through sustainable aquaculture and marine tourism (Nham et al., 2023); climate mitigation via marine renewable energy (offshore wind, tidal, wave) (Li & Wang, 2022; Pandey & Yadav, 2023); and biodiversity conservation through initiatives like blue carbon for coastal wetland restoration (Choudhary et al., 2024).

Digital strategies are integral to both economies. The green economy leverages IoT and AI for environmental monitoring, blockchain for supply chain transparency (Cathrine, 2024), remote sensing for tracking environmental changes (Xiao et al., 2023), and VR for education (Dahiya et al., 2024). The blue economy employs blockchain for seafood traceability (Ismail et al., 2023), AI for maritime logistics optimization (Durlik et al., 2023; Isaac et al., 2023), remote sensing and UAVs for monitoring marine health (Li & Li, 2024; Xiao et al., 2023), and digital twins for ecosystem simulation (Ambarita et al., 2024).

Despite their promise, both economies encounter challenges. The green economy faces regulatory hurdles in digital adoption (Whig et al., 2024), technological gaps, particularly in rural areas (Isaac et al., 2023; Yadav et al., 2025), and economic constraints for small businesses (Azam & Ponnam, 2023). The blue economy grapples with data privacy and cybersecurity concerns (Whig et al., 2024), the need for cross-border governance in the maritime domain (Pace et al., 2023), and funding limitations for marine technologies (Nham et al., 2023).

Ultimately, the synergy between these complementary approaches, bolstered by interdisciplinary research, robust policies, and collaborative partnerships, is essential for realizing a holistic and sustainable future.

These initiatives substantiate significant improvements in resource efficiency, enormous cost savings, and enhanced protection of the environment overall.

2.1 Shared Goal of Climate Change Mitigation

blue and green economies show synergies as they share the goal of mitigating climate change. The blue economy can significantly contribute to this goal by developing marine renewable energy sources such as offshore wind, tidal, and wave energy. These technologies provide clean energy alternatives that reduce reliance on fossil fuels, thus decreasing greenhouse gas emissions. Similarly, the green economy promotes using renewable energy sources like solar, wind, and bioenergy, which can complement marine renewables in creating a diversified and resilient energy portfolio. Integrating offshore wind farms with onshore renewable energy sources can create a stable and continuous supply of green energy. Offshore wind farms can generate significant power, particularly in regions with strong and consistent wind patterns, while onshore solar farms can provide energy during peak sunlight hours. By combining these resources, energy grids can be stabilized, reducing the need for fossil fuel-based backup power and lowering overall carbon emissions.

2.2 Ecosystem Services and Conservation

Coastal and marine ecosystems, such as mangroves, coral reefs, and seagrass beds, provide crucial services, including carbon sequestration, storm protection, and biodiversity conservation. These ecosystems can be integrated with terrestrial green infrastructure projects to enhance resilience against climate change impacts. For instance, mangrove restoration projects can align with watershed management efforts to control soil erosion and improve water quality, benefiting marine and terrestrial environments. There are highly effective at sequestering carbon, often called "blue carbon." Their restoration helps mitigate climate change and provides a habitat for numerous marine species, enhancing biodiversity. Furthermore, mangroves act as natural barriers against storm surges and coastal erosion, protecting inland areas from the impacts of extreme weather events. Integrating mangrove restoration with green infrastructure projects like the construction of wetlands or reforestation can create a network of natural buffers that enhance overall ecosystem resilience.

2.3 Innovations in Sustainable Practices

Integrating blue and green economies can drive innovation in sustainable practices by leveraging advanced digital technologies. The convergence of technologies such as the IoT, AI, and blockchain can optimize resource management across marine and terrestrial sectors (Arvind, 2024). Precision agriculture techniques using IoT sensors can be adapted for sustainable aquaculture, improving productivity while minimizing environmental impact. Blockchain technology can ensure transparency and traceability in supply chains, whether in sustainable fisheries or organic farming, thereby enhancing consumer trust and market access for sustainable products. In the case of sustainable aquaculture, IoT sensors can monitor water quality, temperature, and fish health in real-time, allowing for precise adjustments to feed and environmental conditions. Similarly, blockchain technology can track the journey of seafood from ocean to plate, ensuring that consumers are informed about the sustainability and legality of their purchases. This transparency can drive demand for sustainably sourced products, encouraging more producers to adopt environmentally friendly.

2.4 Resource Efficiency and Circular Economy

The blue and green economies emphasize resource efficiency and the principles of the circular economy, which aim to minimize waste and maximize the reuse and recycling of materials. Integrating these principles can lead to more efficient use of resources across sectors, reducing environmental impact and enhancing economic resilience. Waste from fish processing in the blue economy can be converted into valuable products such as fishmeal and fish oil, which can be used in agriculture as animal feed or fertilizers, closing the loop between marine and terrestrial systems. Similarly, byproducts from agricultural activities in the green economy, such as crop residues, can be utilized in aquaculture as feed or bioenergy production, creating synergies that enhance resource efficiency and sustainability.

2.5 Collaborative Governance and Policy Development

Effective integration of blue and green economies requires collaborative governance and policy development that transcends traditional sectoral boundaries. Policies that promote integrated coastal zone management, marine spatial planning, and ecosystem-based management can ensure that marine and terrestrial resources are coordinated and sustainably. Collaborative governance structures involving stakeholders from both the marine and terrestrial sectors, including government agencies, industry, and local communities, can facilitate the development and implementation of policies that balance economic development with environmental conservation.

2.6 Economic Diversification and Job Creation

Blue and green economy principles can drive economic diversification and job creation by fostering new industries and opportunities. Marine renewable energy projects, sustainable aquaculture, and ecotourism are industries that can generate income and employment while promoting environmental sustainability. For instance, the development of offshore wind farms not only provides clean energy but also creates jobs in construction, maintenance, and operation. Similarly, sustainable tourism initiatives that promote marine and coastal conservation can attract tourists, generate revenue, and create jobs in local communities. Integrated approaches to the blue and green economies lead to improved ecosystem health and resilience. These strategies can enhance biodiversity, improve water quality, and increase carbon sequestration by aligning marine and terrestrial conservation efforts. For instance, the restoration of mangroves and coastal wetlands protects against coastal erosion, supports marine biodiversity, and sequesters significant amounts of carbon, contributing to climate change mitigation.

3. DIGITAL STRATEGIES IN THE BLUE ECONOMY

Digital strategies in the blue economy represent a comprehensive approach to maximizing efficiency, promoting sustainability, and driving innovation across maritime and ocean-related sectors. These strategies harness cutting-edge technologies to address complex challenges while ensuring the responsible use and conservation of marine resources. Central to these efforts is integrating digital solutions that enhance operational efficiencies and contribute to ocean ecosystems' overall health and resilience. One of the primary pillars of digital strategies in the blue economy is optimizing resource use through advanced technologies. By improving monitoring and surveillance, digital strategies enable proactive conservation measures and contribute to achieving marine conservation targets outlined in international agreements like the Sustainable Development Goals (SDGs).

Furthermore, digital strategies foster sustainable economic growth by promoting innovation and entrepreneurship in maritime industries. Emerging technologies such as blockchain enhance transparency and traceability in seafood supply chains, reducing the risk of illegal fishing and promoting fair trade practices. Advanced data analytics and AI-driven predictive models support informed decision-making in maritime logistics, port operations, and offshore energy production, optimizing efficiency and reducing operational costs.

Figure 1.

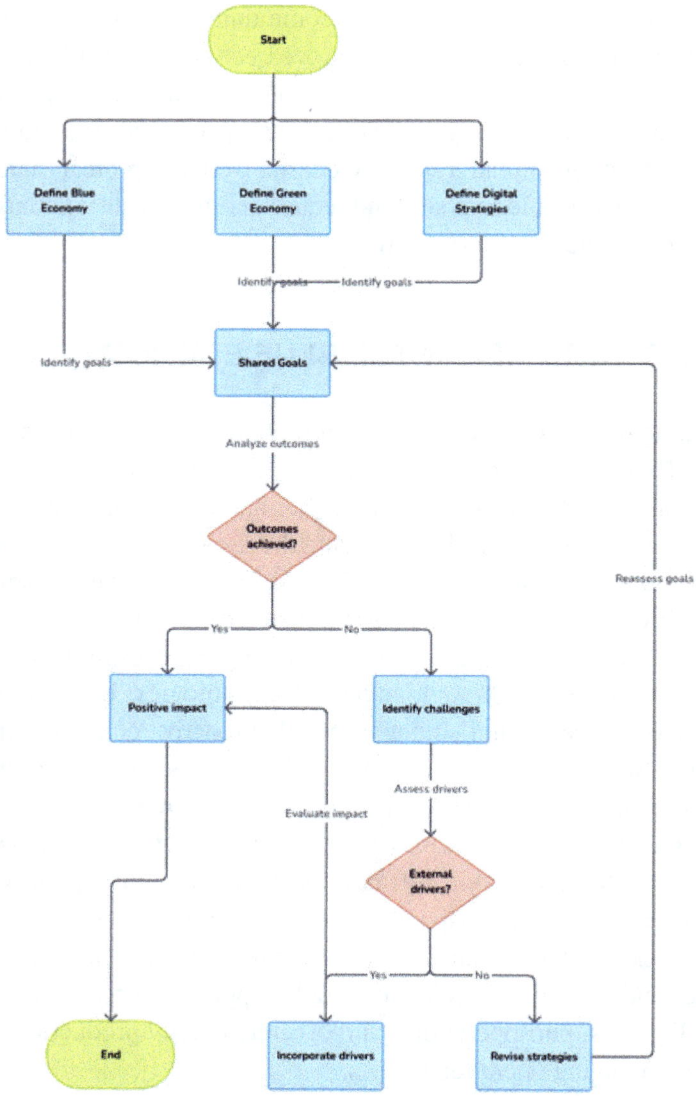

Digital strategies of blue economies are as follows:

3.1 Smart Shipping and Autonomous Vessels

Smart shipping technologies significantly advance maritime operations, integrating sensors, AI, and the IoT to revolutionize vessel management and navigation (Isaac et al., 2023). These technologies enhance the shipping industry's efficiency, safety, and environmental sustainability. Autonomous vessels, a key component of smart shipping, utilize sophisticated navigation systems and AI algorithms to navigate and operate with minimal human intervention (Durlik et al., 2023). One example of smart shipping technology is IoT sensors monitoring vessel performance in real-time. These sensors collect data on engine efficiency, fuel consumption, weather conditions, and cargo status. By analyzing this data, ship operators can optimize operational parameters, such as speed and route, to minimize fuel usage and reduce emissions. For instance, Maersk, a prominent global shipping company, has implemented IoT sensors to monitor engine efficiency and fuel consumption, significantly reducing fuel use and greenhouse gas emissions. Autonomous vessels take smart shipping a step further by integrating AI-driven navigation systems. Smart shipping technologies contribute to sustainability goals by reducing the carbon footprint of shipping activities. Efficient route planning and optimized speed profiles based on real-time data analytics help minimize fuel consumption and emissions. This lowers operational costs and aligns with international efforts to mitigate climate change and promote environmental stewardship in maritime transport.

3.2 Marine Resource Management

Marine resource management is transforming by integrating digital technologies such as sensor networks and IoT devices. These technologies enable real-time monitoring and data collection across marine ecosystems, providing critical insights into fish stocks, oceanographic conditions, and habitat health. By leveraging these digital tools, stakeholders can make informed decisions that optimize resource use, minimize environmental impact, and promote sustainable practices in marine resource exploitation. Sensor networks deployed throughout marine environments gather vast data on various ecological parameters. These sensors measure water quality, temperature, salinity, and nutrient levels, among other variables, providing a comprehensive understanding of marine conditions. The Integrated Ocean Observing System (IOOS) in the United States utilizes sensor networks to monitor and forecast oceanographic conditions. This data supports fisheries management by predicting fish migration patterns, identifying spawning grounds, and assessing environmental factors influencing fish populations. IoT devices play a crucial role in enhancing the efficiency and accuracy of marine resource management. These devices are embedded in fishing gear, buoys, and underwater platforms to track marine activities and monitor ecosystem health in real-time (Durlik et al., 2023).

3.3 Environmental Monitoring and Surveillance

Environmental monitoring and surveillance in marine environments have significantly advanced through integrating remote sensing technologies, satellite imagery, and Unmanned Aerial Vehicles (UAVs) (Li & Li, X.-Z., 2024). These digital tools play a pivotal role in detecting and assessing various environmental parameters, including marine pollution, illegal fishing activities, and changes in ocean health. Remote sensing technologies, such as multispectral and hyperspectral imaging, provide detailed insights into oceanographic conditions and marine habitats from a distance. Satellites equipped with these sensors capture high-resolution images of coastal and open ocean areas, allowing for the monitoring of water quality, coral reefs, and marine biodiversity. Satellite imagery is also instrumental in detecting and monitoring marine pollution. Oil spills, plastic debris, and other pollutants can be identified and tracked using satellite images, enabling authorities to assess the extent of contamination and plan remedial actions.

3.4 Blockchain for Traceability and Transparency

The seafood industry is experiencing a transformation through blockchain technology, which enhances transparency and tracking capabilities in supply chains. This innovation is tackling persistent issues associated with illegal, unreported, and unregulated (IUU) fishing activities. By leveraging blockchain, stakeholders can record and verify transaction data securely, imminently, and transparently, enhancing accountability and promoting sustainable sourcing practices throughout the seafood industry. Fundamentally, blockchain technology operates as a distributed digital database that logs transactions across numerous computers transparently and tamper-resistantly (Vashishth et al., 2024). Each entry, or “block,” is connected to its predecessor, forming a chain of blocks that cannot be modified retroactively without altering all subsequent blocks. By recording data such as catch location, fishing vessel information, and processing details on the blockchain, stakeholders can ensure that seafood products are sourced sustainably and legally (Yang et al., 2024). This system allows consumers to scan QR codes on seafood packaging to access information about the fishery's sustainability practices and verify their authenticity. Consumers can access detailed information about each product's journey, including its origins, processing methods, and environmental impact, fostering informed purchasing decisions that support sustainable fisheries management.

3.5 Predictive Analytics and AI in Maritime Operations

Predictive analytics and AI are revolutionizing maritime operations by enhancing efficiency, safety, and sustainability across various sectors, including logistics, port operations, and offshore energy production. These technologies leverage advanced data analytics and AI-driven models to predict outcomes, optimize resource allocation, and improve real-time decision-making processes. Predictive analytics in maritime operations involve analyzing historical and real-time data to forecast future events and trends. This enables proactive maintenance of maritime infrastructure, such as ships, ports, and offshore platforms, to prevent breakdowns and reduce downtime. Shipping companies use predictive maintenance algorithms to monitor engine performance, identify potential failures before they occur, and schedule maintenance activities during optimal times. This approach extends the lifespan of maritime assets, enhances operational reliability, and reduces maintenance costs.

3.6 Renewable Energy Technologies

Digital strategies are pivotal in advancing renewable energy technologies in offshore environments, focusing on harnessing clean energy sources like offshore wind, tidal, and wave energy. These technologies aim to generate sustainable electricity while decreasing dependence on fossil fuels and mitigating environmental effects typically associated with conventional power generation methods. Offshore wind farms represent a prominent example of renewable energy integration in maritime settings. These farms utilize large wind turbines installed in offshore waters, where wind speeds are typically higher and more consistent than onshore locations. Digital technologies optimize offshore wind farms' design, construction, and operation by conducting detailed feasibility studies, site assessments, and wind resource assessments using advanced modeling and simulation tools. For instance, the London Array, one of the world's largest offshore wind farms, utilizes digital tools to optimize turbine placement and layout, maximizing energy output and minimizing environmental impact. Marine energy systems, including tidal and wave energy converters, harness the kinetic energy of tides and waves to generate electricity (Pandey & Yadav, 2023).

3.7 Blue Carbon Initiatives

Blue carbon initiatives focus on conserving and enhancing coastal and marine ecosystems, such as mangroves, seagrasses, and salt marshes, which are crucial in carbon sequestration and climate change mitigation. These ecosystems capture and store significant amounts of atmospheric carbon dioxide, making them essential in global efforts to combat climate change (Choudhary et al., 2024). Digital strategies are instrumental in enhancing monitoring, restoration, and conservation efforts of blue carbon habitats, maximizing their carbon sequestration potential and supporting sustainable environmental practices. Coastal and marine ecosystems like mangroves, seagrasses, and salt marshes are highly effective in trapping carbon dioxide through photosynthesis and sedimentation.

3.8 Aquaculture Innovation

Aquaculture, farming fish, shellfish, and aquatic plants, is transforming with digital technologies to optimize production efficiency, ensure sustainability, and minimize environmental impacts. Digital strategies such as IoT sensors and AI-powered analytics are revolutionizing aquaculture practices by enabling real-time monitoring, precision management of resources, and proactive disease prevention measures. IoT sensors play a crucial role in aquaculture by continuously monitoring water quality parameters such as temperature, dissolved oxygen levels, pH, and salinity (Vo et al., 2021). These sensors are deployed throughout aquaculture facilities, including fish ponds, net pens, and recirculating aquaculture systems (RAS). Real-time data from IoT sensors provide aquaculturists with insights into environmental conditions, allowing them to adjust feeding regimes, optimize water quality management, and detect early signs of stress or disease among aquatic organisms.

3.9 Maritime Safety and Navigation Systems

Maritime safety and navigation systems have undergone significant advancements with the integration of digital strategies aimed at enhancing efficiency, mitigating risks, and improving overall safety in marine transportation. These digital technologies, including GPS, AIS, and collision avoidance systems, facilitate safe navigation, reduce accidents, and ensure environmental protection in congested waterways and open seas.

3.10 Blue Economy Education and Capacity Building

Digital strategies are pivotal in enhancing accessibility to education and training opportunities for marine professionals, policymakers, and stakeholders worldwide (Autsadee et al., 2023). These strategies leverage online platforms, virtual simulations, and e-learning modules to impart knowledge, develop skills, and empower coastal communities to participate effectively in sustainable blue economy practices.

4. DIGITAL SOLUTIONS IN THE GREEN ECONOMY

Digital strategies in the green economy aim to leverage technology to enhance sustainability, reduce environmental impact, and promote green growth. Here are key types of digital strategies in the green economy:

4.1 Smart Grid and Energy Management Systems

Digital solutions like smart grids and energy management systems are pivotal in revolutionizing how energy is distributed, monitored, and consumed. These technologies are crucial for enhancing efficiency, reducing environmental impact, and promoting sustainable energy practices (Khalid, 2024). This foresight allows grid operators to optimize the use of renewable energy by adjusting supply and demand in real-time. Energy Management Systems (EMS) complement smart grids by optimizing energy consumption locally within buildings, industries, and residential complexes. These systems integrate hardware like smart meters and sensors with sophisticated software that analyzes real-time energy usage data. EMS also supports energy storage, like batteries, to reserve surplus renewable energy for future use or peak demand times (Yadav, et. al., 2025) .

4.2 Internet of Things (IoT)

IoT emerges as a transformative digital solution, particularly through its application in environmental monitoring. IoT involves the deployment of interconnected sensors and devices that collect and transmit real-time data on various environmental parameters such as air quality, water quality, soil health, and biodiversity (Shuja et al., 2017). Deploying IoT Sensors enables comprehensive monitoring across diverse ecosystems. These sensors are strategically placed in urban areas, industrial zones, agricultural lands, and natural habitats to gather data continuously. Air quality sensors measure particulate matter (PM), nitrogen oxides (NOx), and ozone levels, providing insights into urban air pollution patterns and potential health impacts. IoT enhances manufacturing firms' technological innovation capability and production efficiency and increases environmental conciseness (Cardona et al., 2013; Li et al., 2014). Collecting Data from IoT sensors is a valuable resource for policymakers, environmental agencies, and researchers. This data-driven approach informs evidence-based decision-making and policy formulation (Lennerfors et al., 2015). For instance, environmental agencies can use air quality data to identify pollution hotspots and implement targeted interventions to reduce emissions from industrial sources or traffic congestion.

4.3 Artificial Intelligence (AI) and Machine Learning (ML)

AI and ML are pivotal digital solutions driving industries' efficiency, sustainability, and innovation. Applying AI to optimize resource use involves using algorithms to analyze large datasets and optimize manufacturing, agriculture, and energy production processes. AI-powered systems can monitor and adjust resource consumption in real-time, optimizing energy usage, reducing water waste, and minimizing material inputs (Shuja et al., 2017). AI can analyze soil data, weather patterns, and crop conditions in agriculture to optimize irrigation schedules and fertilizer application, improving crop yields while conserving water and minimizing environmental impact. Reducing waste is another area where AI plays a crucial role. AI algorithms can analyze production processes to identify inefficiencies and opportunities for waste reduction (Singh, et. al., 2025).

Enhancing efficiency across industries is a key benefit of AI. By analyzing historical data and real-time information, AI systems can optimize operations, streamline workflows, and identify areas for improvement. AI-driven predictive analytics can optimize maintenance schedules for renewable energy infrastructure, reducing downtime and maximizing energy output. AI can optimize waste collection routes based on real-time data in waste management, reducing fuel consumption and greenhouse gas emissions (Isaac et al., 2023).

4.4 Blockchain for Supply Chain Transparency

Blockchain technology offers significant potential in the green economy by enhancing supply chain transparency and sustainability through its immutable and decentralized ledger system. Utilizing blockchain for supply chain transparency involves creating a secure, transparent, and auditable record of transactions across the supply chain. The blockchain records every supply chain step as individual blocks, from acquiring raw materials to delivering the finished product (Cathrine, 2024). This transparency allows stakeholders, including consumers, to trace the journey of products, verify their authenticity, and ensure compliance with sustainability standards. In the agriculture sector, blockchain can track the origin of organic produce, providing assurance to consumers about the authenticity of organic certifications and promoting fair trade practices. Blockchain also facilitates sustainable sourcing by enabling companies to verify and authenticate the origin of raw materials such as minerals, metals, and timber (Yadav & Pandey, 2022).

4.5 Remote Sensing and Satellite Technology

Remote sensing and satellite technology are pivotal digital solutions in the green economy, offering critical tools for monitoring and managing environmental resources and impacts. Using satellite imagery and remote sensing involves capturing high-resolution images and data from satellites orbiting the Earth. These technologies provide a comprehensive view of landscapes, ecosystems, and environmental changes over large areas and extended periods. Satellite imagery can monitor deforestation by capturing changes in forest cover and identifying areas affected by logging, agriculture expansion, or wildfires. Similarly, remote sensing techniques can track land use changes, such as urbanization, mining activities, and agricultural practices, providing valuable insights into human impacts on natural habitats and biodiversity. Providing data for conservation efforts and sustainable land management is another key application of remote sensing and satellite technology.

4.6 Digital Platforms and Marketplaces

Digital platforms and marketplaces are pivotal in advancing the green economy by facilitating the exchange of renewable energy credits and carbon offsets and promoting sustainable practices across various sectors. Creating online platforms for trading renewable energy credits and carbon offsets is essential for promoting renewable energy adoption and mitigating carbon emissions. Renewable energy credits (RECs) prove that a unit of electricity was generated from a renewable energy source, such as wind or solar. These credits can be traded on digital platforms, allowing businesses and individuals to purchase renewable energy and support clean energy projects even if they cannot directly access renewable sources. Similarly, carbon offsets enable organizations to compensate for their greenhouse gas emissions by investing in projects that reduce emissions elsewhere, such as reforestation or renewable energy installations.

Facilitating the sharing economy through digital platforms promotes sustainable transportation and tourism practices. Carpooling and ride-sharing platforms optimize vehicle occupancy, reducing traffic congestion and emissions per passenger mile. Bike-sharing platforms encourage cycling as a low-carbon alternative to motorized transport, promoting active lifestyles and reducing urban air pollution. Sustainable tourism platforms connect travelers with eco-friendly accommodations, local experiences, and responsible tour operators, supporting destinations that prioritize environmental conservation and community well-being.

4.7 Virtual Reality (VR) and Augmented Reality (AR)

Virtual Reality (VR) and Augmented Reality (AR) are innovative digital solutions in the green economy, leveraging immersive technologies to enhance environmental education, awareness, and conservation efforts. Using VR and AR for environmental education and training transforms traditional learning experiences by offering immersive simulations and interactive environments. VR allows users to explore ecosystems, witness environmental changes, and interact with virtual habitats, providing a firsthand experience of environmental issues such as deforestation, climate change impacts, and wildlife conservation. Creating virtual experiences through VR and AR promotes eco-friendly behaviors and encourages conservation efforts by fostering empathy and understanding. Virtual experiences can simulate sustainable practices, such as renewable energy installations or sustainable agriculture techniques, allowing users to observe the benefits of green technologies firsthand. VR can showcase the process of solar panel installation or wind turbine operations, illustrating their environmental benefits and promoting renewable energy adoption. AR applications can overlay information on recycling bins or sustainable products in stores, educating consumers about eco-friendly choices and encouraging responsible consumption habits. VR can immerse users in coral reefs threatened by climate change, highlighting the urgency of marine conservation efforts and inspiring action to protect fragile ecosystems (Dahiya, et. al., 2024).

4.8 Cyber-Physical Systems (CPS)

Cyber-Physical Systems (CPS) represent a transformative digital solution in the green economy by integrating physical infrastructure with advanced digital technologies, thereby creating smarter and more sustainable cities, buildings, and transportation systems. Integrating physical infrastructure with digital technologies underpins CPS, enabling seamless communication and interaction between physical components and digital systems. In smart cities, CPS connects urban infrastructure, such as traffic lights, public transportation networks, and energy grids, with sensors, actuators, and data analytics platforms. This integration allows cities to gather real-time data on traffic flow, energy consumption, air quality, and other parameters critical for sustainable urban planning and management. CPS can optimize traffic signals based on real-time traffic data, reducing congestion and lowering vehicle emissions. Similarly, in buildings, CPS utilizes sensors and smart meters to monitor energy usage, adjust HVAC systems based on occupancy patterns, and optimize lighting to maximize energy efficiency while maintaining comfort.

Enhancing efficiency and sustainability is a core benefit of CPS in the green economy. By leveraging real-time data analytics and automation, CPS enables predictive maintenance of infrastructure, reducing downtime and extending the lifespan of equipment. In transportation systems, CPS can optimize public transit routes, promote electric vehicles through smart charging infrastructure, and facilitate multimodal transportation options that reduce reliance on private cars. These initiatives contribute to lower carbon emissions, improved air quality, and enhanced mobility options for urban residents.

4.9 Digital Twins

Digital Twins represents a cutting-edge digital solution in the green economy by creating virtual replicas of physical assets such as wind turbines, solar farms, and industrial plants. These digital replicas, or twins, are exact digital copies that simulate their physical counterparts' behavior, performance, and condition in real time or through historical data. This technology revolutionizes asset management and operational efficiency by enabling comprehensive monitoring, predictive maintenance, and scenario planning (Ambarita et al., 2024). Digital twins simulate various operating conditions, weather patterns, and energy production scenarios for renewable energy infrastructure like wind turbines and solar farms. This allows operators to optimize energy generation by adjusting operational parameters such as turbine blade angles or solar panel orientation based on real-time weather forecasts and historical performance data. Digital twins also support the design and deployment of new renewable energy projects by simulating different layouts and configurations, optimizing efficiency, and predicting energy output under different environmental conditions (Pandey, Yadav, & Reddy, 2024).

Moreover, operational efficiency is enhanced through digital twins by optimizing resource use, minimizing energy consumption, and improving overall performance. In industrial plants, digital twins simulate production processes, monitor energy usage, and identify opportunities for efficiency improvements. This includes optimizing supply chain logistics, reducing waste, and enhancing operational workflows based on real-time data insights (Kashif et al., 2024).

4.10 Big Data and Analytics

Big Data and Analytics are foundational digital solutions driving innovation and sustainability in the green economy by harnessing large volumes of data to analyze environmental trends, monitor emissions, and guide decision-making processes (Shuja et al., 2017). Leveraging big data involves collecting and analyzing vast amounts of information from diverse sources such as sensors, satellites, social media, and public records. In the context of the green economy, big data analytics provide insights into environmental trends, climate change impacts, and ecosystem dynamics. Satellite imagery combined with weather data can monitor deforestation rates, track land use changes, and assess habitat fragmentation, enabling conservationists and policymakers to identify at-risk areas and prioritize conservation efforts. Similarly, sensors measuring air and water quality provide real-time data on pollution levels, helping authorities implement targeted interventions to improve environmental health.

Big data analytics also play a crucial role in tracking emissions and assessing industry environmental impacts (Xiao et al., 2023). By analyzing emissions data from power plants, factories, and transportation networks, stakeholders can measure carbon footprints, identify sources of pollution, and develop strategies to reduce greenhouse gas emissions.

4.11 Green Software and Cloud Computing

Green Software and Cloud Computing are pivotal digital solutions in the green economy, focusing on developing energy-efficient technologies and optimizing digital infrastructure to reduce environmental impact (Shuja et al., 2017). Developing energy-efficient software involves designing applications and systems prioritizing energy conservation during operation. Green software minimizes computational resources, optimizes code efficiency, and implements power-saving algorithms to reduce energy consumption. Developers can design software that automatically adjusts processing power based on workload demands or implement sleep modes during idle periods to conserve energy. By reducing the energy footprint of software applications, organizations can lower operational costs, decrease carbon emissions associated with digital operations, and contribute to overall environmental sustainability.

Green cloud computing services enhance environmental stewardship by leveraging energy-efficient data centers and renewable energy sources. Cloud computing providers offer services that optimize server utilization, reduce cooling requirements, and implement energy-efficient hardware designs.

4.12 E-Government and Digital Public Service

E-Government and Digital Public Services are integral digital solutions driving sustainability and efficiency in the green economy by transforming governmental operations and public service delivery. Implementing digital public services entails transitioning traditional government services and administrative processes to digital platforms, reducing paper use, enhancing accessibility, and improving operational efficiency. Digital services enable citizens to access government information, submit forms, and complete transactions online, eliminating the need for paper-based documentation and physical visits to government offices. This shift reduces paper waste and streamlines service delivery, saving citizens and government agencies time and resources. For example, digital platforms for tax filings, permit applications, and public utility payments minimize administrative overheads and enable real-time processing, enhancing overall service efficiency while reducing environmental impact (Latupeirissa et al., 2024). E-governance platforms facilitate the dissemination of environmental policies, regulations, and guidelines to stakeholders, promoting awareness and ensuring compliance with environmental laws (Singh, et. al., 2025).

Furthermore, e-governance initiatives enhance public participation in environmental decision-making processes through digital platforms for public consultations, feedback mechanisms, and citizen engagement. These platforms enable stakeholders, including communities, non-governmental organizations (NGOs), and businesses, to contribute insights, voice concerns, and collaborate on sustainable development initiatives. E-governance initiatives promote informed decision-making and collective action toward achieving environmental sustainability goals by fostering transparency, accountability, and inclusivity in environmental governance.

5. CHALLENGES AND BARRIERS TO ADOPTING DIGITAL STRATEGIES IN BLUE AND GREEN ECONOMY

5.1 Ethical Dilemmas

5.1.1 Data Privacy and Security

Data privacy and security pose significant challenges and barriers in the adoption of digital strategies within both the blue and green economies, for which one of the primary concerns is data collection and consent (Whig et al., 2024). Implementing robust encryption, secure servers, and stringent access controls becomes imperative to safeguard sensitive environmental, personal, and economic data (Whig et al., 2024). Despite these measures, the ever-present threat of cybersecurity vulnerabilities persists, including risks of hacking, malware, and data breaches, which can compromise the integrity and privacy of collected information. Addressing these challenges requires technological solutions, comprehensive regulatory frameworks, and ethical guidelines to ensure digital strategies uphold privacy rights while advancing SDGs in both sectors.

5.1.2 Digital Divide

The digital divide presents significant challenges and barriers to adopting digital strategies in the blue and green economies. Access inequality is a primary concern, as many communities, especially in rural or underserved areas, lack the necessary infrastructure and connectivity to fully engage in digital initiatives aimed at environmental conservation and sustainable resource management. Moreover, there is a notable skills gap, where technical expertise required for effectively using digital tools is often lacking in these communities, hindering their participation and decision-making capabilities. Additionally, cultural and language barriers can marginalize certain populations from effectively engaging with digital platforms and technologies.

5.1.3 Job Displacement

Job displacement presents a significant challenge and barrier to adopting digital strategies in the blue and green economies. As advanced digital technologies such as automation and AI are integrated into environmental and marine conservation efforts, there is a risk of displacing traditional roles and industries reliant on manual labor. This transformation can impact sectors such as agriculture, fishing, forestry, and tourism, where automation and data-driven processes may replace or reduce the need for human intervention. The shift towards digitalization also necessitates new skill sets, including proficiency in data analytics, programming, and technology management, which may not align with the existing workforce's capabilities. By fostering inclusive economic development and ensuring equitable access to the benefits of digital transformation, stakeholders can mitigate the negative impacts of job displacement while harnessing the potential of digital strategies to drive environmental conservation and economic sustainability in the blue and green economies.

5.1.4 Resource Allocation

Resource allocation presents significant challenges and barriers to adopting digital strategies within blue and green economies. These sectors strive to leverage digital technologies for environmental monitoring, sustainable resource management, and conservation efforts, allocating resources effectively becomes crucial yet complex. Financial constraints often hinder the acquisition of necessary technology infrastructure, the development of digital tools, and the implementation of robust cybersecurity measures, particularly for smaller organizations and those in developing regions. Moreover, balancing investments in digital initiatives with competing priorities such as conservation projects and community development poses dilemmas in resource allocation. By fostering inclusive and sustainable resource allocation practices, stakeholders can effectively harness the transformative potential of digital strategies to achieve environmental sustainability goals while addressing socio-economic needs.

5.1.5 Transparency and Accountability

Transparency and accountability are critical considerations in adopting digital strategies within the blue and green economies, where these technologies play pivotal roles in environmental monitoring, resource management, and conservation efforts. A primary challenge lies in ensuring robust data privacy and security measures. To safeguard sensitive environmental data and personal information, stakeholders must navigate complex ethical terrain. The algorithms and AI systems utilized in digital strategies must be transparent and accountable to mitigate biases that could perpetuate inequalities or inaccuracies in decision-making processes. Transparent algorithms ensure fairness in resource allocation and conservation planning, fostering equitable outcomes for all stakeholders. Digital platforms should facilitate accessible channels for stakeholders to provide input and access information, enhancing transparency in decision-making and fostering collaborative governance in environmental matters.

5.1.6 Stakeholder Involvement

Stakeholder involvement presents significant challenges and barriers in adopting digital strategies within the blue and green economies, where effective engagement is crucial for successful implementation and sustainable outcomes. One of the primary challenges lies in ensuring inclusive participation across diverse stakeholder groups. Digital strategies often require collaboration among governments, businesses, non-governmental organizations (NGOs), local communities, and academic institutions. However, coordinating these stakeholders with varying interests, priorities, and levels of digital literacy can be complex and time-consuming. Inadequate stakeholder engagement can lead to resistance misunderstandings and, ultimately, hinder the adoption and effectiveness of digital initiatives aimed at environmental conservation and sustainable resource management. Equitable access to digital platforms and technologies is essential but often unevenly distributed. Rural and marginalized communities may face limited internet connectivity, lack of access to digital devices, or insufficient training in digital literacy. Collaborative platforms, community consultations, and capacity-building initiatives can empower stakeholders to contribute effectively to decision-making processes and co-create socially, economically, and environmentally sustainable.

5.2 Regulatory Challenges

5.2.1 Compliance with Data Protection Laws

Compliance with data protection laws presents a formidable regulatory challenge and barrier to adopting digital strategies within the blue and green economies. As these sectors increasingly rely on digital technologies for environmental monitoring, sustainable resource management, and conservation efforts, the responsible handling of sensitive personal and environmental data becomes paramount. The regulatory landscape is complex and varied, with stringent requirements like the GDPR in Europe and the CCPA in California setting high data privacy and security standards. Organizations must allocate resources to conduct privacy risk evaluations, establish strong data security measures and access restrictions, and educate staff on data protection guidelines. The resource-intensiveness of compliance efforts, including ongoing monitoring and adaptation to evolving regulations, poses significant financial and operational challenges, particularly for smaller entities or those with limited technological infrastructure. Transparent communication about data practices and proactive measures to mitigate risks of data breaches is essential to fostering trust among stakeholders, including governments, businesses, and local communities. By prioritizing compliance with data protection laws and ethical considerations, stakeholders can navigate regulatory complexities effectively, mitigate legal risks, and harness the transformative potential of digital technologies to achieve SDGs in the blue and green economies while safeguarding individual privacy and environmental integrity.

5.2.2 Cybersecurity Regulations

Cybersecurity regulations pose significant challenges and barriers to adopting digital strategies within the blue and green economies. As these sectors increasingly integrate digital technologies for environmental monitoring, sustainable resource management, and conservation efforts, safeguarding against cyber threats becomes imperative. Key aspects of this challenge include: Firstly, the evolving nature of cybersecurity threats necessitates robust regulatory frameworks to protect sensitive environmental and personal data. Regulations such as the European Union's Network and Information Security (NIS) Directive and the Cybersecurity Information Sharing Act (CISA) in the United States aim to enhance the resilience of critical infrastructure against cyber incidents. Secondly, the complexity of digital ecosystems in the blue and green economies, involving diverse stakeholders and interconnected systems, amplifies cybersecurity risks. Adhering to cybersecurity regulations entails securing digital infrastructure and fostering a culture of cyber awareness and proactive risk management among stakeholders. Thirdly, the global nature of digital strategies often involves cross-border data flows and collaboration, complicating compliance with cybersecurity regulations across different jurisdictions. Organizations must navigate legal complexities related to data protection laws, data sovereignty, and international standards for cybersecurity, ensuring alignment with regulatory requirements while facilitating secure data exchange and collaboration on a global scale.

5.2.3 Intellectual Property Rights

Intellectual property rights (IPR) pose significant regulatory challenges and barriers to adopting digital strategies within the blue and green economies. These sectors increasingly rely on innovation and technology to drive environmental sustainability, resource management, and conservation efforts. Firstly, innovations in digital technologies used for environmental monitoring, data analytics, and sustainable practices often involve new inventions, designs, or processes that may qualify for intellectual property protection. Securing patents, copyrights, or trademarks is essential for organizations to safeguard their innovations and incentivize continued investment in research and development. Secondly, the intersection of intellectual property and digital technologies introduces unique data ownership and access challenges. Digital strategies may involve collecting, analyzing, and sharing large volumes of data, including environmental data, raising questions about ownership rights, licensing agreements, and data sovereignty. Clear policies and contractual frameworks are needed to address these issues and ensure equitable access to data while protecting intellectual property rights (Whig et al., 2024). Thirdly, intellectual property rights can also impact the adoption of open innovation models and collaborative partnerships within the blue and green economies. Balancing the need to foster innovation through knowledge sharing and collaboration with the protection of proprietary information and technologies requires careful consideration of intellectual property strategies and licensing arrangements.

5.2.4 Cross-Border Data Flow

Cross-border data flows present significant regulatory challenges and barriers in adopting digital strategies within the blue and green economies. These sectors increasingly rely on digital technologies for environmental monitoring, sustainable resource management, and conservation efforts, necessitating large volumes of data exchange across geographical boundaries. Firstly, differing data protection laws and regulations across jurisdictions can complicate compliance for organizations involved in cross-border data transfers. Transferring personal data to countries with insufficient data protection is strictly regulated, as the European Union's

General Data Protection Regulation (GDPR) shows. Secondly, concerns over data sovereignty and national security further complicate cross-border data flows. Some countries impose restrictions on the storage and processing of data within their borders, requiring organizations to navigate regulatory hurdles to ensure lawful and secure data handling practices. Thirdly, cultural and ethical considerations play a role in shaping regulatory frameworks for cross-border data flows. Differences in cultural attitudes toward privacy, data ownership, and intellectual property rights influence how countries approach data governance and international data transfers. Addressing these diverse perspectives requires diplomatic efforts, international agreements, and frameworks that promote interoperability and mutual recognition of data protection standards.

5.3 Technological Barriers

Technological barriers present substantial regulatory challenges and obstacles in adopting digital strategies within the blue and green economies, where leveraging advanced technologies is pivotal for sustainable resource management and environmental conservation.

5.3.1 Infrastructure Limitations

Infrastructure limitations pose a significant barrier to deploying digital technologies effectively, especially in remote or underserved areas. These regions often lack reliable internet connectivity and stable power supply, essential for the operation of IoT devices and data transmission (Isaac et al., 2023). Without robust infrastructure, the real-time monitoring capabilities of sensors and devices for environmental data collection can be severely compromised. Addressing these infrastructure gaps requires substantial investments in broadband expansion, energy infrastructure, and technological adaptation tailored to local conditions, ensuring equitable access to digital tools across diverse geographical settings.

5.3.2 Interoperability

Interoperability issues among digital platforms and technologies hinder seamless data integration and stakeholder collaboration. Proprietary systems and incompatible data formats can impede the sharing and analysis of environmental data across organizations, governments, and international jurisdictions. Achieving interoperability involves developing standardized protocols, open data formats, and application programming interfaces (APIs) that facilitate data exchange and interoperable solutions. This collaborative approach fosters a more cohesive digital ecosystem, enabling stakeholders to leverage combined data insights for informed decision-making and coordinated environmental actions.

5.3.3 Cybersecurity Vulnerabilities

Cybersecurity vulnerabilities in digital ecosystems pose significant risks to data integrity, privacy, and operational continuity. The interconnected nature of digital platforms and IoT devices increases exposure to cyber threats such as data breaches, ransomware attacks, and unauthorized access. Cybersecurity resilience requires robust measures, including encryption protocols, regular vulnerability assessments, and incident response plans. Compliance with regulatory frameworks such as the GDPR in Europe or the NIST Cybersecurity Framework in the United States is essential for safeguarding sensitive environmental and personal data against evolving cyber threats.

5.3.4 Technological Innovation

The rapid pace of technological innovation exacerbates challenges related to skills gaps and workforce readiness. Organizations and stakeholders must continuously adapt to emerging technologies, data analytics, and cybersecurity practices to implement and manage digital strategies effectively. Investing in workforce training, capacity-building programs, and cross-sector collaboration enhances stakeholders' digital literacy and technical expertise, empowering them to harness technology for sustainable development and resilience in the face of technological advancements.

6. DISCUSSION AND CONCLUSION

Digital strategies are pivotal in advancing the blue and green economies, offering innovative solutions for environmental sustainability and resource management. Key findings underscore the transformative impact of digital technologies such as IoT, AI, and big data analytics in enhancing environmental monitoring, optimizing resource utilization, and promoting conservation efforts. These technologies enable real-time data collection, analysis, and decision-making, improving efficiency, reducing environmental impact, and fostering sustainable practices across sectors.

The contributions to both theory and practice are substantial. From a theoretical perspective, digital strategies contribute to a deeper understanding of how technological advancements can drive environmental sustainability. They illuminate new pathways for integrating environmental sciences with digital innovations, promoting interdisciplinary approaches to address complex ecological challenges. In practice, digital solutions empower stakeholders—from governments and businesses to local communities and NGOs—to implement evidence-based policies, optimize resource allocation, and engage in collaborative conservation efforts. By harnessing digital strategies, organizations can achieve operational efficiencies, enhance transparency, and strengthen stakeholder engagement in environmental governance.

Looking ahead, the implications for future research and policy development are profound. Further research is needed to explore the long-term impacts of digital technologies on ecosystem health, biodiversity conservation, and climate resilience. Emphasis should be placed on developing scalable and interoperable digital solutions adapted to diverse geographical and socio-economic contexts. Additionally, policy frameworks must evolve to address regulatory challenges related to data privacy, cybersecurity, and cross-border data flows. Governments and international bodies play a crucial role in fostering enabling environments that support innovation, collaboration, and ethical use of digital technologies for sustainable development.

REFERENCES

Abhinav, K.. (2020). Blue economy: Opportunities and challenges. *International Journal of Management, 11*(7), 1348–1357.

Ambarita, A. A.. (2024). Digital twin development towards integration into blue economy: A bibliometric analysis. *Sustainability, 16*(18), 8072.

Ambarita, E. E., Karlsen, A., Scibilia, F., & Hasan, A. (2024). Industrial digital twins in offshore wind farms. *Energy Informatics, 7*, 5. Advance online publication. DOI: 10.1186/s42162-024-00005-4

Arvind Mallik, D. M. (2024). Promoting Green Innovation in India's Industry 4.0: Paving the Way to a Net-Zero Economy. In Singh, R., Khan, S., Kumar, A., Luthra, S., & Chokshi, H. (Eds.), *Net Zero Economy, Corporate Social Responsibility and Sustainable Value Creation. CSR, Sustainability, Ethics & Governance*. Springer., DOI: 10.1007/978-3-031-55779-8_13

Autsadee, Y., Jeevan, J., Mohd Salleh, N. H. B., & Othman, M. R. B. (2023). Digital tools and challenges in human resource development and its potential within the maritime sector through bibliometric analysis. *Journal of International Maritime Safety, Environmental Affairs, and Shipping, 7*(4), 2286409. DOI: 10.1080/25725084.2023.2286409

Azam, M. S., & Ponnam, A. (2023). Disparity in Agri-Marketing Challenges in India: Organic vs. Conventional Food Producers. *Journal of International Food & Agribusiness Marketing*, •••, 1–29. DOI: 10.1080/08974438.2023.2228783

Cardona, M., Kretschmer, T., & Strobel, T. (2013). ICT and productivity: Conclusions from the empirical literature. *Information Economics and Policy, 25*, 109–125. DOI: 10.1016/j.infoecopol.2012.12.002

Cathrine, C. (2024). *Blockchain Technology as a Catalyst for Sustainable Development: Exploring Economic*. Social, and Environmental Synergies.

Cathrine Williams. (2024). How Web3 Technology Reinvents Supply Chain Management in 2024? *Published in Coinmonks*. https://medium.com/coinmonks/how-web3-technology-reinvents-supply-chain-management-in-2024-e5af5f275e07 (Accessed on 20th July).

Chen, W., Huang, X., Liu, Y., Luan, X., & Song, Y. (2019). The impact of high-tech industry agglomeration on green economy efficiency—Evidence from the Yangtze river economic belt. *Sustainability, 11*(19), 5189.

Chen, Y., Xiao, H., & Zhang, N. (2019). A bibliometric analysis of research on green economy. *International Journal of Environmental Science and Technology, 16*(12), 7815–7830.

Choudhary, B., Dhar, V., & Pawase, A. S. (2024). Blue carbon and the role of mangroves in carbon sequestration: Its mechanisms, estimation, human impacts and conservation strategies for economic incentives. *Journal of Sea Research, 199*, 102504. DOI: 10.1016/j.seares.2024.102504

Dahiya, S., Yadav, M., & Dahiya, S. (2024). Exploring the Use of Virtual Reality to Support Environmentally Sustainable Behavior Change. *Sustainability, 16*(3), 1096.

Dahiya, V. K., Dahiya, R., Dev, R., Sharma, A., Sharma, A., Kiran, P. B. N., . . . Yadav, S. (2024, October 24). Exploring the role of artificial intelligence in predictive analytics for financial markets. 2024 International Conference on Computing, Sciences and Communications (ICCSC), 1–5. Presented at the 2024 International Conference on Computing, Sciences and Communications (ICCSC), Ghaziabad, India. doi:DOI: 10.1109/iccsc62048.2024.10830442

Durlik, I., Miller, T., Cembrowska-Lech, D., Krzemińska, A., Złoczowska, E., & Nowak, A. (2023). Navigating the sea of data: A comprehensive review on data analysis in maritime IoT applications. *Applied Sciences (Basel, Switzerland), 13*(17), 9742. DOI: 10.3390/app13179742

Durlik, I., Miller, T., Cembrowska-Lech, D., Krzemińska, A., Złoczowska, E., & Nowak, A. (2023). Navigating the Sea of Data: A Comprehensive Review on Data Analysis in Maritime IoT Applications. *Applied Sciences (Basel, Switzerland), 13*(17), 9742.

Fang, X., Zhang, Y., Yang, J., & Zhan, G. (2024). An evaluation of marine economy sustainable development and the ramifications of digital technologies in China coastal regions. *Economic Analysis and Policy, 82*, 554–570.

Haque, M., Akhtar, M. W., Bala, R., & Azam, M. S. (2023). Impact of Green Marketing on Market Performance in Rural India. *Academy of Marketing Studies Journal, 27*(2), 01-11.

Isaac, A., Mascarenhas, R., & Kamble, S. S. (2023). An interpretive model to assess the barriers to ocean energy toward blue economic development in India. *Renewable Energy, 211*, 822–830.

Ismail, S., Reza, H., Salameh, K., Zadeh, H. K., & Vasefi, F. (2023). Toward an intelligent blockchain IoT-enabled fish supply chain: A review and conceptual framework. *Sensors (Basel), 23*(11), 5136. DOI: 10.3390/s23115136 PMID: 37299864

Kashif, M., David, A., Azam, M. S., & Kumar, S. (2024). Utilization of Robo-Advisory Tools in Decision Support Systems. In *Robo-Advisors in Management* (pp. 76–89). IGI Global., DOI: 10.4018/979-8-3693-2849-1.ch005

Khalid, M. (2024). Smart grids and renewable energy systems: Perspectives and grid integration challenges. *Energy Strategy Reviews*, *51*, 101299.

Khalid, M. A. (2024). *Deciphering the Dynamics of Human-Environment Interaction in China: Insights into Renewable Energy*. Sustainable Consumption Patterns, and Carbon Emissions.

Latupeirissa, J. J. P., Dewi, N. L. Y., Prayana, I. K. R., Srikandi, M. B., Ramadiansyah, S. A., & Pramana, I. B. G. A. Y. (2024). Transforming public service delivery: A comprehensive review of digitization initiatives. *Sustainability*, *16*(7), 2818. DOI: 10.3390/su16072818

Lennerfors, T. T., Fors, P., & Rooijen, V. J. (2015). ICT and environmental sustainability in a changing society: The view of ecological World Systems Theory. *Information Technology & People*, *28*, 758–774. DOI: 10.1108/ITP-09-2014-0219

Li, B., & Wang, R. (2022). Marine renewable energy development in China: Status, challenges and policy recommendations. *Renewable & Sustainable Energy Reviews*, *167*, 112747.

Li, H. S., Tian, Y. X., & Li, W. J. (2014). Internet thinking and traditional enterprise reengineering. *China Ind. Econ.*, *10*, 135–146. DOI: 10.19581/j.cnki.ciejournal.2014.10.011

Li, J., Zhou, W., & Cai, Z. (2014). The impact of environmental regulation on firm's green innovation and financial performance: Evidence from China's listed companies. *Journal of Cleaner Production*, *112*, 1569–1577.

Li, Y., & Li, X.-Z. (2024). Utilizing unmanned aerial vehicle technology for environmental monitoring: Future trends, methods, and applications. *Internet Technology Letters*. Advance online publication. DOI: 10.1002/itl2.526

Li, Z., & Li, L. (2024). Remote sensing of coastal litter based on constrained energy minimization detector. *Frontiers in Marine Science*, *11*, 1336030.

Li, Z. G., & Wang, J. (2022). The dynamic impact of digital economy on carbon emission reduction: Evidence city-level empirical data in China. *Journal of Cleaner Production*, *351*, 131570. DOI: 10.1016/j.jclepro.2022.131570

Nham, N. T. H., Hoa, T. T. M., & Ha, L. T. (2023). Influences of digitalization on sustaining marine minerals: A path toward sustainable blue economy. *Ocean and Coastal Management*, *239*, 106589.

Nham, T. H., Hoa, H. V., & Ha, D. T. (2023). Factors Influencing Blue Economy Investment Decisions: Evidence From Egypt. *Journal of Risk and Financial Management*, *16*(11), 484.

Pace, L. A., Borch, K., & Deidun, A. (2023). Bridging Knowledge Gaps towards 2030: The Use of Foresight for the Strategic Management of a Sustainable Blue Economy. *Sustainability*, *15*(13), 10026.

Pace, L. A., Saritas, O., & Deidun, A. (2023). Exploring future research and innovation directions for a sustainable blue economy. *Marine Policy*, *148*, 105433.

Pandey, K. K., & Yadav, S. (2023). An interpretive model to assess the barriers to ocean energy toward blue economic development in India. *Renewable Energy*, *211*, 822–830.

Pandey, M., & Yadav, P. S. (2023). Understanding the role of individual concerns, attitude, and perceived value in green apparel purchase intention; the mediating effect of consumer involvement and moderating role of generation Z&Y. *Cleaner and Responsible Consumption*, *9*(100120), 100120. DOI: 10.1016/j.clrc.2023.100120

Pandey, M., Yadav, P. S., & Pothireddy, R. R. (2024). Role of gamification in influencer marketing. In Marketing and Gamification (pp. 157–169). doi:DOI: 10.4324/9781032694238-13

Shuja, J., Ahmad, R. W., Gani, A., Ahmed, A. I. A., Siddiqa, A., Nisar, K., Khan, S. U., & Zomaya, A. Y. (2017). Greening emerging IT technologies: Techniques and practices. *Journal of Internet Services and Applications*, *8*, 9. Advance online publication. DOI: 10.1186/s13174-017-0059-2

Shuja, J., Alam, M. M., & Khan, F. H. (2017). Greening emerging IT technologies, techniques, and practices: A survey. *Journal of Internet Services and Applications*, *8*(1), 1–11.

Singh, J., Kumar, A., & Singh, S. (2025). Digital platforms for sustainable waste management in a circular economy: A review. *Environmental Science and Pollution Research International*, *32*(1), 1–17. PMID: 39663305

Singh, M., Michael, R. A., Saheb, S. S., Yadav, P. S., Kiran, P. B. N., & Malhi, A. (2025). A study on digital intelligence and influencer marketing for sustainable diversification of India's retail economy. In *Advances in Logistics* (pp. 1–22). Operations, and Management Science., DOI: 10.4018/979-8-3693-8492-3.ch001

Singh, M., Syed, S. M., Saheb, S. S., Yadav, P. S., & Kiran, P. B. N. (2025). Role of influencer marketing in the Indian retail business sector. In *Advances in Marketing* (pp. 105–130). Customer Relationship Management, and E-Services., DOI: 10.4018/979-8-3693-8542-5.ch005

Spalding, M. J. (2016). The new blue economy: The future of sustainability. *Journal of Ocean and Coastal Economics, 2*(2). *Article, 8*, 1–21.

Van Hoof, L. (2019). *Blue growth: opportunities and challenges for the EU*. European Parliament.

Van Hoof, L., Fabib, G., Johansen, V., Steenbergen, J., Irigoien, X., Smith, S., Lisbjergg, D., & Kraush, G. (2019). Food from the ocean; towards a research agenda for sustainable use of our oceans' natural resources. [REMOVED BIBLIOGRAPHY FIELD]. *Marine Policy, 105*, 44–51.

Vashishth, T. K., Sharma, V., Sharma, K. K., Kumar, B., Chaudhary, S., & Panwar, R. (2024). Security and Privacy Challenges in Blockchain-Based Supply Chain Management: A Comprehensive Analysis. In Khan, M., Khan, N., & Ghouri, A. (Eds.), *Achieving Secure and Transparent Supply Chains With Blockchain Technology* (pp. 70–91). IGI Global Scientific Publishing., DOI: 10.4018/979-8-3693-0482-2.ch005

Vo, T. T. E., Ko, H., Huh, J.-H., & Kim, Y. (2021). Overview of smart aquaculture system: Focusing on applications of machine learning and computer vision. *Electronics (Basel), 10*(22), 2882. DOI: 10.3390/electronics10222882

Whig, P., Sharma, P., Aneja, N., Elngar, A. A., & Silva, N. (Eds.). (2024). *Artificial Intelligence and Machine Learning for Sustainable Development: Innovations, Challenges, and Applications* (1st ed.). CRC Press., DOI: 10.1201/9781003497189

Whig, P. S., Ahmad, S., & Mishra, S. (2024). The Legal Implications of Data Privacy Laws, Cybersecurity Regulations, and AI Ethics in a Digital Society.

Xiao, J., Shen, Y., Wang, Y., Yuan, W., Zhang, Y., & Wu, S. (2023). Large discrepancies in quantifying mountain vegetation growth dynamics using multiple remote sensing indices. *Ecological Indicators, 154*, 110697.

Xiao, Y., Wu, S., Liu, Z. Q., & Lin, H. J. (2023). Digital economy and green development: Empirical evidence from China's cities. *Frontiers in Environmental Science, 11*. Advance online publication. DOI: 10.3389/fenvs.2023.1124680

Yadav, M., & Dahiya, S. (2025). Can green finance and innovations promote environmental sustainability: Empirical evidence from India. *Social Responsibility Journal, 21*(1), 167–184.

Yadav, P. S., Kiran, P. B. N., Vemula, R., Kumari, P., Wazir, R., & Sharma, A. (2025). A deep understanding of virtual reality's role in human resource management, with a specific focus on recruitment. In The Future of HRM in a World of Persistent Virtual Reality (pp. 87–107). doi:DOI: 10.1108/978-1-83662-110-220251004

Yadav, P. S., & Pandey, M. (2021). Influencer Marketing: Social-media-Influencer On Shopper stress Deviation and Purchase Intention. *Turkish Online Journal of Qualitative Inquiry*, *12*(8), 6926–6947.

Yang, H., He, S., Feng, Q., Xia, S., Zhou, Q., Wu, Z., & Zhang, Y. (2024). Navigating the depths of seafood authentication: Technologies, regulations, and future prospects. *Measurement Food*, *14*, 100165. DOI: 10.1016/j.meafoo.2024.100165

Yi, M., Liu, Y. F., Sheng, M. S., & Wen, L. (2022). Effects of digital economy on carbon emission reduction: New evidence from China. *Energy Policy*, *171*, 113271. DOI: 10.1016/j.enpol.2022.113271

Chapter 3 Digital Nomadism and AI Pioneering the Future of Global Industry Transitions

Tiago Cardoso
https://orcid.org/0009-0008-5223-2299
Secretary General for Environment, Portugal

ABSTRACT

The digital age, driven by artificial intelligence (AI) and digital nomadism, is reshaping global industries and societies. AI enhances productivity, optimizes processes, and enables real-time decision-making, fostering innovation and economic growth. Simultaneously, digital nomadism challenges traditional work models by promoting a mobile, borderless workforce that drives creativity and technological adoption. Despite these opportunities, disparities in digital access and ethical concerns demand inclusive policies to ensure equitable growth and societal cohesion. Addressing job displacement, skills development, and ethical AI implementation is crucial for a sustainable future. This chapter highlights the transformative potential of AI and digital nomadism while emphasizing the need for strategies that align technological progress with human-centric values and sustainability.

DOI: 10.4018/979-8-3373-0159-4.ch003

INTRODUCTION: THE CONVERGENCE OF DIGITAL NOMADISM AND ARTIFICIAL INTELLIGENCE (AI)

The modern workplace has undergone transformative changes driven by rapid technological advancements, globalization, and evolving societal values. Among these transformations, digital nomadism, a lifestyle characterized by location-independent work, has emerged as a significant trend. Concurrently, artificial intelligence (AI) has risen to prominence, reshaping industries and enabling innovative solutions across diverse sectors. Together, these forces are pioneering a new era of global industry transitions, where traditional paradigms of work are being redefined.

Digital nomadism represents a seismic shift in how work is perceived and executed. This lifestyle, which blends professional flexibility with global mobility, has flourished due to advances in communication technologies, the proliferation of high-speed internet, and the growing normalization of remote work. As of 2023, the global population of digital nomads exceeded 35 million, with hotspots such as Lisbon, Bali, and Chiang Mai attracting a thriving community of location-independent professionals (Gupta, S., Jaiswal, R., & Gupta, S. K. (2024). This trend is further bolstered by the post-pandemic acceptance of hybrid and remote work models, which have become integral to organizational resilience and employee satisfaction.

Simultaneously, the rise of artificial intelligence has redefined the capabilities of global industries. From automating mundane tasks to enabling hyper-personalized services, AI systems have proven indispensable across fields such as healthcare, finance, education, and creative industries. By 2024, the global AI market is projected to reach $500 billion, underscoring its ubiquity and transformative potential (Statista, 2023). For digital nomads, AI tools such as language processors, automated scheduling systems, and virtual assistants have enhanced productivity, enabling professionals to navigate a dynamic and often unpredictable work environment with ease.

The convergence of these two trends—digital nomadism and AI—presents a unique interplay of opportunities and challenges. AI serves as both an enabler and a disruptor, amplifying the potential for nomadic work while raising concerns about the ethical implications of workforce automation and global economic inequities. Digital nomadism, in turn, represents a testbed for AI applications, showcasing their ability to enhance professional autonomy while fostering innovation.

Despite the transformative potential of these forces, their integration is not without challenges. Issues such as algorithmic bias, access to AI tools in developing economies, and regulatory complexities for borderless workers necessitate critical examination. Moreover, the socio-economic divide remains a significant hurdle, as the benefits of digital nomadism and AI often remain concentrated in developed nations.

This chapter explores how digital nomadism and AI intersect to drive industry transitions on a global scale. Through a detailed analysis of theoretical frameworks, industry case studies, and emerging trends, it provides a nuanced understanding of the opportunities and challenges presented by these phenomena. By contextualizing their convergence, the chapter seeks to shed light on their implications for global industries and the future of work.

Key questions guiding this exploration include:

How does AI empower digital nomads to thrive in an increasingly complex global work environment?
In what ways do digital nomadism and AI collectively disrupt traditional industries and economies?
What ethical and policy considerations arise from the integration of AI into nomadic work?

The findings will contribute to ongoing discussions about the future of work, offering insights into how AI and digital nomadism can foster inclusive and sustainable industry transitions. This chapter advocates for interdisciplinary collaboration to address the challenges and maximize the benefits of these transformative forces.

The intersection of digital nomadism and artificial intelligence (AI) represents a transformative shift in global labor markets, reshaping how professionals engage with work, mobility, and technology. Several theoretical frameworks help contextualize these phenomena, illustrating how digital nomadism reflects broader socio-economic changes and how AI simultaneously acts as an enabler and a challenge.

Globalization and Digital Nomadism

Digital nomadism is intrinsically tied to the processes of globalization, which have accelerated the flow of information, capital, and people across borders. Castells (1996) conceptualized globalization as the emergence of a "network society," in which digital infrastructures foster the seamless transfer of knowledge and resources. Digital nomadism exemplifies this concept, as professionals leverage technologies such as cloud computing and high-speed internet to work remotely from virtually any location.

However, globalization is not an equalizing force. World-systems theory, developed by Wallerstein (2004), highlights the hierarchical structure of global economies, where core nations dominate innovation and technological development, while peripheral nations often provide labor and resources to sustain these systems. This disparity manifests in digital nomadism, where professionals from developed countries disproportionately benefit from remote work opportunities due to superior access to AI tools, digital infrastructure, and global networks. In contrast, individuals in developing nations face barriers such as unreliable internet, limited access to advanced AI technologies, and systemic economic inequities (Chakravorti et al., 2017).

For instance, a software developer based in Silicon Valley has greater access to cutting-edge AI tools and training compared to a counterpart in sub-Saharan Africa. This disparity not only limits the latter's ability to compete in global markets but also reinforces existing socio-economic divides (Schor, 2020). Thus, while digital nomadism symbolizes the potential of globalization, it also underscores its inherent inequities.

Digital Nomadism and the Gig Economy

The rise of digital nomadism aligns with the growth of the gig economy, a labor market characterized by freelance and short-term contractual work facilitated by digital platforms. Katz and Krueger (2016) define the gig economy as a system that emphasizes flexibility, autonomy, and project-based engagements. Platforms such as Upwork, Fiverr, and Toptal exemplify this model, using AI-driven algorithms to match freelancers with clients based on skills, experience, and project requirements.

While these platforms expand opportunities for digital nomads, they also expose structural vulnerabilities inherent in gig work. Standing (2011) critiques the gig economy for perpetuating precarity, as freelancers often lack access to traditional employment benefits such as healthcare, pensions, and job security. AI exacerbates this precarity by fostering hyper-competition. As Autor (2015) explains, algorithmic systems prioritize cost-efficiency, often favoring lower-cost providers in developing economies. This dynamic drives a "race to the bottom," where freelancers are pressured to undercut their rates to secure projects, further entrenching economic instability.

For example, an AI-driven platform may recommend a freelance web developer from Southeast Asia over a competitor in North America due to lower costs, regardless of comparable skill levels. While this creates opportunities for some, it also raises ethical questions about wage disparities and exploitative practices in the gig economy.

Technological Determinism and the Role of AI

Technological determinism, a concept articulated by McLuhan (1994), posits that technology is not merely a tool but a force that fundamentally reshapes society. AI exemplifies this theory by transforming professional norms, workflows, and industry structures. Digital nomads, for instance, utilize AI tools such as Grammarly for content refinement, Jasper AI for marketing strategies, and predictive analytics for project optimization (Brynjolfsson & McAfee, 2017).

While AI enhances productivity and enables greater autonomy, it also raises concerns about overdependence. Zuboff (2019) warns that an excessive reliance on AI may erode critical thinking and creativity, as professionals delegate decision-making to algorithms. This dynamic is particularly pronounced in creative industries, where digital nomads often rely on AI for ideation and content generation, potentially limiting human originality.

Moreover, the deterministic perspective prompts critical questions about the societal implications of automation. For example, as AI systems increasingly dictate hiring decisions, project allocations, and client recommendations, they risk reinforcing biases and reducing transparency in professional ecosystems (Noble, 2018).

The Capability Approach and Digital Nomadism

Amartya Sen's (1999) capability approach provides a human-centered framework for understanding digital nomadism, emphasizing the expansion of individual freedoms and opportunities. AI enhances this agency by democratizing access to resources and enabling professionals to transcend geographical limitations. For instance, a freelance graphic designer in Brazil can use Adobe Sensei's AI tools to create high-quality designs that rival those produced by counterparts in more resource-rich regions (Tapscott & Tapscott, 2016).

However, the capability approach also highlights structural inequities in access to technology. Schor (2020) notes that while AI democratizes certain aspects of work, it often excludes individuals without access to reliable internet, advanced devices, or AI training. This disparity disproportionately affects professionals in rural or underserved areas, limiting their participation in global digital economies.

Socio-Technical Systems and Hybrid Workspaces

The socio-technical systems theory posits that technological advancements must be analyzed in conjunction with the social systems they influence. This framework is particularly relevant to digital nomadism, where AI tools interact with cultural, economic, and political dynamics to shape work environments. Hybrid workspaces, blending physical and virtual settings, epitomize this interaction. Digital nomads increasingly rely on AI-driven platforms like Slack, Trello, and Miro to collaborate with teams across time zones and cultures, creating decentralized but interconnected work ecosystems (Lanier, 2017).

However, this reliance on AI raises concerns about privacy and surveillance. Zuboff (2019) critiques the pervasive data collection practices of AI tools, warning that digital nomads often unknowingly trade privacy for convenience. For example, location-tracking features in scheduling apps or data analytics in project management platforms can expose sensitive information, leaving professionals vulnerable to exploitation.

Synthesis and Implications

The theoretical frameworks discussed above converge to illuminate the dual narrative of empowerment and inequity in digital nomadism and AI. While these phenomena foster innovation, flexibility, and global collaboration, they also exacerbate systemic inequalities, ethical dilemmas, and socio-economic divides. Understanding these dynamics is crucial for designing policies and technologies that balance innovation with inclusion and sustainability. As digital nomadism and AI continue to shape the future of work, these frameworks provide valuable insights for navigating the challenges and opportunities ahead.

The Evolution of Digital Nomadism: Past, Present, and Future

Digital nomadism has emerged as a significant socio-economic phenomenon, reflecting technological advancements, shifting cultural attitudes toward work, and the growing integration of artificial intelligence (AI) into professional life. Its evolution illustrates a broader transformation in how individuals perceive professional mobility, autonomy, and the role of technology in reshaping daily life. By examining its historical development, present dynamics, and future potential, we can gain a deeper understanding of its influence on global industries and society.

Historically, digital nomadism finds its roots in the technological revolutions of the late 20th century. The advent of personal computers in the 1980s revolutionized workplace productivity, allowing certain tasks to be completed remotely. This period marked the beginning of telecommuting, particularly within industries such as technology, media, and writing, where physical presence was not essential (Toffler, 1980). The proliferation of the internet in the 1990s further accelerated the feasibility of remote work, enabling virtual collaboration through email and early messaging platforms. Despite these advancements, however, the concept of location-independent work remained limited in scope and was largely inaccessible to the broader workforce.

The term “digital nomad” was popularized with the publication of The Digital Nomad by Makimoto and Manners (1997), which envisioned a future where professionals could work untethered from traditional office spaces. While visionary, this concept remained niche throughout the early 2000s, as technological infrastructure—particularly high-speed internet—was not yet widespread. By the late 2010s, however, advances in mobile technology, cloud computing, and collaboration tools such as Slack, Zoom, and Google Drive transformed the potential for remote work. These tools enabled seamless communication and resource-sharing across time zones, laying the groundwork for a broader adoption of digital nomadism (Lanier, 2017).

The COVID-19 pandemic in 2020 proved to be a pivotal moment in the evolution of digital nomadism. As lockdowns and social distancing mandates disrupted traditional work arrangements, organizations rapidly transitioned to remote work. This shift normalized the idea of working from anywhere, accelerating the adoption of digital nomad lifestyles on a global scale. By 2023, major corporations such as Twitter, Spotify, and Shopify had embraced fully remote or hybrid work models, enabling employees to work outside centralized offices (Gallacher & Hossain, 2020). These developments allowed millions of professionals to explore location-independent careers, fostering the growth of digital nomad communities.

Contemporary digital nomadism is characterized by several defining trends. First, geographic hotspots such as Lisbon, Bali, and Medellín have become hubs for digital nomads due to their affordable living costs, reliable internet infrastructure, and vibrant expatriate communities. Governments in these regions have recognized the economic potential of attracting skilled remote workers, introducing specialized “digital nomad visas” that simplify residency requirements and encourage long-term stays (Gupta, S., Jaiswal, R., & Gupta, S. K. (2024). Additionally, digital nomadism has expanded beyond its original demographic of tech-savvy millennials. Increasingly, professionals from diverse industries—including healthcare, education, and finance—are adopting this lifestyle, supported by AI tools that streamline tasks such as client communication, project management, and data analysis (Stephany, 2021).

AI has become an indispensable component of modern digital nomadism, enabling professionals to operate efficiently across borders. Tools such as Grammarly, Asana, and ChatGPT have redefined productivity by automating repetitive tasks, providing real-time insights, and enhancing content creation. These platforms empower digital nomads to manage complex workflows and collaborate with clients globally, regardless of time zone differences (Brynjolfsson & McAfee, 2017). However, the adoption of AI has also highlighted significant disparities. Access to advanced digital tools and reliable internet infrastructure remains unevenly distributed, particularly in developing regions. Schor (2020) notes that this “digital divide” excludes many professionals from participating in the global remote work economy, perpetuating socio-economic inequalities (Wirtz, B. W., et al 2020).

While digital nomadism offers unparalleled flexibility, it is not without challenges. Legal uncertainties surrounding taxation, residency, and work permits are significant hurdles for many digital nomads. Existing frameworks are often ill-suited to address the complexities of cross-border work, exposing individuals to risks such as double taxation or legal disputes (Kolomic et al., 2022). Additionally, the blending of work and travel can blur boundaries between personal and professional life, increasing the risk of burnout. Many digital nomads struggle to establish routines or disconnect from work, leading to adverse mental health outcomes (Reichenberger, 2018). Furthermore, frequent travel, a hallmark of digital nomadism, raises concerns about environmental sustainability. The carbon footprint associated with international travel underscores the need for more eco-friendly practices, such as slow travel and remote-first work models (Susskind, 2020).

Looking ahead, the future of digital nomadism will be shaped by emerging technologies and evolving societal norms. Decentralized platforms powered by blockchain and artificial intelligence are expected to provide greater autonomy and security for digital nomads. Tapscott and Tapscott (2016) argue that blockchain-based payment systems and decentralized autonomous organizations (DAOs) could reduce reliance on traditional banking systems, offering digital nomads greater financial flexibility. Immersive technologies such as virtual reality (VR) and augmented reality (AR) are also poised to transform collaboration. Lanier (2017) envisions fully immersive virtual workspaces that mimic physical office environments, enabling digital nomads to engage with clients and teams as though they were co-located.

AI will continue to play a central role in the evolution of digital nomadism, enabling hyper-specialization and enhancing professional opportunities. Advanced AI tools capable of analyzing global job trends will allow digital nomads to identify niche opportunities and refine their expertise, increasing their market value and competitiveness (Brynjolfsson & McAfee, 2017). Additionally, as concerns about the environmental impact of digital nomadism grow, technology-driven solutions will be critical in promoting sustainable practices. Carbon offset programs, remote-first work strategies, and energy-efficient AI systems will likely shape the future of this lifestyle (Schor, 2020).

Despite these promising developments, the future of digital nomadism depends on addressing socio-economic divides. While professionals from developed nations dominate this space, initiatives such as Google's "Next Billion Users" program aim to democratize access to digital tools and infrastructure in underserved regions (Chakravorti et al., 2017). Bridging these gaps will require collaborative efforts from governments, corporations, and international organizations.

The evolution of digital nomadism has far-reaching implications for global industries. Education providers are increasingly adopting AI-powered e-learning platforms to cater to mobile students, while healthcare services are leveraging telemedicine to deliver care remotely (Topol, 2019). Creative industries, too, are embracing remote collaboration tools to produce content across borders. For businesses, adapting to the rise of digital nomadism necessitates rethinking traditional organizational structures, fostering flexible policies, and investing in technologies that support decentralized work.

By examining its historical roots, present dynamics, and future potential, we can appreciate how digital nomadism is reshaping the global workforce. As AI continues to amplify the possibilities of this lifestyle, digital nomadism is poised to play an increasingly central role in defining the future of work.

AI as an Enabler of Digital Nomadism

Artificial intelligence (AI) has become an indispensable force in shaping the modern workplace, influencing how tasks are performed, decisions are made, and industries evolve. Its role in digital nomadism is particularly transformative, as it enables professionals to overcome challenges associated with remote work, including productivity, communication, and global collaboration. By providing tools that simplify workflows, facilitate cross-cultural interactions, and expand access to opportunities, AI empowers digital nomads to thrive in increasingly complex and dynamic professional environments(Curtis, 2019).

One of AI's most significant contributions to digital nomadism is its ability to enhance productivity. Through automation and optimization, AI-driven tools reduce the time spent on repetitive and administrative tasks, enabling professionals to focus on higher-value activities. For instance, platforms like Asana and Trello integrate AI-powered features that assist with task prioritization, deadline prediction, and resource allocation (McKinsey & Company, 2022). These tools are invaluable for digital nomads who often juggle multiple clients and projects across diverse time zones. Similarly, content creation tools such as Jasper AI, ChatGPT, and Grammarly streamline the writing process, ensuring high-quality output with minimal effort. These technologies are especially beneficial for professionals in creative industries, where language precision and speed are critical to maintaining client satisfaction and meeting tight deadlines (Brynjolfsson & McAfee, 2017).

AI has also revolutionized how digital nomads navigate the challenges of global communication and collaboration. Effective communication is paramount for professionals operating across borders, often in multilingual and multicultural settings. AI-powered language translation tools such as Google Translate and DeepL break down language barriers, facilitating seamless interactions with clients and colleagues worldwide. By providing accurate, real-time translations, these tools enable digital nomads to build stronger relationships and expand their client base across linguistic boundaries (Stephany, 2021). Virtual meeting platforms, including Zoom and Microsoft Teams, leverage AI to improve the quality of online interactions, offering features like noise cancellation, automated transcriptions, and speaker tracking. These capabilities create inclusive and efficient virtual meeting experiences, essential for maintaining professional engagement in remote work settings.

Beyond communication, AI fosters collaboration through advanced project management and teamwork tools. Software like Slack and Miro integrates AI to suggest relevant resources, analyze team performance, and automate routine tasks such as follow-up reminders. These platforms enable distributed teams to work cohesively, regardless of geographic location, by bridging gaps in coordination and providing real-time insights into project progress (Autor, 2015).

Another critical dimension of AI's impact on digital nomadism is its ability to democratize access to global opportunities. AI-powered freelance marketplaces such as Upwork and Fiverr connect professionals with clients by matching skills, preferences, and work history through sophisticated algorithms. These platforms have not only expanded job markets for digital nomads but also enhanced trust by employing AI for credential verification and fraud detection (Zuboff, 2019). In addition to freelance marketplaces, career platforms like LinkedIn utilize AI to provide personalized job recommendations, networking opportunities, and skills assessments, enabling digital nomads to identify and secure opportunities that align with their expertise and goals. Furthermore, online education platforms such as Coursera and Udemy employ AI to create tailored learning pathways, empowering digital nomads to upskill and remain competitive in an ever-evolving job market (Schor, 2020).

However, while AI offers undeniable advantages, its integration into the digital nomad ecosystem is not without challenges. Algorithmic bias is a significant concern, as AI systems often reflect the biases present in their training data. This can result in unequal opportunities for digital nomads, particularly those from underrepresented backgrounds or regions. For example, job-matching algorithms may inadvertently favor candidates from specific demographics or geographic locations, perpetuating existing inequalities in global labor markets (Zuboff, 2019). Privacy and security are also critical issues, as digital nomads frequently rely on cloud-based AI tools that collect and store sensitive client and personal information. The use of public networks further exacerbates the risk of data breaches, highlighting the need for robust cybersecurity measures (Stephany, 2021). Additionally, overdependence on AI poses risks to creativity and critical thinking. As digital nomads increasingly rely on AI for content creation, decision-making, and project management, there is a danger of diminishing human input and becoming vulnerable to system failures.

To illustrate the transformative role of AI in digital nomadism, several real-world examples highlight its impact. A digital marketing consultant based in Bali, for instance, uses Jasper AI to draft blog posts and social media content for European clients. By automating the initial stages of content creation, the consultant reduces project turnaround times by 40%, enabling them to take on more clients without compromising quality (Stephany, 2021). Similarly, a freelance graphic designer in Lisbon leverages DeepL for seamless communication with clients in Japan and Germany. AI translation tools not only bridge language gaps but also strengthen client relationships, leading to higher project success rates (Brynjolfsson & McAfee, 2017). In another example, a software developer working remotely from Thailand uses AI-powered scheduling tools like Calendly to coordinate with teams across three continents. By automating time zone calculations and sending reminders, these tools streamline collaboration and prevent missed deadlines.

The integration of AI into the digital nomad ecosystem has broader implications for industries and workforce dynamics. It accelerates the shift toward remote-first business models, promoting the adoption of decentralized teams and innovation in service delivery. Industries such as education, healthcare, and technology are already leveraging AI to adapt to the demands of a more flexible and globally distributed workforce. For instance, telemedicine platforms powered by AI enable healthcare professionals to provide remote consultations, while AI-driven e-learning platforms facilitate personalized education for mobile learners (Topol, 2019).

Despite its transformative potential, the integration of AI into digital nomadism underscores the need for new approaches to workforce training, regulatory oversight, and ethical governance. Governments and organizations must prioritize inclusivity and fairness in the design and deployment of AI systems, ensuring that digital nomads from diverse backgrounds have equal access to opportunities. Additionally, policies must address data privacy concerns and promote responsible AI usage to safeguard the interests of remote professionals and their clients.

This means that AI can serve as a critical enabler of digital nomadism, enhancing productivity, communication, and access to opportunities. While it drives industry-wide transformations and empowers individuals to navigate complex work environments, it also presents challenges that require careful consideration. By addressing these challenges and fostering ethical AI practices, the symbiotic relationship between AI and digital nomadism can continue to shape the future of work in meaningful and inclusive ways.

Industry Disruptions: AI and the Nomadic Workforce Across Sectors

The convergence of digital nomadism and artificial intelligence (AI) has significantly disrupted industries worldwide, altering how businesses operate and professionals deliver value. This transformative interplay redefines traditional workflows, decentralizes teams, and introduces innovative methods of productivity and service delivery. While it presents opportunities for growth and efficiency, it also challenges existing regulatory frameworks and workforce dynamics, demanding nuanced responses from industries and policymakers.

The technology sector exemplifies how digital nomadism and AI drive innovation and scalability. With remote work becoming increasingly prevalent, companies now seek professionals with expertise in machine learning, data science, and AI development, fields experiencing exponential demand due to their relevance in automating and optimizing operations (McKinsey & Company, 2022). For instance, digital nomads skilled in AI technologies contribute to startups by implementing scalable AI-driven solutions that reduce time-to-market and enhance product innovation. Tools like GitHub Copilot have revolutionized software development, assisting remote developers in writing, debugging, and optimizing code efficiently, demonstrating the seamless integration of AI into remote workflows. Startups, in particular, benefit from this decentralized approach, leveraging distributed teams of digital nomads to scale operations globally without the need for centralized offices.

In healthcare, the integration of AI and digital nomadism is redefining how medical services are delivered. AI-powered telemedicine platforms like Teladoc and HealthTap enable healthcare professionals to provide consultations remotely, ensuring accessibility in underserved regions (Topol, 2019). These platforms facilitate diagnostics through AI tools such as IBM Watson Health, which analyzes patient data to recommend personalized treatment plans, allowing medical professionals to offer high-quality care from remote locations. Digital nomads in healthcare, including telemedicine providers and health tech developers, participate in global health networks, using AI to share data in real time and collaborate on public health challenges. This model addresses critical shortages in healthcare personnel, particularly in developing regions, while emphasizing the importance of accessible and equitable care.

The creative industries—spanning marketing, design, and entertainment—have undergone profound transformations due to the intersection of AI and digital nomadism. AI tools like Canva and Adobe Sensei simplify graphic design, video editing, and other creative processes, enabling digital nomads to produce professional-quality content without requiring extensive resources. Marketers increasingly rely on AI-driven platforms to analyze consumer behavior and create personalized campaigns that enhance engagement and return on investment (Brynjolfsson & McAfee, 2017). Furthermore, virtual collaboration tools powered by AI facilitate remote partnerships in film production, digital art exhibitions, and other creative projects, enabling geographically dispersed teams to collaborate seamlessly.

Education is another sector that has embraced the dual influence of AI and digital nomadism to revolutionize learning. Online platforms like Coursera and Khan Academy employ AI to deliver personalized educational experiences tailored to individual learners' needs and schedules. Digital nomads working as educators or trainers leverage these tools to conduct interactive virtual classes that transcend geographical and linguistic barriers. Additionally, AI-powered EdTech startups, often led by digital nomads, are transforming traditional pedagogical methods by integrating gamification, analytics, and adaptive testing to enhance learning outcomes (Susskind, 2020). This shift not only democratizes access to education but also underscores the growing importance of lifelong learning in an era of rapid technological change.

The financial sector has also experienced significant disruptions due to AI and the rise of digital nomadism. Companies like Revolut and Wise cater to the financial needs of globally mobile professionals by leveraging AI to offer seamless international transactions and currency exchanges. Digital nomads increasingly adopt decentralized finance (DeFi) solutions powered by blockchain, which provide secure and cost-effective alternatives to traditional banking systems (Tapscott & Tapscott, 2016). AI further supports financial professionals in risk management, market trend analysis, and investment decision-making, allowing analysts to operate remotely while contributing to global financial ecosystems.

Despite these opportunities, the integration of AI and digital nomadism poses challenges across industries. Talent redistribution remains a critical issue, particularly in sectors reliant on physical presence, such as manufacturing and retail, which face difficulties adapting to remote work models. Regulatory hurdles compound these challenges, as companies employing digital nomads must navigate inconsistent international policies regarding taxation, labor rights, and data protection. Moreover, as AI facilitates cross-border collaboration, ensuring cultural sensitivity and inclusivity in diverse teams becomes increasingly important, highlighting the need for ethical AI practices that minimize biases and foster equitable opportunities (Zuboff, 2019).

Real-world examples illustrate the transformative impact of AI and digital nomadism across sectors. For instance, a telemedicine startup led by digital nomads in sub-Saharan Africa leverages AI diagnostics to provide high-quality remote consultations, addressing healthcare disparities in the region. In the marketing sector, a fully remote agency uses AI analytics to optimize campaigns for global clients while relying on digital nomads to execute projects across time zones efficiently. Similarly, an EdTech company founded by a team of digital nomads employs AI to develop multilingual learning modules for students in rural India, expanding educational access while reducing operational costs.

These disruptions have profound implications for industries, signaling a broader shift toward decentralized, technology-driven models of work. To remain competitive, businesses must adopt agile strategies that prioritize investment in AI-driven tools and policies that support remote-first operations. Additionally, addressing the challenges of workforce equity, regulation, and sustainability will be critical to ensuring the long-term success of this transformation.

The integration of AI and digital nomadism underscores the need for industries to rethink traditional paradigms, embrace innovation, and foster inclusivity. While these disruptions offer unprecedented opportunities for growth and efficiency, they also demand careful consideration of their ethical, social, and economic implications. By balancing these dynamics, industries can harness the full potential of AI and digital nomadism to shape a more resilient and adaptive future.

Challenges of Digital Nomadism in an AI-Powered World

The convergence of digital nomadism and artificial intelligence (AI) offers immense potential for innovation and flexibility, but it also introduces complex challenges. These challenges emerge from socio-economic inequalities, psychological pressures, ethical dilemmas, legal ambiguities, and environmental concerns. Together, they reflect the tensions inherent in integrating AI into a globalized, remote workforce, requiring nuanced solutions to mitigate their impacts and ensure equitable outcomes.

A key issue in this ecosystem is the uneven distribution of resources and opportunities. The digital divide remains a persistent barrier, as access to high-speed internet, advanced AI tools, and reliable infrastructure is concentrated in developed nations. This disparity disproportionately affects professionals in developing regions, who are often excluded from competing in the global digital economy due to infrastructural limitations (Chakravorti et al., 2017). For example, while a software engineer in Silicon Valley has access to cutting-edge AI training and tools, their counterpart in rural Africa may struggle with unreliable internet and limited opportunities for upskilling. This inequity reinforces existing socio-economic divides, limiting the transformative potential of digital nomadism as a truly inclusive model of work.

The cost of mobility further exacerbates these inequalities. Despite its image as a flexible and accessible lifestyle, digital nomadism often requires significant financial resources. Expenses related to international travel, accommodations, and technological tools can place this lifestyle out of reach for individuals from lower-income brackets, perpetuating economic disparities (Schor, 2020). Additionally, digital nomads frequently gravitate toward low-cost destinations, where their economic contributions may not align with local development needs. This dynamic, described as economic drain, can lead to dependencies on transient populations without sustainable benefits for host communities (Reichenberger, 2018).

On a personal level, digital nomadism brings notable psychological and social challenges. Its transient nature and remote work often lead to loneliness and disconnectivity. Constant relocation disrupts social stability, with many nomads relying on virtual networks that may lack the depth of in-person support (Wang, 2021). Blurred boundaries between work and leisure increase the risk of burnout and overwork (Gallacher & Hossain, 2020). Although cultural immersion is often a goal, nomads may form isolated "expat bubbles" that hinder meaningful local engagement (Stephany, 2021).

The ethical implications of AI integration into this lifestyle are similarly significant. Algorithmic bias remains a concern, as AI systems used in hiring, evaluation, or content moderation often reflect skewed training data, marginalizing professionals from underrepresented backgrounds (Zuboff, 2019). Privacy risks are heightened by reliance on cloud platforms and public networks. Additionally, automating decisions raises questions of accountability when AI-driven errors or biases negatively impact clients or collaborators.

Legal and regulatory complexities further complicate the integration of digital nomadism and AI. The cross-border nature of remote work exposes digital nomads to taxation ambiguities, as they may be liable in multiple jurisdictions or face double taxation due to inconsistent international policies (Lipniewicz, R. 2024). While some nations have introduced specialized nomad visas, most legal frameworks remain poorly equipped to address the needs of long-term remote workers. Moreover, digital nomads, often classified as freelancers or independent contractors, lack access to traditional labor protections such as healthcare, pensions, and unemployment benefits (Standing, 2011). These gaps highlight the need for global policy reforms that recognize the unique circumstances of digital nomads.

Environmental sustainability presents another pressing challenge. The frequent travel associated with digital nomadism contributes significantly to carbon emissions, raising concerns about its ecological footprint. Air travel, in particular, is a major contributor to greenhouse gas emissions, making the nomadic lifestyle difficult to reconcile with global climate goals (Susskind, 2020). Additionally, popular digital nomad destinations often experience overtourism, leading to environmental degradation and strain on local resources. Addressing these challenges requires a shift toward more sustainable practices, such as slow travel and remote-first work models that minimize physical movement.

Real-world examples underscore these challenges and their broader implications. A digital marketing freelancer in Thailand faced a data breach when their AI-powered scheduling tool was hacked, exposing sensitive client information. This incident highlights the need for stronger security measures in cloud-based platforms. Similarly, a software developer navigating taxation in the European Union encountered significant legal disputes due to inconsistent regulations, illustrating the complexities of cross-border financial compliance. In another case, a graphic designer traveling through Southeast Asia experienced severe burnout after managing demanding client deadlines without adequate support structures, emphasizing the mental health risks associated with the nomadic lifestyle (Yusriadi, Y., et al, (2023).

Despite these challenges, there are opportunities for innovation and reform that can address these issues and promote inclusivity. Bridging the digital divide is a critical first step. Initiatives such as Google's "Next Billion Users" program aim to expand internet access and digital literacy in underserved regions, enabling broader participation in the digital economy (Chakravorti et al., 2017). Advocating for sustainable practices, including carbon offset programs and eco-friendly technologies, can mitigate the environmental impact of digital nomadism. Policy reforms that standardize taxation, visa requirements, and labor protections are also essential to creating a more equitable framework for remote work.

The challenges faced by digital nomads in an AI-powered world reflect broader issues in global industry transitions, including resource inequities, ethical AI practices, and sustainable development. By addressing these challenges through collaborative efforts between governments, businesses, and international organizations, the potential of digital nomadism and AI to drive innovation and inclusivity can be fully realized(Curtis, 2019).

Current Policy Landscape: Governance for Digital Nomadism in an AI-Powered World

The regulatory environment for digital nomadism and AI adoption varies widely across countries, reflecting the fragmented nature of global governance in these rapidly evolving domains. While some nations have pioneered innovative policies to attract digital nomads and regulate AI technologies, others lag in addressing the unique challenges posed by the intersection of remote work and AI. This uneven landscape underscores the need for comprehensive, collaborative, and forward-thinking approaches to governance.

One of the most prominent policy innovations is the introduction of digital nomad visas by countries like Estonia, Portugal, and Barbados. These visas allow remote workers to reside legally while contributing economically, offering benefits such as increased tourism revenue and talent attraction (Kolomic et al., 2022). Estonia's e-residency program exemplifies this trend, enabling digital nomads to establish businesses remotely and access European Union markets without the need for physical presence. Similarly, Portugal has positioned itself as a top destination for digital nomads by combining simplified residency requirements with attractive tax benefits. These initiatives reflect a growing recognition of the economic and cultural value that digital nomads bring to host countries. (Yusriadi, Y., et al, (2023).

In AI governance, governments and international bodies are establishing regulatory frameworks to address ethical and societal impacts. The EU's proposed AI Act, for instance, regulates AI systems by risk level, emphasizing safety, transparency, and accountability (European Commission, 2021). Yet, these frameworks often neglect the specific realities of digital nomads, who rely on AI for work. Algorithmic bias, data privacy, and accessibility remain under-addressed, exposing nomads to inequities and inefficiencies (Zuboff, 2019).

Simultaneously, the growth of gig and freelance work has led some jurisdictions to revise labor laws, adding protections like minimum wage guarantees, benefits access, and safeguards against unfair dismissal (Standing, 2011). However, enforcement is inconsistent—especially for digital nomads operating across borders. This lack of regulatory standardization deepens the vulnerability of remote work, emphasizing the urgent need for robust international policy coordination.

Despite these advancements, several key challenges persist. One of the most significant is taxation complexity, as digital nomads often face unclear obligations across multiple countries. The absence of standardized agreements on cross-border taxation creates risks of double taxation and legal penalties, discouraging compliance and complicating financial planning for nomads (Kolomic et al., 2022). Similarly, regulatory frameworks for AI frequently fail to address issues such as algorithmic bias and data security, disproportionately affecting digital nomads who depend on AI tools for job matching, communication, and project management (Zuboff, 2019). The broader absence of international standards on data protection, labor rights, and remote work further fragments the policy landscape, leaving digital nomads to navigate contradictory and often inadequate regulations.

To address these gaps, policymakers and stakeholders must pursue policy innovation tailored to the dynamic nature of digital nomadism and AI. Harmonized taxation frameworks are a critical first step. Governments could collaborate to establish global standards that prevent double taxation and simplify compliance, potentially leveraging digital platforms to streamline tax reporting. For instance, AI-powered tax calculators could assist nomads in understanding their obligations across jurisdictions, reducing administrative burdens and errors.

In the realm of AI, inclusive governance should prioritize transparency, accountability, and fairness. Special provisions could ensure that AI tools are accessible and affordable for professionals in developing nations, addressing the digital divide (Chakravorti et al., 2017). Policymakers must also consider the ethical implications of AI adoption, including the risks of algorithmic discrimination and the need for robust privacy protections.

Global remote work agreements could further alleviate the challenges faced by digital nomads. International organizations such as the United Nations or the International Labour Organization (ILO) could facilitate agreements that standardize visa requirements, labor protections, and data-sharing practices. These agreements would provide consistent safeguards for digital nomads while enabling countries to benefit equitably from their economic contributions.

Sustainability is another critical area for policy innovation. Policymakers should incentivize slow travel, remote-first work practices, and the adoption of eco-friendly AI tools to mitigate the environmental impact of digital nomadism. Carbon offset programs, for instance, could be linked to visa requirements or travel permits, encouraging nomads to adopt greener practices (Susskind, 2020).

Several pioneering nations offer best practices that could serve as models for others. Estonia's e-residency initiative demonstrates how technology can simplify cross-border work, providing digital nomads with the tools they need to operate globally. Portugal's digital nomad visa program highlights the importance of integrating tax benefits with streamlined residency processes to attract talent. On the AI front, the European Union's AI Act sets a benchmark for ethical governance by emphasizing risk-based regulation and accountability, offering a roadmap for other regions seeking to manage AI adoption responsibly.

The borderless nature of digital nomadism and AI underscores the importance of collaborative governance models. Governments, technology companies, and civil society organizations must work together to develop inclusive and equitable policies. Public-private partnerships could drive the creation of secure and accessible AI tools, while stakeholder engagement could ensure that the perspectives of digital nomads, industry leaders, and local communities are represented in policy-making processes. Global forums for dialogue on issues such as taxation, data privacy, and labor protections could foster international cooperation, laying the groundwork for more cohesive governance(Curtis, 2019).

Technology itself can play a role in improving governance for digital nomadism. AI-powered tools, such as tax calculators and policy simulation models, can help governments design and implement effective regulations. For example, AI could streamline visa applications by analyzing eligibility criteria and verifying documents efficiently, reducing administrative bottlenecks and enhancing transparency. Additionally, governments could use AI to simulate the potential impacts of proposed policies, allowing for evidence-based decision-making that anticipates the needs of digital nomads and their host countries.

Ethical considerations must remain central to these efforts. Policies should prioritize equity, ensuring that governance frameworks do not disproportionately favor certain regions or demographics. Privacy protections must be robust, balancing the need for data collection with the rights of individuals to control their personal information. Finally, mechanisms for accountability should hold governments and organizations responsible for the impacts of their policies on digital nomads, local communities, and the broader ecosystem of remote work.

The successful integration of digital nomadism and AI into global economies requires a proactive, collaborative, and ethical approach to policy-making. By addressing current gaps and fostering innovation, governments can create a sustainable ecosystem that benefits digital nomads, industries, and societies alike. These efforts are not only essential for navigating the complexities of an interconnected world but also for ensuring that the transformative potential of digital nomadism and AI is realized equitably and responsibly.

Ethical Considerations: Balancing Autonomy, Innovation, and Equity

The regulatory environment for digital nomadism and AI adoption varies widely across countries, reflecting the fragmented nature of global governance in these rapidly evolving domains. While some nations have pioneered innovative policies to attract digital nomads and regulate AI technologies, others lag in addressing the unique challenges posed by the intersection of remote work and AI. This uneven landscape underscores the need for comprehensive, collaborative, and forward-thinking approaches to governance.

One of the most prominent policy innovations is the introduction of digital nomad visas by countries like Estonia, Portugal, and Barbados. These visas allow remote workers to reside legally while contributing economically, offering benefits such as increased tourism revenue and talent attraction (Kolomic et al., 2022). Estonia's e-residency program exemplifies this trend, enabling digital nomads to establish businesses remotely and access European Union markets without the need for physical presence. Similarly, Portugal has positioned itself as a top destination for digital nomads by combining simplified residency requirements with attractive tax benefits. These initiatives reflect a growing recognition of the economic and cultural value that digital nomads bring to host countries.

In the realm of AI governance, governments and international organizations have begun to establish regulatory frameworks to address the ethical and societal implications of AI. The European Union's proposed AI Act, for example, seeks to regulate AI systems based on their risk levels, prioritizing safety, transparency, and accountability (European Commission, 2021). However, these frameworks often overlook the specific needs of digital nomads, who rely heavily on AI tools for their professional activities. Issues such as algorithmic bias, data privacy, and accessibility remain underexplored in existing policies, leaving digital nomads vulnerable to inequities and inefficiencies in AI implementation (Zuboff, 2019).

The rise of freelance and gig economy work has also prompted some jurisdictions to update labor laws to protect independent contractors. Minimum wage guarantees, access to benefits, and protections against unfair termination are increasingly being integrated into policy frameworks (Standing, 2011). However, enforcement remains inconsistent, particularly for international freelancers and digital nomads who operate across multiple jurisdictions. This lack of standardization exacerbates the precarity of remote work, highlighting the need for more robust global agreements.

Despite these advancements, several key challenges persist. One of the most significant is taxation complexity, as digital nomads often face unclear obligations across multiple countries. The absence of standardized agreements on cross-border taxation creates risks of double taxation and legal penalties, discouraging compliance and complicating financial planning for nomads (Kolomic et al., 2022). Similarly, regulatory frameworks for AI frequently fail to address issues such as algorithmic bias and data security, disproportionately affecting digital nomads who depend on AI tools for job matching, communication, and project management (Zuboff, 2019). The broader absence of international standards on data protection, labor rights, and remote work further fragments the policy landscape, leaving digital nomads to navigate contradictory and often inadequate regulations.

To address these gaps, policymakers and stakeholders must pursue policy innovation tailored to the dynamic nature of digital nomadism and AI. Harmonized taxation frameworks are a critical first step. Governments could collaborate to establish global standards that prevent double taxation and simplify compliance, potentially leveraging digital platforms to streamline tax reporting. For instance, AI-powered tax calculators could assist nomads in understanding their obligations across jurisdictions, reducing administrative burdens and errors.

In the realm of AI, inclusive governance should prioritize transparency, accountability, and fairness. Special provisions could ensure that AI tools are accessible and affordable for professionals in developing nations, addressing the digital divide (Chakravorti et al., 2017). Policymakers must also consider the ethical implications of AI adoption, including the risks of algorithmic discrimination and the need for robust privacy protections.

Global remote work agreements could further alleviate the challenges faced by digital nomads. International organizations such as the United Nations or the International Labour Organization (ILO) could facilitate agreements that standardize visa requirements, labor protections, and data-sharing practices. These agreements would provide consistent safeguards for digital nomads while enabling countries to benefit equitably from their economic contributions.

Sustainability is another critical area for policy innovation. Policymakers should incentivize slow travel, remote-first work practices, and the adoption of eco-friendly AI tools to mitigate the environmental impact of digital nomadism. Carbon offset programs, for instance, could be linked to visa requirements or travel permits, encouraging nomads to adopt greener practices (Susskind, 2020).

Several pioneering nations offer best practices that could serve as models for others. Estonia's e-residency initiative demonstrates how technology can simplify cross-border work, providing digital nomads with the tools they need to operate globally. Portugal's digital nomad visa program highlights the importance of integrating tax benefits with streamlined residency processes to attract talent. On the AI front, the European Union's AI Act sets a benchmark for ethical governance by emphasizing risk-based regulation and accountability, offering a roadmap for other regions seeking to manage AI adoption responsibly.

The borderless nature of digital nomadism and AI underscores the importance of collaborative governance models. Governments, technology companies, and civil society organizations must work together to develop inclusive and equitable policies. Public-private partnerships could drive the creation of secure and accessible AI tools, while stakeholder engagement could ensure that the perspectives of digital nomads, industry leaders, and local communities are represented in policy-making processes. Global forums for dialogue on issues such as taxation, data privacy, and labor protections could foster international cooperation, laying the groundwork for more cohesive governance.

Technology itself can play a role in improving governance for digital nomadism. AI-powered tools, such as tax calculators and policy simulation models, can help governments design and implement effective regulations. For example, AI could streamline visa applications by analyzing eligibility criteria and verifying documents efficiently, reducing administrative bottlenecks and enhancing transparency. Additionally, governments could use AI to simulate the potential impacts of proposed policies, allowing for evidence-based decision-making that anticipates the needs of digital nomads and their host countries.

Ethical considerations must remain central to these efforts. Policies should prioritize equity, ensuring that governance frameworks do not disproportionately favor certain regions or demographics. Privacy protections must be robust, balancing the need for data collection with the rights of individuals to control their personal information. Finally, mechanisms for accountability should hold governments and organizations responsible for the impacts of their policies on digital nomads, local communities, and the broader ecosystem of remote work.

The successful integration of digital nomadism and AI into global economies requires a proactive, collaborative, and ethical approach to policy-making. By addressing current gaps and fostering innovation, governments can create a sustainable ecosystem that benefits digital nomads, industries, and societies alike. These efforts are not only essential for navigating the complexities of an interconnected world but also for ensuring that the transformative potential of digital nomadism and AI is realized equitably and responsibly.

Ethical Considerations: Balancing Autonomy, Innovation, and Equity

The rapid integration of digital nomadism and artificial intelligence (AI) into global workforces presents significant ethical challenges. These include maintaining autonomy, ensuring equitable access, fostering innovation with ethical oversight, protecting privacy, and mitigating environmental impacts. Addressing these requires governance that balances inclusivity, transparency, and accountability without hindering innovation. AI technologies offer great potential to enhance autonomy for digital nomads by automating routine tasks and enabling focus on creative, strategic work. Freelancers often use AI tools to manage schedules, draft proposals, and analyze feedback efficiently (Brynjolfsson & McAfee, 2017). However, this empowerment has limits. AI systems that match jobs, evaluate performance, or set rates can constrain autonomy. Many platforms use opaque algorithms that favor certain skills, regions, or pricing models, restricting freedom and flexibility (Zuboff, 2019). This algorithmic control may reduce independent judgment, leading to overreliance on automated systems and weakening critical thinking, adaptability, and innovation in an increasingly dynamic global economy.

The promise of AI and digital nomadism to democratize opportunities is undermined by significant disparities in access. The global digital divide remains one of the most critical ethical challenges, with unequal access to reliable internet, advanced AI tools, and robust digital infrastructure disproportionately excluding professionals in rural or developing regions. These individuals face barriers that their urban or developed-world counterparts do not, perpetuating systemic inequalities in the global digital economy (Chakravorti et al., 2017). Algorithmic bias compounds these disparities, as AI systems often reflect the prejudices embedded in their training data. This bias can lead to discriminatory outcomes based on gender, ethnicity, or geographic origin. For instance, an AI-powered freelance platform might prioritize candidates from North America over equally skilled professionals from Southeast Asia, limiting access to global opportunities for underrepresented groups (Noble, 2018). Additionally, economic stratification arises when AI-driven freelance platforms prioritize cost efficiency over skill, creating a "race to the bottom" that undervalues expertise in favor of lower-cost labor (Autor, 2015).

The relentless pace of AI innovation often outstrips the establishment of robust ethical and regulatory frameworks, resulting in unintended consequences. Privacy violations, exploitative practices, and the misuse of AI technologies are frequent outcomes of a market-driven approach that prioritizes competitiveness over ethics. The lack of transparency in AI system design and deployment exacerbates these risks. For example, platforms that influence job selection or compensation rarely disclose the decision-making criteria of their algorithms, leaving users unaware of the biases or assumptions shaping their opportunities (European Commission, 2021). Ethical AI design must address these gaps by embedding transparency, fairness, and accountability into every stage of development and deployment. Rigorous testing of AI systems to identify and minimize algorithmic bias is essential to ensuring that these technologies promote inclusivity and equitable outcomes for all users (Bostrom & Yudkowsky, 2011).

Privacy and data protection are critical ethical concerns in the digital nomad ecosystem, where AI-powered platforms and cloud services are widely used. These platforms often collect extensive user data without transparent policies on storage, use, or sharing, leaving nomads exposed to breaches and unauthorized surveillance—especially when using public Wi-Fi during travel (Zuboff, 2019). AI's surveillance capabilities intensify these risks. Productivity monitoring, location tracking, and behavior analysis can undermine privacy and autonomy, particularly in countries with weak data laws (Topol, 2019). Strengthening global data protection standards and enforcing high levels of security are essential to safeguarding digital nomads and their clients.

The environmental impact of digital nomadism and AI development is another critical ethical dimension. Frequent international travel, a defining characteristic of digital nomadism, contributes significantly to carbon emissions, raising questions about the sustainability of this lifestyle. Advocating for sustainable practices such as slow travel, carbon offset programs, and remote-first work models can help mitigate these environmental costs (Susskind, 2020). AI technologies, while enabling innovation, also carry an environmental footprint. Training large AI models requires substantial computational power and energy consumption, with a single training session capable of producing as much carbon dioxide as multiple transatlantic flights. Ethical considerations must include designing energy-efficient AI systems and implementing strategies to offset their environmental impact (Brynjolfsson & McAfee, 2017).

Real-world examples illustrate these ethical dilemmas. A digital nomad from Southeast Asia experienced repeated rejections on a global freelance platform due to an AI algorithm favoring candidates from North America, despite possessing comparable qualifications. This instance highlights the systemic inequalities embedded in algorithmic decision-making. Another case involved a freelance writer in Europe who faced a data breach when their cloud storage platform was hacked, exposing sensitive client information. The incident underscores the urgent need for robust encryption and stronger security measures in cloud-based tools. Environmental concerns are also evident in the case of a digital nomad in the creative industries who traveled to over 12 countries in a year, contributing significantly to their carbon footprint. This tension between professional mobility and environmental responsibility raises critical questions about the sustainability of digital nomadism.

Addressing these challenges requires the adoption of ethical principles in the design, deployment, and governance of AI-driven digital nomadism. Transparency in AI operations, including disclosure of decision-making criteria and data usage policies, is crucial for building trust and accountability. Developers must prioritize inclusive design to ensure that AI tools are accessible to diverse populations and actively work to minimize algorithmic bias. Sustainability initiatives, such as reducing unnecessary travel, supporting renewable energy, and integrating energy-efficient AI systems, should be embraced by digital nomads and companies alike. Strengthening data protection laws is essential to safeguarding privacy and ensuring that platforms adhere to rigorous security standards.

The ethical challenges of AI-driven digital nomadism emphasize the importance of global collaboration and stakeholder engagement. Policymakers, developers, and industry leaders must work together to create governance frameworks that evolve alongside technological advancements. By prioritizing inclusivity, transparency, and sustainability, these frameworks can ensure that innovation benefits all stakeholders equitably while safeguarding fundamental rights. As AI and digital nomadism continue to reshape global workforces, ethical governance will play a pivotal role in balancing the competing demands of autonomy, innovation, and equity.

Future Trends: AI and the Next Frontier of Digital Nomadism

The convergence of digital nomadism and artificial intelligence (AI) marks a transformative era in the global economy, reshaping the foundations of work, industry structures, and societal norms. This relationship is both a catalyst for innovation and a source of disruption, as it challenges traditional paradigms while opening new frontiers of possibility. By examining their intersection, this chapter has illuminated the profound ways these forces collectively redefine productivity, collaboration, and equity. However, alongside these opportunities come significant challenges, demanding a nuanced and inclusive approach to governance and innovation.

AI has emerged as a pivotal enabler of digital nomadism, enhancing productivity, flexibility, and global accessibility. By automating routine tasks, facilitating seamless communication, and expanding access to niche opportunities, AI empowers professionals to operate in a borderless work environment (Brynjolfsson & McAfee, 2017). Tools such as AI-powered collaboration platforms, predictive analytics, and personalized learning systems have created unprecedented opportunities for digital nomads to thrive across industries. This technological synergy has disrupted sectors including technology, healthcare, education, and creative fields, decentralizing traditional workforces and fostering innovation. However, these advancements have also unsettled established business models, requiring organizations to adapt to more dynamic and decentralized systems.

Despite its potential, the integration of AI into digital nomadism raises significant ethical and social challenges. Algorithmic bias continues to perpetuate inequities, disproportionately affecting underrepresented groups and professionals from developing regions (Noble, 2018). Data privacy risks intensify as digital nomads depend on AI-powered platforms and cloud services, exposing sensitive personal and client information (Zuboff, 2019). Socio-economic disparities endure, with unequal access to digital infrastructure and AI tools reinforcing the global digital divide (Chakravorti et al., 2017). Policy and governance frameworks struggle to keep pace with these transformations. While initiatives like digital nomad visas and the EU's AI Act offer promising models, regulation remains fragmented (European Commission, 2021). Addressing these issues requires coordinated international efforts to harmonize standards and ensure inclusive, equitable participation.

Looking ahead, emerging technologies and shifting cultural attitudes will shape the next frontier of AI-driven digital nomadism. Immersive virtual environments, decentralized platforms, and AI-driven hyper-specialization will redefine how professionals collaborate, learn, and innovate. These advancements promise to create more sustainable and inclusive models of work, addressing environmental concerns through energy-efficient systems and promoting equitable access to resources and opportunities (Susskind, 2020). AI-powered e-learning platforms and localized marketplaces will empower professionals in developing regions to participate in global economies, bridging the digital divide and fostering socio-economic inclusivity.

The future of work is increasingly defined by flexibility, autonomy, and global collaboration. AI dissolves barriers to communication and coordination, enabling digital nomads to build extensive networks that drive cultural exchange, innovation, and economic growth. However, this future must also prioritize sustainability, ensuring that technological advancements align with global environmental goals. As the frequency of international travel and energy-intensive AI deployments grows, adopting environmentally conscious practices such as slow travel, carbon offset programs, and green technology integration will be essential (Tapscott & Tapscott, 2016).

To fully harness the transformative potential of AI-driven digital nomadism, governments, industries, and communities must collaborate on multiple fronts. Policy innovation is essential to creating harmonized tax frameworks, inclusive AI governance, and standardized visa policies that address the unique needs of digital nomads. Companies must prioritize transparency, fairness, and accountability in AI system design, ensuring these tools are accessible to diverse populations and free from biases that perpetuate inequity (Bostrom & Yudkowsky, 2011). Digital nomads and businesses should adopt sustainable practices, reducing their environmental footprint and promoting the use of renewable energy and eco-friendly AI technologies. Additionally, educational institutions must invest in lifelong learning programs and AI literacy initiatives, equipping individuals with the skills needed to navigate an increasingly digital and decentralized economy.

The intersection of digital nomadism and AI presents an unprecedented opportunity to reimagine work in ways that prioritize creativity, inclusivity, and sustainability. By addressing the challenges outlined in this chapter and embracing innovation responsibly, society can pioneer a future where technology empowers individuals, transforms industries, and fosters global collaboration. This vision of a balanced future requires concerted efforts to align technological progress with ethical principles, ensuring that the benefits of AI-driven digital nomadism are shared equitably across borders and generations.

REFERENCES

Autor, D. H. (2015). Why are there still so many jobs? The history and future of workplace automation. *The Journal of Economic Perspectives*, *29*(3), 3–30. DOI: 10.1257/jep.29.3.3

Bostrom, N., & Yudkowsky, E. (2011). The ethics of artificial intelligence. Cambridge Handbook of Artificial Intelligence, 1–20. Retrieved from https://nickbostrom.com/ethics/artificial-intelligence.pdf

Brynjolfsson, E., & McAfee, A. (2017). *The Second Machine Age: Work, Progress, and Prosperity in a Time of Brilliant Technologies*. W.W. Norton & Company.

Chakravorti, B., & Chaturvedi, R. S. (2017). Digital planet.

Curtis, S. (2019). Digital transformation—The silver bullet to public service improvement? *Journal Public Money & Management*, *39*(5), 322–324.

European Commission. (2021). Proposal for a regulation laying down harmonized rules on artificial intelligence (Artificial Intelligence Act). Retrieved from https://ec.europa.eu

Gallacher, G., & Hossain, I. (2020). Remote work and employment dynamics under COVID-19: Evidence from Canada. *Canadian Public Policy*, *46*(S1), S44–S54. PMID: 38629973

Gupta, S., Jaiswal, R., & Gupta, S. K. (2024). Digital nomads: a systematic literature review and future research agenda. *Tourism Review*.MBO Partners. (2023). The State of Independence in America 2023. MBO Partners. Retrieved from https://www.mbopartners.com

Lanier, J. (2017). *Dawn of the New Everything: Encounters with Reality and Virtual Reality*. Henry Holt and Company.

Lipniewicz, R. (2024). Digital Nomads and International Taxation of Income from Employment. *Krytyka Prawa*, *16*(2), 268–285.

Makimoto, T., & Manners, D. (1997). The Digital Nomad. Wileyand sons.

McLuhan, M. (1994). *Understanding media: The extensions of man. MIT press. Noble, S. U. (2018). Algorithms of Oppression: How Search Engines Reinforce Racism*. NYU Press.

Reichenberger, I. (2018). Digital nomads–a quest for holistic freedom in work and leisure. Annals of Leisure Research, 21(3), 364-380.Schor, J. B. (2020). After the Gig: How the Sharing Economy Got Hijacked and How to Win It Back. University of California Press.

Susskind, R. (2020). *The Future of the Professions: How Technology Will Transform the Work of Human Experts*. Oxford University Press.

Tapscott, D., & Tapscott, A. (2016). *Blockchain Revolution: How the Technology Behind Bitcoin Is Changing Money, Business, and the World*. Portfolio Penguin.

Topol, E. (2019). *Deep Medicine: How Artificial Intelligence Can Make Healthcare Human Again*. Basic Books.

Wallerstein, I. (2004). *World-Systems Analysis: An Introduction*. Duke University Press.

Wang, J. (2021). Nomadic work and the isolation paradox: A cultural critique. *Cultural Studies in Work*, *19*(3), 45–59.

Wirtz, B. W., Weyerer, J. C., & Sturm, B. J. (2020). The dark sides of artificial intelligence: An integrated AI governance framework for public administration. *International Journal of Public Administration*, *43*(9), 818–829.

Yusriadi, Y., Rusnaedi, R., Siregar, N., Megawati, S., & Sakkir, G. (2023). Implementation of artificial intelligence in Indonesia. *International Journal of Data and Network Science*, *7*(1), 283–294.

Zuboff, S. (2019). *The Age of Surveillance Capitalism: The Fight for a Human Future at the New Frontier of Power*. PublicAffairs.

Chapter 4
AI-Driven Digital Nomads:
Transforming Labor Markets and Industrial Growth in the Digital Economy

Muhammad Usman Tariq
https://orcid.org/0000-0002-7605-3040
Abu Dhabi University, UAE & University College Cork, Ireland

ABSTRACT

This chapter discovers the transformative effect of AI-driven digital nomadism on global labor markets and industrial development in the digital economy. AI technologies empower digital nomads by aiding flexible, location-independent work and breaking down terrestrial and socioeconomic barriers. This change is driving a revolution across technology, healthcare, and creative sectors, as digital nomads control AI to access global prospects, work together remotely, and contribute to particular fields. The chapter studies how AI simplifies the growth of freelance economies, supports cross-border mobility, and nurtures inclusivity, allowing marginalized groups to participate in the digital economy. Moreover, it addresses issues relevant to labor laws, taxation, and healthcare accessibility, supporting AI-driven policy reforms to defend digital nomads' rights.

DOI: 10.4018/979-8-3373-0159-4.ch004

INTRODUCTION

The interchange of artificial intelligence (AI) and digital nomadism is intensely reforming global labor markets, changing how work is performed, planned, and distributed. As a disruptive technology, AI redefines industries by allowing automation, improving decision-making, and nurturing innovation. In the interim, digital nomadism, simplified by technological advances, signifies a new paradigm of labor mobility and flexibility. Together, these phenomena focus on the transformative power of technology in reimagining work, offering both prospects and challenges in an era of quick change. Artificial intelligence is a fundamental force in the current transformation of labor markets worldwide. AI includes various technologies that duplicate and improve human abilities, including machine learning, natural language processing, and robotics. By automating repetitive tasks, offering predictive analytics, and optimizing workflows, AI has become essential across industries, from manufacturing and healthcare to finance and retail (Adams, 2024).

AI's impact ranges beyond operational competence; it drives innovation and creates new economic prospects. For example, AI-powered tools in healthcare are transforming diagnostics and treatment planning, while in agriculture, AI is refining crop yields through accurate farming techniques. These progressions underline AI's role in nurturing industrial transitions as firms adapt to technological changes and readjust their workforce requirements (Tariq, 2025).

However, AI's transformative potential also brings issues. Automation threatens to shift jobs into routine and manual jobs, creating a skills gap that could extend socioeconomic discrimination. As AI reforms job functions, workers must attain new data analysis, programming, and AI ethics skills to remain competitive. Policymakers, educational institutes, and firms must collaborate to address these issues through workforce reskilling initiatives and unbiased access to prospects.

Background

Digital nomadism exemplifies the flexibility and agility presented by the digital economy. Digital nomads utilize technology to work remotely while maintaining a location-independent lifestyle. This phenomenon has gained grip with the spread of high-speed internet, cloud-based tools, and collaborative mediums that allow continuous communication and yield across borders (Tariq, 2024). The digital nomad lifestyle has substantial inferences for labor markets and economies. Digital nomads contribute to the global economy by providing specialized skills and services in software development, content creation, marketing, and consulting. By embracing remote work, they challenge conventional employment ideas and validate the feasibility of distributed workforces. Also, their capability to integrate into diverse cultural and economic environments nurtures cross-cultural collaboration and innovation.

Host countries and cities have also recognized the economic prospect of digital nomads. Popular destinations such as Bali, Lisbon, and Chiang Mai have become hubs for digital nomads, enticing talent and inspiring local economies. Governments have presented digital nomad visas to take benefit of this trend, offering incentives for remote workers to exist in and contribute to their economies. However, the invasion of digital nomads can also stress local resources and intensify housing affordability and cultural displacement problems. and tools. This mobility lets global talent access and challenges conventional labor market structures.

The shifts and revolutions within industries are driven by technological progressions, economic trends, and developing consumer needs. These transitions involve applying new technologies, changes in job roles, and the rise of innovative business models. Digital nomads play a dynamic role in driving innovation and economic progress across industries in the digital economy. By leveraging technology and embracing non-traditional work arrangements, they demonstrate a shift toward more active and flexible labor markets. Their contributions are primarily evident in industries where creativity, technical expertise, and remote collaboration are essential.

Digital nomads nurture innovation by introducing diverse perspectives and experiences into their work. Functioning in different cultural and economic contexts lets them approach issues with exceptional insights and solutions. For example, a digital nomad in a co-working space in Bali might work with people from different nationalities and industries, resulting in innovative ideas and cross-disciplinary associations.

Digital nomads contribute to entrepreneurial environments by supporting local businesses and involving with startup communities. Many digital nomads are entrepreneurs who provide freelancing services or build their ventures. This entrepreneurial spirit inspires economic activity and boosts the development of ancillary industries such as co-working spaces, tourism, and technology services (Mallisetty, 2023).

Furthermore, digital nomads serve as early adopters of developing technologies comprising AI. They depend on AI-powered tools to improve productivity, rationalize workflows, and steer the complexities of remote work. For instance, AI-driven project management mediums allow digital nomads to coordinate tasks proficiently with global teams. At the same time, language translation apps simplify communication in diverse linguistic environments (Tariq, 2025).

The junction of AI and digital nomadism represents how technology and mobility are reforming the nature of work. AI-powered tools authorize digital nomads to function efficiently in remote and distributed settings, improving their efficiency and expanding their skills. From AI-driven content generation tools for writers to predictive analytics for consultants, these technologies are essential to the digital nomad experience. On the contrary, digital nomads contribute to developing and modifying AI technologies. As early adopters, they provide valuable feedback that helps developers create user-centric solutions. Many digital nomads also work in AI-related fields, driving innovations in machine learning, data analysis, and software development. This symbiotic relationship underscores the mutual influence of AI and digital nomadism on labor markets (Nandwani & Bhatnagar, 2023).

Digital labor mobility, simplified by digital technologies, is a defining feature of the contemporary economy. It allows workers to access global prospects, breaking down geographic and organizational barriers. This mobility is mainly substantial in digital transformation industries, with a high demand for dedicated skills and expertise. The gig economy demonstrates the effect of digital labor mobility, as mediums such as Upwork, Fiverr, and Toptal connect freelancers with clients worldwide. These mediums democratize accessibility to work prospects, letting individuals in developing regions strive in global markets. However, they also increase competition and highlight wage disparities and labor protections.

Industrial transitions determined by digital technologies need a flexible and digitally skilled workforce. Workers must steer a landscape categorized by automation, growing job roles, and new business models. For instance, e-commerce has transformed retail, creating demand for logistics, data analysis, and digital marketing roles. Likewise, progressions in renewable energy technologies are reforming the energy sector, stressing the requirement for workers with expertise in green technologies. The connection of AI, digital nomadism, and labor market transitions signifies a reflective shift in the global economy. AI is transforming industries by allowing automation, innovation, and efficiency. At the same time, digital nomadism demonstrates the flexibility and adaptability of the contemporary workforce. Together, these phenomena focus on the opportunities of a connected, technology-driven labor market (Tariq, 2024).

However, comprehending the full potential of these trends needs addressing challenges such as job shifts, skills gaps, and regulatory disparities. Policymakers, firms, and educational institutions must work together to create inclusive policies, invest in digital infrastructure, and prioritize workforce development. By nurturing an environment that balances innovation with equity, the global labor market can adapt to the requirements of the digital economy, ensuring that the aids of these transitions are widely shared (PiSit, 2024).

AI and Digital Nomads: Catalysts for Global Workforce Transformation

The junction of artificial intelligence (AI) and digital nomadism has deeply partially affected the development of the global workforce. AI technologies authorize digital nomads by allowing continuous, location-independent work, nurturing unparalleled flexibility and efficiency. Digital nomads, in turn, are leveraging AI-driven tools to redefine professional models, tapping into prospects across industries and exceeding conventional work limitations. From allowing collaboration to creating new career avenues, AI and digital nomads jointly drive the revolution of the global workforce into a more active, flexible, and comprehensive ecosystem. AI technologies are fundamental to the digital nomad lifestyle, providing tools and systems that improve competence, connectivity, and problem-solving skills. These technologies simplify the remote execution of complex tasks that formerly needed on-site presence. For example, AI-powered virtual assistants like ChatGPT help digital nomads draft documents, generate ideas, manage administrative tasks, and streamline workflows. Similarly, machine learning algorithms can assess large datasets, allowing digital nomads working in data-centric fields to provide actionable insights efficiently (Tariq, 2024).

One of AI's most substantial contributions to digital nomadism is its capability to allow real-time communication and collaboration across time zones. AI-powered language translation tools like Google Translate and DeepL let nomads get involved with clients and colleagues worldwide without language barriers. Furthermore, AI-based scheduling mediums like Calendly improve meeting arrangements by accounting for time zone variances and individual availability.

Beyond individual productivity, AI augments the flexibility of digital nomads in diverse work environments. AI-powered tools can curate personalized learning resources, allowing professionals to attain new skills affiliated with emerging market demands. For instance, mediums such as Coursera and Udemy use AI algorithms to suggest courses customized to individual career objectives. This adaptability is critical for digital nomads, who generally navigate dynamic professional landscapes requiring constant upskilling. AI's incorporation into numerous industries has created new prospects for digital nomads, allowing remote work in sectors conventionally bound to physical locations. Some of the most prominent industries impacted by AI involve technology, healthcare, and creative fields.

The technology industry is at the lead of AI implementation, providing abundant prospects for digital nomads. Remote roles are progressively predominant in software development, data analysis, cybersecurity, and machine learning. AI-powered development mediums like GitHub Copilot assist programmers by generating code snippets, debugging errors, and optimizing workflows. These tools allow developers to work competently from any location, nurturing innovation without the restraints of office settings. Digital nomads in the tech industry also benefit from AI-driven project management tools like Monday.com and Asana. These mediums rationalize task allocation, progress tracking, and team communication, confirming that geographically disseminated teams remain cohesive and productive.

AI revolutionizes healthcare, enabling digital nomads to contribute remotely to this critical field. Medical transcriptionists, healthcare consultants, and data scientists are among the roles accessible to remote professionals. AI-powered tools like IBM Watson Health and Natural Language Processing (NLP) systems assist healthcare workers in assessing patient data, generating reports, and recognizing treatment suggestions.

For digital nomads with expertise in telemedicine, AI simplifies remote patient consultations via diagnostic tools that assess symptoms and medical histories. AI's ability to interpret radiological images and offer preliminary assessments has also opened avenues for radiologists and medical specialists to work remotely, providing critical services across borders.

AI has suggestively impacted creative professions, making them more accessible to digital nomads. AI-powered tools have democratized access to resources and improved productivity in graphic design, content creation, and digital marketing. For example, mediums like Canva and Adobe Sensei leverage AI to generate design templates, recommend visual elements, and optimize layouts, allowing digital nomads to provide professional-quality work competently.

AI has also transformed content creation. Writers and marketers use AI-driven mediums like Jasper AI to generate copy, draft articles, and brainstorm ideas. Likewise, AI video editing and animation tools like Runway ML allow creative professionals to produce high-quality visual content from remote locations.

AI-powered mediums and tools enable collaboration and productivity in a globally mobile workforce. These technologies cater to the exceptional requirements of digital nomads, simplifying remote work while fostering connectivity and efficiency.

Collaboration is a foundation of practical remote work. AI-powered tools have continuously enabled digital nomads to be involved with global teams. Mediums like Microsoft Teams and Slack use AI to prioritize messages, recommend responses, and integrate third-party apps, creating an interconnected workspace. Advanced features such as real-time transcription and meeting summaries, offered by tools like Otter.ai, ensure effective communication even in asynchronous environments (Fidalgo & Thormann, 2024).

AI also improves collaboration through shared document mediums such as Google Workspace, where machine learning algorithms optimize document editing, version tracking, and file sharing. These capabilities allow digital nomads to collaborate on real-time projects, irrespective of location.

AI-powered productivity tools help digital nomads manage their workloads and optimize their time. For instance, tools like Trello and ClickUp use AI to suggest task priorities, predict project timelines, and automate recurring procedures. These features let digital nomads emphasize high-value tasks while maintaining a balanced work-life dynamic.

In addition, AI-driven financial management tools like QuickBooks and Expensify assist digital nomads in tracking income, managing expenses, and preparing for taxes. These mediums streamline financial operations, a vital aspect for professionals across multiple jurisdictions (Hutson & Rains, 2024).

AI has also transformed job discovery and networking for digital nomads. Mediums like LinkedIn employ AI algorithms to suggest job prospects, connect professionals with related contacts, and provide insights into industry trends. Specialized gig economy mediums such as Upwork and Toptal use AI to match freelancers with clients based on skillsets, experience, and project requirements, confirming mutually beneficial partnerships (Bankins et al., 2024).

While AI offers immense potential for digital nomads, its adoption raises challenges and ethical concerns. The dependence on AI-powered mediums can create vulnerabilities, comprising data security risks and biases in algorithmic decision-making. Digital nomads must exercise caution when sharing sensitive information and advocate for transparency in AI systems.

Furthermore, the increasing occurrence of AI may lead to over-reliance on automation, lessening the human creativity and intuition central to many professions. Striking a balance between leveraging AI and maintaining a human-centric approach is critical for digital nomads and the broader workforce (Bergan et al., 2021).

AI and digital nomadism are promoters for transforming the global workforce, providing unparalleled flexibility, productivity, and innovation prospects. AI technologies empower digital nomads to perform complex tasks remotely. At the same time, the growth of AI-powered mediums simplifies continuous collaboration and connectivity. Across industries, AI is creating new avenues for remote work, redefining the potential of location-independent professions.

To fully realize these trends' potential, stakeholders must address the related challenges. Policymakers, businesses, and technology developers must collaborate to confirm ethical AI practices, reasonable access to prospects, and robust digital infrastructure. By nurturing an environment that supports technological innovation and human adaptability, the global workforce can advance into a more inclusive and robust system, meeting the demands of a quickly changing world (Jayasekara & Hansson, 2024).

The Economic Impact of AI-Driven Digital Nomadism

In current years, the swift rise of AI technologies has reformed how individuals work, providing unparalleled flexibility and allowing the phenomenon of digital nomadism to flourish. Digital nomads use technology to work distantly from different locations and reform economies worldwide, mainly in evolving markets. By leveraging AI-driven tools, digital nomads contribute to their professional progress and play a significant role in economic expansion in numerous industries and nations. In this analysis, we discover the economic benefits of digital nomads, mainly in developing economies, and observe the regional impacts across the Gulf region, Southeast Asia, and Europe. Moreover, we measure how AI nurtures innovation and boosts industrial competitiveness through the proliferation of digital nomadism (Rosen & Alvarez León, 2024).

The rising workforce of digital nomads has far-reaching economic inferences, chiefly in industries that depend profoundly on technology, innovation, and mobility. By offering location-independent work, digital nomads contribute to economic progress through multiple channels: job creation, foreign exchange inflows, talent migration, and the development of new business models (Kumar et al., 2024).

One of digital nomadism's most substantial economic effects is job creation in developed and emerging economies. In traditional economies, remote work was generally limited to explicit sectors, such as technology or academia. Digital nomads now span diverse industries, from creative arts and marketing to consulting, design, and software development. The demand for digital services has led to new job roles and business models, mainly in regions where the digital infrastructure is growing. These new employment prospects allow countries to tap into global talent pools while confirming that their economies remain competitive in the digital age.

The influx of digital nomads has further allowed economic diversification in emerging economies. These regions depend profoundly on specific industries, such as manufacturing or agriculture. The digital nomad phenomenon provides the prospects to introduce new sectors into the economy. Digital nomads bring skills in high demand globally, such as web development, marketing, data analysis, and financial consulting. As these workers move to developing regions, they provide services and create demand for local businesses, comprising housing, hospitality, and co-working spaces, stimulating local economies (Oakes, 2024).

Evolving economies, particularly those in the Global South, generally benefit from the inflow of foreign currency due to the rising number of digital nomads who choose these regions as their base of operations. Many digital nomads earn incomes from clients or firms in high-income countries, such as the United States, Western Europe, and Australia. This income is spent locally in emerging markets, generating foreign exchange and stimulating domestic economic activity (Sánchez-Vergara et al., 2023).

The existence of digital nomads also opens up opportunities for foreign businesses and investors to tap into emerging markets. For example, as more remote workers move into cities with a growing tech scene, global tech companies may establish offices or collaborate with local entrepreneurs. It increases foreign direct investment (FDI) and drives technological and industrial development (Mishra & Singh Kaurav, 2024).

The flexibility of digital nomads nurtures the exchange of knowledge, skills, and expertise between countries. In many emerging economies, there is an influx of highly skilled professionals who work distantly for international companies or start their digital businesses. This movement inspires local talent development, provides mentorship, and transfers knowledge to local workers, particularly in the technology, finance, and marketing industries.

In countries with partial access to advanced education or specialized training, digital nomads provide invaluable mentorship and knowledge-sharing prospects that enhance the skill sets of the local workforce. This knowledge transfer helps to link the gap between developed and developing countries, inspiring innovation and entrepreneurship within the host economy (Jaiswal et al., 2024).

CASE STUDIES ON THE IMPACT OF DIGITAL NOMADS IN KEY REGIONS

The Gulf Region

The Gulf Cooperation Council (GCC) countries, comprising the United Arab Emirates (UAE), Qatar, and KSA, have long been known for their oil-rich economies. However, as these countries seek to expand their economies away from oil dependency, they have gradually embraced digital transformation. Digital nomadism is critical in this transition, attracting skilled workers worldwide (Eager et al., 2022).

The UAE, mainly Dubai, has become a hub for digital nomads due to its infrastructure, tax incentives, and strategic location as a gateway between Europe, Asia, and Africa. The country introduced a "virtual working program" in 2020, letting foreign nationals live and work in Dubai while employed by companies outside the UAE. This initiative aims to attract high-skilled professionals in technology, marketing, and finance, thus diversifying the economy and reducing reliance on the oil sector (Lin & Tao, 2025).

Digital nomads in the Gulf region also contribute to the growing technology and startup ecosystems, mainly in cities like Dubai and Abu Dhabi. The influx of digital entrepreneurs and remote workers has driven innovation and fostered the progress of co-working spaces, technology hubs, and tech accelerators. Moreover, the UAE's adoption of AI technologies in the transportation, healthcare, and finance sectors has been further fueled by the influx of AI-skilled digital nomads. It has allowed the country to stay competitive in global markets, positioning itself as a leader in the region for innovation.

Southeast Asia

Southeast Asia is another region that is promoting the digital nomad trend. Countries like Thailand, Vietnam, and Indonesia have seen substantial increases in digital nomads opting to settle in cities like Bali, Ho Chi Minh City, and Chiang Mai. These destinations provide reasonable living costs, lively digital nomad communities, and accessibility to fast internet, making them attractive options for remote workers (Alfaraz & Tully, 2024).

In Bali, for instance, the government has progressively catered to the requirements of digital nomads by developing infrastructure and creating visa options for long-term stays. The presence of digital nomads in Bali has improved local industries such as real estate, hospitality, and retail. The progress of co-working spaces in Bali has explicitly been distinguished, with over 50 spaces now available across the island, providing the required infrastructure for digital nomads to flourish. Also, the rise of digital nomadism in Southeast Asia has contributed to the local knowledge economy. Many digital nomads work in the tech, finance, and marketing sectors, offering services to clients worldwide. This trend drives local economic progress and helps enhance the local workforce's skills via collaboration and networking (Masera, 2024).

Europe

Europe has long been a common destination for digital nomads due to its well-established digital infrastructure, high quality of life, and rich cultural multiplicity. Cities like Lisbon, Barcelona, and Tallinn have appeared as digital nomad hotspots, attracting talent from across the globe. In Portugal, the government has presented visa schemes that facilitate remote work, letting digital nomads live and work in the country for prolonged periods.

The economic impact of digital nomads in Europe is prominent in terms of tourism, property markets, and local businesses. Digital nomads generally rent apartments, spend money on services like cafes and co-working spaces, and participate in tourism activities, all generating income for local economies. In Lisbon, for instance, the influx of remote workers has inspired the growth of the hospitality sector, providing jobs in both the accommodation and leisure industries (Hannonen, 2023).

Moreover, AI technologies have played a fundamental role in driving industrial competitiveness in Europe. Digital nomads in artificial intelligence, data science, and software development contribute directly to European innovation ecosystems. Their proficiency helps European businesses stay competitive in the global economy by developing cutting-edge AI solutions and technologies. AI is essential in driving innovation, mainly in digital nomads' industries, such as technology, marketing, finance, and healthcare. By automating tasks, optimizing procedures, and generating insights from vast amounts of data, AI has authorized digital nomads to operate more efficiently, collaborate more efficiently, and access new business prospects (Bernovskis et al., 2024).

For instance, AI-powered tools for data analysis let digital nomads working in marketing or finance offer businesses deeper insights into customer behavior, market trends, and investment prospects. Likewise, digital technology and software development nomads depend on AI-powered mediums to rationalize code writing, automate testing, and speed up software deployment (Oltean & Taylor, 2023).

AI-driven innovation also increases industrial competitiveness as firms and digital nomads access sophisticated tools that improve productivity, reduce costs, and enhance decision-making. Industries that embrace AI are better placed to respond to global market demands, revolutionize faster, and create high-quality products or services. As digital nomads contribute to this procedure, they catalyze the broader economic revolution AI brings (Chen & Pun, 2024).

The financial impact of AI-driven digital nomadism is complicated, benefiting industries and nations by nurturing job creation, attracting foreign investment, stimulating local economies, and driving innovation. In emerging economies, digital nomads play a pivotal role in economic diversification, knowledge transfer, and the development of new industries. Regions such as the Gulf, Southeast Asia, and Europe are mainly profiting from this trend, as digital nomads contribute to the growth of local businesses, increase infrastructure development, and boost global competitiveness (Oltem and Taylor, 2023). AI technologies are a vital enabler of this shift, simplifying remote work, refining collaboration, and authorizing digital nomads to contribute implicitly to global economies. As digital nomadism continues to nurture, its financial impact will likely expand, creating new prospects for innovation and development in advanced and emerging markets. To harness this potential, governments and businesses must continue investing in digital infrastructure, regulatory frameworks, and policies supporting this dynamic workforce's progress.

Industry Specialization and AI: Opportunities for Growth in the Digital Age

Through the power of AI, digital nomadism quickly transforms specialized industries as it accelerates their development and the dynamism of sectors. Consequently, as digital nomads increasingly apply AI to manage leading industries to solve global problems efficiently, they use industries in the blue economy, green economy, sustainable transport, and robotics to rank niche sectors. Their assimilation of AI allows them to enhance their capacities for independent work while also addressing the specific needs of these sectors. The following explores how digital nomads, enabled by AI, drive innovation and growth in specialized industries.

The blue economy is defined as using ocean resources sustainably, which leads to economic growth and improved livelihoods and jobs while conserving the health of ocean ecosystems. AI is a central booster of such advancement to all these sectors, where digital nomads can act by implementing AI in developing solutions that improve the health of oceans, biodiversity conservation, and optimize marine-based industries (Sood & Juneja,2024).

Case Study: AI in Marine Conservation and Fisheries Management

It involves using AI technologies in marine conservation, where AI helps digital nomads work on real-time data analyses to monitor the health of the oceans. For example, machine learning algorithms can process satellite images to illegally monitor the condition of coral reefs, sea level, and even fish patterns. AI-driven marine biology freelance professionals associated with digital nomads are based in non-governmental organizations and government agencies. For this, they must develop predictive models of sustainable fisheries management to assess fishing practices for sustainability and their impact on marine ecosystems' health (Orel, 2023).

AI can be used in fisheries to analyze marine data, which may contribute to predicting fish stocks, detecting and monitoring overfishing, and providing decision support for resource management in fisheries. It would enable local governments and global organizations through improved regulation based on protecting marine biodiversity with regulations seen from data analyses. Specialists in AI and remote sensing technologies within the blue economy as digital nomads can work with scientists, environmentalists, and policymakers from wherever they are to develop solutions that help reduce ocean industries' environmental impacts (Shaer et al.., 2023).

The Green Economy: AI for Environmental Sustainability

While the world is more than ever participating in actions towards climate change and promoting sustainable development, the green economy has acquired a very vital area of growth. AI is central to that, allowing these digital nomads to be a part of developing sustainable energy, waste management, and environmentally friendly agriculture. Where AI meets digital nomadism, some new solutions to environmental problems come, mainly in energy optimization, resource conservation, and man ecosystem management (Cook, 2023).

Case Study: AI in Renewable Energy Optimization

AI in renewable energy lies in enhancing solar panels, wind turbines, and energy grids to increase efficiency. Artificial intelligence algorithms experts and machine learning digital nomads are working on building weather forecasting systems, optimizing energy output for renewable sources, and reducing inefficiencies in storage and distribution. It is also certain that artificial intelligence tools will be used to predict the availability of solar and wind power— this will make planning much easier for energy companies and help gradually reduce the use of fossil fuels.

An AI-based predictive maintenance system, for instance, can be used to identify a fault in the wind turbine or solar panel before it goes out of hand. It lessens downtime, increases energy production, and reduces overall operational costs. Energy companies, environmental researchers, and utilities are other examples of where digital nomads will be working, applying AI to ensure sustainable and cost-effective energy production (Aloisi & De Stefano, 2022).

Case Study: AI in Smart Agriculture

Agriculture is another sector where AI is completely changing the means of practice and reducing the environmental impact. Digital nomads in artificial intelligence and agricultural technology apply machine learning and sensors. They use it to create systems for monitoring soil conditions, predicting crop diseases, and managing irrigation optimization. It results in future waste-free technologies in water and pesticides, with efficiency at the core supporting sustainable agricultural practices. AI can also create systems for precision agriculture that collect and process satellite imagery, drone imagery, and sensor data from multiple sources to improve crop yields and reduce farming carbon footprints. Innovators in digital nomadism, especially people working from places in near-to-far rural transformation areas, have become assimilators of these innovations by the farmer to allow for better environmental stewardship and productivity (Shaer et al., 2023).

The Sustainable Transport Transition is one of the most critical global efforts to reduce carbon emissions and mitigate climate change. AI empowers the digital nomad to work from distances on various means of transport across different transport sectors, where it improves infrastructure, improves how vehicles perform, and creates new and more efficient, environmentally friendly transportation systems.

Case Study: AI in Electric Vehicles (EVs) and Smart Cities

Sustainable transport would include the contribution of digital nomads in designing electric vehicles and their supporting infrastructure. Another significant contribution of AI in the electric vehicle domain is battery management and route optimization. For instance, AI algorithms help electric vehicles put energy to their best use by altering performance and considering parameters such as landscape and traffic. It ensures that vehicles operate more efficiently and with reduced emission levels.

In smart cities, AI-driven systems support improved traffic flow and more efficient modes of transportation. As a coincidence, the digital nomads working in AI and data science fields help to develop intelligent transportation systems that can ensure zero-congestion traffic with optimized flow, thereby improving public transport systems' efficiency and lowering commuting's environmental impact. All this relies heavily on real-time data from sensors and the rest of it—plus AI to predict traffic patterns and manage schedules for buses and trains, as well as all-around increased safety and efficiency for urban transport networks (Vogl & Micek, 2023).

Robotics and Automation: Driving Innovation Across Industries

AI stands at the heart of this wave—all those digital nomads, working with companies or research institutions where from the comfort of their homes, enable the development of smarter robots and automation systems that drive efficiency improvements, cost reductions, and productivity enhancements in fields as disparate as manufacturing, healthcare, and logistics, among many others.

Case Study: AI in Manufacturing Automation

In manufacturing, robots are increasingly tasked with more repetitive jobs— but also quality control— at the assembly line. AI and robotics digital nomads work on the algorithms to enable the robots to navigate new conditions, spot flaws in produced items, and even make on-the-spot choices. These developments allow businesses to improve production efficiency, eliminate human error, and lower operating costs. In other words, the implementation of AI-powered robots results in the elimination of manual routine work. Subsequently, it creates the opportunity for the human workforce to engage in higher value-added activities (Pacheco & Azevedo, 2023).

In manufacturing, AI plays a role in predictive maintenance by analyzing machine data to forecast failure just before it occurs. The digital nomads operating within the industrial companies remotely use AI models to spot irregularities in machinery, preempting costly downtime and, in return, enhancing efficiency at operations. It contributes to industrial competitiveness by keeping manufacturing operations at the cutting edge of the technological revolution (Matsushita, 2023).

Case Study: AI in Healthcare Robotics

AI-powered robotics are also of great importance to the healthcare sector. Digital nomads in health tech use AI to develop robots capable of performing delicate surgical operations with micro precision. These robots can analyze patient data, respond to real-time changes in the operating room, and support the surgeon with more assistance in complex operations. It will decrease the chance of errors and improve the patient's outcomes (Holleran & Notting, 2023).

Furthermore, AI in robotics enhances the healthcare system at nursing homes and hospitals. Robots functioning with AI can initiate tasks related to medicine by helping to deliver medications to the patient, keeping track of the patient's condition, and assisting in mobility for an older patient. It would improve efficiency in healthcare, reduce the workload on staff, and improve satisfaction among patients. AI is transforming traditional industries while promoting digital inclusion and creating new job markets in underdeveloped regions. In its work, digital nomads work with tools powered by AI remotely, contributing to forming job markets span sectors such as education, freelancing, and entrepreneurship (Nembe & Idemudia, 2024).

Case Study: AI in Education and Remote Learning

AI is critical in providing quality learning resources to remote and underserved communities in education. Digital nomads specializing in educational technology are using AI to develop personalized learning platforms that adapt to student's individual needs, making education more accessible to learners worldwide. AI can analyze students' progress and provide tailored feedback, improving educational outcomes (Yu et al., 2024). Moreover, AI-powered tools enable teachers in developing regions to access global curricula and collaborate with other educators. These tools provide training, support, and resources to enhance teaching effectiveness, even in areas with limited access to traditional education infrastructures.

Case Study: AI in Remote Work Platforms

In education, AI has a critical role in ensuring the availability of quality learning resources for remote and underserved communities. AI and data science digital nomads work for companies that build intelligent systems through which project requirements and the appropriate expertise and experience of prospective employees are matched. Their contribution to such platforms fuels the gig economy by implying that many more people can access flexible work opportunities.

As discussed, artificial intelligence is a part of the development of specialized industries. With AI, digital nomads change the blue economy, green economy, and robotics through innovation and growth within those sectors. That is to say; remote workers apply artificial intelligence to help them resolve intertwined problems that are complicated with problems and make possible previously untapped opportunities for businesses and communities worldwide while increasing efficiencies (Hong, 2023).

It creates new job opportunities through the gig economy and enhances access to education and employment. Digital nomads are more than just members of this global workforce; they are also innovators and problem-solvers who likely play an important role in creating a sustainable and rational world for all its members. With current and evolving AI, these digital nomads will have more say in potential industry thrust, ultimately setting future work precedents globally.

Digital Nomads and the Future of Work: Opportunities and Challenges

Influenced by digital technologies, especially artificial intelligence, the future of work is influenced significantly by the rise of digital nomads among the significant actors in overhauling the global workforce. Leveraging technology to work remotely and lead a location-independent life is what digital nomads do. Increasingly, they use AI for enhanced productivity, smoother workflows, and opening up new opportunities in diverse sectors. AI has brought much greater flexibility, global mobility, and access to freelance work, changing the nature of work itself. Many opportunities aside, labor laws, taxation, and healthcare access remain some of the most significant challenges that can be addressed through innovative policy reforms for digital nomads. This article will discuss how AI will shape the future of work for digital nomads and shed light on the nascent trends redefining the nomadic workforce (Sood and Juneja, 2024).

The convergence of AI and digital nomadism has paved the way for a more flexible and dynamic workforce. As AI technologies evolve, they are making it easier for digital nomads to manage their work remotely, collaborate with teams across the globe, and participate in a more decentralized labor market. AI-powered tools, platforms, and systems are enhancing the quality of work, optimizing workflows, and enabling digital nomads to scale their businesses or freelance careers without being tied to a single location.

One of the most significant ways AI is shaping the future of work for digital nomads is by offering unprecedented flexibility and mobility. AI-driven tools would cover project management software (Trello, Asana) and communication applications (Slack, Zoom) that enable digital nomads to manage activities seamlessly, stay in touch with their remote teams, and collaborate on projects in real-time, no matter where they are situated. Such tools also apply machine learning algorithms to automate routine tasks and workflow suggestions, wherein work prioritization by these tools drastically reduces time spent on administrative duties.

AI is also revolutionizing travel and mobility for digital nomads. AI-powered travel and accommodation booking platforms optimize movements for the nomads. Since these systems allow digital nomads to access user-specific recommendations based on preferences and real-time insights, users can find cost-efficient flexible housing, modes of transport, and related workspaces. The rise of "smart cities" and digital hubs plays a central role in the rise of the digital nomad trend, creating ecosystems specific to the needs of a digital nomad. In such cities, street traffic to public service management can be run by an AI, thus making it easier for nomads to walk around new environments.

Freelancing and gig work are at the heart of digital nomadism, and AI might improve opportunities within these sectors. AI-oriented freelance platforms, among others, include Upwork, Fiverr, Toptal, etc., and are changing the game in how work and projects are found for digital nomads. These platforms use algorithms to integrate both the freelancer's skills and experience with the demands of the job and the client. In this sense, big data is finally in the picture; from freelancers and clients, an enormous amount of data is culled to ensure the matching process is much more efficient. These digital nomads discover Opportunities much more quickly, and the collaborations are likely to yield successful results since several volumes of implicit data are analyzed.

AI also optimizes pricing and fee structures within the freelance economy. Freelancers use AI to calculate fair market rates using real-time data and determine that they are adequately compensated for their skills and work. Such tools can also help monitor earnings and automate invoicing and calculating taxes.

The AI incorporation brings forth a basket of opportunities for the nomadic workers. However, this equally means that a set of challenges is introduced that need to be addressed to realize the full potential of this new mode of work. For example, legal and social challenges make it difficult for digital nomads to do their work efficiently and securely. These include labor laws, taxation, and legal protection; these are what much viability in a digital-nomad lifestyle requires.

Clear-cut labor laws that recognize precisely what they are doing are a significant challenge facing the digital nomad. The labor law, predicated on a fixed relationship between employers and employees within a physical workplace, leaves room for too many questions to effectively govern the relationship between employers and employees when the latter works as a freelancer in the former's place. For example, it is not always clear whether they are entitled to the complete protection that labor laws extend to local workers— covering areas such as minimum wage laws, laws about overtime pay, and social security benefits.

The same can be applied to this issue: AI can help governments and businesses design more flexible and adaptive labor policies. With data available, AI can identify facts concerning gig work trends—for example, the rise of a new kind of gig worker, the digital nomad—and suggest how existing labor laws need to change so that they can provide better protection for such workers. The same intelligence could also suggest how to streamline channels so that digital nomads may access legal support or navigate complicated regulations tied to cross-border employment.

Taxation is a significant issue for digital nomads, especially when the work is done across different countries. Often, they find themselves trapped within various tax jurisdictions of different countries. Hence, it becomes a challenge to understand the liabilities of taxes and filing procedure into different nations, complying with international tax agreements. Because there is no set framework for the taxation of digital nomads, this situation can easily lead to double taxation — or even fines or criminal charges in some extreme cases.

AI can also help calculate taxes automatically, track income from various regions, and ensure the tax man gets paid. Multiple countries' tax data merged into the systems could give digital nomads real-time information on their tax liabilities and the country that gets the taxing rights, depending on their residency status. The AI platforms could help digital nomads find the tax benefits or exemptions available as remote workers in specific countries, ensuring optimally coordinated financial planning.

Access to healthcare is another issue for digital nomads because, more often than not, they do not have a traditional employer who provides health insurance. Most countries require either a residence permit or employment status to qualify for public healthcare; thus, digital nomads are often left behind with no access to health services. Most of the time, these people operate in countries that do not provide healthcare services at relatively low costs, especially in developing regions.

By making it possible for developers to create telemedicine platforms that enable remote consultation, diagnosis, and prescription of medication, AI can facilitate the provision of access to healthcare for digital nomads through the implementation of such technologies. Other aspects include AI-powered health apps that may track health data for these digital nomads, give recommendations on wellness, and even assist in diagnostics with AI-driven tools to note their health situation. Platforms driven by artificial intelligence may also provide an individualized approach to healthcare for those who need insurance by offering insurance policies for workers irrespective of their working location.

Integrating AI is not merely improving the tools available for digital nomads. However, it also ushers in new trends that will transform their work. These include AI-based co-working spaces, smart cities, and digital hubs catering to the infrastructure and community support the nomads need for successful lives as location-independent professionals.

Co-working spaces are a crucial part of the whole digital nomad deal. Take all that you need for flexible office space and a place to work with other remote workers. AI will automate everything for you, from operations to booking systems and work environment optimization. From booking rooms to setting the right temperature for people working in the space, AI systems can ensure digital nomads have access to comfortable and productive workspaces.

In addition to upgrading the physical aspects of co-working spaces, AI facilitates networking and more effective collaboration opportunities for digital nomads. Other workers—whether matching professional interests or their skill sets—can be connected by an AI-driven platform, thus creating collaboration and knowledge exchange opportunities. Such spaces are increasingly a center for exchanging ideas between entrepreneurs, freelancers, and other digital nomads, sharing partnerships in business development activities.

A trend is rapidly growing among cities worldwide, and the adaptation to it is the accommodation of digital nomadism. Therefore, more and more attention is being paid to creating "smart cities" and digital hubs to meet remote workers' needs. Those cities provide installations conducted with AI, such as autonomous transportation, intelligent waste management systems, and high-speed internet access, which make them very attractive destinations for digital nomads.

Smart cities should enable mobility, connectivity, and efficiency for all users, including digital nomads accessing public services, workspaces, and amenities. Lisbon, Bali, and Mexico City offer very explicitly designed policies that orient them to the potential of becoming hotspots for digital nomads who can work collaboratively in a tech-enabled environment.

The increasing recognition of digital nomadism has also taken a toll on policymakers who need to rethink labor regulations, taxation, and social protection schemes for remote arrangements. AI can also participate in this reformation by offering data-driven insights that should inform policy and regulation changes to ensure equity for digital nomads. AI systems will help the government monitor the remote worker trend, realize where there are shortfalls in the legal system, and develop policies that cover the peculiar needs of digital migrants.

With the advent of AI in changing industries, creating new opportunities and tools for equipping a more elastic and mobile workforce, digital nomads will be at the center of where work is headed. Through surging global mobility, bolstering freelance economies, and offering solutions to hairy problems like taxation and access to healthcare for the new world, AI is helping build for those who can work from anywhere. However, with the rise of digital nomadism, the government, companies, and individual digital nomads should begin to look at the necessary legal, financial, and even social adjustments that must be made for this work structure. Policy shifts and tech advancements would ensure harmonious contributions between the digital nomad and AI, thus perpetuating a future of work that is dynamic and sustainable.

The Role of AI in Building Inclusive Digital Labor Markets

Artificial Intelligence contributes to a broader conception of more inclusive and accessible labor markets. It helps break the traditional barriers of geographically and socioeconomically regionalized labor markets. Conventionally, labor markets cannot involve people from underrepresented or remote regions due to locational constraints on opportunities or skill disparities. That is precisely the kind of door AI-driven platforms open around the globe for every person, regardless of where they are situated or standing socioeconomically. They make opportunities for jobs and training available to all the world's people. Thus, it allows for building a more global and inclusive workforce by placing suitable jobs for workers through AI.

AI also has a great potential to help narrow gender divides and to support efforts to bring underrepresented groups into the digital nomad ecosystem. AI tools can analyze data for more equitable access to opportunities by targeting underrepresented groups, e.g., women, racial minorities, and persons with disabilities. Such tools can recommend specific educational material resources and mentors connecting individuals from diverse backgrounds into sectors such as tech and high-demand areas like digital marketing.

However, the deployment of AI in labor markets raises ethical concerns primarily regarding equal pay, fairness to workers, and digital labor mobility regarding the potential for exploitation. There is an urgent need for AI systems that enable fair pay, protect workers' rights, and ensure that labor mobility does not end up causing exploitation or inequality. Ethical AI should ensure fairness in treatment, access to benefits, and protection against discrimination in digital labor markets.

Policy Implications for AI and Digital Nomadism

With the continuous growth of digital nomadism, forward-looking AI and labor policies are increasingly needed to support this emerging workforce and to foster industrial innovation in the spirit of the 21st-century economy. The current regulations are typically not designed to cope with the fluid and transnational aspects of digital nomad work; as such, they often create blind spots in areas such as labor rights, taxation, and social protection. The issue should urge policymakers to develop applicable regulatory structures that appreciate the fluidity of location-independent work by changing labor regulations that can extend various labor protections, including health care, to which digital nomads might not have an office.

The recommendations would involve developing inclusive and sustainable economies to build places attractive to digital nomads and provide opportunities for all. Governments should concentrate on policies supporting the required digital infrastructure, incentivizing businesses, and ensuring that workers can transition easily between industries and geographies. More so, government partnerships with technology companies and educational institutions can further enhance these workers' access to AI-driven learning resources.

Moreover, AI can guide industrial policy development in the directions of the Sustainable Development Goals (SDGs) and green economy initiatives. The use of AI technologies in carrying out industrial transitions will allow the implementation of sustainable practices along with resource optimization and innovation development in green industries. The development of AI-driven digital nomadism will also enable the mobility of such labor to drive sustainable development in those regions where they are urgently needed, thereby fostering economic growth in emerging economies while furthering global challenges.

CONCLUSION: THE FUTURE OF AI, DIGITAL NOMADS, AND INDUSTRIAL GROWTH

Artificial Intelligence (AI) and digital nomadism cross over to redefine the global labor market and all the challenges and opportunities it entails. AI technology allows those workers to break free from geography and social status constraints to work from anywhere on earth - or beyond it. These tools empower more people to participate in the global economy by opening access to jobs and resources and driving innovation in all industries. Whether it is AI-enabled freelancing platforms or tools for better remote collaboration, the rise of the digital nomad has quickened the pace of AI, transforming every sector, from tech to healthcare to the creative industries.

In the future, AI will continue to be critical to support the cause of digital nomads and help industrial transitions. In ushering in newer, sustainable, more tech-oriented industries, such industries will use expertise in green energy, sustainable transport, and blue economy with the help of AI to enable digital nomads. Also, AI can boost mobility flexibility and innovation to make it easier for workers to adjust to new job markets and emerging sectors. This change will probably initiate the rise of digital hubs, smart cities, and AI-driven co-working spaces. Acquiring the infrastructure needed to succeed in a dynamic, globalized work environment will allow nomads to thrive.

The call to action for academia, business, and government—that is, stakeholders—in AI is to work collectively to seize the opportunity for a reset that benefits all by putting in place sustainable, inclusive policies for everyone's protection of digital nomads fostering innovation and ensuring equal access to opportunities. It can guide the building of a robust, responsive, and varied workforce that will drive sustained long-term industrial development.

REFERENCES

Adams, R. (2024). *The new empire of AI: the future of global inequality*. John Wiley & Sons.

Alfaraz, C., & Tully, C. (2024). Mobilizing social transformation with technology. The shaping of social processes since the development of industrial society and beyond: Innovation input and social processes. *Innovation (Abingdon)*, •••, 1–17.

Aloisi, A., & De Stefano, V. (2022). *Your boss is an algorithm: artificial intelligence, platform work and labour*. Bloomsbury Publishing.

Bankins, S., Jooss, S., Restubog, S. L. D., Marrone, M., Ocampo, A. C., & Shoss, M. (2024). Navigating career stages in the age of artificial intelligence: A systematic interdisciplinary review and agenda for future research. *Journal of Vocational Behavior*, •••, 104011.

Bergan, T. L., Gorman-Murray, A., & Power, E. R. (2021). Coliving housing: Home cultures of precarity for the new creative class. *Social & Cultural Geography*, *22*(9), 1204–1222.

Bernovskis, A., Sceulovs, D., & Stibe, A. (2024). Society 5.0: Shaping the future of e-commerce. *Journal of Open Innovation*, *10*(4), 100391.

Chen, P., & Pun, N. (2024). 'Re-coupling site'of social media and the workplace in digital nomadism: Chinese female workers' self-produced vlogs with class and gender connotations. *Information Communication and Society*, •••, 1–17.

Cook, D. (2023). What is a digital nomad? Definition and taxonomy in the era of mainstream remote work. *World Leisure Journal*, *65*(2), 256–275.

Eager, B., Maritz, A., & Millemann, J. (2022). The silver economy on wheels: A narrative review of the mature-aged, hypermobile gig worker phenomena. *Small Enterprise Research*, *29*(1), 68–85.

Fidalgo, P., & Thormann, J. (2024). The Future of Lifelong Learning: The Role of Artificial Intelligence and Distance Education.

Hannonen, O. (2023). Emergent geographies of digital nomadism: Conceptual framing, insights and implications for tourism. *Tourism Geographies*, •••, 1–11.

Holleran, M., & Notting, M. (2023). Mobility guilt: Digital nomads and COVID-19. *Tourism Geographies*, *25*(5), 1341–1358.

Hong, R. (2023). Road warriors to digital nomads: Portable computers, habitats, and remote work. *Cultural Studies*, *37*(3), 508–535.

Hutson, J., & Rains, T. J. (2024). *Charting the AI Transition in Education and Business Environments: Navigating the Generative Inflection Point for Industry 4.0 Success*. Taylor & Francis.

Jaiswal, R., Gupta, S., & Gupta, S. K. (2024). The impending disruption of digital nomadism: Opportunities, challenges, and research agenda. *World Leisure Journal*, •••, 1–31.

Jayasekara, D., & Hansson, F. (2024). The Digital Economy Takes Over. In *THE CITY REBOOTED* (pp. 65–104). Networks, Connectivity and Place Identities in Singapore.

Kumar, S., Verma, A. K., & Mirza, A. (2024). Digital Transformation. *AI & Society*. PMID: 39302202

Lin, X., & Tao, N. (2025). Audiobooks in the Cultural Metaverse: Reimagining New Quality Productive Forces and the Future of the Audio Culture Industry. In *International Conference on Metaverse* (pp. 124-133). Springer, Cham.

Mallisetty, M. S. (2023). *Digital transformation: advancements in business*. Book Saga Publications.

Masera, M. L. (2024). Redefining Tomorrow: A Comprehensive Analysis of AI's Impact on Employment and Identity.

Matsushita, K. (2023). How the Japanese workcation embraces digital nomadic work style employees. *World Leisure Journal*, *65*(2), 218–235.

Mishra, V., & Singh Kaurav, R. P. (2024). Leveraging Disruptive Technologies and Strategies for Competitive Advantage. In *Review of Technologies and Disruptive Business Strategies* (pp. 1–16). Emerald Publishing Limited.

Nandwani, P., & Bhatnagar, D. (2023). Comprehensive and Psychological Review and its Impact on Technology Driven Applications on Business Development and Diversities of Tourism and Hospitality Industry during Pandemic in Indian Prospective. *Journal for ReAttach Therapy and Developmental Diversities*, *6*(8s), 405–418.

Nembe, J. K., & Idemudia, C. (2024). Designing effective policies to address the challenges of global digital tax reforms. *World Journal of Advanced Research and Reviews*, *22*(3), 1171–1183.

Oakes, T. (2024). Toward a critical geopolitics of smart tourism. *Tourism Geographies*, •••, 1–12.

Oltean, O., & Taylor, A. (2023). Back to the Future: How the Convergence of Globalization and Technology is Changing Labour and Mobility. *Social Change Review, 20*(1), 19–44.

Orel, M. (2023). Wanderlust workforce: A journey into understanding digital nomadism. *World Leisure Journal, 65*(2), 143–149.

Pacheco, C., & Azevedo, A. (2023). Mapping the journey of the CoLiving experience of digital nomads, using verbal and visual narratives. *World Leisure Journal, 65*(2), 192–217.

PiSit. N. (2024). Remote Work and Its Implications on Personal Financial Planning Beyond Covid-19. *Available at* SSRN *4845642*.

Rosen, J., & Alvarez León, L. F. (2024). Signaling hinterlands and the spatial networks of digital capitalism. *Annals of the Association of American Geographers, 114*(8), 1841–1853.

Sánchez-Vergara, J. I., Orel, M., & Capdevila, I. (2023). "Home office is the here and now." Digital nomad visa systems and remote work-focused leisure policies. *World Leisure Journal, 65*(2), 236–255.

Shaer, S., O'Neil, A., Salem, F., Akrout, Z., & Shibl, E. (2023). Advancing Artificial Intelligence Impact in Dubai: Future Directors Towards Strengthening the Digital Economy. *Future of Government Series*.

Sood, D., & Juneja, M. (2024). Bleisure Travel: The Rise of Flexible Work and Its Impact on Tourism. In *Bleisure Tourism and the Impact of Technology* (pp. 22-45). IGI Global.

Tariq, M. U. (2024). Smart Transportation Systems: Paving the Way for Sustainable Urban Mobility. In Munuhwa, S. (Ed.), *Contemporary Solutions for Sustainable Transportation Practices* (pp. 254–283). IGI Global., DOI: 10.4018/979-8-3693-3755-4.ch010

Tariq, M. U. (2024). Generative AI in Curriculum Development in Higher Education. In Fields, Z. (Ed.), *Impacts of Generative AI on Creativity in Higher Education* (pp. 227–258). IGI Global., DOI: 10.4018/979-8-3693-2418-9.ch009

Tariq, M. U. (2025). Navigating Bias and Fairness in Digital AI Systems. In Bhattacharya, P., Hassan, A., Liu, H., & Bhushan, B. (Eds.), *Ethical Dimensions of AI Development* (pp. 127–156). IGI Global., DOI: 10.4018/979-8-3693-4147-6.ch006

Tariq, M. U. (2025). *AI-Driven Learning and Engagement in Higher Education*. IGI Global., DOI: 10.4018/979-8-3693-4074-5

Tariq, M. U., & Sergio, R. P. (2025). Ethical Considerations and Social Impact of AI and Computational Intelligence in Society 5.0. In Pandey, R., Srivastava, N., Prasad, R., Prasad, J., & Garcia, M. (Eds.), *Open AI and Computational Intelligence for Society 5.0* (pp. 225–248). IGI Global Scientific Publishing., DOI: 10.4018/979-8-3693-4326-5.ch010

Tariq, M. U., & Sergio, R. P. (2025). Nurturing Digital Citizenship in Society 5.0 Through AI and Computational Intelligence Education. In Pandey, R., Srivastava, N., Prasad, R., Prasad, J., & Garcia, M. (Eds.), *Open AI and Computational Intelligence for Society 5.0* (pp. 59–84). IGI Global Scientific Publishing., DOI: 10.4018/979-8-3693-4326-5.ch003

Vogl, T., & Micek, G. (2023). Work-leisure concepts and tourism: Studying the relationship between hybrid coworking spaces and the accommodation industry in peripheral areas of Germany. *World Leisure Journal*, *65*(2), 276–298.

Yu, K., Zhang, J., & Hannam, K. (2024). Welcome to 'Dalifornia': Chinese digital nomads as mobile entrepreneurs. *Current Issues in Tourism*, •••, 1–15.

KEYWORDS AND DEFINITIONS

Nomadism: The way of life where individuals shift between different locations regularly.

Digital Economy: The economic activity that is done virtually.

Freelancing: A form of self-employment.

Chapter 5
The Rise of Digital Nomad Visas:
Transforming Global Work, Travel, and Local Economies

S. Thandayuthapani
https://orcid.org/0000-0001-9559-745X
Kristu Jayanti College, India

P. Thirumoorthi
https://orcid.org/0000-0001-5783-3984
Periyar University, India

ABSTRACT

The coming of computerized Wanderer Visas denotes an extraordinary change in worldwide work and travel elements, reshaping both nearby economies and labor force versatility. These visas enable telecommuters to thrive in new environments and contribute financially, free from traditional business constraints. This paper examines the evolution and impact of advanced migrant visas, focusing on their role in promoting financial flexibility in developed nations, enhancing local labor markets, and promoting sustainable travel industry models. Through examination of contextual investigations and strategy structures, it surveys what these visas mean for social and financial scenes, upholding versatile approaches that upgrade shared benefits for advanced travelers and host networks.

DOI: 10.4018/979-8-3373-0159-4.ch005

INTRODUCTION

The computerized transformation has empowered individuals to live and work in ways that were impossible even years and years prior. Perhaps the most remarkable advancement in this computerized era is the rise of computerized nomadism, a lifestyle where experts, often in fields such as technology, writing, counseling, and showcasing, leverage innovation to work remotely while traveling to various locations. This developing pattern has led to computerized migrant visas—unique licenses presented by state-run administrations to draw in telecommuters, especially the people who can uphold themselves monetarily while adding to nearby economies through their spending.

Various Innovative, Monetary, and Social Movements Have Pushed for Advanced Nomadism

The multiplication of the rapid web, reasonable worldwide travel, and the ascent of an independent-driven gig economy have added to the possibility and allure of an area-free way of life. The coronavirus pandemic, which standardized remote work across various businesses, has further advanced the trend towards computerized nomadism, prompting numerous legislators to recognize the potential benefits of welcoming these telecommuters. With computerized migrant visas, nations desire to invigorate their economies by drawing in another segment of shoppers who spend on conveniences, nearby organizations, and administrations without straightforwardly rivaling the neighborhood labor force.

The Concept of the Advanced Migrant Visa Clearly Differs From Traditional Work or Traveler Visa

Though work visas frequently require a task inside the host nation and traveller visas limit the length of stay, Digitalized wanderer visas permit people to remain in a country for stretched-out periods while proceeding to turn out from a distance for unfamiliar bosses or clients. Since the introduction of the primary programs in 2020, an increasing number of countries, ranging from popular tourist destinations such as Barbados and Estonia to less well-known ones like Malta and Georgia, have developed computerized traveler visas to accommodate this trend. Not only are these visas designed to attract high-spending, low-influence travelers, but they also aim to alleviate the financial impact of the pandemic's reduced travel industry.

Development of Work in the Advanced Period

The advanced period has re-imagined work elements, empowering consistent coordinated effort and correspondence across geographic limits. Technological advancements such as video conferencing, project management software, and distributed computing have made remote work feasible, if not ideal, for a vast number of experts worldwide (Baldry, 2021). As remote work has proven successful, especially during the pandemic, organizations across various industries have become more receptive to flexible work arrangements, enabling employees to work from any location with a reliable internet connection. This change has not only expanded the scope of open positions accessible to people regardless of their location, but it has also redefined working in a globalised, Digitalized economy (Courier and Gschwind, 2016).

The development of computerized travelers should be seen as an extension of this advancement in work. At first comprising specialists and business visionaries who preferred adaptable working circumstances, advanced nomadism has extended to include customary representatives, who are progressively allowed to remotely work. Living in one country while working for clients or managers in another has subsequently gained authenticity as a lifestyle choice and a viable financial model. In this new worldview, public boundaries become less applicable, permitting people to join work and travel in manners that add to individual satisfaction and expert efficiency (Reichenberger, 2018).

The Allure of Advanced Wanderer Visas

Computerized wanderer visas serve as a crucial response to these changes, aiming to attract a growing segment of mobile experts. For computerized migrants, these visas offer a novel chance to dwell in a country longer than would be conceivable with a common vacationer's visa, frequently with fewer regulatory obstacles than work visas. By giving legitimate residency, computerized migrant visas furnish these telecommuters with the security to lay out transitory roots, cultivating a sense of having a place that supports further spending and interest in the nearby local area (Petriglieri, 2019).

For many nations, the allure lies in the financial boost that computerized wanderers can bring. Telecommuters typically earn higher-than-average incomes from their jobs in financially developed nations, despite living in areas where the cost of everyday items may be significantly lower. This disparity can lead to increased spending power, which can benefit local organizations, community centers, and specialty cooperatives. Importantly, advanced migrants typically do not compete for jobs with local residents due to the unfamiliar nature of their work. This is especially appealing to more modest countries or those with economies vigorously dependent on the travel industry, as computerized wanderers can assist in counterbalancing misfortunes brought about by worldwide travel limitations or monetary slumps (Hannonen, 2020).

The Financial and Social Effects on the Neighborhood People Group

With the introduction of advanced traveller visas, the financial impact on neighbourhood networks has begun to emerge, providing insights into both the benefits and anticipated challenges of this model. On the positive side, advanced wanderers frequently bring new abilities and points of view, which can animate information trade and development in nearby networks. Neighbourhood entrepreneurs may modify their offerings to cater to this new segment, potentially enhancing the quality of services available to residents. Furthermore, advanced travellers indirectly contribute to the neighbourhood's revenue base by spending on convenience, dining, and various sporting activities (Kong, 2021).

Nonetheless, this inundation of telecommuters can likewise present difficulties. An increase in demand for lodging and co-working spaces could increase rental costs, potentially leading to a rise in well-known objections. At times, local people may feel undervalued or underestimated as well-off Digitalized wanderers increase the cost of many everyday items. This peculiarity highlights the significance of insightful metropolitan preparation and guidelines to adjust the advantages of advanced nomadism according to the requirements of neighborhood occupants (Thornthwaite, 2022).

Strategy Contemplations and Future Bearings

The outcome of advanced traveller visas generally depends on how legislators plan and implement these projects. Important considerations include the duration of the visa, the requirements for pay and medical coverage, and the availability of social services for computerized wanderers. Policymakers face the challenge of formulating regulations that stimulate the influx of telecommuters while maintaining the government's support for local networks. Some countries, for instance, mandate computerized wanderers to pay a nominal neighbourhood charge or contribute to government-managed retirement funds, ensuring that they contribute to the economy even as non-resident laborers (Ojala, 2022).

Further, as advanced nomadism develops, there might be an expanded interest in global guidelines overseeing computerized wanderer visas. Normalization could improve application processes, making it easier for telecommuters to move between nations without delayed visa processes. Laying out uniform rules around pay confirmation, medical coverage, and admissible work exercises could make these projects more open and valuable for the two wanderers and host nations. Such administrative structures could likewise give clarity to organizations utilizing telecommuters, easing worries around tax assessment, work regulations, and government-backed retirement.

Finishing Up Considerations

The rise of computerized migrant visas is leading to a shift in the global labor force, with a growing standardization and celebration of area freedom. By profiting from this pattern, nations can change their economies, transforming impermanent guests into monetary supporters who infuse new spending and abilities into nearby networks. However, comprehending these benefits necessitates a sophisticated approach that addresses the financial, social, and administrative aspects of digital nomadism. Future exploration and continuous strategy assessments will be fundamental for refining computerized migrant visa projects and making a decent connection between advanced travelers and the networks they occupy.

BACKGROUND OF THE STUDY

The rise of computerized migrant visas has reshaped how individuals live, work, and travel. Computerized wanderers, experts who influence innovation to work from a distance while voyaging, have generally experienced difficulties while exploring visa guidelines intended for customary or momentary work in the travel industry. Perceiving the monetary potential and extraordinary effect of drawing in advanced travelers, a few nations have committed to computerized wanderer visas. These visas empower area-free laborers to lawfully dwell and work in unfamiliar nations, encouraging new elements of worldwide work, travel, and nearby economies. This part dives into the development of advanced wanderer visas, factors driving their reception, and their more extensive ramifications.

1. The Digitalized Migrant Peculiarity

The concept of computerized nomadism gained momentum in the mid 2000s due to advancements in computerized communication and remote work capabilities (Mouratidis, 2021). However, the coronavirus pandemic accelerated this trend, making remote work necessary and even impossible. Organizations and workers adapted to virtual environments, preparing for a growing population seeking a balance between professional responsibilities and personal fulfillment through mobility. Computerized wanderers regularly work in information-based fields such as IT, showcasing, planning, and counseling, which do not require physical presence in a specific area (Cook, 2022).

This segment's desire for flexibility, experience, and social interactions has sparked a global trend, with an estimated 35 million people identifying as digital migrants by 2022 (MBO Accomplices, 2022). As this way of life gained popularity, the demand for administrative designs that facilitate long-term visits without violating visa requirements also increased.

2. The Development of Advanced Migration Visas

A relatively recent development, the computerized traveller visa aims to bridge the gap between traditional work visas and vacationer visas. Early adopters of these visas, like Estonia, Barbados, and Bermuda, understood the financial advantages of drawing in telecommuters who could add to the nearby economy without competing for neighborhood occupations (Reichenberger, 2021). Estonia sent off its computerized migrant visa in 2020, allowing telecommuters to dwell in the country for as long as a year provided they meet explicit pay and business models (Marr, 2020).

Computerized traveler visas regularly expect candidates to demonstrate work with an organization outside the host country or show stable pay for remote work. By drawing in higher-paying people who contribute to nearby economies through leases, the travel industry, and way-of-life spending, these visas can animate neighborhood economies without troubling the neighborhood work market. Rather than conventional movement strategies that emphasize talented work for homegrown businesses, computerized Wanderer Visas focus on transient, autonomous pay sources (O'Brien, 2023).

3. Factors Driving the Ascent of Digitalized Migrant Visas

A few variables have contributed to the surge in popularity of Digitalized wanderer visas. These elements range from the monetary potential of the computerized travel proposition to changing inclinations for adaptable work game plans.

a. Monetary Policies Provide Opportunities for Host Nations

Computerized wanderers bring extra cash with them, which they likely spend on local goods, services, and experiences. For more modest economies, especially in the travel industry's subordinate locales like the Caribbean, computerized migrant visas address a technique to broaden and balance out income streams, particularly notwithstanding worldwide disturbances like the coronavirus pandemic. By drawing in advanced migrants, these areas can exploit the travel industry framework while empowering longer, financially useful stays (Hayden, 2022).

b. Remote Work is Another Norm

The pandemic's push for remote work has fundamentally changed how organizations and representatives perceive the need for physical presence. As associations progressively embrace adaptable work arrangements, representatives have more opportunity to work from different areas (Sullivan and Lewis, 2021). This shift adjusts well to computerized traveler visas, which take care of telecommuters who are not bound to an office and are equipped to add to the worldwide economy, paying little heed to their area.

c. Moving Way of Life Inclinations

Current laborers, particularly those aged twenty to thirty and Gen Z, are increasingly prioritizing a balance between fun and serious activities, individual flexibility, and social interactions over traditional professional practices (Richter and Richter, 2023). This segment's shift towards valuing encounters and adaptability has contributed to the growing popularity of advanced nomadism. Computerized migrant visas allow these laborers to legally reside in countries that provide a high quality of life, a robust infrastructure, and social or natural attractions.

4. The Effect on Neighborhood Economies

The convergence of advanced wanderers can animate nearby economies through spending on lodging, eating, and diversion. This financial boost is especially crucial in regions where global emergencies or sporadic fluctuations have affected the travel industry. Digitalized wanderers contribute a consistent progression of pay, supporting neighbourhood organisations year-round, unlike during peak travel seasons. A concentrate by the Croatian The travel industry service found that computerized migrants contributed 12%; a lot of it went to neighborhood spending sightseers, mostly because of their long-term visits (Baričević and Tadić, 2022).

Moreover, advanced migrants often interact with local business people and consultants, fostering a variety of trades and skill sharing that can stimulate development and the growth of private companies (Korpela, 2021). However, there are concerns about potential improvements and rising living expenses, particularly among well-known advanced migrants, as the demand for short-term rentals and convenient accommodations increases. Policymakers should take these factors into account to ensure that advanced traveler programs benefit both local residents and visiting telecommuters.

5. Changing Worldwide Work and Travel Ideal Models

Computerized migrant visas are reclassifying the crossing point between work and travel by offering a formalized, lawful structure for area-free experts. This change lines up with patterns in the worldwide labor force, where adaptability, independence, and work-life reconciliation have become increasingly significant. By empowering labourers to legitimately live in different social settings, Digitalized migrant visas advance a worldwide outlook, empowering experts to expand their perspectives and participate in cross-line information trade (MacIntyre, 2023).

Additionally, advanced wanderer visas have had a significant impact on the travel industry, shifting the focus from high-volume, transient sightseers to long-haul guests who integrate more deeply into local networks. This approach aligns with manageable travel industry practices, as advanced wanderers often seek meaningful social interactions and are more likely to invest in local goods and services, thereby contributing significantly to the local economy compared to transient sightseers.

6. Difficulties and Contemplations

Although computerized traveller visas provide significant opportunities, they also pose challenges. Floods among advanced travelers can prompt rising rental expenses and interest for framework enhancements, putting tension on nearby assets. A few pundits contend that computerized nomadism, if left unregulated, could compound disparities in lodging and pay dissemination. Nations executing advanced wanderer visas should cautiously deal with these projects to offset financial advantages with the requirements of nearby networks.

Additionally, advanced travellers may face unique challenges related to tax collection and social benefits, as they often lack eligibility for the same insurance policies as local residents. Managing these administrative complexities is crucial for developing practical advanced migrant projects that benefit both host countries and visiting experts.

OBJECTIVES OF THE STUDY

Digitalized traveler visas have arisen as an answer for telecommuters looking for adaptability, permitting experts to live in outside nations while working for bosses or clients somewhere else (Mohn, 2021). This pattern denotes a takeoff from customary work ideal models, reshaping how people and organizations view efficiency and area (Reichenberger, 2018).

The review tries to comprehend what these visas mean for neighborhood economies by breaking down monetary commitments from advanced wanderers, like convenience, eating, and relaxation spending, which can prompt expanded income for nearby organizations (Williams, 2022). Furthermore, this examination will survey the social and social effect of coordinating unfamiliar telecommuters inside nearby networks, including both positive connections and possible difficulties (Kavita and Gupta, 2022). At long last, the review expects to investigate the strategy structures encompassing advanced migrant visas and how states can upgrade these to draw in talented specialists while guaranteeing shared benefits for occupants and unfamiliar experts (Alach, 2020).

REVIEW OF LITERATURE

1. Prologue to Computerized Traveler Visas

The idea of advanced nomadism, where people work from a distance while voyaging, has developed fundamentally, especially following the Coronavirus pandemic. Computerized wanderer visas are particular allows that empower people to work legitimately inside a far off country for broadened periods without the typical business visa imperatives. Dissimilar to customary work licenses, computerized migrant visas take care of telecommuters whose pay is created external the host country, accordingly making them less subject to the nearby work market (Reichenberger, 2018; Mancinelli, 2022). This shift has made computerized nomadism more open and formalized, permitting people to encounter new societies while supporting their expert interests.

2. Verifiable Foundation and Development of Advanced Nomadism

The beginnings of computerized nomadism follow back to the mid 2000s, with progresses in advanced innovation, web availability, and the expansion of compact gadgets working with remote work. With the beginning of the pandemic in 2020, remote work turned into a need as opposed to a decision, filling a worldwide flood in computerized nomadism. Mancinelli (2022) examines the quick reception of computerized wanderer visas as a reaction to the expanded number of telecommuters looking for adaptability in where they reside and work. By 2021, more than 25 nations had presented computerized migrant visa programs (Makimoto and Habits, 2021).

3. Influence on Worldwide Work Patterns

The ascent of computerized traveler visas has altogether impacted worldwide work patterns by moving viewpoints on the need of actual presence in the working environment. Concentrates by Saltzman and Beltran (2023) demonstrate that computerized nomadism cultivates another kind of work-life mix, permitting telecommuters to investigate different societies without forfeiting their vocations. This shift has driven organizations to embrace adaptable work approaches to hold representatives looking for additional independence and portability in their expert lives (Mancinelli, 2022).

Moreover, computerized nomadism has uplifted interest in offbeat work models, which decrease reliance on severe time-region arrangements and advance adaptable planning across appropriated groups (Chen, 2023). Subsequently, organizations are more open to recruiting ability from various regions of the planet, in this manner expanding labor force variety and cooperation on a worldwide scale.

4. Monetary Effect on Host Nations

One of the essential inspirations for nations to offer computerized wanderer visas is the expected financial lift. Advanced wanderers add to neighborhood economies through spending on convenience, food, transportation, and the travel industry administrations without seeking nearby positions. Research by López et al. (2022) features the huge monetary advantages of facilitating advanced migrants, assessing that an individual computerized traveler contributes a normal of $1,500 to $3,000 each month to the host economy.

Past direct financial commitments, computerized wanderers likewise act as casual brand envoys, drawing in additional travel industry and interest in their host nations through virtual entertainment and different channels (Patterson, 2022). In districts where the travel industry declined because of the pandemic, advanced wanderer visas have introduced an elective way to deal with financial recuperation. In any case, this deluge of unfamiliar specialists can likewise make difficulties, like expansion in rental costs and improvement, especially in little urban communities and emerging countries (Reichenberger, 2018; Mancinelli, 2022).

5. Computerized Nomadism and Social Trade

Computerized travelers add to social variety inside have nations, advancing diverse comprehension and trade. As per Mancinelli (2022), computerized migrants frequently coordinate themselves into nearby networks, going to language classes, taking part in widespread developments, and shaping associations with local people.

This mix has encouraged intercultural ability, which fortifies worldwide citizenship values.

In any case, there are likewise concerns with respect to "social the travel industry," where computerized migrants might regard nearby networks as brief attractions as opposed to taking part in significant social trades. Reichenberger (2018) noticed that a few computerized migrants make isolated networks that coincidentally lead to social false impressions or separation from nearby society. This peculiarity calls for additional investigation into encouraging maintainable and socially deferential computerized wanderer rehearses.

6. Difficulties and Dangers Related with Computerized Traveler Visas

While advanced migrant visas bring many advantages, they additionally present expected dangers and difficulties. An essential concern is the possible stress on neighborhood assets and foundation, particularly in famous computerized migrant centers. Expanded interest for lodging, combined with restricted supply, can drive up rental costs and make it hard for local people to manage the cost of lodging (Saltzman and Beltran, 2023). Besides, since computerized travelers are less put resources into the drawn out government assistance of the networks they possess, there is a gamble of compounding social imbalances.

Moreover, nations offering computerized traveler visas should address charge and administrative issues. Since computerized wanderers by and large acquire pay outside the host country, there is many times vulnerability with respect to burden commitments and government backed retirement commitments. Reichenberger (2018) contends that nations with advanced wanderer visas ought to consider approaches to manage the monetary commitments of computerized travelers to forestall financial lopsided characteristics.

7. Lawful and Administrative Systems for Computerized Wanderer Visas

The execution of advanced migrant visas brings up issues about the legitimate and administrative structures important to help and deal with this new class of worldwide specialists. As per Mancinelli (2022), one of the difficulties in planning computerized migrant visa strategies is laying out an unmistakable comprehension of duty commitments and freedoms for computerized wanderers. Given the variety in charge regulations and work guidelines across nations, have countries should guarantee that their visa arrangements line up with global expense settlements and work regulations to stay away from lawful difficulties.

Moreover, online protection is a developing worry, as computerized wanderers frequently work on open organizations, possibly uncovering themselves and their bosses to digital dangers. López et al. (2022) accentuate the requirement for have nations to give secure advanced foundation and teach computerized migrants on accepted procedures to relieve network safety gambles.

8. Future Possibilities and Maintainability of Advanced Traveler Visas

As advanced nomadism keeps on developing, nations are probably going to extend their visa contributions and acquaint strategies with draw in telecommuters. Future exploration ought to analyze the manageability of computerized migrant visas, zeroing in on creating guidelines that offset financial advantages with social and natural contemplations. Concentrates by Patterson (2022) recommend that nations embracing advanced wanderer visas ought to execute approaches to guarantee fair admittance to lodging, safeguard neighborhood work showcases, and urge computerized migrants to effectively add to nearby networks.

Also, the drawn-out supportability of computerized nomadism relies upon limiting its environmental impression. As advanced wanderers frequently travel habitually, there are worries about the ecological effect of expanded air travel and asset utilization in have nations (Chen, 2023). Future examinations ought to investigate procedures to empower earth capable way of behaving among advanced travelers and survey the job of green the travel industry rehearses in this unique circumstance.

Koskela, K., & Beckers, P. (2024) This paper conducts a comparative analysis of the Digital Nomad Visas (DNVs) from Croatia together with Thailand and Spain. The research distinguishes between three different policy frameworks that influenced their development by linking them to tourism needs and wealth-building efforts and immigration policy. The research develops a two-factor classification system for DNVs by linking civic affiliation with time-dependent factors which shows DNVs turned from pandemic emergency measures into permanent economic drivers for social development.

RESEARCH GAP

Regardless of the developing prominence of computerized migrant visas and their effect on worldwide work and travel designs, significant exploration holes remain. To start with, there is restricted exact examination on how advanced migrant visas impact neighborhood economies in have nations, especially as far as monetary advantages, work market impacts, and nearby business potential open doors (Mayer and Flynn, 2023). Current examinations center around expansive financial effects however need nitty gritty investigations of explicit areas impacted by the flood of advanced wanderers, like cordiality, lodging, and nearby administrations (Smith, 2022). Second, the job of computerized nomadism in molding long haul movement strategies and work regulations is underexplored, leaving inquiries on legitimate ramifications, charge approaches, and laborers' freedoms unsettled (Johnson and Pereira, 2021). Third, the social and social impacts on have networks, remembering possible improvement and movements for nearby culture because of transient populaces, are not surely known (Roth and Dvorak, 2023). Tending to these holes could yield basic experiences for policymakers and neighborhood partners trying to saddle the advantages while dealing with the difficulties presented by advanced nomadism.

PROBLEMS, ISSUES, AND CONTROVERSIES

The rise of digital nomad visas (DNVs) signifies a transformative approach to immigration, work, and tourism in an increasingly interconnected world. These visas enable individuals to reside in one country while working remotely for employers based elsewhere, fostering a new category of global workers. While the adoption of DNVs brings numerous advantages for both individuals seeking flexible lifestyles and host countries aiming to bolster their economies, they also present a range of challenges that require thorough exploration. This analysis delves into the multifaceted implications of DNVs, addressing economic impacts, social dynamics, legal issues, environmental concerns, and health and safety considerations.

Economic Impacts

One of the primary economic concerns associated with digital nomad visas is the potential disruption they can cause within local labor markets. The influx of skilled digital nomads may lead to competition for jobs, particularly in lower-skilled sectors, resulting in wage suppression for local workers (Taneja et al., 2021). While host countries may experience short-term economic benefits from the spending power of these nomads, the long-term effects can be detrimental if local talent is sidelined. Moreover, the unequal distribution of economic benefits often leads to adverse outcomes, such as inflated housing prices in popular destinations like Bali or Lisbon. Reports indicate that the rise in demand for rentals can lead to "touristification," which drives local residents out of their communities and exacerbates socioeconomic disparities (The New York Times, 2021). Additionally, many countries may become overly reliant on the revenue generated by digital nomads, making them vulnerable to economic fluctuations that can significantly impact local economies.

Social Dynamics

The arrival of digital nomads can also result in complex social dynamics, particularly in terms of cultural tensions and community fragmentation. As digital nomads often bring their own values and lifestyles, they may inadvertently clash with local customs, leading to misunderstandings and resentment among residents. Leung et al. (2019) highlight the risk of cultural imperialism, where nomadic populations impose their norms on local communities, threatening cultural identities. Furthermore, the phenomenon of gentrification frequently accompanies the influx of wealthier nomads into lower-income neighborhoods, raising property values and displacing long-term residents. A case study in Barcelona underscores this issue, as local protests emerged over concerns about housing affordability and community cohesion (The Guardian, 2020). Moreover, the transient nature of digital nomadism can hinder the formation of meaningful connections with local communities, resulting in superficial interactions rather than genuine cultural exchanges.

Legal and Regulatory Issues

Legal frameworks governing digital nomadism remain ambiguous, presenting significant challenges for both nomads and host countries. Existing labor laws often do not adequately address the unique circumstances surrounding remote work, leading to confusion regarding taxation, labor rights, and compliance with local regulations. Many digital nomads operate under the assumption that they are exempt from local laws, which can result in potential legal conflicts (Wang, 2022). Taxation dilemmas further complicate matters, as nomads often face the possibility of being taxed in both their home and host countries, creating double taxation scenarios that deter potential relocators (OECD, 2021). Additionally, the enforcement of DNV regulations poses challenges for governments, as many lack the resources to monitor compliance effectively, leading to potential abuses of the system and strained relationships between authorities and foreign workers.

Environmental Concerns

The environmental implications of digital nomadism are another critical area of concern. While remote work reduces the need for daily commutes, the frequent travel associated with nomadic lifestyles can lead to an increased carbon footprint due to flights and tourism-related activities. Gössling et al. (2020) emphasize the importance of considering the environmental costs of such travel when evaluating the overall benefits of DNVs. Furthermore, the sudden influx of digital nomads can place substantial strain on local resources, such as water, energy, and waste management systems, particularly in destinations with limited infrastructure. Sustainable practices may be challenging to maintain as local systems struggle to accommodate the increased demand (Sustainable Travel International, 2021).

Health and Safety Issues

Digital nomads often face significant health and safety challenges in their host countries. Access to healthcare services can be problematic, as visa requirements may exclude nomads from local healthcare programs, leaving them with inadequate coverage. Additionally, language barriers and unfamiliarity with local healthcare systems complicate access to necessary medical services (Smith et al., 2020). Safety concerns also arise from the transient nature of digital nomadism; individuals may lack the local knowledge needed to navigate unfamiliar environments, exposing them to risks such as crime or natural disasters. Reports of harassment or discrimination against digital nomads further complicate their experiences, highlighting the need for improved awareness and support mechanisms in host countries (Bishop, 2022).

SUGGESTIONS FOR RESEARCH

The concept of digital nomad visas has emerged as a significant trend in global mobility, allowing individuals to work remotely while traveling across countries. This phenomenon has implications for work culture, travel patterns, and local economies. The following suggestions outline key areas for further research to better understand the impact of digital nomad visas and how they can be optimized to benefit various stakeholders.

1. Comprehensive Policy Analysis

One of the first areas of research should focus on the policy frameworks surrounding digital nomad visas. This includes examining the different types of visas offered by various countries, the eligibility criteria, application processes, and the duration of stay. Comparative studies can be conducted to assess the effectiveness of these policies in attracting digital nomads. Such analyses should consider factors like ease of application, tax implications, and access to local services. This will help identify best practices that countries can adopt to enhance their visa programs.

2. Impact on Local Economies

Research should investigate the economic impact of digital nomads on host countries. This includes examining how the influx of remote workers affects local businesses, housing markets, and tourism. Data collection can involve surveys of local business owners to understand changes in consumer spending patterns and how they adapt their services to cater to digital nomads. Additionally, studies could assess the longer-term effects on real estate prices and availability in popular nomad destinations, providing insights into potential socio-economic challenges.

3. Cultural Exchange and Integration

The rise of digital nomad visas also opens opportunities for cultural exchange between nomads and local populations. Research could explore how digital nomads interact with local communities and how these interactions affect cultural dynamics. Studies could focus on the potential for mutual learning and exchange of ideas, skills, and practices. Furthermore, understanding the challenges digital nomads face in integrating into local cultures can provide insights for policymakers to create more inclusive environments.

4. Work Patterns and Productivity

Understanding how digital nomadism affects work patterns and productivity is another critical area for research. Studies could investigate the working habits of digital nomads, such as preferred work environments, hours of work, and the tools they use. Additionally, research could examine how the flexibility of remote work impacts productivity and job satisfaction. Surveys and interviews can help gather qualitative data on these aspects, providing insights into the work-life balance experienced by digital nomads.

5. Sustainability Considerations

As the number of digital nomads rises, there is a need to assess the environmental implications of this trend. Future research should explore the sustainability of nomadic lifestyles, including their carbon footprints, consumption patterns, and effects on local ecosystems. Investigating how digital nomads can engage in environmentally responsible practices while traveling could offer valuable guidelines for promoting sustainable tourism and work habits.

6. Technological Infrastructure and Support

The success of digital nomad visas is heavily reliant on technological infrastructure. Research should assess the adequacy of internet connectivity, coworking spaces, and digital services in host countries. Studies can focus on how these factors influence the choice of destination for digital nomads. Understanding the role of local governments and private sectors in enhancing technological support can inform strategies to attract remote workers.

7. Legal and Tax Implications

Digital nomads often navigate complex legal and tax landscapes when working across borders. Future research should delve into the legal frameworks that impact digital nomads, including taxation, employment rights, and social security benefits. Comparative studies could evaluate how different countries address these issues and the implications for digital nomads' rights and responsibilities. Providing clarity on these aspects can help digital nomads make informed decisions about their travel and work arrangements.

8. Impact on Tourism Trends

The rise of digital nomad visas may also alter traditional tourism patterns. Research should investigate how the influx of long-term remote workers influences local tourism industries, including hospitality, leisure, and recreation. Understanding whether digital nomads contribute to off-peak tourism and their preferences for local experiences can provide valuable insights for tourism stakeholders to adapt their offerings.

9. Community and Network Development

Digital nomads often seek community and networking opportunities while traveling. Future research could focus on the formation of communities among digital nomads, including how they connect with one another and share resources. Studies could explore the role of social media and digital platforms in facilitating these connections and how such communities influence the experiences of nomads in various destinations.

10. Future Trends and Challenges

Finally, research should address the future of digital nomadism in light of emerging trends and challenges. This includes exploring the potential impact of global events, such as pandemics or economic downturns, on the mobility of digital nomads. Studies could also investigate how changing attitudes toward work, travel, and remote employment will shape the evolution of digital nomad visas.

RECOMMENDATIONS

The emergence of digital nomad visas represents a significant shift in the landscape of work and travel, enabling individuals to live and work remotely while exploring new countries. As this trend continues to grow, it is essential for governments, businesses, and local communities to develop strategies that maximize the benefits of digital nomadism while addressing potential challenges. The following recommendations provide a comprehensive framework for stakeholders to harness the transformative potential of digital nomad visas effectively.

1. Develop Comprehensive Policy Frameworks

Governments should establish clear and comprehensive policy frameworks for digital nomad visas. These policies should outline eligibility criteria, application processes, and tax regulations to ensure transparency and accessibility for potential applicants. Collaboration between government agencies, such as immigration, tourism, and economic development departments, is crucial to create a cohesive strategy that aligns with national and local economic goals (Huang, 2021).

2. Promote Digital Nomad Friendly Infrastructure

Investing in digital infrastructure is critical for attracting digital nomads. Governments and local authorities should prioritize the development of high-speed internet, co-working spaces, and reliable telecommunications. Additionally, enhancing public amenities, such as transportation, healthcare, and safety, will create a conducive environment for remote workers (Hassan, 2022). Public-private partnerships can be instrumental in funding and facilitating these infrastructure projects.

3. Encourage Local Business Engagement

Local businesses should actively engage with digital nomads to create a welcoming environment. This can include offering discounts or incentives to remote workers, organizing events, and providing services tailored to their needs. Local chambers of commerce can facilitate networking opportunities that connect nomads with businesses, fostering collaboration and economic growth (Baker, 2023). By integrating digital nomads into the local economy, communities can diversify their customer base and stimulate growth.

4. Foster Community and Networking Opportunities

Creating platforms for community engagement is essential for digital nomads to connect with one another and the local population. Governments and local organizations should facilitate networking events, workshops, and cultural exchanges that encourage interaction between nomads and residents. Such initiatives can enhance the sense of belonging among digital nomads and promote cultural exchange, enriching the local community (Fuchs, 2022).

5. Implement Supportive Taxation Policies

To attract digital nomads, governments should consider implementing favorable taxation policies. This may include tax exemptions or reduced rates for remote workers to incentivize them to choose their country as a base. Ensuring that taxation policies are simple and transparent will help avoid confusion and potential legal issues for digital nomads (Baker, 2023). Furthermore, consultations with digital nomads can provide valuable insights into their preferences regarding taxation.

6. Conduct Research and Data Collection

Governments and academic institutions should prioritize research on the impact of digital nomadism on local economies and communities. Collecting data on spending patterns, economic contributions, and demographic profiles of digital nomads can inform policymakers and stakeholders about the benefits and challenges associated with this trend. This evidence-based approach will aid in the development of targeted policies and initiatives that maximize the positive impact of digital nomads (Huang, 2021).

7. Develop Marketing Strategies

To attract digital nomads, countries must develop targeted marketing strategies that highlight the unique advantages of their locations. This can include showcasing the local lifestyle, culture, and amenities that appeal to remote workers. Social media campaigns, influencer partnerships, and participation in digital nomad conferences can effectively promote the country as a desirable destination for remote work (Fuchs, 2022).

8. Promote Sustainability and Responsible Tourism

As digital nomadism grows, it is essential to promote sustainable practices that minimize the environmental impact of increased tourism. Governments should encourage responsible tourism initiatives, such as supporting local businesses, participating in community service projects, and respecting local cultures and environments. By fostering a culture of sustainability, countries can ensure that the influx of digital nomads benefits both the local economy and the environment (Hassan, 2022).

9. Provide Resources and Support for Digital Nomads

Governments and local organizations should offer resources and support for digital nomads, including information on visa applications, housing options, and local services. Creating an online platform that aggregates this information can enhance the experience for remote workers and help them navigate the challenges of relocating to a new country (Baker, 2023). Additionally, providing access to legal and financial advice can empower digital nomads to make informed decisions.

10. Monitor and Evaluate the Impact of Digital Nomad Policies

Finally, it is crucial for governments to continuously monitor and evaluate the impact of digital nomad visa policies. This can involve gathering feedback from digital nomads and local businesses, analyzing economic indicators, and adjusting policies based on the findings. By adopting a responsive approach, governments can ensure that their strategies remain effective and aligned with the evolving landscape of remote work and travel (Huang, 2021).

CONCLUSION

The rise of digital nomad visas marks a significant shift in the global work and travel landscape, presenting new opportunities for both individuals and host countries. By allowing remote workers to live and work in different countries without the constraints of traditional employment models, these visas foster a more flexible and interconnected workforce. This transformation not only enhances work-life balance for digital nomads but also stimulates local economies by increasing tourism, supporting local businesses, and promoting cultural exchange (Friedman, 2020).

As countries compete to attract skilled remote workers, they can harness the economic benefits that come with this influx. For instance, cities like Lisbon and Bali have seen a surge in local startups, co-working spaces, and service industries tailored to the needs of digital nomads (Benson, 2021). Moreover, digital nomadism encourages a more diverse and adaptable workforce, essential for innovation in an increasingly globalized economy (Baker & Wall, 2021).

However, challenges such as regulatory frameworks, infrastructure, and community integration must be addressed to maximize the benefits of digital nomad visas. Future research should focus on understanding the long-term impacts of this trend on local communities, including potential strains on housing and public services. By navigating these challenges thoughtfully, countries can leverage the rise of digital nomadism to build resilient economies and foster sustainable growth in a rapidly evolving world of work.

SCOPE FOR FURTHER RESEARCH

The emergence of digital nomad visas (DNVs) presents an evolving landscape that warrants comprehensive exploration. Future research could focus on the socio-economic impacts of DNVs on host countries, assessing how these programs influence local economies, labor markets, and service sectors. Studies could utilize quantitative methods to measure changes in tourism revenues, local business growth, and employment dynamics as a result of digital nomads settling temporarily in these regions (González & Eguizábal, 2022).

Moreover, the implications of DNVs on digital nomads themselves—such as their lifestyle choices, community integration, and mental health—deserve attention. Qualitative research methodologies, including interviews and case studies, can provide insights into the lived experiences of digital nomads, exploring challenges and opportunities associated with their unique work-travel arrangements (Böcker & Meisner, 2019).

Additionally, examining the policy frameworks that govern DNVs across different countries could inform best practices for implementation. Comparative studies of DNV policies in various nations could yield insights into how regulatory environments impact the success and attractiveness of these visa programs (Bajpai & Ghosh, 2021).

Finally, future research could investigate the environmental implications of increased mobility due to DNVs, analyzing how this trend aligns with sustainability goals and responsible tourism practices. This multifaceted approach will contribute to a deeper understanding of the implications of digital nomadism on a global scale.

REFERENCES

Adler, P. A., & Adler, P. (2020). The Role of Ethnography in Understanding the Global Community of Digital Nomads. *Journal of Global Mobility*, *8*(3), 267–282.

Alach, P. (2020). Digital Nomad Visas: A Comparative Analysis of National Policies and Programs. *Journal of International Mobility*, *3*(1), 45–63.

Bajpai, R., & Ghosh, A. (2021). Digital Nomads: The Impact of Visa Programs on Tourism. *Journal of Tourism Research*, *12*(3), 345–362.

Baker, J. (2023). The impact of digital nomads on local economies: Strategies for engagement and growth. *Journal of Economic Development*, *45*(1), 45–58.

Baker, S., & Wall, A. (2021). The impact of digital nomadism on local economies: A case study approach. *Journal of Tourism and Cultural Change*, *19*(2), 142–158. DOI: 10.1080/14766825.2021.1949533

Baldry, C. (2021). Work and technology: The impact of remote work on global employment. *Journal of International Employment Studies*, *5*(3), 211–234.

Baričević, M., & Tadić, M. (2022). Economic impact of digital nomads on local tourism: A case study from Croatia. *Tourism Economics*, *28*(4), 943–959. DOI: 10.1177/13548166221104790

Bénassy-Quéré, A., & Coulibaly, S. (2021). The rise of digital nomad visas: New opportunities for mobility. *European Economic Review*, *130*, 103579. DOI: 10.1016/j.euroecorev.2021.103579

Benson, A. (2021). Exploring the benefits of digital nomad visas for host countries. *International Journal of Hospitality Management*, *95*, 102927. DOI: 10.1016/j.ijhm.2021.102927

Bishop, R. (2022). Digital Nomads and Their Safety Concerns: A Qualitative Study of Experiences Abroad. *Journal of Travel Research*, *61*(4), 789–802.

Böcker, L., & Meisner, L. (2019). The Digital Nomad: Lifestyle and Work-Travel Balance. *Tourism Management Perspectives*, *31*, 100–109. DOI: 10.1016/j.tmp.2019.05.001

Buckley, R., & Bexton, R. (2021). Digital nomads: A new paradigm for tourism and work. *Tourism Management Perspectives*, *38*, 100834. DOI: 10.1016/j.tmp.2021.100834

Cacá, A., & Matias, J. C. (2022). The economic impact of digital nomads on local economies: Evidence from emerging destinations. *Journal of Economic Geography*, *22*(3), 501–525. DOI: 10.1093/jeg/lbab029

Chen, D. (2023). Remote work and the digital nomad phenomenon: An analysis of global work trends. *International Journal of Remote Work*, *15*(2), 104–125.

Connell, J. (2020). Digital nomads and the changing landscape of work: A global perspective. *Global Networks*, *20*(3), 349–368. DOI: 10.1111/glob.12308

Cook, J. (2022). Digital nomads: The rise of location-independent work. *Journal of Global Mobility*, *10*(2), 157–174. DOI: 10.1108/JGM-12-2021-0062

Friedman, S. (2020). The rise of remote work: How digital nomad visas are shaping the future of travel. *Tourism Management Perspectives*, *35*, 100724. DOI: 10.1016/j.tmp.2020.100724

Fuchs, C. (2022). Digital nomadism: Community and cultural exchange in a globalized world. *International Journal of Cultural Studies*, *25*(2), 120–136.

González, M. E., & Eguizábal, A. (2022). Digital Nomad Visas and Their Economic Impacts on Local Communities. *Tourism Economics*, *28*(6), 1323–1340. DOI: 10.1177/13548166211035939

Gössling, S., Scott, D., & Hall, C. M. (2020). Global Trends in Sustainable Tourism: A Review of the Literature. *Journal of Sustainable Tourism*, *28*(12), 1749–1765.

Hannonen, O. (2020). In search of a digital nomad: Defining the phenomenon. *Information Technology & Tourism*, *22*(3), 335–353. DOI: 10.1007/s40558-019-00177-z

Hassan, S. (2022). Building a digital nomad-friendly infrastructure: Key considerations for governments. *Journal of Urban Planning*, *34*(4), 210–226.

Hayden, C. (2022). Remote workers and economic resilience in tourism economies. *Journal of Travel Research*, *61*(5), 1158–1175. DOI: 10.1177/00472875221103714

Huang, L. (2021). The rise of digital nomad visas: Implications for global work and travel. *Journal of International Business Studies*, *52*(3), 345–362.

Hwang, J., & Lee, J. (2021). Community building among digital nomads: The role of social media. *Journal of Business Research*, *126*, 494–502. DOI: 10.1016/j.jbusres.2020.12.051

Johnson, K., & Pereira, L. (2021). Digital nomad visas: Redefining the boundaries of work and travel. *Journal of Global Mobility*, *9*(2), 134–149. DOI: 10.1108/JGM-05-2021-0029

Kavita, S., & Gupta, M. (2022). Social and Cultural Impacts of Remote Work Migration: Insights from Digital Nomads. *The Global Studies Journal, 14*(2), 134–148.

Kinsella, K. (2021). The sustainability of digital nomad lifestyles: An environmental perspective. *Sustainability, 13*(14), 7592. DOI: 10.3390/su13147592

Kong, L. (2021). The economic impact of digital nomad visas on small nations. *Economic Development Quarterly, 35*(2), 124–138.

Korpela, K. M. (2021). Digital nomadism and local economic development: Opportunities and challenges. *Urban Studies (Edinburgh, Scotland), 58*(6), 1125–1141. DOI: 10.1177/0042098020970789

Koskela, K., & Beckers, P. (2024). Typologizing Digital Nomad Visas: Comparing Policy Rationales from Tourism to Wealth Accumulation to Immigration. *Journal of Comparative Policy Analysis, 26*(5), 407–425. DOI: 10.1080/13876988.2024.2343696

Leung, D., Weiler, B., & Kim, H. (2019). Cultural Identity and Interaction: A Study of Digital Nomads in Southeast Asia. *Annals of Tourism Research, 78*, 102738.

López, A., Jiménez, J., & Schmidt, M. (2022). The economic impact of digital nomadism: A case study of Portugal's digital nomad visa. *Journal of Economic Development, 42*(3), 112–136.

Makimoto, T., & Manners, D. (2021). *Digital nomadism and the transformation of the workplace*. Routledge.

Mancinelli, S. (2022). Digital nomad visas: A comparative study of their role in post-pandemic recovery and global mobility. *Journal of Tourism & Hospitality (Los Angeles, Calif.), 12*(1), 67–83.

Marr, B. (2020). How Estonia became the first country to offer a digital nomad visa. *Forbes*. Retrieved from https://www.forbes.com

Mayer, J., & Flynn, T. (2023). Economic impacts of digital nomadism on local economies: A case study. *Economic Development Quarterly, 37*(1), 27–42. DOI: 10.1177/08912424221110583

Messenger, J. C., & Gschwind, L. (2016). Three generations of telework: New ICTs and the (r)evolution from home office to virtual office. *New Technology, Work and Employment, 31*(3), 195–208. DOI: 10.1111/ntwe.12073

Mohn, T. (2021). The Rise of the Digital Nomad: How Remote Work is Transform

Partners, M. B. O. (2022). Digital nomad report. MBO Partners. Retrieved from https://www.mbopartners.com

Chapter 6
Digital Leadership in Education AI and Digital Nomadism Transforming Global Learning Landscapes

Ahmed M. Alkaabi
https://orcid.org/0000-0001-7220-8087
United Arab Emirates University, UAE

Ahmad M. Qablan
https://orcid.org/0000-0002-2780-9796
United Arab Emirates University, UAE

Hesham R. I. Badawy
https://orcid.org/0000-0002-0311-7496
United Arab Emirates University, UAE

Hosam R. I. Badawy
https://orcid.org/0000-0001-5107-4016
United Arab Emirates University, UAE

Khawla M. Hassan Almaazmi
United Arab Emirates University, UAE

Sumayya Robbin Andi
https://orcid.org/0009-0005-8098-375X
United Arab Emirates University, UAE

Asma Asma Gul Yousaf Khan
https://orcid.org/0000-0002-9978-0566
United Arab Emirates University, UAE

ABSTRACT

The educational sector has witnessed a paradigm shift with the advent of Artificial Intelligence (AI) and digital leadership. In this chapter, we explore how AI technologies are reshaping leadership practices, curriculum delivery, and workforce management in the educational sphere. Special emphasis is placed on digital nomadism and its implications for leadership in globally interconnected institutions.

DOI: 10.4018/979-8-3373-0159-4.ch006

By analyzing case studies from the UAE, KSA, and Qatar, the chapter examines how educational systems in these countries integrate AI and digital strategies to address localized and global challenges. Policy recommendations are provided to guide effective AI adoption and inclusive educational practices globally.

INTRODUCTION

In the evolving global education landscape, the integration of Artificial Intelligence (AI) and digital leadership has become central to institutional transformation, workforce preparedness, and the pursuit of inclusive and adaptive learning environments. AI, once viewed as a futuristic enhancement, now reconfigures the foundational structures of education through personalized learning systems, predictive analytics, and adaptive instruction. Concurrently, digital leadership has shifted from a peripheral competency to a strategic imperative, empowering leaders to navigate complexities associated with digital transformation, equity, and technological governance (Chen et al., 2020; Ghamrawi & Tamim, 2022).

In the context of early education, equipping children with skills in computational thinking, AI, and STEM is increasingly recognized as essential for future readiness. Badawy et al. (2024) emphasize that computational thinking supports analytical and problem-solving capabilities, while AI fosters personalized and adaptive learning experiences. STEM education, meanwhile, ignites curiosity and hands-on exploration. The authors also highlight that despite barriers such as limited access to resources, insufficient teacher training, and challenges in curriculum integration, these obstacles can be overcome through collaborative efforts among educators and policymakers. Their study advocate for inclusive technological access, ongoing professional development, and cohesive curriculum design to ensure children are well-prepared for a rapidly evolving digital world (Badawy et al., 2024).

Across the Gulf Cooperation Council (GCC), particularly in the United Arab Emirates (UAE), Kingdom of Saudi Arabia (KSA), and Qatar, AI integration is pursued not merely as a technological upgrade but as a catalyst for national innovation strategies, human capital development, and economic diversification (UAE Government, 2024; Nawaz et al., 2020). The UAE's AI Strategy 2031 and Qatar's National AI Strategy articulate this vision explicitly, framing AI as instrumental to achieving Sustainable Development Goals (SDGs), enhancing institutional agility, and democratizing access to education through digital equity and cultural sensitivity (Ahmed, 2020; UNESCO, 2022).

This section introduces the core inquiry of this scholarly study: how AI and digital nomadism converge to reshape educational leadership, organizational governance, and global workforce transitions. The conceptual lens integrates the Technology

Acceptance Model (TAM), Diffusion of Innovations Theory (Rogers, 2003), and Responsible Research and Innovation (RRI) to analyze how AI is diffused and accepted within educational systems and how ethical imperatives are navigated in tandem with digital transformation (Venkatesh & Davis, 2000; European Commission, 2020).

Digital nomadism—the ability to work remotely across borders through digital tools—adds a critical dimension to this inquiry. Educational nomadism, as an extension of digital labor mobility, challenges traditional paradigms of institutional leadership and geographical tethering (Choudhury, 2022; De Sousa et al., 2025). It enables educational leaders to reconceptualize workforce management through decentralized, agile, and culturally attuned strategies, reflecting broader shifts in the gig economy and platform work ecosystems (Aroles et al., 2020).

The UAE has emerged as a global testbed for AI adoption in education, pioneering initiatives such as the AI Tutor platform, Alef Education, and the Smart Learning Program. These projects reflect a commitment to ethical, inclusive, and scalable educational innovations (Emara et al., 2023; UAE Government, 2024). Saudi Arabia's Madrasati platform demonstrates how AI can be deployed for data-informed leadership and curricular responsiveness, while Qatar's integration of AI in research-intensive learning environments highlights a strategic shift toward knowledge-based economies (Alswedani et al., 2022; Ahmad et al., 2023).

Globally, institutions like Georgia Tech, through projects such as "Jill Watson," and policy frameworks by the OECD and WEF underscore the dual mandate of AI: to augment human capability and uphold equity, privacy, and transparency (Goel & Polepeddi, 2016; OECD, 2023; WEF, 2025). These efforts resonate with ethical imperatives in AI governance, including fairness in algorithmic systems, equitable access to AI-enhanced education, and the need for human oversight in automated decision-making processes (West et al., 2019; Wang, 2021).

Purpose of the Study

This study critically investigates how AI-driven leadership and digital nomadism are transforming educational leadership, institutional governance, and workforce dynamics, with a particular focus on the UAE, Saudi Arabia, and Qatar. It explores the nexus of technological innovation, ethical governance, and global mobility in education, offering a theory-informed and policy-relevant framework for managing these transitions.

The UAE exemplifies national strategies advancing AI integration in education, notably through the UAE Strategy for Artificial Intelligence 2031 and the DUB. AI framework, aimed at enhancing learning outcomes and global competitiveness (UAE Government, 2024). Concurrently, digital nomadism—understood as mobile professional work—has expanded in the post-pandemic era, generating new models of transnational teaching, remote school leadership, and distributed academic collaboration (Choudhury, 2022; De Sousa et al., 2025).

The study pursues three core aims. First, it examines how AI reconfigures educational leadership roles, augmenting decision-making, administrative efficiency, and personalized learning through predictive systems (Chen et al., 2020; Satya & Mohammed, 2024), while also posing ethical concerns related to algorithmic bias, privacy, and the erosion of human judgment (West et al., 2019; Grace et al., 2023). Second, it interrogates the implications of digital nomadism for leadership, focusing on how leaders manage geographically dispersed teams, ensure equity, and adapt institutional cultures to support remote education (Fernandez & Shaw, 2020; Butcher, 2021). Third, it draws on the Technology Acceptance Model (Venkatesh & Davis, 2000), Diffusion of Innovations Theory (Rogers, 2003), and Responsible Research and Innovation framework (European Commission, 2020) to assess how AI and digital mobility are adopted, governed, and institutionalized.

By integrating global insights with Gulf regional case studies, the study contributes to both theoretical and applied discourse. It provides strategic guidance for embedding ethical AI governance, fostering inclusive digital infrastructures, and aligning leadership practices with evolving labor markets in AI-intensive contexts.

Theoretical and Conceptual Frameworks

Technology Acceptance Model (TAM)

The Technology Acceptance Model (TAM), introduced by Davis (1989) and extended by Venkatesh and Davis (2000), offers a foundational framework for analyzing how educational leaders engage with AI technologies. TAM posits that perceived usefulness (PU) and perceived ease of use (PEOU) shape individuals' intentions to adopt a given technology. Within educational contexts, these constructs are critical for understanding how leaders integrate AI into governance, curriculum design, assessment, and strategic decision-making.

In the AI-integrated systems of the UAE, KSA, and Qatar, TAM explains institutional variation in the uptake of tools like Alef Education's intelligent tutoring systems, DUB.AI's teacher training platforms, and Madrasati's predictive analytics dashboards. Leaders who find these tools both beneficial (high PU) and intuitive (high PEOU) are more likely to support their implementation (Satya & Mohammed, 2024; Wang, 2021).

TAM is particularly pertinent in policy-driven systems like the UAE, where large-scale AI investments, such as those outlined in the UAE Strategy for Artificial Intelligence 2031, depend on local leadership engagement. Resistance often emerges when AI tools are perceived as complex or misaligned with institutional culture, despite national endorsement and infrastructure support (Emara et al., 2023; Tarisayi, 2024). TAM thus provides a framework to evaluate how professional development, technological literacy, and support systems influence AI adoption at leadership levels.

The model also accommodates external variables—such as ethical trust, pedagogical alignment, and professional training quality—that indirectly shape PU and PEOU. These factors are particularly salient in Gulf educational systems, where bilingual environments, centralized governance, and diverse stakeholder expectations affect AI integration (Chen et al., 2020; Grace et al., 2023).

Moreover, TAM offers insight into digital nomadism by explaining how remote educators interact with AI-mediated platforms. For geographically mobile professionals, acceptance depends on platform usability, interoperability, and responsiveness—core elements of the PEOU construct (Choudhury, 2022; De Sousa et al., 2025). TAM thus enables a scalable analysis of AI acceptance across both localized and transnational educational settings.

Diffusion of Innovations Theory

The Diffusion of Innovations Theory, developed by Everett Rogers (2003), offers a systemic lens for analyzing how AI technologies are communicated, adopted, and institutionalized across educational contexts. The model classifies adopters into five categories—innovators, early adopters, early majority, late majority, and laggards—and identifies key innovation attributes (relative advantage, compatibility, complexity, trialability, and observability) alongside communication channels, time, and social systems as core determinants of adoption.

In Gulf nations like the UAE, KSA, and Qatar, AI adoption in education has been catalyzed by national strategies and high-level policy initiatives. However, as Rogers (2003) emphasizes, adoption is shaped less by policy mandates than by organizational culture, leadership vision, and contextual fit. For instance, the UAE's Alef Education and Qatar's research-based AI platforms have experienced varied uptake based on institutional readiness, leadership competence, and stakeholder perceptions of value (Emara et al., 2023; Ahmad et al., 2023), reflecting the theory's constructs of relative advantage and compatibility.

The model also accounts for resistance. Emerging technologies such as generative AI and predictive learning systems may be viewed as complex or misaligned with entrenched pedagogical norms. In such contexts, digital leaders and AI-trained principals serve as change agents—early adopters who influence others through modeling and peer engagement (Fullan et al., 2023; Milton & Al-Busaidi, 2023). Diffusion is thus mediated by relational and experiential dynamics, not merely structural directives.

In globalized and hybrid education systems—including those employing digital nomads—diffusion assumes a transnational character. Mobile educators, equipped with high digital fluency, often adopt AI tools early, transferring knowledge through reverse mentoring and collaborative design (Choudhury, 2022; Papanikolaou et al., 2023). These cross-border interactions reaffirm Rogers' emphasis on social systems and interpersonal networks in shaping innovation trajectories.

Furthermore, the trialability and observability of AI innovations—such as AI tutors piloted in UAE classrooms—enhance their potential for adoption. When tools demonstrate tangible benefits (e.g., improved retention, reduced workload), they gain institutional traction (WAM, 2024; UAE Government, 2024). Rogers' theory underscores how diffusion is contingent upon broader policy ecosystems. While the UAE has established ethical AI frameworks to support responsible integration, other regions may lack standardized governance, influencing both the pace and legitimacy of adoption. Diffusion, in this sense, is a multi-level process shaped by national cultures, institutional trust, and leadership agency.

Responsible Research and Innovation (RRI) Framework

The Responsible Research and Innovation (RRI) framework, developed by the European Commission (2020), offers an ethical, anticipatory, and participatory approach to technological governance, increasingly relevant to AI integration in education. Unlike models centered on efficiency or market utility, RRI prioritizes societal values, inclusivity, and democratic engagement by embedding foresight, reflexivity, transparency, and stakeholder co-design throughout innovation processes.

In Gulf educational ecosystems—where AI initiatives such as the UAE's AI Tutor platform and Qatar's AI research consortia are expanding rapidly—RRI serves as a normative anchor. It ensures that AI adoption aligns with ethical imperatives, not just technological advancement. The UAE's AI Principles and Ethics policy, emphasizing data protection and algorithmic accountability, and Qatar's mandate for regular ethical audits of AI systems illustrate RRI-informed governance (UAE Government, 2024; Nawaz et al., 2020).RRI becomes particularly salient in addressing algorithmic bias, data privacy, and autonomy—issues magnified in educational settings due to student vulnerability and the asymmetry between technology providers and users. AI tools relying on behavioral data raise concerns about consent and surveillance. RRI calls for transparent algorithms, robust data governance, and the inclusion of educators and learners in decision-making (Grace et al., 2023; UNESCO, 2022).

The framework also complements digital leadership in transnational and nomadic education contexts. As learning environments grow more virtual and decentralized, leaders face questions of jurisdiction, cultural sensitivity, and social impact. RRI's emphasis on contextual deliberation and stakeholder responsiveness enables ethical navigation of these complexities (Choudhury, 2022; Wang, 2021).In public-private partnerships—such as those between UAE institutions and global tech firms like Microsoft and OpenAI—RRI is vital for maintaining democratic oversight and institutional autonomy. Policies promoting transparency and participatory review mirror RRI principles and prevent the entrenchment of inequality or external dependency (Education Middle East, 2023).

Aligned with the UN Sustainable Development Goals, particularly Goals 4, 9, and 10, RRI ensures AI in education contributes to equitable and inclusive development rather than reinforcing digital divides. For educational leaders, RRI reframes their role from implementers of technology to ethical stewards—responsible for equity, societal impact, and community engagement—especially in regions like the Gulf, where AI is both a reform instrument and a marker of national innovation.

THE ROLE OF AI AND DIGITAL NOMADISM IN TRANSFORMING EDUCATIONAL LEADERSHIP

AI-Driven Educational Leadership: Paradigmatic Shifts in Strategy and Practice

Artificial Intelligence (AI) is fundamentally reshaping educational leadership, shifting it from administrative support toward data-informed strategic governance. Unlike earlier technologies, AI systems now personalize learning, drive predictive analytics, and automate decision-making at scale. Theoretical models such as the Technology Acceptance Model (Venkatesh & Davis, 2000) and Diffusion of Innovations Theory (Rogers, 2003) offer critical insights into the conditions that influence AI adoption across educational institutions.AI applications, such as the UAE's Alef Education platform, exemplify this shift. Real-time analytics enable school leaders to track student progress, implement targeted interventions, and recalibrate curricula dynamically (Chen et al., 2020; Ahmad, 2020). Predictive modeling informs resource allocation and staffing, enhancing institutional efficiency and equity (Gyanamurthy & Radhanath, 2023). This evolution redefines leadership agency through the lens of algorithmically driven insight rather than reactive oversight.

Digital leadership, therefore, requires new competencies in AI tools, ethical governance, and strategic foresight (Jones & Kennedy, 2023; Du et al., 2023). National strategies like the UAE's AI Strategy 2031 and the DUB.AI initiative exemplify how AI has become embedded in educational policy and institutional practice, integrating governance mechanisms, teacher upskilling, and data-driven planning (WAM, 2024).This shift is further anchored by the Responsible Research and Innovation (RRI) framework, which mandates ethical, inclusive, and anticipatory governance (European Commission, 2020; OECD, 2023). Leaders are thus tasked not only with optimizing efficiency but safeguarding equity, transparency, and moral accountability in AI integration (Tarisayi, 2024; Wang, 2021). This is especially critical in domains such as student assessment and curriculum design, where human judgment remains indispensable. AI's role in advancing inclusive education is evident in platforms like Alef, which adapt content for diverse linguistic and cognitive needs. These efforts align with OECD and UNESCO guidance on using AI to foster equity for multilingual and neurodiverse learners (Holmes et al., 2021; UNESCO, 2022).

However, ethical and technical challenges persist. Algorithmic bias, data privacy, and digital inequality threaten to reinforce systemic disparities. Leaders must address these risks through algorithm audits, GDPR-compliant data governance, and stakeholder inclusion in AI design (Grace et al., 2023; West et al., 2019; Nguyen et al., 2022). Gulf case studies illustrate both opportunity and responsibility in AI-driven leadership. In Saudi Arabia, the Madrasati platform supports performance tracking while institutional oversight mitigates ethical risks (Alswedani et al., 2022). In Qatar, AI tools at Qatar University foster interdisciplinary research with embedded safeguards for academic integrity and cultural responsiveness (Ahmad et al., 2023; Nawaz et al., 2020). AI is not a neutral tool but a transformative force that redefines leadership itself. The future of educational leadership lies in integrating technological innovation with ethical stewardship—aligning data with judgment, efficiency with inclusion, and digital transformation with human-centered values.

Digital Nomadism and the Evolution of Educational Leadership in a Mobile World

Once considered marginal, digital nomadism has evolved into a significant force reshaping educational leadership in an increasingly globalized, post-pandemic context. Defined by mobility, autonomy, and digitally mediated collaboration, it challenges traditional notions of institutional structure, labor geography, and pedagogy across both higher education and K–12 systems (De Sousa et al., 2025; Hensellek & Puchala, 2021).Digital nomadism now manifests through remote teaching, cross-border academic partnerships, and globally distributed knowledge networks. These developments disrupt conventional spatial and temporal constraints, requiring leaders to build digitally fluent, culturally adaptive learning communities (Choudhury, 2022). Leading distributed teams demands "e-leadership" strategies—models grounded in asynchronous communication, trust-building, and outcome-based evaluation (Phelps, 2014; Robinson & Reisdorf, 2024).

The rise of "knowledge nomads" further signals the pedagogical potential of mobility. These globally engaged educators and learners drive intercultural learning and institutional innovation, as evidenced by models like the Erasmus nomadic university (Papanikolaou et al., 2023). Effective leadership in such contexts demands intercultural competence, strategic agility, and technological literacy to sustain inclusive, transnational educational ecosystems.

Leadership paradigms must also evolve. Traditional supervisory models give way to transformational leadership that prioritizes vision, innovation, and emotional intelligence in managing remote teams (Antonopoulou et al., 2021; Erhan et al., 2022). Digital well-being, flexible scheduling, and fair performance assessment become central concerns (Ghamrawi & Tamim, 2022).

AI-enabled platforms play a critical role in this transformation, supporting collaborative planning, real-time feedback, and instructional coherence. The UAE's Mohammed Bin Rashid Smart Learning Program exemplifies this integration, combining remote instruction, adaptive learning, and predictive analytics (Fullan et al., 2023; UAE Ministry of Education, 2023).

Nonetheless, digital nomadism also surfaces equity and ethical challenges. Access to digital tools, fair compensation, and legal protections remain uneven, requiring inclusive policies that support all remote educators regardless of location (Butcher, 2022; Robinson & Reisdorf, 2024).

In the Gulf, digital nomadism aligns with national strategies for innovation, such as the UAE's DUB.AI initiative, yet also introduces leadership demands related to cybersecurity, cultural sensitivity, and ethical AI governance (WAM, 2024). The digital nomadism redefines educational leadership. It calls for leaders who can navigate fluid geographies, harness AI for cohesion, and foster borderless, inclusive learning communities. As a catalyst for global collaboration and institutional resilience, digital nomadism offers both a challenge and an opportunity for visionary leadership in education.

The Evolution of Digital Leadership in the AI Era

Digital leadership in education has evolved markedly with the rise of artificial intelligence (AI), shifting from ICT integration and infrastructure modernization to strategic foresight, ethical governance, and transformative innovation (Chauhan & Thangavelu, 2024; Ellis, 2024). Initially centered on promoting digital literacy and supporting e-learning, digital leadership now requires competencies in data analytics, algorithmic decision-making, and AI ethics (Karakose & Tülübaş, 2023; Jones & Kennedy, 2023; Tarisayi, 2024). Contemporary frameworks, such as Ghamrawi and Tamim's (2022) 5D Typology—Digital Competence, Culture, Differentiation, Governance, and Advocacy—reflect this expanded role. AI integration intersects these domains, with leaders overseeing algorithm audits, ethical AI deployment, and personalized learning systems (Nguyen et al., 2022; Wang, 2021).

Adoption dynamics are further clarified by the Technology Acceptance Model (Venkatesh & Davis, 2000), which emphasizes the importance of demonstrating AI's pedagogical value, and the Diffusion of Innovations Theory (Rogers, 2003), which underscores the role of institutional culture and leadership adaptability in fostering innovation (Du et al., 2023; Gyanamurthy & Radhanath, 2023). In the UAE, this evolution is embedded in national strategies such as the AI Strategy 2031 and initiatives like Alef Education and DUB.AI. These programs redefine leadership as a systemic function involving AI-enhanced teacher training, performance monitoring, and alignment with national education goals (WAM, 2024; UAE Government, 2024).

Digital leaders today must also address challenges related to the digital divide, algorithmic bias, and cybersecurity. The RRI framework and OECD AI Principles call for anticipatory, inclusive, and transparent leadership that mitigates inequality and ensures responsible innovation (OECD, 2019; European Commission, 2020). Empirical studies affirm this expanded paradigm. Fullan et al. (2023) highlight the importance of human judgment, innovation culture, and data fluency in AI integration. The rise of remote and mobile learning further reinforces the need for e-leadership—capable of managing virtual teams and sustaining equitable learning across dispersed contexts (Fernandez & Shaw, 2020; Robinson & Reisdorf, 2024).

Ethical and Governance Dimensions of AI and Digital Nomadism in Education

The rapid adoption of artificial intelligence (AI) and the rise of digital nomadism in education present not only unprecedented opportunities for innovation and inclusivity but also profound ethical and governance challenges. These transformations require educational leaders, policymakers, and institutions to rethink traditional frameworks of accountability, equity, privacy, and institutional oversight. At the intersection of these evolving technologies and workforce models lies the urgent need for robust governance systems rooted in ethical principles and international policy standards.

AI Ethics and Educational Leadership Responsibilities

AI systems in education enhance personalization, efficiency, and data-informed decision-making but also raise significant ethical concerns. Risks include algorithmic bias, surveillance, data privacy breaches, and diminished human oversight—particularly when systems are trained on non-representative datasets or applied without cultural sensitivity (West et al., 2019; Wang, 2021). Without embedded fairness, tools like automated grading and adaptive learning may reinforce existing inequalities (Grace et al., 2023). Ethical governance frameworks such as the OECD AI Principles (2019), UNESCO's Futures of Learning (2022), and the Responsible Research and Innovation (RRI) model (European Commission, 2020) call for transparency, accountability, inclusivity, and human-centric AI oversight. In practice, this demands policies that protect student data, ensure algorithmic fairness, and maintain human judgment in AI-assisted decisions (Nguyen et al., 2022; Jones & Kennedy, 2023).

National strategies like the UAE AI Strategy 2031 and the DUB.AI Blueprint operationalize these principles through teacher training, algorithm audits, and GDPR-compliant data protocols. Alef Education's implementation reflects this alignment, combining ethical AI practices with sensitivity to local cultural values (Alyammahi, 2019; Emara et al., 2023).

Digital Nomadism and the Ethics of Educational Labor

Digital nomadism introduces further ethical complexity, particularly around labor equity, governance, and cultural sensitivity. As educators engage in transnational work, institutions must address fair contracts, infrastructure access, and inclusive digital environments. Without safeguards, digital nomadism risks replicating neocolonial dynamics, especially when affluent educators serve marginalized communities without local engagement or accountability (Butcher, 2022; Aroles et al., 2020).

Ethical digital leadership requires inclusive hiring, cross-cultural competence, and attention to the well-being of remote educators. Policies must address labor rights, remote onboarding, asynchronous performance assessment, and psychological safety (Robinson & Reisdorf, 2024). The UAE's AI governance models, including the Dubai Universal Blueprint for AI, exemplify how equity and well-being can be embedded in AI-enhanced educational labor systems (WAM, 2024).

Toward a Responsible and Inclusive AI Future in Education

The ethical integration of AI and digital nomadism requires governance at institutional, national, and international levels. Educational leaders must adopt a proactive ethical stance—one that anticipates social consequences, promotes inclusivity, and upholds democratic values in technology use (Roshanaei et al., 2023; Sposato, 2024).This demands comprehensive educator training in AI ethics, data literacy, and algorithmic accountability, enabling critical engagement with AI systems. Equally important is the inclusion of diverse stakeholders in AI design to prevent bias and ensure alignment with principles of equity and justice. As AI and digital nomadism reshape education, ethical leadership and responsible governance will be critical to harnessing their benefits while safeguarding fairness, dignity, and democratic participation.

AI-DRIVEN EDUCATIONAL LEADERSHIP AND THE DIGITAL NOMAD PARADIGM

AI-Driven Decision-Making and Strategic Leadership in Education

Artificial Intelligence (AI) is transforming educational leadership by enabling proactive, data-informed governance. Tools such as predictive analytics and intelligent learning systems allow leaders to analyze large-scale data—ranging from student performance to institutional efficiency—supporting strategic planning, early intervention, and policy development (Chen et al., 2020; Wang, 2021).

In the UAE, platforms like Alef Education facilitate real-time data analysis and personalized instruction in K–12 settings, enhancing pedagogical differentiation and enabling targeted support (Alyammahi, 2019; Emara et al., 2023). Higher education institutions employ predictive modeling to identify at-risk students and align retention strategies with national objectives such as the UAE AI Strategy 2031 and the National Program for Artificial Intelligence (UAE Government, 2024).

International benchmarks, including Georgia Tech's Jill Watson and China's Squirrel AI, demonstrate the scalability of AI-augmented decision-making in tutoring and support services (Goel & Polepeddi, 2016; Zhou et al., 2021). These efforts align with OECD guidelines emphasizing ethical governance, inclusion, and strategic foresight in AI deployment (OECD, 2023). AI also automates administrative functions—admissions, scheduling, feedback—freeing leaders to focus on innovation and stakeholder engagement (Roshanaei et al., 2023; Tarisayi, 2024). This shift requires educational leaders to develop competencies in AI literacy, data ethics, and digital strategy, evolving from traditional decision-makers to collaborative, tech-savvy strategists (Madanchian et al., 2024; Chauhan & Thangavelu, 2024).

However, increasing reliance on AI raises ethical concerns around transparency, privacy, and fairness. Regulatory alignment with frameworks like the OECD AI Principles and the European Commission's RRI model is essential (European Commission, 2020; OECD, 2019). The UAE's AI Ethics Framework institutionalizes these standards, mandating accountability in AI decision-making across sectors, including education (UAE Legislation, n.d.). AI-driven leadership represents a paradigm shift—requiring educational leaders to balance innovation with ethical responsibility, ensuring that technological advancement remains grounded in human-centric values.

Personalized Learning and Educational Transformation through AI

Artificial Intelligence (AI) is reshaping education by enabling personalized learning—adapting content, pace, and instruction to individual learner needs. AI-powered platforms analyze real-time data to tailor learning experiences, enhancing engagement, retention, and achievement (Chen et al., 2020; Katiyar et al., 2024). At the core of this transformation are adaptive learning systems and intelligent tutoring platforms that adjust instruction based on a student's knowledge, style, and progress. In the UAE, Alef Education delivers bilingual, curriculum-aligned instruction while optimizing content through continuous data analysis (Alyammahi, 2019; Emara et al., 2023). These systems promote inclusive, data-driven learning responsive to linguistic and cognitive diversity.

International models, such as Squirrel AI in China and Georgia Tech's Jill Watson, demonstrate the scalability of AI-personalized instruction in high-enrollment contexts (Goel & Polepeddi, 2016; Zhou et al., 2021). Their success aligns with WEF (2025) findings on AI's role in fostering 21st-century skills like collaboration and problem-solving. In the Gulf, platforms like Saudi Arabia's Madrasati and Qatar University's AI-driven research assistants extend personalization across educational levels. Madrasati supports adaptive instruction through predictive analytics, while Qatar's tools aid research productivity in higher education (Alswedani et al., 2022; Ahmad et al., 2023).

However, concerns persist regarding equity, algorithmic bias, and data commodification. Without equitable infrastructure, under-resourced schools may be excluded from these benefits. Ensuring transparency, data protection, and algorithmic fairness is essential for ethical implementation (Wang, 2021; Grace et al., 2023). Leadership plays a pivotal role in enabling this shift. Supporting AI literacy, ethical AI governance, and professional development are crucial. UAE initiatives like DUB.AI teacher training and AI tutor hackathons exemplify this commitment (WAM, 2024).

Personalized AI systems also support digital nomad learners by offering flexible, location-agnostic education—linking AI to global workforce mobility and digital transformation (Papanikolaou et al., 2023; Shawkat et al., 2021). AI-powered personalization is both a pedagogical innovation and a strategic imperative. Its transformative potential depends on ethical safeguards, inclusive infrastructure, and forward-looking leadership.

Ethical Governance and Human-Centered AI in Educational Leadership

As AI adoption accelerates in education, ethical governance becomes essential to address risks such as algorithmic bias, data misuse, and opaque decision-making (Grace et al., 2023; OECD, 2019). Educational leaders must ensure that AI systems are aligned with transparency, equity, and human-centered values.

In the Gulf region, particularly the UAE, AI ethics is embedded in national strategies like the UAE AI Strategy 2031 and the DUB.AI Blueprint. These frameworks mandate fairness, accountability, and privacy, supported by regulatory tools such as algorithm audits and legal provisions for bias (UAE Government, 2024; UAE Legislation, n.d.). Effective AI governance requires balancing automation with human oversight. Predictive analytics must be contextualized through educator judgment to preserve moral integrity, as advocated by the Responsible Research and Innovation (RRI) framework (European Commission, 2020; Wang, 2021; Nguyen et al., 2022).

Localized applications—such as Alef Education and Madrasati—demonstrate ethical implementation through GDPR-aligned data policies, stakeholder transparency, and consent-based data use (Alyammahi, 2019; Alswedani et al., 2022). Qatar's AI strategy similarly enforces annual ethical audits to ensure fairness and cultural relevance (Nawaz et al., 2020). Persistent concerns include algorithmic bias, which may marginalize underrepresented learners, and surveillance, which threatens autonomy. Inclusive design, opt-in data practices, and adherence to frameworks like GDPR and UNESCO's AI and the Futures of Learning are critical safeguards (West et al., 2019; UNESCO, 2022; Wang, 2021).

Human-centered leadership reframes AI not as a replacement but as a complement to educators. Empathy, moral reasoning, and critical thinking remain distinctly human domains that must be preserved (Fullan et al., 2023; Tarisayi, 2024). To lead ethically, educators need training in AI literacy, algorithmic fairness, and stakeholder engagement. UAE initiatives, including the AI Educator Training Framework and DUB. AI guidelines, exemplify institutional models for embedding ethics into leadership development (WAM, 2024; Fadlelmula & Qadhi, 2024). Ethical governance in AI education must be anticipatory, not reactive—grounded in foresight, inclusion, and the unwavering commitment to human dignity in an increasingly automated world.

Digital Nomadism, Remote Work, and Leadership in Education

Digital nomadism—driven by technological change and global labor shifts—represents a structural transformation in how education is delivered and led. Characterized by location-independent, digitally mediated work, it is redefining the boundaries of learning, teaching, and institutional governance (Hensellek & Puchala,

2021; De Sousa et al., 2025). In education, digital nomadism enables broader access to global expertise, fosters intercultural collaboration, and enhances system resilience. Virtual universities, AI-enabled platforms, and remote teaching hubs allow educators to operate across borders, as seen in models like the Erasmus "Nomadic University" (Choudhury, 2022; Papanikolaou et al., 2023).

However, managing a distributed academic workforce introduces challenges: time zone coordination, communication consistency, digital equity, and institutional cohesion (Robinson & Reisdorf, 2024; Fernandez & Shaw, 2020). Adaptive leadership models—particularly e-leadership—emphasize digital fluency, empathy, and decentralized decision-making for effective virtual engagement (Phelps, 2014).In the Gulf, national strategies like the UAE's Vision 2031 and initiatives such as NAFIS and the AI Tutor platform support remote educator recruitment, aligning digital nomadism with broader goals of internationalization and educational accessibility (UAE Cabinet, 2021; WAM, 2024).

AI technologies play a central role in enabling nomadic education. Intelligent scheduling, automated feedback, multilingual bots, and predictive analytics facilitate seamless remote operations and data-driven leadership (Jones & Kennedy, 2023; Ghamrawi et al., 2023). Yet digital nomadism also raises regulatory and ethical concerns—taxation, labor classification, data jurisdiction, and access equity. Institutional collaboration with policymakers is essential to develop frameworks that legitimize and support nomadic academic labor (De Sousa et al., 2025).Pedagogically, leadership must support adaptive, mobile-responsive curricula that include asynchronous content, AI translation tools, and global credent ialing—blending digital pedagogy with mobile learning strategies. Culturally responsive and emotionally intelligent leadership is critical in diverse, distributed teams. Trust-building, inclusion, and psychological safety are essential to sustaining collaborative, human-centered virtual environments (Antonopoulou et al., 2021; Allal-Chérif et al., 2021).

AI in Predictive Analytics for Educational Leadership

The integration of predictive analytics into education marks a pivotal shift from reactive to anticipatory leadership. Powered by AI, predictive analytics uses machine learning and statistical models to forecast outcomes from historical and real-time data, enhancing decision-making in resource management, learner support, and policy formation (Baker et al., 2022; Wang, 2021). In the UAE, platforms like Alef Education and the Mohammed Bin Rashid Smart Learning Program utilize AI to identify at-risk students, guide personalized interventions, and monitor instructional effectiveness. These tools enable early intervention, improving student success and institutional efficiency (Alyammahi, 2019; Emara et al., 2023).Higher education institutions apply predictive models for enrollment forecasting, academic advising, and curriculum planning. UAE universities, for instance, use AI to allocate resources and tailor course recommendations based on student data (Satya & Mohammed, 2024).

Globally, Georgia State University's success platform exemplifies the impact of predictive analytics—using over 800 indicators to support at-risk students and improve graduation rates (Goel & Polepeddi, 2016). In Saudi Arabia, the Madrasati platform supports data-informed adjustments in teaching and resource allocation, aligning with Vision 2030 (Alswedani et al., 2022). Qatar's AI platforms help forecast research outputs and guide academic strategy (Ahmad et al., 2023). Despite its benefits, predictive analytics raises ethical concerns, including algorithmic bias and data privacy risks. Biased datasets can produce inequitable predictions, disproportionately affecting marginalized learners (West et al., 2019). Ethical frameworks like the OECD AI Principles and the UAE's national AI ethics guidelines are essential for ensuring fairness, accountability, and human oversight (OECD, 2019; UAE Government, 2024).

In order to use predictive tools responsibly, educational leaders must cultivate data literacy and ethical awareness. UAE initiatives, such as DUB.AI, offer training to build institutional capacity in data-driven and ethical decision-making (WAM, 2024). Predictive analytics is not just a technical advancement—it is a strategic tool for responsive, equitable, and future-ready educational leadership. When ethically embedded, it enables institutions to anticipate needs, improve outcomes, and support diverse learners effectively.

Teacher Empowerment and Upskilling Programs in AI-Driven Educational Leadership

As AI becomes integral to education, empowering and upskilling teachers has become a strategic and ethical imperative. Educators must be equipped not only with technical proficiency but also with the pedagogical and ethical competencies to lead AI integration effectively (Fadlelmula & Qadhi, 2024; Gamage & Vithanage, 2023). In the UAE, initiatives like the Dubai Universal Blueprint for AI and the 2024 AI Teacher Training Initiative aim to build AI literacy, enabling teachers to design and implement intelligent learning systems. Recognizing their pivotal role, educators are incentivized through awards such as the AED 1 million AI Educator Innovation Prize (WAM, 2024).

Effective upskilling goes beyond technical training. Teachers must understand AI's implications for instruction, data ethics, and algorithmic bias (Grace et al., 2023; Chen et al., 2020). Platforms like Alef Education support this shift by offering real-time learning analytics, transforming teachers into data-informed facilitators (Alyammahi, 2019; Emara et al., 2023). Across the Gulf, similar efforts are evident. Qatar University offers interdisciplinary AI workshops aligned with its national strategy, while Saudi Arabia's Madrasati platform embeds AI literacy into CPD for K–12 educators (Ahmad et al., 2023; Aldawsari, 2023).

However, teacher empowerment must be embedded within sustained professional development ecosystems that include mentorship, collaboration, and reflective practice. Leadership must foster a culture of innovation and provide time and resources for AI-focused inquiry (Milton & Al-Busaidi, 2023; Ghamrawi & Tamim, 2022). Ethical dimensions are also central. As AI systems influence assessment and instruction, educators must retain their autonomy and be trained to critically engage with algorithmic recommendations (Tarisayi, 2024; Wang, 2021). Equity remains a challenge. Disparities in access to upskilling—especially in remote or under-resourced schools—require inclusive policies and differentiated training. The UAE's use of online CPD portals, AI micro-credentials, and school-based AI leadership teams offers scalable models (Li et al., 2024). Empowering teachers through continuous, ethical upskilling ensures that AI serves as a pedagogical enabler—not a substitute. Leadership that invests in teacher agency will drive responsible and transformative AI integration in education.

Digital Transformation Leadership Attributes: The 5D Typology

In the context of AI-driven educational transformation, digital leadership is not merely a technical capacity but a multidimensional competency framework that guides institutional change, pedagogical innovation, and ethical governance. One of the most comprehensive models for conceptualizing digital leadership in education is the 5D Typology, which delineates five core leadership attributes: Digital Competence, Digital Culture, Digital Differentiation, Digital Governance, and Digital Advocacy (Ghamrawi & Tamim, 2022). This typology serves as a strategic framework for navigating the complexities of digital transformation in schools, universities, and ministries.

Digital Competence

Digital competence refers to a leader's ability to effectively utilize digital technologies for instructional, managerial, and strategic purposes. This includes mastery of AI-based platforms, data analytics tools, cloud-based systems, and learning management environments. In the UAE, the Alef Education platform and the Smart Learning Program exemplify how digital competence enables principals and instructional leaders to analyze student data, track learning progression, and personalize instruction (Alyammahi, 2019; Emara et al., 2023). Leaders must also possess the capacity to evaluate technological tools critically, ensuring their alignment with learning objectives and institutional visions.

Digital Culture

Digital culture reflects a leader's ability to foster a climate of innovation, experimentation, and technological fluency within the school community. It involves promoting openness to change, encouraging risk-taking, and building collective efficacy around digital transformation. In the UAE, this attribute is institutionalized through the AI Teacher Training Initiative and the Dubai AI Innovation Awards, which recognize and reward schools that embed AI into teaching and leadership practices (WAM, 2024). By modeling digital fluency and supporting capacity-building initiatives, leaders normalize the integration of AI technologies across their institutions.

Digital Differentiation

This attribute involves the customization of teaching and learning processes through technology to meet the diverse needs of learners and staff. AI enables differentiated instruction by providing personalized learning pathways, adaptive assessments, and multilingual support. Digital differentiation also applies to leadership—leaders must adapt their management styles to accommodate remote educators, diverse cultural contexts, and hybrid work models, especially in digitally nomadic and international schools (Papanikolaou et al., 2023). The UAE's AI Tutor Platform exemplifies digital differentiation by tailoring content to individual students in both Arabic and English, reflecting sensitivity to linguistic and cultural diversity.

Item Generation and Construct Alignment

The initial stage involved drafting survey items directly from the qualitative data, specifically from the coded themes and subthemes that emerged during the analysis. This process, referred to as item generation, was designed to ensure conceptual fidelity between qualitative narratives and quantitative constructs. For example, participants' accounts of "invisibility" and "cultural mismatch" informed the creation of items within the Cultural Identity Pressures domain. This grounding in authentic participant language enhanced the contextual sensitivity and content relevance of the items.

Digital Governance

Digital governance encompasses the policies, structures, and ethical protocols that regulate the use of digital technologies. It includes data privacy, cybersecurity, algorithmic transparency, and compliance with international and national AI ethics frameworks (Nguyen et al., 2022; OECD, 2019). In the Gulf region, particularly in the UAE, ethical AI leadership is codified through national strategies such as the UAE AI Strategy 2031 and the Generative AI Policy in Education, which guide schools and universities in deploying AI responsibly (UAE Government, 2024). Leaders must ensure that AI systems adhere to principles of fairness, accountability, and inclusivity, and that staff and stakeholders are aware of their digital rights and responsibilities.

Digital Advocacy

Digital advocacy involves a leader's role as a change agent who champions the integration of digital technologies for societal and institutional improvement. It includes lobbying for infrastructure investments, mobilizing communities to support AI-enhanced education, and influencing policy. Leaders act as intermediaries between classroom-level innovation and system-level reform, advocating for technology that advances equity, access, and global competitiveness (Karakose & Tülübaş, 2023). In the UAE, advocacy is reflected in the cross-sectoral partnerships between the Ministry of Education and global AI firms such as Microsoft and OpenAI, aimed at co-developing tools like GPT-based tutoring systems and teacher dashboards (WAM, 2024).

The 5D Typology thus offers a holistic and actionable framework for cultivating digital leadership in AI-enriched environments. It not only supports the operationalization of AI tools but anchors leadership practices in ethical governance, pedagogical differentiation, and strategic innovation. As educational systems across the GCC and beyond embrace digital transformation, the 5D model provides both a diagnostic and developmental roadmap for future-ready educational leadership.

DIGITAL NOMADISM AND EDUCATIONAL WORKFORCE MOBILITY

Digital Nomadism and the Reconfiguration of Academic Labor

Digital nomadism marks a structural shift in educational labor, decoupling academic work from fixed institutions and national systems. Enabled by AI, cloud computing, and global connectivity, educators, curriculum designers, and technologists increasingly operate as "knowledge nomads"—delivering instruction and services across borders in alignment with platform economies and digital globalization (Shawkat et al., 2021; Hensellek & Puchala, 2021).

These education-focused nomads engage in teaching, consulting, and content design across multiple ecosystems—universities, edtech firms, and course marketplaces—without fixed institutional affiliation. Leveraging AI-assisted platforms, adaptive learning systems, and collaborative cloud tools, they conduct synchronous and asynchronous learning across linguistic and cultural boundaries (Papanikolaou et al., 2023; De Sousa et al., 2025). AI technologies—real-time translation, learning analytics, and personalized content delivery—enable mobile educators to engage diverse learners globally, reinforcing a labor market defined by flexibility and digital fluency (Holmes et al., 2021; Li et al., 2024). This evolution challenges traditional norms of tenure, pedagogical standardization, and institutional loyalty. Platforms like Outschool and Udemy have formalized the gigification of educational labor, where freelancers compete for visibility and compensation based on algorithmic metrics. While offering flexibility, these arrangements raise ethical concerns about income precarity, legal protections, and governance in digital education marketplaces (Butcher, 2021; Aroles et al., 2019).

Policy frameworks are adapting. Initiatives like the UAE's Remote Work Visa and Estonia's Digital Nomad Visa institutionalize cross-border academic mobility, prompting the need for rethinking teacher certification, credential portability, and regulatory compliance (Choudhury, 2022). As institutions increasingly rely on mobile expertise, leadership must evolve to manage asynchronous workflows, remote collaboration, and intercultural pedagogy. Knowledge nomads function as nodes in global learning networks, requiring educational systems to reconceptualize their roles not only as employers but as strategic partners in a transnational educational landscape.

Institutional Strategies for Remote Leadership and Virtual Collaboration

The institutionalization of remote educational work has required significant adaptation of leadership models, digital infrastructures, and organizational cultures. As educational institutions across the globe confront the realities of hybrid work, cross-border instruction, and mobile academic labor, new frameworks for remote leadership and virtual collaboration have become imperative. These strategies are not only reactive measures to post-pandemic disruption but proactive responses to the structural evolution of the global educational workforce catalyzed by AI, cloud-based systems, and platform-mediated pedagogy (Fernandez & Shaw, 2020; Robinson & Reisdorf, 2024).

Remote Leadership as Distributed Governance

Remote leadership in education has evolved into a form of distributed governance, wherein authority and decision-making are diffused across geographically dispersed teams. This model requires leaders to pivot from traditional hierarchical control toward empowering decentralized units, embracing principles of flexibility, emotional intelligence, and trust-building in virtual contexts. Research underscores that effective remote leaders exhibit competencies in asynchronous communication, digital project management, and the orchestration of collaborative technologies (Phelps, 2014; Karakose et al., 2022). E-leadership, as it is increasingly termed, entails guiding staff through complex technological ecosystems while remaining attuned to socio-emotional cues often lost in digital communication channels.

Technological Scaffolding for Collaboration

AI-powered platforms play a critical role in enabling virtual collaboration across institutional and national boundaries. Tools such as Microsoft Teams, Zoom, Miro, and AI-enhanced learning management systems (e.g., Moodle with predictive analytics) facilitate synchronous and asynchronous interaction. Moreover, AI-enabled scheduling assistants, real-time translation features, and automated documentation systems optimize communication among diverse, multilingual teams (Wang, 2021; Holmes et al., 2021). These systems mitigate logistical barriers while providing insight-rich dashboards that aid leaders in monitoring team engagement, learner satisfaction, and progress toward institutional goals.

Educational institutions are also deploying collaborative knowledge-management systems (e.g., Notion, Confluence, and AI-curated repositories) to ensure continuity, transparency, and institutional memory in distributed work environments. The integration of AI-based sentiment analysis tools, now used in academic HR departments, supports leadership in identifying morale trends, burnout risks, and team cohesion levels—allowing timely interventions.

Capacity-Building and Faculty Empowerment

To manage the transition to remote and hybrid modalities, many institutions have developed structured capacity-building programs to upskill academic staff in both technical competencies and remote leadership practices. In the UAE, for example, the Dubai Universal Blueprint for Artificial Intelligence (DUB.AI) and associated teacher AI-literacy initiatives reflect a state-level strategy to empower faculty to operate effectively in digital and decentralized learning environments (WAM, 2024; Fadlelmula & Qadhi, 2024). Similar models are emerging across Europe and Asia, where academic institutions offer micro-credentialing in virtual pedagogy, AI integration, and collaborative platform use.

These programs not only support operational adaptation but also cultivate a new form of educational professionalism, where instructors are seen as co-designers of learning environments rather than passive deliverers of content. Institutional strategies that incorporate mentorship, peer-review mechanisms, and reflective practice contribute to sustaining collaboration in the absence of physical co-location.

Governance and Accountability in Remote Educational Contexts

A persistent challenge in remote educational leadership is governance—how to ensure accountability, quality assurance, and alignment with institutional missions when faculty and staff are dispersed across time zones and jurisdictions. To address this, institutions are developing comprehensive remote operations frameworks, which include clearly articulated performance indicators, transparent evaluation protocols, and inclusive feedback systems. AI plays a role here as well, offering leaders dashboards that aggregate key metrics across virtual teams, course performance, and learner analytics to support evidence-based oversight (Chen et al., 2020; Roshanaei et al., 2023).

Virtual leadership also raises questions about inclusivity and accessibility. Ensuring that all staff—regardless of their geographical or technological situation—can participate equitably in decision-making and collaborative initiatives is essential. Institutions adopting participatory governance models often embed inclusive digital leadership charters, diversity-sensitive scheduling practices, and cloud-based collaboration tools that accommodate users in low-bandwidth environments (Jaworski et al., 2022; Ghamrawi & Tamim, 2022).

Reframing Institutional Identity in a Post-Place Paradigm

Perhaps one of the most profound implications of institutional strategies for remote leadership is the reconfiguration of institutional identity itself. With educators no longer confined to campuses, the spatial boundaries of the university or school become porous, giving rise to what can be described as post-place education. Institutions are responding by rebranding themselves as "global campuses," adopting visual and narrative strategies that reflect their reach, diversity, and technological sophistication. This evolution demands new leadership literacies—leaders must understand cultural nuance, negotiate hybrid institutional logics, and integrate multiple temporalities into strategic planning. In these contexts, digital nomadism is not a peripheral anomaly but a defining feature of the contemporary educational ecosystem.

COMPARATIVE CASE STUDIES FROM THE GULF REGION

United Arab Emirates: AI Innovation and Remote Leadership Ecosystems

AI-Driven Educational Transformation in the United Arab Emirates

The United Arab Emirates (UAE) has emerged as a global leader in AI integration within education, guided by the UAE Strategy for Artificial Intelligence 2031. Its approach prioritizes not only technological adoption but also ethical governance, teacher empowerment, and data-informed pedagogy (UAE Government, 2024). A flagship initiative is the Alef Education platform, which uses machine learning to personalize instruction based on student learning patterns. Deployed across public and private schools, Alef provides predictive insights to teachers, enabling targeted interventions and individualized support—marking a shift toward student-centered, analytics-driven pedagogy (Alyammahi, 2019; Emara et al., 2023).

The AI Tutor Platform, developed by the Ministry of Education, complements Alef by delivering bilingual, culturally relevant content aligned with the national curriculum. At the 2024 World Economic Forum, Minister Ahmad Al Falasi underscored AI tutors' role in expanding access to personalized learning (WAM, 2024). The Smart Learning Program and NAFIS further align education with labor market needs. Smart Learning integrates AI into school operations for data-driven decision-making, while NAFIS provides AI-related training in fields like cloud computing and cybersecurity to prepare a future-ready workforce (Satya & Mohammed, 2024; UAE Cabinet, 2021).

To accelerate innovation, the AI and Robotics Award for Good incentivizes educational AI solutions, such as gamified tools and inclusive platforms, reinforcing the UAE's leadership in socially impactful EdTech. Predictive analytics also underpin governance in higher education. AI dashboards help administrators track learning gaps and support at-risk students, enabling strategic decision-making at scale (Ahmed, 2020; Chen et al., 2020). The UAE's AI agenda reflects a pedagogical and systemic transformation. Educational leadership is redefined through AI-enabled foresight and coordination, balancing innovation with equity, cultural relevance, and global competitiveness—positioning the UAE as a leading model of AI-enabled education in the Gulf and beyond.

Digital Nomadism and Mobile Educational Workforces in the United Arab Emirates

Alongside its AI leadership, the UAE is emerging as a hub for educational digital nomadism, integrating mobile work into a remote-capable educational ecosystem. National strategies such as the Remote Work Visa and the Projects of the 50 extend residency and employment rights to globally mobile educators, fostering a cadre of "knowledge nomads" who contribute to UAE-based education without geographic permanence (UAE Cabinet, 2021; Papanikolaou et al., 2023).

Digital nomadism is operationalized through AI-enabled platforms and virtual infrastructures at institutions like UAE University and Khalifa University. These systems support smart classrooms, real-time collaboration, and distributed academic leadership across emirates and international borders (Choudhury, 2022; Ahmed, 2020).

Initiatives like the Dubai Centre for AI's Teacher Training Program equip educators with skills in automation and AI pedagogy, preparing them for flexible, remote teaching roles. Such programs foster a digitally agile workforce aligned with the UAE's innovation agenda (WAM, 2024). This shift redefines educational leadership. Principals now lead through data dashboards and AI-generated analytics, managing performance and engagement asynchronously. Leadership becomes distributed and tech-enabled, supporting scalability and transnational educational delivery (Roshanaei et al., 2023). Challenges remain, particularly in sustaining cohesion, cultural integration, and relational accountability in K–12 settings. Leaders must balance digital flexibility with inclusive, student-centered practices that support well-being and community connection (Fernandez & Shaw, 2020; Robinson & Reisdorf, 2024).

Ethical Governance and Policy Alignment in the United Arab Emirates

The UAE's AI integration in education is strategically anchored in ethical governance, aligning national objectives with international standards such as the OECD AI Principles (2019) and UNESCO's Ethics of AI Recommendation (2021). The UAE's AI Principles and Ethics framework emphasizes fairness, accountability, inclusivity, and human-centered design in educational technologies (UAE Government, 2024). This commitment is operationalized through mandated audits of AI platforms like Alef and smart learning systems, ensuring algorithmic fairness, bias detection, and GDPR-aligned data protection. Institutional review boards and ethics committees oversee these audits, and educational leaders are trained to act on findings to support adaptive, responsible governance (Alyammahi, 2019; Deri et al., 2024).

Data privacy is central to the UAE's strategy. Student data is anonymized, securely stored, and subject to transparent consent protocols. The Generative AI in Education Policy (2023) offers additional safeguards for the ethical use of large language models in classrooms (Education Middle East, 2023). Public engagement further reinforces ethical governance. Events such as the AI Retreat and Alef Education Summit facilitate dialogue among educators, students, parents, and developers, aligning with the Responsible Research and Innovation (RRI) model's emphasis on anticipatory and inclusive policymaking (European Commission, 2020).

Leadership practices reflect this framework. School leaders are expected to embed ethical AI literacy in teacher training, curriculum development, and performance evaluation. Programs from the Dubai Centre for AI include modules on algorithmic bias, data sovereignty, and human-AI collaboration, equipping educators with both technical and ethical competencies (WAM, 2024). Aligned with the UAE AI Strategy 2031, the nation's ethical infrastructure advances both innovation and societal trust. By institutionalizing audits, stakeholder engagement, and leadership training, the UAE exemplifies proactive, responsible digital governance—positioning itself as a global model for ethically integrated AI in education.

Kingdom of Saudi Arabia: AI-Powered Platforms and Distributed Leadership

AI-Driven Educational Transformation in Saudi Arabia

Saudi Arabia's education sector is undergoing significant transformation through the strategic integration of AI, anchored in Vision 2030 and led by the Madrasati platform. Initially launched during the COVID-19 pandemic, Madrasati has evolved into a comprehensive AI-enabled learning ecosystem, supported by the Saudi Data and Artificial Intelligence Authority (SDAIA) and the Ministry of Education (Alswedani, Mehmood, & Katib, 2022). Madrasati employs AI-driven analytics to monitor student engagement, performance, and classroom interactions. Real-time data allows school leaders to implement early interventions, personalize support, and enhance institutional efficiency—key hallmarks of 21st-century educational leadership (Gyanamurthy & Radhanath, 2023).

Its adaptive learning capabilities adjust content based on learner profiles, promoting equity and engagement, particularly in addressing geographic and socio-economic disparities (Aldawsari, 2023). These personalized pathways support differentiated instruction and reduce dropout risk. Aligned with SDAIA's national AI strategy, the platform also supports predictive modeling for enrollment, academic forecasting, and curriculum planning—integrating AI into system-wide educational planning (Alswedani et al., 2022). Teacher empowerment is central to this transformation. Professional development programs train educators to use learning analytics, manage virtual classrooms, and co-design AI-enhanced pedagogy—advancing Vision 2030's Human Capability Development Program.

AI also streamlines administrative functions such as grading and scheduling, enabling school leaders to focus on strategic initiatives and stakeholder engagement (Singh, 2023). Cloud-based infrastructure ensures scalability and access across the Kingdom.

Overall, Saudi Arabia's AI integration reflects a dual focus on innovation and systemic reform. By embedding AI across classroom, institutional, and national levels, the Kingdom is reshaping leadership, redefining teacher roles, and positioning education as a driver of national talent development.

Digital Nomadism and Virtual Academic Leadership in Saudi Arabia

Saudi Arabia's education sector is gradually embracing digital nomadism through hybrid governance and geographically flexible instructional models, aligned with Vision 2030 and the Human Capability Development framework. While distinct from entrepreneurial nomadism, this institutionalized form enables mobile educators and virtual leadership within both K–12 and higher education contexts.

Central to this shift is the Madrasati platform, which evolved from a pandemic response into a core digital infrastructure. It enables synchronous and asynchronous instruction, allowing educators to teach and lead remotely across provinces, thereby redefining spatial constraints in school management (Alswedani et al., 2022). Virtual academic leadership is reinforced by cloud-based systems and AI dashboards that offer real-time analytics and communication tools. These technologies support data-informed decision-making and enable school leaders to manage distributed teams without physical proximity—signaling a shift toward outcomes-driven, digitally fluent leadership (Gyanamurthy & Radhanath, 2023). To sustain this transition, national training initiatives now include modules on remote supervision, digital communication, and virtual team coordination. These are delivered through e-learning platforms and teacher academies to prepare educators and administrators for future-ready, flexible workforce roles (Aldawsari, 2023).

While Saudi Arabia has not formalized digital nomad visas, it is fostering internal mobility by enabling teachers and supervisors to work remotely—particularly in underserved regions—through virtual staffing models that optimize national talent distribution. Cultural adaptation remains ongoing, shaped by religious norms, gender dynamics, and traditional leadership expectations. Nevertheless, the Kingdom is steadily building the digital infrastructure and leadership capacity to support a culturally attuned, decentralized model of educational digital nomadism—one that balances institutional integrity with technological adaptability.

Ethical Frameworks and Oversight Mechanisms in Saudi Arabia

Saudi Arabia's advancement in AI-enabled education is guided by a growing emphasis on ethical governance, algorithmic accountability, and culturally aligned implementation. As AI platforms like Madrasati become integral to learning and decision-making, the Kingdom has prioritized transparency, equity, and data protection in alignment with Vision 2030 and SDAIA's responsible innovation framework (Alswedani et al., 2022; Aldawsari, 2023).

The Ministry of Education has established algorithmic review committees to audit AI systems for bias and ensure equitable recommendations across socio-economic, regional, and cognitive learner profiles. In Madrasati, particular attention is given to fair student performance tracking and inclusive adaptive content (Alswedani et al., 2022). Parental consent protocols—modeled on GDPR standards—require explicit approval for AI-driven data use, accompanied by public education efforts to improve digital literacy and trust in data governance (Singh, 2023). Ethical alignment with Islamic values and national goals is central to SDAIA's strategy, which mandates regular AI risk assessments and value-sensitive design across public-sector AI applications, including education (Aldawsari, 2023).

Institutionally, school leaders and IT coordinators are trained in bias detection, data ethics, and the responsible use of predictive analytics. These professional development programs promote reflective, student-centered leadership that integrates moral judgment with digital fluency (Gyanamurthy & Radhanath, 2023). Inclusivity is also a core priority. AI tools within Madrasati are designed to support students with disabilities, multilingual learners, and those in remote areas—mitigating digital exclusion amid rapid tech adoption. Challenges remain, particularly in balancing centralized oversight with institutional autonomy and ensuring transparency in proprietary AI tools. In response, Saudi policymakers are exploring open-source audits, third-party evaluations, and public reporting to enhance accountability without compromising national strategic interests. Saudi Arabia's evolving ethical AI governance model demonstrates a culturally rooted, policy-aligned approach to ensuring that digital transformation in education advances equity, trust, and student well-being.

Qatar: Research-Oriented AI and Knowledge Nomadism

AI-Driven Educational Transformation in Qatar

Qatar's approach to AI in education is distinguished by its emphasis on research-led innovation, higher education reform, and alignment with sustainability goals. Unlike the UAE's K–12 focus or Saudi Arabia's national platforms, Qatar's transformation is led by institutions like Qatar University and guided by its National AI Strategy, emphasizing academic productivity, ethical governance, and interdisciplinary integration (Ahmad et al., 2023).

A core element is the deployment of intelligent research assistants and digital academic tools that support literature reviews, data analysis, and hypothesis generation. These AI systems enhance research efficiency and position AI as a driver of knowledge production and innovation. Qatari institutions also integrate AI into sustainability-focused disciplines—such as environmental science and urban development—using AI to analyze complex datasets and inform research and policy on climate and energy (Ahmad et al., 2023; Nawaz et al., 2020). This supports Qatar's vision of becoming a knowledge-based, environmentally responsible society. Adaptive learning platforms and intelligent tutoring systems provide personalized instruction and real-time analytics, fostering inclusion across Qatar's multilingual and multicultural academic landscape (Nawaz et al., 2020).

The National AI Strategy, introduced by the Ministry of Transport and Communications, outlines ethical safeguards, including bias prevention, cultural alignment, and mandatory audits to ensure fairness and transparency in AI applications (Nawaz et al., 2020). Global academic-industry partnerships further support Qatar's AI ecosystem. Collaborations in areas such as natural language processing and AI-enhanced simulation enable access to advanced tools and accelerate implementation across teaching and research (Ahmad et al., 2023). To ensure sustainability, capacity-building programs train educators and researchers in AI literacy, predictive analytics, and ethical deployment. This cultivates a digitally competent academic workforce capable of advancing AI integration locally and globally. Qatar's model reflects a strategic, ethics-driven application of AI in higher education—leveraging research, sustainability, and global collaboration to shape a future-ready, knowledge-based society.

Digital Nomadism in Higher Education and Knowledge Mobility in Qatar

Qatar's higher education strategy integrates digital nomadism into a research-driven, knowledge-based framework aligned with its national vision for global competitiveness and innovation. Rather than focusing on freelance remote work, Qatar supports mobile scholars and transnational academic collaboration through AI-enabled infrastructure and institutional flexibility. Initiatives such as Qatar University's partnerships with global institutions facilitate joint virtual research, hybrid conferences, and online mentoring—creating "knowledge nomads" who operate internationally while maintaining ties to Qatari academia (Ahmad et al., 2023). AI tools underpin this model, enabling real-time translation, adaptive course design, and multilingual content delivery. These platforms bridge cultural and linguistic gaps, promoting inclusion and international engagement in Qatar's academic ecosystem (Nawaz et al., 2020).

Qatar also emphasizes mobile research productivity. Digital labs, AI-supported research assistants, and virtual data repositories allow faculty to conduct interdisciplinary and sustainability-focused research remotely—aligning agile academic mobility with national development goals (Ahmad et al., 2023). To support this shift, Qatar invests in faculty training on digital pedagogy, AI integration, and virtual classroom management. These programs equip educators to lead globally distributed teams while maintaining academic integrity and cultural sensitivity. Policy infrastructure, guided by the National AI Strategy, promotes decentralized academic work. Though lacking formal digital nomad visas, Qatari universities allow faculty to collaborate and teach abroad during sabbaticals or joint appointments—expanding Qatar's intellectual reach. Digital nomadism contributes to educational equity by extending AI-powered distance learning to rural and underserved populations. This decentralization fosters inclusive access and strengthens national cohesion beyond Doha's urban academic centers. Qatar's model exemplifies how academic mobility and digital infrastructure can be strategically harnessed to build a globally integrated, equitable, and future-ready higher education system.

Ethical AI and Cultural Sensitivity in Qatar

Qatar's integration of AI in education is firmly grounded in ethical governance, cultural sensitivity, and inclusive innovation, as outlined in its National AI Strategy. Rather than treating ethics as supplementary, Qatar embeds them into its digital transformation agenda to foster public trust, equity, and educational integrity (Nawaz et al., 2020). Annual audits of AI systems assess algorithmic fairness, data privacy, and transparency. Overseen by the Ministry of Transport and Communications, these reviews address bias related to gender, race, and socioeconomic status, ensuring equitable AI deployment in a multicultural academic landscape.

Cultural contextualization is central. Adaptive learning platforms and intelligent tutors are designed to respect local norms and function bilingually (Arabic and English), supporting culturally congruent teacher-student interactions and inclusive content delivery. Data sovereignty is a key pillar. Institutions must comply with national privacy laws and enforce strict data-sharing agreements when collaborating with third-party platforms—aligning with international standards such as the OECD AI Principles (OECD, 2019). At the institutional level, universities appoint AI ethics officers or committees to monitor risks and promote ethical literacy through workshops and curriculum integration. These structures embed accountability, transparency, and human dignity in AI use (Ahmad et al., 2023).

Qatar also encourages diverse stakeholder involvement in AI development. Cross-functional teams in university–industry partnerships integrate varied cultural and disciplinary perspectives to reduce bias and enhance the relevance of AI tools. Aligned with the UN Sustainable Development Goals—particularly Goals 4, 9, and 10—Qatar's ethical AI approach ensures that educational innovation advances quality, inclusion, and sustainability. Educational leaders are thus expected to integrate ethics into digital transformation planning to serve the broader societal good.

CHALLENGES, RISKS, AND ETHICAL CONSIDERATIONS

Bias and Discrimination in Algorithms and Nomadic Systems

AI Challenges

AI integration in education introduces risks of algorithmic bias, particularly in areas such as admissions, personalized instruction, performance tracking, and resource allocation. These biases often stem from training data that reflect historical inequalities or demographic imbalances, resulting in discriminatory outcomes for marginalized student groups (West et al., 2019; Grace et al., 2023). Adaptive learning platforms are especially susceptible. When trained on culturally narrow datasets, they may misinterpret the needs of bilingual or underrepresented students, such as Arabic-first learners in the UAE, leading to inequitable learning trajectories (Chen, Wang, & Lin, 2020; Fadlelmula & Qadhi, 2024).Bias also affects AI-enabled teacher evaluations. LMS-integrated appraisal tools may undervalue differentiated or culturally grounded teaching approaches, disproportionately impacting expatriate educators from the Global South by privileging Western pedagogical norms (Ayeni et al., 2024; Milton & Al-Busaidi, 2023).

To mitigate these risks, ethical governance must be central to AI policy and design. Frameworks like the OECD AI Principles (2019) and UNESCO's AI and the Futures of Learning (2022) call for transparency, inclusivity, and algorithmic explainability. In the UAE, platforms like Alef Education adopt GDPR-aligned data protections and conduct regular algorithm audits to ensure fairness (Alyammahi, 2019; UAE Government, 2024). However, ethical AI requires more than technical safeguards. Educational leaders must develop competencies to critically assess algorithmic outputs, advocate for inclusive datasets, and lead participatory AI design processes involving educators, students, and communities (Jones & Kennedy, 2023; Du et al., 2023). Addressing algorithmic bias is thus a leadership responsibility—essential for fostering trust, equity, and culturally responsive innovation in AI-enhanced learning environments.

Digital Nomadism Challenges

Despite its promise of flexibility and decentralization, digital nomadism in education often reinforces systemic inequities. Dominated by narratives of Western mobility, it marginalizes educators and learners from the Global South or politically restricted regions, who face visa constraints, economic exclusion, and limited access to transnational networks (Butcher, 2022; Aroles, Granter, & de Vaujany, 2020). Policy frameworks—such as taxation, health coverage, and employment eligibility—rarely accommodate mobile professionals. Many institutions require local residency for contracts, excluding nomadic educators from leadership roles and institutional benefits, relegating them to precarious, project-based work (Choudhury, 2022).

Digital platforms and credentialing systems compound this exclusion. Nomadic educators may face skepticism over non-traditional qualifications or struggle with platforms designed for standardized environments—neglecting time zone differences, inconsistent internet access, and multilingual needs (Hensellek & Puchala, 2021). Gender and family status further intensify barriers. Female digital nomads often lack access to child care, maternity protections, or culturally appropriate work environments. In conservative contexts, mobility itself may challenge normative expectations of professionalism (De Sousa et al., 2025).

AI-enabled systems can also encode structural bias. Productivity trackers and feedback algorithms may penalize mobile educators working asynchronously or creatively across cultures. Such systems often fail to value pedagogical adaptability, multilingualism, or intercultural fluency (Jones & Kennedy, 2023). To address these disparities, educational institutions must reform governance to legitimize mobile teaching roles, recognize transnational credentials, and embed nomadic educators' strengths into hiring and evaluation policies (Ghamrawi & Tamim, 2022). AI platforms must be redesigned to support distributed workflows and inclusive pedagogical models. Without such reforms, digital nomadism risks reproducing digital colonialism, extracting labor from the Global South without offering agency, protections, or recognition (Butcher, 2022). A rights-based, culturally responsive approach is essential to ensure digital nomadism contributes equitably to global education.

Equity and the Digital Divide

AI Challenges

While AI holds transformative potential in education, it often exacerbates digital inequities. High-speed connectivity, infrastructure, and AI literacy—prerequisites for effective integration—remain unevenly distributed across and within countries, privileging well-resourced institutions while marginalizing underfunded schools and learners (Li, Fengchao, & Zhang, 2024). Students in rural areas, marginalized communities, and those with disabilities frequently lack access to adaptive platforms due to limited broadband, outdated hardware, and the absence of inclusive design features like translation tools or screen readers (Grace, Vidhyavathi, & Malathi, 2023). Even in high-income settings, disparities persist between urban and rural districts, and between mainstream and special education.

Algorithmic bias further deepens these divides. AI systems trained on homogenous datasets often misclassify or overlook minority and indigenous learners, reinforcing systemic inequities under the appearance of objectivity (West et al., 2019; Wang, 2021). Educator readiness is another critical gap. Teachers in underfunded schools often lack access to AI training or adequate tools, limiting their ability to interpret data or apply AI-driven insights effectively (Fadlelmula & Qadhi, 2024). This undermines the potential of AI-enhanced teaching, particularly in underserved contexts. Addressing these disparities requires systemic solutions beyond hardware provision. Investments must support inclusive design, culturally relevant content, and governance frameworks that prioritize equity. The UAE's Smart Learning Program and AI Tutor platform exemplify efforts to deliver adaptive, bilingual AI tools to diverse learners (WAM, 2024).

International bodies such as UNESCO and the OECD advocate for equity-by-design, calling for universal design standards, language inclusion, and bias auditing in AI development (UNESCO, 2022; OECD, 2023). Ethical governance must ensure representation in training data and enforce mechanisms to monitor and correct disparities in access. Equity must be treated as foundational—not peripheral—to AI integration in education. Without intentional policies and sustained investment, AI risks becoming a barrier rather than a catalyst for inclusive, high-quality learning.

Digital Nomadism Challenges

While digital nomadism offers global teaching and learning flexibility, it also exposes deep inequalities in digital access, labor protections, and systemic support. Operating in transnational, often unregulated contexts, nomadic educators frequently lack stable infrastructure, legal recognition, and institutional inclusion—challenges especially acute in the Global South (De Sousa et al., 2025).

Connectivity asymmetries are a key barrier. Educators from low- and middle-income countries face unreliable internet, limited digital tools, and power disruptions, while peers from high-income regions benefit from seamless access to secure, cloud-based systems (Hensellek & Puchala, 2021). This disparity constructs a digital hierarchy, privileging geographic and economic capital. Regulatory exclusions further marginalize nomadic educators. Many lack formal residency or work rights, leaving them without health insurance, job security, or professional recognition—particularly in freelance and transnational teaching contexts that fall outside labor protections (Choudhury, 2022).

Digital nomadic learners encounter similar barriers, including IP-based credential rejection, language mismatches, and infrastructure constraints that exclude them from MOOCs and online degree programs (Papanikolaou et al., 2023). Women, caregivers, and persons with disabilities face additional obstacles related to safety, accessibility, and caregiving support (Butcher, 2022). Market-driven platforms often favor Western credentials, native English fluency, and familiarity with dominant ed-tech systems, marginalizing skilled professionals from non-Western contexts whose qualifications remain undervalued (Aroles et al., 2020).

Addressing these disparities requires coordinated policy reform. Governments should modernize labor and visa frameworks to support nomadic educators, especially in high-mobility regions like the GCC. Ed-tech firms must prioritize platform accessibility, multilingual support, and offline functionality to serve diverse user needs (Taha et al., 2023). Without inclusive governance and structural safeguards, digital nomadism risks reproducing global labor inequities—extracting expertise without ensuring equity, agency, or representation. Bridging this divide demands a justice-oriented approach to global mobility, centered on rights, participation, and reform.

Faculty Resistance, Upskilling, and Change Management

AI Challenges

As AI becomes embedded in education, faculty resistance has emerged as a key barrier—not due to technophobia, but as a reasoned response to concerns about job displacement, ethical ambiguity, and diminished professional autonomy (Fullan et al., 2023; Muhammad & Orji, 2024). A primary concern is redundancy. Automation of grading, tutoring, and content delivery fosters fears that AI substitutes, rather than supports, human expertise—especially when framed in institutional discourse on cost efficiency (Jones & Kennedy, 2023; Ghamrawi et al., 2023). Insufficient, non-contextualized professional development also drives resistance. Generic training often fails to equip educators with competencies in AI ethics, algorithmic reasoning, or instructional design, leading to superficial or reluctant adoption (Katiyar et al., 2024).

Moreover, AI tools can compromise pedagogical autonomy. Predictive analytics and algorithm-driven recommendations may override instructor discretion, standardize content, and erode the relational, interpretive dimensions of teaching (Wang, 2021). Resistance is also shaped by institutional culture. Educators often react not to AI itself, but to top-down mandates and celebratory narratives that ignore implementation challenges. Faculty disengagement may reflect opposition to the politics of adoption rather than the technology per se (Du et al., 2023; Ellis, 2024). Addressing resistance requires participatory and developmental change management. Faculty should co-design, evaluate, and critique AI initiatives, supported by upskilling programs that blend technical training with ethical reflection and pedagogical application (Gamage & Vithanage, 2023).

Initiatives like the UAE's DUB.AI and AI Tutor platform model effective integration by combining AI literacy with instructional innovation (WAM, 2024). Distributed leadership is essential—shifting from enforcement to empowerment, and from compliance to co-evolution.To succeed, AI adoption must frame faculty as partners in innovation—not obstacles to it—ensuring that AI enhances rather than replaces the human core of teaching and learning.

Digital Nomadism Challenges

Digital nomadism offers faculty professional autonomy and global engagement, yet it disrupts institutional norms rooted in geographic fixity. Unlike AI-related resistance, which often centers on automation and ethics, resistance to nomadism stems from concerns over legitimacy, accountability, and organizational coherence (Choudhury, 2022; Fernandez & Shaw, 2020). Many institutions lack policies to support mobile educators, requiring physical presence for benefits, leadership roles, or resource access. Nomadic faculty may be excluded from curriculum design, mentorship, or professional development, leading to perceptions of disengagement or disloyalty (Butcher, 2022). Tensions also arise from perceived inequities. The resident faculty may view nomads as enjoying flexibility without shared burdens, especially when nomadic educators gain global recognition or short-term appointments, intensifying institutional divides (De Sousa et al., 2025).

Digital nomads face unique barriers to upskilling and institutional integration. Operating across time zones and infrastructure constraints, they often lack access to training, updates, and LMS platforms, complicating participation in institutional processes (Hensellek & Puchala, 2021).Without structured mentorship or peer networks, nomadic educators risk professional isolation and burnout. Navigating asynchronous, virtual environments requires skills not always developed in traditionally trained faculty (Phelps, 2014).

To address these challenges, institutions must formalize hybrid work policies, expand digital access to professional learning, and foster geographically inclusive peer networks. Erasmus and Virtual Exchange models demonstrate how distributed academic communities can thrive through shared governance and transnational collaboration (Papanikolaou et al., 2023). Educational leadership must evolve to embrace distributed, culturally responsive, and participatory models. Servant and transformational leadership approaches—emphasizing inclusion, emotional intelligence, and autonomy—can reduce resistance and legitimize nomadic faculty contributions (Fernandez & Shaw, 2020). Resistance to digital nomadism reflects deeper cultural tensions. By reimagining leadership and institutional structures, educational systems can harness mobility and diversity as catalysts for innovation rather than sources of disruption.

Human-AI Collaboration: Preserving Emotional Intelligence and Creativity

AI Challenges

While AI enhances educational systems through automation, analytics, and personalization, it raises concerns about the erosion of core human capacities in leadership—especially emotional intelligence, empathy, creativity, and ethical judgment. These attributes are central to relational leadership and institutional culture, and cannot be replicated by machines (Madanchian et al., 2024; Fullan et al., 2023). Emotional intelligence (EI) underpins trust, motivation, and conflict resolution. AI may simulate social behaviors via sentiment analysis or chatbots, but it lacks the moral nuance and cultural sensitivity necessary in diverse educational contexts like the Gulf (Du et al., 2023; Satya & Mohammed, 2024).

Creativity in leadership involves visionary problem-solving and cultural innovation—capacities AI cannot authentically replicate. Over-reliance on AI risks reducing leadership to managerial efficiency, weakening its moral and imaginative dimensions (Quaquebeke & Gerpott, 2023). AI-driven decision tools may also displace empathy-based engagement. For example, automated student support systems risk bypassing relational understanding, narrowing the leader's role to algorithm validation rather than holistic care (Wang, 2021). This shift can diminish the depth of human connection in educational practice.

To address this, ethical frameworks such as UNESCO's AI and the Futures of Education (2022) and the OECD AI Principles (2019) advocate for "human-in-the-loop" protocols that preserve human oversight, especially in decisions affecting well-being, equity, and ethics. Effective models are emerging. AI coaching tools offer feedback on communication tone, and creativity platforms simulate decision outcomes—augmenting, rather than replacing, human insight. Their success depends on leadership cultures that prioritize reflection, emotional awareness, and complexity over optimization (Pago, 2024; Sposato, 2024). Preparing leaders for human-AI collaboration requires professional development that integrates technical skills with emotional and ethical literacy. As Du et al. (2023) argue, "AI leadership education must include not just the coding of systems but the coding of values." Sustaining emotional intelligence and creativity is not about resisting AI, but about reaffirming the human essence of education. Leadership in the AI era must evolve by amplifying—rather than outsourcing—its moral and relational foundations.

Digital Nomadism Challenges

While digital nomadism expands flexibility in education, it challenges the cultivation of emotional intelligence and creativity—both central to effective teaching and leadership. Operating remotely, nomadic educators often experience fragmented human connection and diminished opportunities for collaborative innovation (Choudhury, 2022; Robinson & Reisdorf, 2024). Emotional labor in education—responding to students' affective needs, mediating tensions, and fostering inclusion—is rooted in embodied interactions. Digital nomads, detached from institutional settings, lose access to informal cues like hallway conversations or spontaneous peer support, limiting responsive, empathetic pedagogy (Hensellek & Puchala, 2021). AI tools, such as chatbots or automated monitoring systems, cannot replicate the nuance of relational engagement.

Creativity also suffers in dispersed digital environments. Asynchronous communication, cross-cultural dynamics, and platform fragmentation constrain improvisation, risk-taking, and co-creative planning. AI-driven instruction can further reduce educators' capacity for reflection or adaptation, especially when time zones and connectivity issues limit spontaneity (De Sousa et al., 2025; Fernandez & Shaw, 2020). Nomadic educators frequently report emotional strain due to professional invisibility, weakened institutional ties, and limited influence on change. These affective dimensions—loneliness, imposter syndrome, or fatigue—are rarely captured by AI performance systems focused on output metrics (Butcher, 2022).

To address these gaps, institutions must design intentional strategies that center emotional connection and creativity. Asynchronous co-creation tools—collaborative whiteboards, reflective journals, and digital storytelling—can foster cultural exchange and emotional expression. AI systems can be adapted to detect affective signals (e.g., sentiment in student feedback) and inform nomadic educators' relational engagement (Ghamrawi & Tamim, 2022). Inclusive leadership is essential. Servant and e-leadership models offer frameworks for empowering distributed teams through empathy, visibility, and shared purpose (Fernandez & Shaw, 2020; Phelps, 2014). In the context of digital nomadism, these human-centered approaches help preserve the emotional and creative capacities that AI cannot replace.

Data Privacy and Security Frameworks

AI Challenges

As AI becomes integral to education, data privacy and cybersecurity have emerged as critical ethical challenges. AI systems depend on extensive data collection—from academic records to biometric and socio-emotional indicators—raising concerns about rights protection, data security, and governance adequacy (Wang, 2021; Grace et al., 2023). AI applications like predictive analytics and adaptive platforms often involve third-party vendors and cloud hosting, complicating data ownership, jurisdictional compliance, and accountability. Without strong safeguards, institutions risk breaches, identity theft, and violations of data protection laws (OECD, 2023). Many educational AI systems function as opaque "black boxes," lacking transparency in decision-making. When students are algorithmically flagged or tracked without clear justification, procedural fairness is undermined—especially for marginalized groups vulnerable to biased models (Jones & Kennedy, 2023; West et al., 2019).

Inconsistent institutional practices further exacerbate risk. While some schools adopt GDPR-aligned policies, others rely on vendor agreements with minimal oversight. In the Gulf, platforms like Alef Education have prompted policy reforms, with the UAE aligning AI implementation with international data protection standards (Alyammahi, 2019; UAE Government, 2024).

Cybersecurity threats compound these vulnerabilities. AI-enhanced systems are attractive targets for cyberattacks, as demonstrated by the 2020 ransomware attack on Baltimore County Public Schools. Institutions prioritizing AI innovation without investing in cybersecurity may jeopardize both safety and institutional trust (Li et al., 2024). Addressing these issues requires multilayered governance: privacy-by-design, informed consent, algorithm audits, and human oversight. OECD (2023) and UNESCO (2022) frameworks stress explainability, equity, and ethical AI development grounded in learners' rights.

Leadership is central to this agenda. School leaders and policymakers must coordinate protocols for AI adoption, vendor selection, and data retention, while cultivating a culture of ethical digital stewardship that values transparency, student agency, and data justice. Safeguarding data privacy is not merely technical—it is foundational to human-centered educational leadership in the AI era. The right to equitable and secure learning must not be compromised in pursuit of algorithmic efficiency.

Digital Nomadism Challenges

Digital nomadism introduces unique data privacy and cybersecurity challenges, distinct from traditional campus-based contexts. Mobile educators and students often operate across jurisdictions with varying or weak data protection laws, using unsecured networks and personal devices that heighten exposure to breaches, surveillance, and credential theft (Choudhury, 2022; De Sousa et al., 2025). Institutional cybersecurity protocols—typically reliant on protected intranets or VPNs—are difficult to enforce for nomads. Geographic dispersion and inconsistent legal protections complicate governance, especially when educators use third-party cloud platforms for assessment and communication, where data ownership and jurisdiction remain unclear (Phelps, 2014; Fernandez & Shaw, 2020).

Nomadic learners face similar risks. Verification systems tied to fixed identities, such as location-based two-factor authentication, often exclude mobile users from accessing institutional platforms (Hensellek & Puchala, 2021). AI-powered systems further intensify concerns, as they collect behavioral and biometric data across borders with limited consent structures—raising issues of transparency and profiling (Robinson & Reisdorf, 2024). To mitigate these risks, institutions must adopt transnational data protection strategies, including cloud-based identity management, AI-driven anomaly detection, and mobile-optimized cybersecurity training. These systems must be governed ethically to avoid penalizing legitimate mobility (Ghamrawi & Tamim, 2022).

Aligning institutional policies with global frameworks such as GDPR, CCPA, and the UAE Federal Personal Data Protection Law is essential for regulatory coherence (UAE Government, 2024). Human-in-the-loop oversight should be embedded in AI security systems to ensure fairness and contextual sensitivity. Privacy in nomadic education must evolve from a compliance task to a leadership imperative—grounded in relational, ethical practices that protect informational autonomy and uphold academic freedom in an increasingly borderless educational landscape.

Ethical Frameworks and Global Accountability in Transnational AI-Nomadic Systems

The convergence of AI and digital nomadism in global education challenges traditional, nation-bound governance structures, demanding transnational, values-based ethical frameworks. As AI-driven platforms and mobile teaching models proliferate, fragmented national policies prove inadequate to address cross-border risks related to algorithmic bias, data exploitation, and labor precarity (OECD, 2023; UNESCO, 2022). Existing global frameworks—such as the OECD AI Principles and UNESCO's AI Ethics Recommendation—offer foundational values like transparency and fairness, yet remain inconsistently applied across educational contexts. For nomadic educators working across jurisdictions, this results in regulatory gaps and uneven ethical protections (OECD, 2019; UNESCO, 2022).

AI governance must prioritize algorithmic transparency and auditability, especially in systems for student assessment, behavioral analytics, or teacher evaluation. Without enforceable oversight, AI risks perpetuating structural inequities under the guise of objectivity (West et al., 2019). Generative AI tools also require clear attribution norms and cultural safeguards to prevent plagiarism and misinformation (Grubaugh & Levitt, 2023). In parallel, digital nomadism requires ethical labor frameworks that recognize mobile educators as legitimate professionals. The absence of binding international standards enables platform providers to sidestep accountability, leading to informal, exploitative employment conditions (Butcher, 2022).

Addressing these challenges requires transnational coalitions—similar to GDPR's data governance model—bringing together governments, AI experts, nomadic professionals, and civil society to co-create interoperable, enforceable ethical standards (Choudhury, 2022; De Sousa et al., 2025). Ethical leadership must embed these standards institutionally through ethics committees, impact assessments, and integration of AI ethics into leadership training and teacher certification (Du et al., 2023). Just as importantly, institutions must foster cultures of reflexivity, where digital ethics evolve alongside technological change. Ethical governance in AI and digital nomadism requires more than technical compliance—it calls for globally conscious leadership committed to justice, human dignity, and the relational mission of education in an increasingly automated and borderless world.

RECOMMENDATIONS AND POLICY ROADMAP

Strategic Directions for Educational Leaders in the AI and Nomadic Era

Cultivating AI-Competent Leadership and Institutional Agility

The rise of AI in education demands a fundamental shift from hierarchical management to agile, innovation-driven leadership. AI-competent leaders must combine technical proficiency with strategic foresight, ethical awareness, and the ability to manage diverse, digitally connected learning environments. Effective leaders integrate AI tools—such as predictive analytics and intelligent automation—into decision-making to enhance strategic planning, personalized learning, and operational efficiency (Pago, 2024; Wang, 2021). Initiatives like the UAE's Smart Learning Program and AI Tutor platform exemplify how data-informed leadership can drive academic improvement and institutional responsiveness (WAM, 2024; UAE Ministry of Education, 2023).

Beyond technical skill, leadership agility is essential. Digitally agile leaders foster innovation, support adaptive teaching, and build flexible systems that can evolve with technological change (AlNuaimi et al., 2022). This includes agile curriculum design, continuous teacher development, and responsive learner support. Agility also requires embedding ethical AI governance. Leaders must enforce transparency, data privacy, and fairness, guided by frameworks such as those from the OECD (2019) and UNESCO (2022). Alef Education's GDPR-aligned policies and algorithm audits in the UAE exemplify ethical leadership in practice (Alyammahi, 2019; Emara et al., 2023). In a globally mobile educational landscape, leaders must also support digital nomadism by enabling asynchronous collaboration, borderless learning, and inclusive digital infrastructures (Choudhury, 2022; Papanikolaou et al., 2023). Institutions that neglect this shift risk excluding valuable talent and limiting inter-cultural engagement.

National strategies must prioritize AI leadership development. Countries like the UAE and Finland have introduced AI-focused upskilling agendas that promote systems thinking, ethical reasoning, and human-AI collaboration (Fadlelmula & Qadhi, 2024; WEF, 2025). Embedding such competencies into leadership certification and professional development is critical to building AI-empowered institutions.

Supporting Distributed Leadership Models for Mobile and Hybrid Educational Workforces

The rise of hybrid work and digital nomadism is reshaping educational leadership, shifting from centralized hierarchies to distributed models that emphasize collaboration, shared responsibility, and decentralized decision-making across dispersed teams. This shift supports the flexibility and global engagement needed in AI-integrated, transnational educational systems. Distributed leadership empowers educators—including digital nomads—to lead based on expertise rather than location or rank, enhancing institutional agility and responsiveness while maintaining strategic coherence (Antonopoulou et al., 2021). In the UAE, platforms like Alef Education and the Smart Learning Program enable shared access to learner analytics and performance data, allowing virtual teams to operate effectively (Alyammahi, 2019; Emara et al., 2023).

Leaders in distributed settings must cultivate cultural fluency and emotional intelligence to manage asynchronous communication, cross-cultural norms, and diverse regulatory environments (Hensellek & Puchala, 2021; Choudhury, 2022). Inclusive participation protocols, mentoring structures, and equitable feedback systems are essential for fostering team cohesion. AI-powered tools—such as dashboards and collaborative platforms—facilitate transparency, workload management, and access to professional development regardless of geographic location (Suntharalingam, 2024; Jones & Kennedy, 2023). These technologies underpin decentralized leadership while maintaining institutional accountability.

Support for nomadic educators requires policy innovation: portable credentials, virtual supervision frameworks, and digital community-building initiatives must be integrated to ensure inclusion and recognition (Papanikolaou et al., 2023; De Sousa et al., 2025).To sustain distributed leadership, institutions must invest in capacity-building. Leadership training should address hybrid team management, AI-informed governance, and inclusive digital design. Aligned with OECD (2023) recommendations, future-ready leaders must be digitally literate, ethically grounded, and adaptive to globally distributed education environments.

Embedding Ethical AI Use and Data Governance in Institutional Decision-Making

The transformative potential of AI in education hinges on ethical governance that safeguards human dignity, privacy, and equity. As institutions adopt AI for learning personalization and operational efficiency, embedding ethical frameworks into decision-making is essential for trust, legitimacy, and sustainability. Educational leaders must translate global principles—such as the OECD's AI Principles (2019) and UNESCO's AI Ethics Guidelines (2022)—into institutional policies that ensure fairness, transparency, accountability, and privacy. This includes algorithmic impact assessments, AI ethics committees, and regular audits for bias and data security (OECD, 2023; Grace et al., 2023).

The UAE exemplifies ethical AI operationalization. The Alef Education platform applies GDPR-compliant protocols and conducts periodic system audits. These practices reflect national mandates in the UAE AI Strategy 2031 and its "AI Principles and Ethics" framework, which emphasize rights protection and algorithmic transparency (Alyammahi, 2019; Emara et al., 2023; UAE Government, 2024).Effective governa nce also requires participatory approaches. Ethical AI leadership must involve educators, students, parents, and technical experts in shaping deployment, aligned with the Responsible Research and Innovation (RRI) model emphasizing inclusivity and reflexivity (European Commission, 2020).

Robust data governance is critical. Institutions must enforce data minimization, informed consent, and opt-out rights—particularly when handling minors' data. Emerging models of "data dignity" reframe learners as rights-bearing participants, not passive data subjects (Wang, 2021; Nguyen et al., 2022). AI systems must support—not replace—human expertise. Leaders must resist technocentric approaches that undermine pedagogical judgment or amplify historical bias. Ethical governance must foreground student well-being, contextual appropriateness, and educational purpose (Madanchian et al., 2024; Tarisayi, 2024). As mobility increases, ethical AI governance must extend across borders. Institutions must develop interoperable privacy standards, secure data-sharing agreements, and digital identity protections for mobile educators, particularly in cross-border programs and platforms (Choudhury, 2022; Butcher, 2021). Ethical AI leadership demands a human-centered, globally conscious approach—where innovation is guided by justice, transparency, and respect for the rights of all educational stakeholders.

Empowering Nomadic and Remote Educators Through Inclusion, Well-being, and Professional Mobility Frameworks

As transnational and remote education expands, digital nomadic educators play a growing role in advancing curriculum internationalization and global knowledge exchange. Yet, despite their contributions, they often remain on the periphery of institutional structures. To ensure equity and sustainability, educational leadership must implement inclusive, well-being-oriented, and professionally supportive frameworks (De Sousa et al., 2025). Institutional policies must formally integrate nomadic educators, granting equitable access to decision-making, performance evaluations, and workload distribution, regardless of location. Without such inclusion, their roles risk marginalization. must also address psychosocial well-being. Isolation, unclear role expectations, and lack of peer engagement are common stressors for remote faculty (Butcher, 2021; Hensellek & Puchala, 2021). AI tools, including sentiment analysis and virtual mentoring platforms, can monitor well-being and foster digital belonging through timely interventions and community-building (Jones & Kennedy, 2023).

Sustainable engagement requires credential portability, contract flexibility, and clear advancement pathways. Blockchain-enabled credentials and digital badges help verify nomadic educators' achievements across borders (Choudhury, 2022). Outcome-based contracts offer institutions pedagogical continuity while accommodating mobility. AI can further streamline scheduling, workload forecasting, and cross-time-zone collaboration through intelligent calendaring and asynchronous dashboards—enhancing productivity in distributed teams (Suntharalingam, 2024). Culturally responsive leadership is also essential. Nomadic educators navigate diverse institutional norms and pedagogical philosophies. Inclusive leadership must adopt intercultural governance, dialogic engagement, and flexible policy alignment to support diverse teaching identities (Papanikolaou et al., 2023; Aroles et al., 2020).

Scalable models such as Erasmus+, globally networked learning programs, and UAE-based AI hubs demonstrate how mobility can be effectively integrated into national strategies (WAM, 2024).

Legal frameworks must evolve to protect nomadic educators' rights. This includes adapting labor laws, tax policies, and visa systems, and ensuring protections around data sovereignty, social insurance portability, and ethical digital surveillance (OECD, 2023; De Sousa et al., 2025). Empowering digital nomads requires systemic change—blending inclusive leadership, AI-driven tools, and global policy innovation to embed them as core contributors to future-ready education systems.

Policy Imperatives for National Governments and Regional Authorities

Establishing National Ethical AI Guidelines in Education

As artificial intelligence (AI) becomes deeply integrated into educational systems worldwide, national governments bear a critical responsibility to establish comprehensive ethical guidelines that uphold learner rights, ensure equity, and foster responsible innovation. These guidelines must evolve beyond aspirational declarations into concrete, enforceable policies that govern AI's development, deployment, and oversight within education. Effective national frameworks should be grounded in internationally endorsed principles, such as those articulated by the OECD (2019), which include human-centered values, transparency, fairness, accountability, and robustness. However, these principles must be localized to reflect each country's educational goals, legal landscape, and cultural context. The UAE exemplifies this approach through its AI Strategy 2031 and AI Principles and Ethics Framework, which embed data protection, inclusive access, and alignment with Islamic and societal values into national policy (UAE Government, 2024).

A comprehensive ethical AI policy in education should address three core areas. First, algorithmic transparency and explainability must be mandated so that students, educators, and parents understand how decisions—such as personalized learning pathways or behavioral alerts—are made. Second, governments must require bias mitigation protocols, including regular equity audits, to prevent AI from reinforcing systemic discrimination against marginalized learners (West et al., 2019; Wang, 2021). Third, robust privacy protections are essential. National standards should mandate GDPR-aligned data handling practices that limit third-party access, require informed consent, and ensure the right to opt out of automated profiling.

Governments should also institutionalize ethical oversight mechanisms. These may include national AI ethics councils, third-party audit requirements for educational AI systems, and standardized impact assessments that evaluate tools for inclusion, safety, and effectiveness. Such structures are essential for public accountability and the institutionalization of ethical AI practices within ministries and schools. The UAE serves as a leading regional example. Its Alef Education platform operates under international data protection standards, implements frequent algorithmic audits, and trains educators in ethical AI use (Emara et al., 2023). Additionally, the UAE's Generative AI Guide provides over 100 defined ethical use cases and risk protocols for educational and public sector applications, offering a scalable template for other nations (UAE Government, 2024). Inclusive governance must also be a central principle in national AI guidelines. Stakeholders such as teachers, students, parents, and community leaders should be involved in co-designing and evaluating policies. Participatory design processes enhance legitimacy, reveal localized risks, and ensure policies remain attuned to real-world educational contexts (UNESCO, 2022; European Commission, 2020).

Moreover, national policy must extend ethical AI education to students. Curricula should include digital ethics and algorithmic literacy, enabling students to critically engage with the systems shaping their educational experience. This aligns with the World Economic Forum's (2025) recommendation to embed AI ethics within K–12 civic and computational literacy programs, preparing students as responsible users and co-creators of emerging technologies. National ethical AI guidelines are foundational to ensuring inclusive, equitable, and human-centered educational transformation. In their absence, governments risk compromising public trust, perpetuating inequality, and misaligning educational innovation with democratic and cultural values.

Developing AI-Integrated Teacher Education and Upskilling Policies

The successful integration of artificial intelligence (AI) in education depends on parallel investments in teacher professional development. As frontline facilitators of AI-enhanced learning, educators' digital readiness directly influences pedagogical effectiveness, ethical implementation, and student outcomes. National governments must therefore embed AI literacy, ethical awareness, and adaptive pedagogy into all stages of teacher education and professional development.

Empirical research highlights that low digital confidence, ethical concerns, and resistance among teachers often hinder AI adoption (Milton & Al-Busaidi, 2023; Fadlelmula & Qadhi, 2024). Addressing these barriers requires comprehensive national strategies that institutionalize AI competencies in pre-service training, in-service education, and continuous learning systems—moving beyond short-term workshops to sustained, system-wide support. The UAE offers a strong policy example. Through initiatives such as the Dubai Centre for Artificial Intelligence and the DUB.AI framework, teachers receive structured training in automation, machine learning, and personalized learning design (WAM, 2024; UAE Government, 2024). These programs feature hybrid formats, mentorship models, and microcredentials, aligning educational upskilling with national economic priorities.

Equity must also guide AI-focused teacher development. Educators in under-resourced or rural communities often face barriers to access. National policies should provide subsidized AI tools, remote training opportunities, and incentives such as advancement credits to promote inclusive participation (Gamage & Vithanage, 2023; Jones & Kennedy, 2023). AI-integrated teacher training should focus on three inter-related domains. First, technical proficiency—including algorithmic logic, platform navigation, and data interpretation. Second, pedagogical innovation—emphasizing differentiated instruction, personalized feedback, and inquiry-based approaches.

Third, ethical and regulatory literacy—ensuring teachers can manage data privacy, identify algorithmic bias, and integrate AI responsibly (Nguyen et al., 2022; Grace et al., 2023).

Sustainable implementation requires embedding teacher upskilling within broader education reform and cross-sector partnerships. Ministries of education should collaborate with AI developers, universities, and international bodies to co-create modular, scalable training linked to national curricula and global AI trends. Public-private partnerships can further support this by funding innovation hubs, AI labs, and open-source training platforms. Global models offer valuable benchmarks. Finland's integration of AI into teacher competencies and Singapore's digital teacher roadmap provide phased pathways—from awareness and application to educator-led innovation and mentorship (UNESCO, 2022; OECD, 2023). Educators must be recognized not as passive recipients but as co-designers and ethical stewards of AI in education. National upskilling policies that position teachers as leaders in technological transformation are essential to ensuring that AI enhances—rather than displaces—the core values of education.

Institutionalizing Flexible Work and Mobility Policies for Digital Nomads in Education

The rise of digital nomadism is reshaping educational labor markets, requiring national governments to establish flexible, cross-border policy frameworks that support the rights and inclusion of mobile educators. Without such structures, digital nomadic educators—who contribute significantly to international and online education—remain underutilized and insufficiently protected.

Digital nomads often operate outside conventional employment classifications, creating ambiguity around labor protections, residency rights, and social benefits (De Sousa et al., 2025; Butcher, 2021). Governments must establish regulatory pathways that recognize remote educational work, including legal residency, health coverage, and intellectual property protections. Initiatives like Estonia's, the UAE's, and Barbados's digital nomad visas offer promising models that could be adapted to include educators contributing to global learning systems.

Credential portability is another key policy area. Many nomadic educators face barriers in transferring qualifications across borders. Regional frameworks, such as the Bologna Process within the European Higher Education Area (EHEA), and blockchain-based credentials offer scalable mechanisms for verifying professional expertise across jurisdictions (Choudhury, 2022).

National education policies should also mandate the institutional inclusion of remote educators. Many universities and schools exclude nomadic staff from governance and professional development. Governments can require institutions receiving public funds to adopt inclusive HR practices—ensuring fair workload distribution, access to upskilling, and participation in strategic planning regardless of geographic location (Antonopoulou et al., 2021; Ghamrawi & Tamim, 2022).

Technology policy plays a critical enabling role. Investment in secure, high-speed infrastructure is essential for facilitating real-time collaboration. AI-powered platforms can support distributed faculty evaluation, scheduling, and team coordination, while cybersecurity and data sovereignty regulations protect both educators and learners (Jones & Kennedy, 2023; Suntharalingam, 2024).

Fiscal frameworks must also evolve. Digital nomads frequently fall into legal grey zones in income taxation, facing risks of double taxation or non-compliance. National governments should explore bilateral tax treaties, digital worker classifications, and residency-neutral taxation models to accommodate remote educators fairly and transparently (Butcher, 2021).

Labor equity remains a pressing issue. Many nomadic educators work as contractors without job security or benefits. Governments should develop flexicurity policies that ensure mobility while offering baseline protections, including union representation, digital grievance mechanisms, and eligibility for publicly funded training or fellowships (Hensellek & Puchala, 2021).

Mobility frameworks should align with national education and innovation strategies. Countries aspiring to be global education hubs—such as the UAE, Singapore, and Qatar—must ensure that nomadic educators are not only welcomed but also integrated into national research, digital literacy, and curriculum development agendas. Such integration will position nations to leverage mobile intellectual capital in building inclusive, future-ready education systems.

Investing in Equitable Digital Infrastructure and Cross-Border Access Systems

The rapid expansion of AI-driven education and digital nomadism requires national governments to invest in equitable and interoperable digital infrastructure. Without inclusive access to digital tools, platforms, and networks, technological innovation risks reinforcing educational inequalities and excluding marginalized learners and mobile educators from participating in digital transformation.

Equitable infrastructure extends beyond broadband access to include affordable smart devices, cloud computing, AI-enabled learning platforms, cybersecurity systems, and scalable data centers (Gamage & Vithanage, 2023). Governments must integrate infrastructure development with education, labor, and innovation strategies to build sustainable digital learning ecosystems.

Geographic disparities in connectivity, particularly in rural and underserved regions, remain a major barrier. Communities in the Global South often lack access to high-speed internet, hindering their engagement with AI-enhanced education and virtual teaching support networks (Li et al., 2024). Public investment in last-mile connectivity solutions—such as satellite broadband, 5G expansion, and solar-powered routers—should be prioritized. Public-private partnerships are essential to address infrastructure gaps in low-profit regions.

Device accessibility is also critical. To reduce device poverty, governments should subsidize digital devices for disadvantaged learners and educators, and promote shared-use models like school-based device libraries. In the UAE, Smart Learning Programs have increased digital equity by providing cloud-based curriculum access and real-time analytics across K–12 schools, reducing reliance on physical infrastructure (UAE Ministry of Education, 2023).

Cross-border interoperability is vital for supporting nomadic educators and transnational learners. Digital platforms must operate across jurisdictions, ensuring access despite varying regulatory environments. National policies should promote open standards, regional roaming for digital services, and harmonized data protection protocols to facilitate educational continuity for mobile users (OECD, 2023).

Infrastructure development must also support AI scalability. Cloud platforms should be capable of managing large datasets and delivering real-time, personalized learning experiences. National data centers should align with international privacy standards, emphasizing algorithmic explainability, ethical data governance, and secure cross-border data flows (Grace et al., 2023; Wang, 2021).

Inclusive infrastructure is not only technical but also social. Digital citizenship education, teacher training, and community engagement must accompany infrastructure deployment to ensure users—especially first-generation learners—can navigate AI-enhanced systems safely and confidently (UNESCO, 2022).

Sustainable infrastructure development must incorporate long-term fiscal planning and environmental responsibility. Governments should invest in green infrastructure—such as AI-powered energy management, eco-efficient data centers, and climate-resilient networks. The UAE's integration of AI in environmental monitoring and green computing provides a replicable model for sustainable digital infrastructure (UAE Government, 2024).

Robust and equitable digital infrastructure is the foundation of inclusive, resilient, and future-ready education systems. It enables personalized learning, supports a mobile academic workforce, and ensures that digital transformation reaches all learners—regardless of geography, mobility, or socio-economic status.

Governance and Innovation Pathways for Global Organizations and Industry Stakeholders

Building Public-Private Research and Innovation Ecosystems

Accelerating AI integration and supporting digital nomadism in education requires more than top-down policy; it necessitates the creation of dynamic innovation ecosystems that connect governments, private enterprises, and academic institutions. Public-private partnerships (PPPs) are central to this effort, enabling resource sharing, co-development of AI solutions, and scalable responses to the pedagogical and operational demands of digital transformation. Such ecosystems allow ministries of education to benefit from the technical expertise, infrastructure, and adaptability of private sector actors while aligning developments with national educational priorities. These collaborations drive the creation of AI-powered tools—such as adaptive platforms and real-time data dashboards—that increasingly define digitally transformed learning environments (OECD, 2023; UNESCO, 2022).

The UAE demonstrates this approach through its partnerships with Microsoft and OpenAI in developing the DUB.AI framework and GPT-powered AI tutors. Initiatives such as the AI Tutor Hackathon and high-profile collaborations at COP28 and Davos 2024 illustrate how global tech expertise can be harmonized with national policy frameworks to produce ethically aligned, pedagogically grounded innovations (WAM, 2024). Equally important is the development of research ecosystems. Ministries, research councils, and industry partners must co-invest in AI labs, digital pedagogy centers, and nomadic workforce observatories. These institutions function as interdisciplinary incubators for human-centered design, longitudinal research, and policy experimentation (Ahmed, 2020; Ellis, 2024).

Open innovation is a cornerstone of effective ecosystems. Governments should promote open-source AI platforms, data interoperability, and shared development protocols to avoid vendor lock-in and enable collaborative experimentation. The UAE's Falcon LLM initiative offers a model for local access to large language models within ethical and educational parameters (UAE Government, 2024).

Industry also plays a critical role in shaping ethical AI frameworks. Joint governance mechanisms—such as regulatory sandboxes, ethics boards, and advisory councils—ensure shared responsibility in addressing algorithmic bias, data governance, and inclusivity. These mechanisms must include diverse stakeholders, including educators, students, ethicists, and nomadic professionals (OECD, 2023; European Commission, 2020).Talent development is vital to sustaining innovation. Ecosystems should support the co-creation of curricula, AI literacy programs, and professional certification aligned with national workforce needs (WEF, 2025; Ghamrawi & Tamim, 2022). Industry-academia collaborations—through internships, AI bootcamps, and teaching fellowships—help bridge skills gaps and foster AI-literate leadership in education.

In parallel, support for entrepreneurship is essential. Governments should enable edtech startups and AI-enabled educational microenterprises—particularly those led by women, youth, and migrant educators—to scale localized innovations while promoting inclusive economic development. For global impact, innovation ecosystems must facilitate transnational collaboration. Bilateral and multilateral agreements on research mobility, co-innovation funding, and ethical data governance enable cross-border learning platforms, support nomadic educators, and contribute to a globally integrated educational landscape. These systems are key to building equitable, future-ready education at the intersection of AI and mobility.

Supporting AI and Nomadic Work Standards Across Borders: Taxation, Labor Rights, and Digital Sovereignty

The globalization of AI-driven education and the rise of digital nomadism challenge existing legal, labor, and fiscal governance structures. As educators and AI-powered platforms increasingly operate across borders, regulatory inconsistencies in taxation, labor rights, and data governance generate uncertainty and inequity. Coordinated international frameworks are essential to support cross-border mobility, protect digital rights, and balance national sovereignty with global educational collaboration. A primary concern is the taxation of remote educational professionals. Digital nomads often face ambiguous income reporting, double taxation, and jurisdictional compliance issues (Choudhury, 2022). To address this, governments should adopt bilateral tax treaties, simplified nomad-specific tax codes, and income declaration mechanisms tailored to education. Models such as the UAE's digital visa schemes and Estonia's e-residency offer valuable templates for fiscally supporting mobile intellectual labor.

Labor protections are equally urgent. Many nomadic educators lack access to formal employment benefits, grievance procedures, or professional development opportunities (De Sousa et al., 2025). International agencies—including the ILO, UNESCO, and OECD—should establish cross-border labor standards for digital educators, encompassing remote health coverage, research funding eligibility, and academic freedom protections. With AI systems increasingly mediating employment decisions—such as workload allocation, student evaluations, and compensation—educators must be safeguarded against algorithmic opacity, bias, and surveillance. National policies should mandate algorithmic transparency, human-in-the-loop review mechanisms, and enforceable AI ethics guidelines for remote education systems (Nguyen et al., 2022; West et al., 2019).

Digital sovereignty presents another challenge, particularly regarding educational data governance. Cross-border data flows raise concerns over storage, access, and usage rights. Data localization laws, such as those in the EU, UAE, and India, must be reconciled with the operational needs of global education providers. Frameworks like the OECD's AI Policy Observatory and UNESCO's AI Ethics Recommendations (2021) offer guidance for balancing national control with ethical and interoperable data sharing. To advance digital sovereignty while preserving collaboration, governments and education consortia should adopt harmonized data governance protocols. These should include standardized encryption, consent-based data portability, and clearly defined data ownership and usage rights (Wang, 2021; OECD, 2023). This is especially critical for educators and learners navigating jurisdictions with divergent privacy or academic freedom protections.

International professional bodies also play a key role. By certifying cross-border platforms, maintaining global educator registries, and enforcing transnational codes of conduct, such organizations can promote quality assurance, ethical standards, and inclusive participation in AI-mediated digital education (UNESCO, 2022; WEF, 2025). Supporting AI-enabled and nomadic education requires multi-level governance—national, regional, and global. Aligning fiscal, labor, and data policies with transnational realities is vital to ensuring that educational innovation remains equitable, secure, and anchored in human rights and democratic values.

Fostering Collaborative Knowledge Networks and Cross-Cultural Educational Partnerships

In the context of AI-driven educational transformation and rising digital nomadism, fostering collaborative knowledge networks and cross-cultural partnerships is essential for promoting inclusive, globally responsive, and resilient educational systems. These ecosystems of co-creation facilitate professional and epistemic mobility, enabling educators and learners to co-develop educational practices that transcend national and institutional boundaries. Collaborative knowledge networks emphasize decentralized participation, open resource sharing, and co-produced knowledge, ensuring AI-enhanced education evolves in ways that are context-sensitive rather than technocratically imposed (UNESCO, 2022; Ellis, 2024). Cross-border partnerships play a critical role in comparative research, multilingual content development, and culturally responsive pedagogical innovation.

Sustaining these networks requires supportive digital infrastructure and policy frameworks, including interoperable learning management systems, real-time translation tools, and ethical data-sharing protocols (OECD, 2023; Ghamrawi & Tamim, 2022). Regional initiatives such as the UAE's AI retreats, Qatar's interdisciplinary AI clusters, and Saudi Arabia's Madrasati platform exemplify institutional efforts to enable knowledge exchange across AI-enhanced systems. Cross-cultural competence is vital to prevent AI tools from reproducing dominant epistemologies or erasing cultural diversity. Partnerships that co-design educational content rooted in diverse knowledge systems promote pluralism and inclusion (Papanikolaou et al., 2023). Models such as Erasmus+, Asia-Pacific alliances, and GCC-led digital forums offer replicable frameworks for intercultural collaboration.

Nomadic educators serve as critical bridges between systems, diffusing innovation while anchoring it in diverse socio-cultural contexts. Recognizing their contributions requires institutional policies that validate knowledge generated through informal, mobile, and cross-sectoral experiences (Butcher, 2021; De Sousa et al., 2025). Institutionalizing such partnerships demands coordinated investment in academic mobility, joint degrees, and transnational research grants that prioritize AI ethics, equity, and sustainability. Public-private consortia can further support this through fellowships, global teaching labs, and co-teaching programs that foster applied AI experimentation across cultural contexts (UAE Government, 2024; WEF, 2025).

Open educational resources (OER) should be expanded through multilingual content, culturally grounded case studies, and AI-enhanced personalization engines to serve diverse learners. Initiatives like MIT OpenCourseWare and UNESCO's OER Commons exemplify scalable platforms for inclusive knowledge dissemination (UNESCO, 2022; Roshanaei et al., 2023).To ensure legitimacy, these networks must adopt participatory governance models grounded in knowledge democracy—valuing indigenous, practitioner, and local expertise alongside academic and technical knowledge (Ghamrawi & Tamim, 2022; Fullan et al., 2023).In sum, collaborative knowledge networks and cross-cultural partnerships transform AI and digital nomadism from technological trends into catalysts for global citizenship, educational equity, and mutual capacity-building.

Recommendations for Future Research and Interdisciplinary Inquiry

Evaluating the Long-Term Impact of AI-Driven Leadership on Equity and Learning Outcomes

As AI becomes increasingly embedded in educational leadership, there is a critical need to examine its long-term effects on equity, access, and student outcomes. While early studies highlight improvements in efficiency and personalization, the broader structural implications—particularly for marginalized groups—remain insufficiently explored. Future research must adopt longitudinal and interdisciplinary frameworks to assess how AI-driven leadership reshapes institutional cultures, learning ecologies, and educational justice over time. A central concern is equity.

Although AI systems can offer individualized support, biased training data and exclusionary design practices may exacerbate disparities (West et al., 2019; Grace et al., 2023). Research must investigate whether AI-enhanced platforms close or widen achievement gaps across socio-economic, racial, linguistic, and neurodiverse learner populations. Disaggregated analysis by demographic variables is essential to assess these outcomes.

The evolution of leadership practices under AI influence also requires critical inquiry. Predictive analytics, algorithmic dashboards, and automated performance feedback may reshape decision-making, professional autonomy, and institutional accountability. It remains unclear whether these tools support collaborative, inclusive leadership or reinforce managerialist and surveillance-oriented cultures. Mixed-method approaches—combining ethnography and performance metrics—can illuminate these dynamics (Madanchian et al., 2024; Tarisayi, 2024).

Another emerging focus is the impact of AI on teacher-student relationships. As AI is increasingly used to track discipline, monitor attendance, and guide assessment, researchers must explore its effects on trust, empathy, and student agency. Studies should go beyond academic performance to assess affective outcomes such as motivation, well-being, and relational engagement (Fullan et al., 2023; Ghamrawi et al., 2023). AI's role in policy diffusion and reform also warrants attention. Longitudinal studies can trace how AI influences curricular standards, certification criteria, and accountability frameworks. Cross-national comparative research—particularly in GCC, ASEAN, and EU regions—can illuminate how regulatory, cultural, and infrastructural conditions mediate AI's educational impact (OECD, 2023; UNESCO, 2022).

Inclusive research methodologies are vital for capturing AI's social dimensions. Approaches such as community-based participatory research (CBPR), design-based implementation research (DBIR), and critical policy ethnography can center the voices of students, educators, and communities, ensuring that impact assessments reflect lived experience and contextual relevance (Ellis, 2024). AI's global diffusion raises questions of epistemic equity. As Global North-developed tools are exported to low- and middle-income countries, researchers must examine whether such technologies perpetuate epistemic colonialism or foster local innovation. South-South collaborations and decolonial AI frameworks should be integral to this inquiry (Papanikolaou et al., 2023; Butcher, 2021). Long-term, theory-informed research is essential to ensure that the integration of AI in educational leadership advances not only efficiency, but also equity, inclusion, and sustainable transformation.

Investigating the Role of Digital Nomadism in Shaping Global Educational Workforces

As digital nomadism shifts from a peripheral lifestyle to a mainstream mode of academic labor, its impact on global education systems demands systematic scholarly attention. Mobile educators are reshaping knowledge production, delivery, and governance across borders. Future research must examine how this mobility challenges traditional employment models, institutional affiliations, and pedagogical norms while offering new pathways for inclusivity, flexibility, and knowledge democratization.

A critical area of inquiry is the reconfiguration of academic labor. Nomadic educators often operate outside formal contracts and institutional frameworks, raising questions about tenure, professional identity, labor rights, and collective representation. Studies should investigate whether nomadic teaching fosters autonomy and global engagement or deepens precarity and labor segmentation (De Sousa et al., 2025; Butcher, 2021). Institutional adaptation is also key. Research should assess how universities and schools integrate mobile educators into curriculum design, governance, and quality assurance. Comparative case studies across diverse education systems—such as those in the UAE, Finland, and Singapore—can illuminate how legal, cultural, and technological contexts shape recruitment, evaluation, and collaboration structures (Choudhury, 2022; Antonopoulou et al., 2021).

The pedagogical contributions of nomadic educators remain underexplored. Their intercultural competence, multilingualism, and adaptive teaching practices offer valuable assets for curriculum internationalization and student engagement. Longitudinal studies should evaluate the impact of nomadic faculty on learner outcomes, particularly in hybrid and virtual environments (Papanikolaou et al., 2023).

Ethical considerations are also paramount. Digital nomadism may replicate global inequalities, with educators from the Global North benefiting from greater access to mobility infrastructure than their Global South counterparts. Research should critically assess whether nomadic education promotes epistemic inclusion or reinforces extractive labor dynamics and digital privilege (Aroles et al., 2020; Butcher, 2021).

The convergence of AI and nomadism presents new research frontiers. AI increasingly structures the work of nomadic educators through algorithmic scheduling, learning analytics, and automated evaluation. Scholars should examine how these tools affect pedagogical autonomy, labor mobility, and the governance of transnational academic work (Suntharalingam, 2024; Ellis, 2024). Policy research is needed to support this evolving workforce. Studies should identify effective models for taxation, credential portability, data protection, and labor rights suited to global educational mobility. Comparative analyses can guide ministries, accreditation bodies, and international organizations in aligning policy with the realities of digitally mediated and borderless teaching (Wang, 2021; UNESCO, 2022). Advancing interdisciplinary, context-sensitive research on digital nomadism will enable governance systems to balance flexibility with equity and innovation with ethical accountability in the future of global education.

Exploring Responsible AI Governance Models in Multicultural Education Contexts

The integration of artificial intelligence (AI) into educational leadership and learning environments necessitates governance models that are both technically sound and culturally responsive. As AI increasingly mediates pedagogical decisions, student evaluations, and institutional planning, governance frameworks must address linguistic diversity, ethical pluralism, and culturally specific equity concerns—particularly in multicultural education systems. A core research priority is the contextualization of global AI ethics frameworks. While principles such as transparency and fairness outlined by the OECD (2019) and UNESCO (2022) provide foundational guidance, they often reflect Euro-American norms. Adapting these to contexts shaped by Islamic ethics, Confucian traditions, or indigenous epistemologies requires careful reinterpretation that maintains technical rigor while respecting local values (Nguyen et al., 2022; OECD, 2023).

Algorithmic bias in multicultural settings is a critical concern. AI models trained on culturally narrow datasets may misclassify or marginalize learners from underrepresented groups. For instance, predictive systems that flag student "risk" may misread culturally normative behaviors. Research must develop culturally attuned governance mechanisms—such as algorithmic audits, community validation, and inclusive data practices—to mitigate such biases (Grace et al., 2023; West et al., 2019).

Localization of AI tools also warrants attention. Schools serving linguistically diverse populations—including nomadic and expatriate learners—must adapt global AI technologies through translation, culturally responsive interface design, and multilingual scaffolding. Comparative studies in countries like the UAE, Canada, and India can highlight effective localization strategies and best practices (Suntharalingam, 2024). Participatory governance is essential for ethical AI integration. Top-down implementation often marginalizes educators, families, and students—especially in postcolonial or diverse societies. Future research should explore inclusive governance models that involve all stakeholders in the selection, oversight, and evaluation of AI tools, aligning with the principles of Responsible Research and Innovation (European Commission, 2020; Ghamrawi & Tamim, 2022).

Leadership practice in multicultural AI contexts also requires investigation. School leaders must navigate ethical dilemmas involving religious norms, tribal customs, and the lived realities of migrant learners. Research into leadership strategies—especially in regions such as the UAE, KSA, and Malaysia—can illuminate how administrators balance data-driven decision-making with cultural sensitivity and ethical accountability (Fullan et al., 2023). AI governance must be analyzed in relation to national identity and language policy. In regions where education promotes social cohesion—such as the GCC and ASEAN—AI tools can either support or disrupt national curricula and civic education goals. Studies should examine whether AI systems reinforce or complicate identity formation and heritage language instruction (Ellis, 2024; WEF, 2025).The responsible AI governance in multicultural education is an ethical, cultural, and political challenge. Future research must develop frameworks that reconcile global standards with local diversity to ensure that AI supports pluralistic, inclusive, and context-sensitive educational transformation.

Designing Future-Ready Metrics for AI and Mobility Integration in Education Policy and Practice

As artificial intelligence and digital nomadism transform global education systems, traditional metrics—such as standardized test scores, contact hours, and on-site instruction—are increasingly inadequate. To evaluate AI-enhanced learning environments and mobile educational labor, future research must develop context-sensitive, forward-looking frameworks that capture pedagogical, institutional, ethical, and transnational dimensions.

One key area of focus is assessing human-AI collaboration. Rather than measuring AI efficiency in isolation, new indicators should evaluate how AI augments teacher creativity, enhances leadership decision-making, and supports learner engagement in hybrid environments (Madanchian et al., 2024; Sposato, 2024). Multi-modal approaches—combining behavioral analytics, qualitative feedback, and emotional engagement data—can offer a nuanced understanding of these interactions. Metrics must also address the ethical implications of AI deployment. These include algorithmic fairness, data privacy, transparency, and inclusivity in personalized learning. Tools such as algorithmic impact assessments (AIAs), ethical dashboards, and fairness audits should be adapted for institutional use, with policy guidance for ethical benchmarks (OECD, 2023; Wang, 2021).

In the context of digital nomadism, conventional workforce indicators—like FTE status or in-person teaching time—do not reflect the realities of mobile educators. New metrics are needed to capture virtual collaboration, cross-border instructional time, and AI-supported productivity (Choudhury, 2022; De Sousa et al., 2025). These would validate the contributions of nomadic faculty in hybrid and asynchronous formats. Learner agency is another critical dimension. AI-driven personalization enables adaptive learning, but systems must be evaluated for how they support student autonomy. Metrics such as digital self-regulation, AI tool fluency, and engagement with adaptive feedback can gauge the quality of student interaction with AI (Lakshmi et al., 2023; Roshanaei et al., 2023).

Transnational engagement also requires new evaluative tools. Indicators should measure digital citizenship, intercultural collaboration, and virtual academic mobility. Examples include multilingual platform use, participation in global co-teaching, and authorship across time zones (Papanikolaou et al., 2023; UNESCO, 2022). To ensure policy alignment, future-ready metrics must be embedded within national and international quality assurance frameworks. Education ministries and accrediting bodies should integrate AI and mobility indicators into inspection protocols and institutional evaluations, enabling global benchmarking that respects contextual diversity while promoting equity and excellence. Metric development must be participatory and iterative. Co-creation with educators, students, nomadic professionals, AI developers, and policymakers ensures relevance and legitimacy. Continuous validation through real-world testing and stakeholder feedback is essential to adapt metrics to evolving educational landscapes.

CONCLUSION

Synthesis of Integrated Findings

The integrated analysis across the preceding sections reveals the multi-dimensional convergence of artificial intelligence (AI), digital nomadism, and educational leadership in shaping global technological and pedagogical transformations. Drawing from theoretical models such as the Technology Acceptance Model (TAM), Diffusion of Innovations, the OECD's AI Principles, and Responsible Research and Innovation (RRI), this synthesis underscores three major thematic domains: AI-driven transformation of educational leadership, the institutional integration of digital nomadism as a mode of work and learning, and the ethical recalibration of policy frameworks in digitally mediated systems.

The early sections of this study established the foundational premise that AI is no longer a peripheral tool but a core determinant of strategic educational leadership. In Section One, digital leadership was conceptualized as a dynamic competency encompassing vision, technological proficiency, data-informed decision-making, and ethical governance. This foundation was advanced in Section Two, which demonstrated how AI integration supports personalized learning, predictive analytics, and institutional effectiveness. Here, AI emerged as both an administrative enabler and a pedagogical enhancer, supporting school leaders in aligning instructional delivery with real-time learner data while addressing infrastructural constraints, especially within the Gulf Cooperation Council (GCC) region.

Section Three extended this analysis by examining the attributes of digital leadership in the AI era. It introduced the "5D Typology"—digital competence, culture, differentiation, governance, and advocacy—highlighting how educational leaders must navigate tensions between innovation and inclusion. These findings were grounded in empirical examples, including AI-powered platforms such as Alef Education, which offer real-time feedback and data transparency for teacher empowerment. Yet, the same sections revealed that the promise of AI remains tethered to structural challenges: unequal access to digital infrastructure, algorithmic bias, and resistance to change among educators.

Sections Four and Five pivoted to the implications of digital nomadism for education, marking a transition from institutional-centric to mobility-centric frameworks of leadership and work. Section Four argued that digital nomadism—characterized by global mobility, location-independent work, and transnational collaboration—is not merely a labor trend but an epistemic shift. It reshapes the identities and relationships between learners, educators, and institutions. Drawing parallels with remote health and tech sectors, the analysis positioned educational nomads as catalysts for cross-border knowledge exchange and cultural hybridization, while also exposing gaps in governance, credential recognition, and employment protection.

In Section Five, Gulf-based case studies—particularly from the UAE, KSA, and Qatar—illustrated how national AI strategies are translated into educational ecosystems. From UAE's Alef Education and AI Tutor platforms to Saudi Arabia's Madrasati and Qatar's AI-enhanced research infrastructures, each case offered region-specific applications of AI in learning environments. These examples demonstrated that AI, when coupled with local policy vision and ethical oversight, can foster scalable innovations in teaching, assessment, and institutional planning. However, these advances also underscored the need for robust ethical governance, as algorithmic transparency and data sovereignty remain emergent concerns, especially in transnational contexts involving mobile educators and learners.

Section Six offered a comparative lens on sectoral intersections—exploring how the insights from education and digital leadership inform practices in healthcare, logistics, and entrepreneurial ecosystems. These cross-sectoral linkages confirmed that AI-enhanced leadership and distributed team management models are not exclusive to education but reflect broader industrial shifts toward hybridization, cloud-based infrastructures, and algorithmic decision-making. Similarly, the adaptability and resilience required for managing digital nomads mirror leadership demands across industries engaging with remote workforces.

Sections Seven and Eight deepened the ethical and policy-oriented discourse. Section Seven problematized the risks of AI bias, surveillance, inequitable access, and professional marginalization—particularly among nomadic and underrepresented educators. These risks were mapped against international ethical guidelines, such as those articulated by UNESCO, the OECD, and national strategies like DUB.AI and NAFIS. Section Eight responded to these challenges by offering actionable recommendations for institutional leaders, policymakers, and research bodies. It argued for ethical-by-design frameworks, distributed leadership models, and cross-border regulatory coordination to ensure that the adoption of AI and digital nomadism aligns with the principles of equity, transparency, and human dignity.

Reimagining Education through Human-Centric AI and Leadership

As artificial intelligence (AI) becomes increasingly integral to educational systems, reimagining education through a human-centric lens is essential. This approach shifts the focus from technological efficiency to ethically grounded, learner-centered, and culturally responsive practices. AI must serve human values, not replace them—enhancing emotional intelligence, inclusion, and the educator-learner relationship rather than reducing education to automated outputs.

AI offers tools for strategic planning, personalized learning, and administrative efficiency, as discussed in Section Three. However, these benefits come with ethical concerns about algorithmic bias and pedagogical dehumanization. Human-centric leadership, aligned with OECD (2019) and UNESCO (2022) principles, requires educational leaders to balance data-driven insights with empathy, moral judgment, and contextual awareness.

This vision prioritizes holistic student development. Adaptive platforms like the UAE's Alef Education system support differentiated instruction and real-time feedback, enabling educators to focus on learners' cognitive and emotional growth. Yet, such tools must operate within pedagogical frameworks that emphasize creativity, ethical reasoning, and collaboration—core capacities that AI cannot replicate (Grubaugh & Levitt, 2023; Fullan et al., 2023).

Equally important is supporting educators through structured, human-centered professional development. As outlined in Sections Seven and Eight, teacher resistance often reflects concerns about obsolescence and limited training. Initiatives such as the UAE's KHDA-led DUB.AI programs provide upskilling that maintains pedagogical agency while enabling educators to orchestrate adaptive, AI-enhanced learning environments. This model redefines the teacher's role as a mentor and facilitator of personalized learning, not merely a content transmitter.

A human-centric approach also addresses equity in increasingly mobile and digitally mediated education. Section Four highlighted the risks of exclusion in digital nomadism—from visa inequities to gaps in digital access. Leadership must develop inclusive systems such as interoperable credentials, culturally sensitive platforms, and equitable infrastructure to ensure AI expands rather than restricts educational opportunity.

This reimagining also reorients education's purpose. Rather than serving only market demands, AI-enhanced learning must cultivate ethical reasoning, civic engagement, and global citizenship. Echoing the World Economic Forum's "Schools of the Future" framework (2025), this model integrates digital fluency with moral literacy and interpersonal collaboration—framing education as a public good rooted in social cohesion. Human-centric AI and leadership demand reflexive, empathetic, and distributed models that empower communities to co-shape technological change. By embedding AI in ecosystems of care and cultural understanding, education can harness innovation while preserving the ethical foundations of meaningful learning.

The Future of AI, Ethics, and Nomadic Learning/ Work: Toward Resilient, Equitable Global Systems

The convergence of artificial intelligence (AI), ethical governance, and digital nomadism presents a critical frontier for global education and workforce systems. As AI-driven decision-making and mobile learning redefine traditional notions of leadership, labor, and knowledge, institutions must prioritize resilient, equitable frameworks capable of adapting to evolving cultural, ethical, and infrastructural demands.

Sections Four and Six demonstrated that digital nomadism is reshaping workforce structures across education, governance, and other sectors. Yet, current policies—concerning taxation, visa regimes, credential recognition, and labor protections—remain misaligned with the needs of mobile, AI-literate professionals. Cross-border governance is essential to ensure benefit portability, social protection, and regulatory coherence for globally dispersed workers (De Sousa et al., 2025; Choudhury, 2022).

Simultaneously, as highlighted in Section Seven, AI systems increasingly mediate access to learning and employment opportunities through mechanisms such as automated hiring and algorithmic evaluation. These systems risk entrenching inequities without strong ethical oversight. Existing frameworks by the OECD (2019), UNESCO (2022), and national initiatives like the UAE's AI Ethics Guidelines provide foundational guidance but must evolve to address the vulnerabilities of transient users and global learners. Cross-border data governance and algorithmic accountability must become international priorities.

Section Eight emphasized that addressing digital divides requires more than infrastructure—it necessitates cultural and linguistic inclusion. The elitist drift of nomadic education models can be reversed by investing in AI tools tailored to diverse learners, community-based digital hubs, and locally contextualized teacher training. UAE's NAFIS and DUB.AI initiatives exemplify such integrative approaches, combining infrastructure with ethical, multilingual, and inclusive design.

Future leadership must also adapt. As seen in Section Three, effective digital leadership demands fluency in ambiguity, distributed accountability, and intercultural collaboration. Leaders will increasingly manage hybrid teams—blending AI agents, remote professionals, and in-person staff—requiring protocols for ethical coordination, transparency, and shared responsibility. Empathy, reflexivity, and global citizenship are emerging as core leadership literacies.

This study illuminates the transformative intersection of artificial intelligence and digital nomadism in reshaping educational leadership, institutional governance, and workforce mobility. Drawing on theoretical frameworks such as the Technology Acceptance Model, Diffusion of Innovations Theory, and Responsible Research and Innovation, the research demonstrates how AI-driven tools and nomadic work structures are not merely technological trends but fundamental shifts that demand new leadership competencies, ethical frameworks, and inclusive strategies. From the Gulf region's ambitious AI initiatives to the rise of globally mobile educators, the study highlights the dual imperative of innovation and equity. To harness the full potential of AI and digital mobility, educational systems must cultivate ethical governance, invest in educator upskilling, and ensure inclusive access across sociocultural and geographic contexts. The future of education lies in visionary, human-centered leadership that aligns technological advancement with values of justice, inclusivity, and global collaboration.

As we stand at the edge of a digitally redefined educational frontier, it is no longer enough to understand or apply emerging technologies—we must evaluate their societal impact, synthesize human-centered policies, and create future-ready ecosystems where equity, innovation, and ethical intelligence converge. The true measure of educational leadership in the AI era lies not in how swiftly we adopt technology, but in how wisely we harness it to empower diverse learners, transcend boundaries, and reimagine what it means to teach, lead, and belong in a borderless world. Digital nomadism, once a fringe labor phenomenon, now signals a paradigmatic shift—challenging institutions to embrace fluid geographies, distributed expertise, and culturally responsive virtual communities. It is through this lens that educational leaders must rise—not as guardians of tradition, but as architects of an inclusive, mobile, and ethically grounded future.

REFERENCES

Abimbola, C., Eden, C. A., Chisom, O. N., & Adeniyi, I. S. (2024). Integrating AI in education: Opportunities, challenges, and ethical considerations. *Magna Scientia Advanced Research and Reviews, 10*(2), 6–13. DOI: 10.30574/msarr.2024.10.2.0039

Ahmad, Z., Ammar, M., Siby, N., Bhadra, J., Sellami, A., & Al-Thani, N. J. (2023). Do research experience programs promote capacity building in Qatar: Investigating the trend and participation differences. *Heliyon*. https://www.cell.com/heliyon/fulltext/S2405-8440(23)09279-4

Ahmed, F. M. (2020). *The adoption of artificial intelligence in the UAE education sector* [Master's thesis, The British University in Dubai]. https://bspace.buid.ac.ae

Aldawsari, F. I. (2023). *Understanding policy enactment of technology in Saudi Arabia: Three case studies in intermediate schools pursuing the Future Gate Project* (Doctoral dissertation, Flinders University). https://flex.flinders.edu.au/file/62afc95c-6b89-4134-813c-cedb8f7bdde1/1/AldawsariThesis2023.pdf

Allal-Chérif, O., Guijarro-García, M., Ballester-Miquel, J. C., & Carrilero-Castillo, A. (2021). Being an ethical leader during the apocalypse: Lessons from The Walking Dead to face the COVID-19 crisis. *Journal of Business Research, 133*, 354–364. PMID: 36540061

AlNuaimi, B. K., Singh, S. K., Ren, S., Budhwar, P., & Vorobyev, D. (2022). Mastering digital transformation: The nexus between leadership, agility, and digital strategy. *Journal of Business Research, 145*, 636–648. DOI: 10.1016/j.jbusres.2022.03.067

Alswedani, S., Mehmood, R., & Katib, I. (2022). Sustainable participatory governance: Data-driven discovery of parameters for planning online and in-class education in Saudi Arabia during COVID-19. *Frontiers in Sustainable Cities, 871171*. https://www.frontiersin.org/journals/sustainable-cities/articles/10.3389/frsc.2022.871171/full

Alswedani, S., Mehmood, R., & Katib, I. (2022). Sustainable participatory governance: Data-driven discovery of parameters for planning online and in-class Education in Saudi Arabia during COVID-19. *Frontiers in Sustainable Cities*, 871171. https://www.frontiersin.org/articles/10.3389/frsc.2022.871171

Alswedani, S., Mehmood, R., & Katib, I. (2022). Sustainable participatory governance: Data-driven discovery of parameters for planning online and in-class education in Saudi Arabia during COVID-19. *Frontiers in Sustainable Cities*. https://doi.org/DOI: 10.3389/frsc.2022.871171

Alyammahi, A. H. (2019). The impact of Alef Platform on students' performance at Al Asayel School in Abu Dhabi, UAE. Retrieved from https://bspace.buid.ac.ae/buid_server/api/core/bitstreams/e8fc67ed-8575-406a-a1bc-baa383844f3c/content

Antonopoulou, H., Halkiopoulos, C., Barlou, O., & Beligiannis, G. N. (2021). Associations between traditional and digital leadership in academic environments during the COVID-19 pandemic. *Emerging Science Journal*, *5*. Advance online publication. DOI: 10.28991/esj-2021-01286

Aroles, J., Granter, E., & de Vaujany, F. X. (2020). 'Becoming mainstream': The professionalisation and corporatisation of digital nomadism. *New Technology, Work and Employment*, *35*(1), 114–129.

Ayeni, O. O., Al Hamad, N. M., Chisom, O. N., Osawaru, B., & Adewusi, O. E. (2024). AI in education: A review of personalized learning and educational technology. *GSC Advanced Research and Reviews*, *18*(2), 261–271.

Badawy, H. R. I., Alkaabi, A. M., Qablan, A. M., Ndlela, N. P., & Associates. (2024). *Nurturing future innovators: Integrating computational thinking, AI, and STEM in early education*. In *Empowering early education with computational thinking, AI, and STEM* (Chapter 4). IGI Global. https://doi.org/DOI: 10.4018/979-8-3693-6210-5.ch004

Baker, R. S., Wang, Y., & Aleven, V. (2022). *Educational data mining and learning analytics: Improving education through big data*. Springer.

Butcher, T. (2021). *Book review: Rachael A. Woldoff and Robert C. Litchfield, Digital Nomads: In Search of Meaningful Work in the New Economy*. https://doi.org/DOI: 10.1177/09500170211043056

Butcher, T. (2021). Digital nomadism and global labor: Neo-colonial dynamics in remote education and entrepreneurship. *Journal of Global Mobility*, *9*(2), 205–222.

Butcher, T. (2022). *Digital Nomads: In Search of Meaningful Work in the New Economy*. https://doi.org/DOI: 10.1177/09500170211043056

Cabinet, U. A. E. (2021). *The UAE Cabinet: Projects of the 50*. https://uaecabinet.ae/en/the-50-s-projects/second-set-of-projects-of-the-50-nafis

Chauhan, R., & Thangavelu, C. (2024). *Transforming leadership for the digital era: Embracing collaboration and technological proficiency*. Educational Administration: Theory and Practice. https://doi.org/DOI: 10.53555/kuey.v30i6.6033

Chen, L., Chen, P., & Lin, Z. (2020). Artificial intelligence in education: A review. *IEEE Access : Practical Innovations, Open Solutions, 8,* 75264–75278. DOI: 10.1109/ACCESS.2020.2988510

Chen, W., Wang, S., & Lin, Z. (2020). The role of AI in advancing leadership in education. *AI in Education Journal, 15*(4), 256–271. DOI: 10.1016/j.aiedu.2020.06.001

Choudhury, P. (2022). Geographic mobility, immobility, and geographic flexibility: A review and agenda for research on the changing geography of work. *The Academy of Management Annals, 16*(1), 258–296.

Choudhury, P. (2022). Geographic mobility, immobility, and geographic flexibility: A review and agenda for research on the changing geography of work. *The Academy of Management Annals, 16*(1), 258–296.

De Sousa, B. V., Bastida, M., & Vieira, E. (2025). Unraveling digital nomadism: A comprehensive bibliometric review of emerging research and trends. *Journal of Global Mobility: The Home of Expatriate Management Research.* https://doi.org/ DOI: 10.1108/jgm-04-2024-0029

De Sousa, B. V., Bastida, M., & Vieira, E. (2025). Unraveling digital nomadism: A comprehensive bibliometric review of emerging research and trends. *Journal of Global Mobility.* Advance online publication. DOI: 10.1108/jgm-04-2024-0029

Deri, M. N., Singh, A., Zaazie, P., & Anandene, D. (2024). Leveraging artificial intelligence in higher educational institutions: A comprehensive overview. *Revista de Educación y Derecho.* Retrieved from https://revistes.ub.edu/index.php/RED/article/view/45777

Du, X., Alghowinem, S., Taylor, M., Darling, K., & Breazeal, C. (2023). *Innovating AI leadership education. In 2023 IEEE Frontiers in Education Conference.* FIE., DOI: 10.1109/FIE56618.2023.10343238

Education Middle East. (2023, March 4). UAE to introduce policy on generative AI technology in education. https://educationmiddleeast.com/news/uae-to-introduce-policy-on-generative-ai-technology-in-education/

Ellis, R. A. (2024). *The education leadership challenges for universities in a post-digital age.* Postdigital Science and Education., DOI: 10.1007/s42438-024-00461-9

Emara, N., Ali, N., & Abu Khurma, O. (2023). Adaptive learning framework (Alef) in UAE public schools from the parents' perspective. *Social Sciences, 297,* •••. https://www.mdpi.com/2076-0760/12/5/297

Erhan, T., Uzunbacak, H. H., & Aydin, E. (2022). From conventional to digital leadership: Exploring digitalization of leadership and innovative work behavior. *Management Research Review*, *45*(11), 1524–1543. DOI: 10.1108/mrr-05-2021-0338

European Commission. (2020). *Responsible Research and Innovation: Europe's Approach to Science and Innovation*. Publications Office of the European Union. https://op.europa.eu/en/publication-detail/-/publication

Fadlelmula, F. K., & Qadhi, S. M. (2024). A systematic review of research on artificial intelligence in higher education: Practice, gaps, and future directions in the GCC. *Journal of University Teaching & Learning Practice*, *21*(6). Advance online publication. DOI: 10.53761/pswgbw82

Favour Oluwadamilare Usman, F., Adeleke, A., & Bello, B. (2024). AI-driven entrepreneurship in the digital age: Innovation, scalability, and workforce strategies. *Journal of Digital Business Innovation*, *11*(1), 65–82.

Fernandez, A. A., & Shaw, G. P. (2020). Academic leadership in a time of crisis: The coronavirus and COVID-19. *Journal of Leadership Studies*, *14*(1), 39–45. DOI: 10.1002/jls.21684

Fullan, M., Azorín, C., Harris, A., & Jones, M. (2023). Artificial intelligence and school leadership: Challenges, opportunities and implications. *School Leadership & Management*, *44*(4), 339–346. DOI: 10.1080/13632434.2023.2246856

Gamage, D., & Vithanage, K. (2023). AI-based curriculum design in inclusive education. *Journal of Educational Technology Research*, *39*(1), 91–112. DOI: 10.1109/JETR.2023.0101

Ghamrawi, N., Shal, T., & Ghamrawi, N. A. (2023). Exploring the impact of AI on teacher leadership: Regressing or expanding? *Education and Information Technologies*, *29*(7), 8415–8433. DOI: 10.1007/s10639-023-12174-w

Ghamrawi, N., & Tamim, R. M. (2022). A typology for digital leadership in higher education: The case of a large-scale mobile technology initiative (using tablets). *Education and Information Technologies*, *28*, 7089–7110. DOI: 10.1007/s10639-022-11483-w PMID: 36465422

Goel, A., & Polepeddi, L. (2016). *Jill Watson: A virtual teaching assistant for online education*. Georgia Institute of Technology Research Papers.

Government, U. A. E. (2024). *Artificial intelligence in government policies*. https://ai.gov.ae

Government, U. A. E. (2024). *Artificial intelligence in government policies*. https://u.ae/en/about-the-uae/digital-uae/digital-technology/artificial-intelligence/artificial-intelligence-in-government-policies

Grace, E. G., Vidhyavathi, P., & Malathi, P. (2023). AI in education: Opportunities and challenges for personalized learning. *Industrial Engineering Journal, 52*(5), 750–759. DOI: 10.36893/iej.2023.v52i05.750-759

Grace, R., Vidhyavathi, R., & Malathi, D. (2023). Ethical AI for education: Frameworks and governance models. *Journal of Educational Innovation*.

Grubaugh, S., & Levitt, G. (2023). Artificial intelligence and the paradigm shift: Reshaping education to equip students for future careers. *International Journal of Social Sciences and Humanities Invention, 10*(6), 7931–7941. DOI: 10.18535/ijsshi/v10i06.02

Gyanamurthy, V., & Radhanath, S. (2023). Leading change in the AI era: Strategies for transformational leadership. *International Journal of Advanced Engineering Technologies and Innovations*, 164–184. https://scholar.google.com/scholar_lookup?q=Leadership+Challenges+and+Strategies+in+the+Era+of+AI+Transformation

Gyanamurthy, V., & Radhanath, S. (2023). *Leading Change in the AI Era: Strategies for Transformational Leadership*. International Journal of Advanced Engineering Technologies and Innovations.

Hensellek, S., & Puchala, N. (2021). The emergence of the digital nomad: A review and analysis of the opportunities and risks of digital nomadism. In *Human Resource Management* (pp. 195–214). Springer., DOI: 10.1007/978-3-030-62167-4_11

Holmes, W., Bialik, M., & Fadel, C. (2021). *Artificial Intelligence in Education: Promises and Implications for Teaching and Learning*. Center for Curriculum Redesign.

Jaworski, B. K., Webb Hooper, M., Aklin, W. M., Jean-Francois, B., Elwood, W. N., Belis, D., & Hunter, C. M. (2022). Advancing digital health equity: Directions for behavioral and social science research. *Translational Behavioral Medicine, 13*(3), 132–139. DOI: 10.1093/tbm/ibac088 PMID: 36318232

Jones, L., & Kennedy, E. (2023). *Effective technology tools for school leadership: Understanding digital and data-driven strategies*. Routledge.

Karakose, T., & Tülübaş, T. (2023). Digital leadership and sustainable school improvement—A conceptual analysis and implications for future research. *Educational Process International Journal, 12*(1), 7–18. DOI: 10.22521/edupij.2023.121.1

Karakose, T., Yirci, R., & Papadakis, S. (2022). Exploring the emerging field of digital leadership: A bibliometric analysis. *Sustainability*, *14*(15), 9003. DOI: 10.3390/su14159003

Katiyar, N., Awasthi, M. V. K., Pratap, R., Mishra, M. K., Shukla, M. N., & Tiwari, M. (2024). AI-driven personalized learning systems: Enhancing educational effectiveness. *Educational Administration: Theory and Practice*, *30*(5), 11514–11524. DOI: 10.53555/kuey.v30i5.4961

Lakshmi, A. J., Kumar, A., Kumar, M. S., Patel, S. I., Naik, S. L., & Ramesh, J. V. N. (2023). Artificial intelligence in steering the digital transformation of collaborative technical education. *The Journal of High Technology Management Research*, *34*(2), 100467. DOI: 10.1016/j.hitech.2023.100467

Legislation, U. A. E. (n.d.). UAE's international stance on artificial intelligence policy. https://uaelegislation.gov.ae

Li, L., Fengchao, Y., & Zhang, E. (2024). A systematic review of learning task design for K-12 AI education: Trends, challenges, and opportunities. *Computers and Education: Artificial Intelligence*, *100217*. Advance online publication. DOI: 10.26855/jhass.2024.04.039

Li, L., Fengchao, Y., & Zhang, E. (2024). Bridging the digital divide in AI-enhanced learning environments: Policy and practice recommendations. *Computers and Education: Artificial Intelligence*, *5*, 100217.

Madanchian, M., Taherdoost, H., Vincenti, M., & Mohamed, N. (2024). Transforming leadership practices through artificial intelligence. *Procedia Computer Science*, *235*, 2101–2111. DOI: 10.1016/j.procs.2024.04.199

Milton, J., & Al-Busaidi, A. (2023). New role of leadership in AI era: Educational sector. *SHS Web of Conferences, 156*, 09005.

Muhammad, F., & Orji, C. M. (2024). Revolutionizing education in the digital era: The role of AI in promoting inclusivity, equality, and ethical innovation. *The American Journal of Social Science and Education Innovations*, *6*(09), 151–157.

Nawaz, W., Koç, M., Nawaz, W., & Koç, M. (2020). Case Study: Qatar. In *Industry, University and Government Partnerships for the Sustainable Development of Knowledge-Based Society: Drivers, Models and Examples in US, Norway, Singapore and Qatar* (pp. 71–106). Springer. https://link.springer.com/section/10.1007/978-3-030-26799-5_5

Nawaz, W., Koç, M., Nawaz, W., & Koç, M. (2020). *Case Study: Qatar.* In *Industry, University and Government Partnerships for the Sustainable Development of Knowledge-Based Society* (pp. 71–106). Springer.

Nguyen, A., Ngo, H. N., Hong, Y., Dang, B., & Nguyen, B.-P. T. (2022). Ethical principles for artificial intelligence in education. *Education and Information Technologies*, *28*(4), 4221–4241. DOI: 10.1007/s10639-022-11316-w PMID: 36254344

OECD. (2019). OECD principles on artificial intelligence. https://www.oecd.org/going-digital/ai/principles/

OECD. (2023). *Artificial intelligence in education: Global policy perspectives.* OECD Publishing. https://www.oecd.org/

Organisation for Economic Co-operation and Development (OECD). (2019). *OECD Principles on Artificial Intelligence.* https://www.oecd.org/going-digital/ai/principles/

Organisation for Economic Co-operation and Development (OECD). (2023). *Artificial intelligence in education: Global policy perspectives.* OECD Publishing. https://www.oecd.org/

Pago, L. M. (2024). Artificial intelligence empowerment in leadership: A systematic review of positive impacts and applications. *International Journal of Multidisciplinary Research and Analysis*, *7*, 4118–4125. DOI: 10.47191/ijmra/v7-i08-57

Papanikolaou, V., Roussakis, Y., & Tzionas, P. (2023). Knowledge nomads: An educational cultural fusion of the local with the global to promote democratic cooperation. *Globalisation, Societies and Education*, •••, 1–21. DOI: 10.1080/14767724.2023.2166464

Phelps, K. C. (2014). "So much technology, so little talent"? Skills for harnessing technology for leadership outcomes. *Journal of Leadership Studies*, *8*(2), 51–56. DOI: 10.1002/jls.21331

Quaquebeke, N. V., & Gerpott, F. H. (2023). The now, new, and next of digital leadership: How artificial intelligence (AI) will take over and change leadership as we know it. *Journal of Leadership & Organizational Studies*, *30*(3), 265–275. DOI: 10.1177/15480518231181731

Robinson, L., & Reisdorf, B. (2024). The double digital divide: Technology, marginalized populations, and inclusive education. *Digital Inclusion Studies Quarterly*, *3*(1), 1–19.

Robinson, L., & Reisdorf, B. C. (2024). Digital equity in education: Navigating remote learning and access in post-pandemic institutions. *Educational Policy Futures*, *14*(1), 48–64.

Robinson, L., & Reisdorf, B. C. (2024). Digital inclusion and equity: Lessons from post-pandemic education. *Journal of Digital Equity and Leadership*, *3*(1), 45–67.

Robinson, L., & Reisdorf, B. C. (2024). Prejudice, impression management, and digital communications: Leadership challenges in marginalized remote communities. *Journal of Communication and Social Change*, *12*(1), 29–46.

Robinson, L., & Reisdorf, B. C. (2024). Remote education and inclusion: Impacts of digital access and autonomy. *Education and Information Technologies*, *29*(2), 189–204.

Rogers, E. M. (2003). *Diffusion of innovations* (5th ed.). Free Press.

Roshanaei, M., Olivares, H., & Lopez, R. R. (2023). Harnessing AI to foster equity in education: Opportunities, challenges, and emerging strategies. *Journal of Intelligent Learning Systems and Applications*, *15*(4), 123–143. DOI: 10.4236/jilsa.2023.154009

Roshanaei, M., Olivares, H., & Lopez, R. R. (2023). Harnessing AI to foster equity in education: Opportunities, challenges, and emerging strategies. *Journal of Intelligent Learning Systems and Applications*, *15*(4), 123–143. DOI: 10.4236/jilsa.2023.154009

Satya, R., & Mohammed, L. A. (2024). Interdisciplinary insights: The convergence of AI and educational leadership. *International Journal of Research and Innovation in Social Science*, *8*(4), 1872–1887. DOI: 10.47772/ijriss.2024.804131

Shawkat, S., Rozan, M. Z. A., Salim, N. B., & Shehzad, H. M. F. (2021). Digital nomads: A systematic literature review. *IEEE*, 1–6. https://doi.org/DOI: 10.1109/icriis53035.2021.9617008

Singh, S. (2023). Leadership challenges and strategies in the era of AI transformation. In *2023 International Conference on Computational Science and Computational Intelligence (CSCI)*, 119–124. https://ieeexplore.ieee.org/abstract/document/10590476/

Singh, S. (2023). Leadership challenges and strategies in the era of AI transformation. In *2023 International Conference on Computational Science and Computational Intelligence (CSCI)*, 119–124. https://ieeexplore.ieee.org/abstract/document/10590476/

Sposato, M. (2024). *AI leadership for education 4.0: Strategic perspectives*. Springer.

Sposato, M. (2024). Leadership training and development in the age of artificial intelligence. *Development and Learning in Organizations*, *38*(4), 4–7. DOI: 10.1108/dlo-12-2023-0256

Suntharalingam, H. (2024). Enhancing digital learning outcomes through the application of artificial intelligence: A comprehensive review. *International Journal of Innovative Science and Research Technology*, *9*(4), 718–727. DOI: 10.38124/ijisrt/ijisrt24apr530

Taha, S., Abulibdeh, E., Qunais, J., Skaik, H., Alghazo, E. M., Daoud, S., & Bouzenoun, A. (2023). Exploring the utilization of augmented reality in higher education: Perceptions of media and communication students. *Emerging Science Journal*, *7*, 204–216. DOI: 10.28991/esj-2023-sied2-016

Tarisayi, K. S. (2024). Strategic leadership for responsible artificial intelligence adoption in Higher Education. *CTE Workshop Proceedings, 4–14.* https://acnsci.org/journal/index.php/cte/article/view/616

UAE Ministry of Education. (2023). *AI implementation in education: Progress report.* https://www.moe.gov.ae

UNESCO. (2022). *AI and the futures of learning: Ensuring inclusion and equity.* UNESCO. https://unesdoc.unesco.org

UNESCO. (2022). *Recommendation on the Ethics of Artificial Intelligence*. https://unesdoc.unesco.org

Venkatesh, V., & Davis, F. D. (2000). A theoretical extension of the technology acceptance model: Four longitudinal field studies. *Management Science*, *46*(2), 186–204. DOI: 10.1287/mnsc.46.2.186.11926

Venkatesh, V., & Davis, F. D. (2000). A theoretical extension of the technology acceptance model. *Management Science*, *46*(2), 186–204. DOI: 10.1287/mnsc.46.2.186.11926

Venkatesh, V., & Davis, F. D. (2000). A theoretical extension of the technology acceptance model: Four longitudinal field studies. *Management Science*, *46*(2), 186–204. DOI: 10.1287/mnsc.46.2.186.11926

WAM. (2024, January 12). Hamdan bin Mohammed launches initiative to expand teacher AI training. *Emirates News Agency*. https://www.wam.ae/en/article/b3mmuob-hamdan-bin-mohammed-launches-initiative-expand

WAM. (2024, January 17). Minister of Education highlights AI's role in revolutionising education at Davos 2024. Retrieved from https://www.wam.ae/en/article/13pwt81-minister-education-highlights-ai%E2%80%99s-role

Wang, Y. (2021). Artificial intelligence in educational leadership: A symbiotic role of human-artificial intelligence decision-making. *Journal of Educational Administration, 59*(3), 256–270. DOI: 10.1108/JEA-10-2020-0216

Wang, Y. (2021). Data privacy challenges in AI-based education systems. *Journal of Information Privacy and Security.*

Wang, Y. (2021). When artificial intelligence meets educational leaders' data-informed decision-making: A cautionary tale. *Studies in Educational Evaluation, 69*, 100872. DOI: 10.1016/j.stueduc.2020.100872

WEF. (2025). *Future of Jobs Report 2025*. World Economic Forum. https://www.weforum.org

WEF. (2025). *Future of Jobs Report 2025*. World Economic Forum. https://reports.weforum.org/docs/WEF_Future_of_Jobs_Report_2025.pdf

WEF. (2025). *Schools of the future: Defining new models of education for the Fourth Industrial Revolution*. World Economic Forum. https://www.weforum.org

West, S. M., Whittaker, M., & Crawford, K. (2019). *Discriminating systems: Gender, race, and power in AI*. AI Now Institute. https://ainowinstitute.org/discriminatingsystems.html

World Economic Forum. (2025). *Schools of the Future: Defining New Models of Education for the Fourth Industrial Revolution*. https://www.weforum.org/

Zhou, Z., Li, L., & Huang, X. (2021). Personalized learning with Squirrel AI: Opportunities and challenges. *Chinese Journal of Education Technology.*

Chapter 7
Human-Centric Innovations and Sustainable Transformations:
Bridging Industry 5.0 and Society 5.0 for Smart Manufacturing and Resilient Communities

Raffi Mohammed
https://orcid.org/0000-0003-2826-6065
Ramachandra College of Engineering, India

Prasad Babu Bayrisetti
https://orcid.org/0009-0008-3612-4503
Ramachandra College of Engineering, India

Chiranjeevi Aggala
https://orcid.org/0009-0006-6630-7330
Ramachandra College of Engineering, India

Sarma S. Subramanya
https://orcid.org/0000-0002-4619-466X
Ramachandra College of Engineering, India

Kiran Kumar Bunga
https://orcid.org/0009-0001-7419-0666
Sasi Institute of Technology and Engineering, India

Subhani Mohammed
https://orcid.org/0009-0009-5350-6068
Sasi Institute of Technology and Engineering, India

Ranga Jarabala
Ramachandra College of Engineering, India

Jagan Mohan Rao Saride
https://orcid.org/0000-0003-4763-9277
Ramachandra College of Engineering, India

DOI: 10.4018/979-8-3373-0159-4.ch007

ABSTRACT

The fusion of Industry 5.0 and Society 5.0 is driving sustainable transformations and human-centric innovations that enhance smart manufacturing and resilient communities. This chapter explores how AI, IoT, blockchain, and digital twins boost human-machine collaboration, leading to improved efficiency and industrial resilience. Innovations also introduce challenges, such as ethical AI and workforce adaptation. Society 5.0 aims to create smart ecosystems that foster economic progress, while Industry 5.0 emphasizes human-driven decision-making and circular economy practices to minimize environmental impact. The chapter analyzes challenges and opportunities, providing strategies to bridge gaps and accelerate sustainable innovations for an intelligent future.

1. INTRODUCTION

The concept of Industry 5.0 is the focus of this essay. Moving from the factory to the laboratory, Industry 5.0 is broadly defined here as the exploration of new pathways for industrialization. At present, questions are being asked as to how we can move forward into Industry 5.0. It is increasingly clear that, wherever we are located, this movement will only be realized if it is more attuned to the complex processes of life than Industry 4.0. Instead of claiming superiority based on the speed of reactions or the secret superpowers of artificial intelligence, new forms of innovation should work to make technologies – including digital technologies - sounder for us and the planet on which we depend (Leng et al., 2022).

Important aspects of this proposition are indicated in the concepts of 'human-centric innovation' and 'sustainability'. The 'human-centric' part of the label refers to the full gamut of those enterprises which are only partly human or where the 'human' element is only seen as a series of interactions-transactions, interfaces, motivations, or service encounters. The emphasis in this context is on those interconnected practices which direct the deployment of technologies in the factories of the future, the type of technologies that will be harnessed, and the ways in which humans and inhuman things and processes will co-exist. The concept of 'innovation' has also become popular in recent years. 'Innovation systems' and 'innovation indicators' are now important mechanisms in most industrialized countries for providing policy leaders with a sense of the social engine rooms of the economy and productive human endeavor (Kumar, n.d.).

Figure 1. Components of Industry 5.0

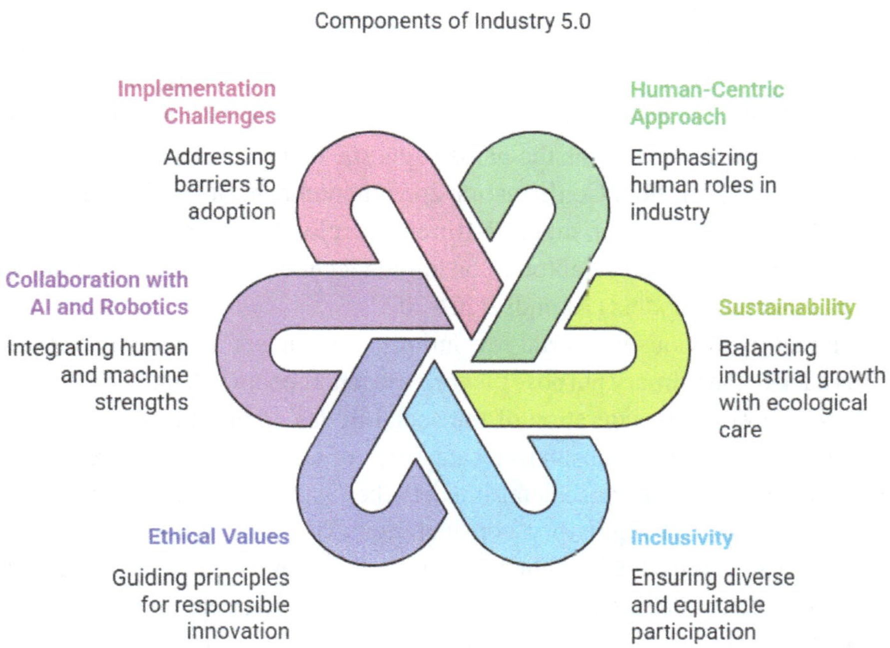

The evolution towards Industry 5.0 signifies a notable transformation from a previously technology-driven industrial revolution to one that embraces a human-centered framework, with emphasis on sustainability, inclusivity, and ethical values. In contrast to Industry 4.0, which primarily focused on automation and decisions informed by data, Industry 5.0 seeks to blend human intellect with artificial intelligence and robotics, thereby fostering a collaborative and resilient industrial environment. This chapter delves into the key characteristics of Industry 5.0, the hurdles it faces during implementation, and the critical regulatory structures required to facilitate a seamless transition. Industry 5.0 is not just an incremental progress from Industry 4.0; it signifies a profound reorientation of industrial operations. It positions humans at the core of technological progress, ensuring that the journey of digital transformation is in harmony with societal requirements and ecological sustainability. This transition is essential for addressing important issues like job displacement, the ethical use of AI, and the environmental impact of industrial activities as shown in Figure 1.

2. UNDERSTANDING INDUSTRY 5.0

The emergence of Industry 5.0 over the characteristic waves of the Information Age has been driven by the digital transformation or fourth industrial revolution, an era described by pervasive intelligent automation ecosystem of advanced software and AI-based robotics that are increasingly employed to displace human labor and democratize automation. 5.0, as the name suggests, is the subsequent chapter and innovation in this evolution. Confirmation and inherent benefits of the industry 5.0 conceptual direction have been suggested through exploration of industry magazines and contemporary research on automation, digital technologies, robotics, manufacturing, and business models (Akundi et al., 2022).

In contrast to previous industrial revolutions, the concept of Industry 5.0 shifts the focus back to the primary purpose of work and labor: people. A movement within Industry 4.0 towards consideration of the social in design and manufacturing has given momentum to more substantive categories of automation being recognized for the positive and negative societal impacts they have as entities. The formally recognized ethical and regulatory considerations of such systems as "socially adaptive agents" signify the returning shift in industry evolution back towards the human-centric direction. Industry 5.0 is concerned with augmenting the traditional needs of the worker at the beginning of Industry 1.0 with society's more recent emphasis on labor reform for the general good (Leng et al., 2022; Xu et al., 2021). The transition from Industry 4.1, 4.2, and 4.3 is not qualitative like the transition from 3.0 to "4.0" but discussed in terms of the long-term and increasing importance of the socio-technical system. The rapid evolution of digital technologies and the average level of technological competence have further expedited movement towards Industry 5.0 (Sarkar et al., 2024).

2.1. Definition and Evolution

In recent years, new actors including production sites and service start-ups have moved the definition of new industrial paradigms. This led to discussions about Industry 4.0 as a continuation and expansion of factory automation. However, Industry 4.0 also highlights a number of limitations such as excessive mechanization and the lack of human presence in production activities. This has resulted in additional interest in a human-centric environment, with one of the origins of our discussion being Industry 5.0. A rather broad and comprehensive definition of Industry 5.0 was given on the basis of social, economic, and industrial trends. Industry 5.0 is an evolutionary extension of the quasi-human system, a new system where both humans and AI are co-evolving and, above all, circulate with each other and cooperate. In the age of Industry 5.0, humans can regain adequate importance in the workplace, as the redundant, dangerous, dirty, and hard work is managed with the help of direct support from automation (Krichevsky, 2020).

The Fourth Industrial Revolution, which is prominently recognized and characterized by Industry 4.0, is fundamentally automated, resulting in a significant replacement of traditional work roles with advanced technology. In contrast, Industry 5.0 revisits the foundational idea of automation that was centered around human labor during the first industrial revolution and seeks to implement these concepts in a refreshed manner. Industry 5.0 effectively harnesses the wisdom accumulated over thousands of years of labor evolution, spanning various industrial eras, and amalgamates automated systems to enhance the experiences associated with human tasks that date back to the earlier industrial times.

This shift in perspective towards labor and workforce management, particularly focusing on the unnecessary migration of jobs, entails a thorough examination of the social context, ethical considerations, and economic repercussions. It discusses the geographical aspects of this transformation, presenting a narrative on the co-evolution of human beings and technology, which remains highly relevant to the selective changes previously observed within the industrial landscape. Furthermore, the distinctive specialized skills possessed by the human workforce are forecasted to have a bright and promising future, as advanced technology is predicted to enrich roles rather than entirely replace them within the work environment.

The direct assistance provided by automation in this new era diverges radically from the industry 4.0 concept known as the "Factory of Things," as well as from the previous industry 3.0 notion referred to as the "Factory of Machines." Instead, Industry 5.0 emphasizes the significance of integrating tools and technological innovations across all processes and interactions among people, consequently offering opportunities for extensive data collection and fostering greater transparency in operations (Martini et al., 2024; Maddikunta et al., 2022).

Industry 4.0 marked a significant transformation with the advent of automation, the Internet of Things (IoT), and artificial intelligence (AI) in decision-making processes, resulting in the emergence of smart factories and digital supply chains. Nevertheless, this surge in mechanization has raised important issues related to workforce displacement and the ethical application of AI technology. In response, Industry 5.0 seeks to address these challenges by focusing on several key areas:

Figure 2. Transition from Industry 4.0 to Industry 5.0

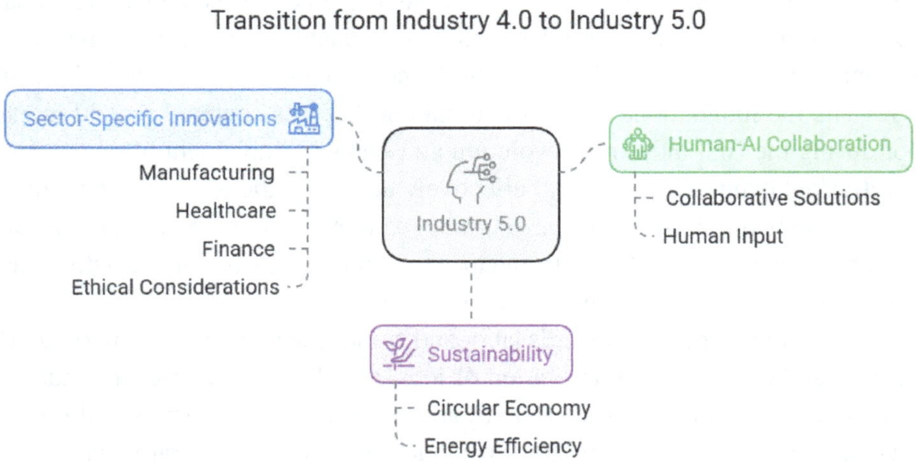

1. Human-AI Collaboration: This approach fosters a partnership between human workers and intelligent systems to collaboratively develop solutions, rather than solely relying on automation for task execution.
2. Sustainability: Principles of a circular economy and designs that maximize energy efficiency are prioritized to promote environmentally friendly practices.
3. Sector-Specific Innovations:
   - Manufacturing: The integration of human input in decision-making processes within smart factories is emphasized.
   - Healthcare: AI-driven diagnostics are employed to improve patient care while preserving the role of healthcare professionals.
   - Finance: Ethical considerations are incorporated into algorithmic trading to guide responsible investment strategies.

The evolution from Industry 4.0 to Industry 5.0 is defined by a greater synergy between AI and human decision-making, rather than a shift toward complete automation. This integrated approach enables industries to uphold a balance between operational efficiency and social responsibility.

3. KEY PRINCIPLES OF INDUSTRY 5.0

Recent research conducted in 2024 and 2025 sheds light on the increasing importance of collaboration between humans and machines across various sectors, including manufacturing, healthcare, and services. Scholars such as Martini et al. (2024) and Sarkar et al. (2024) delve into the ethical considerations and societal effects prompted by the advent of Industry 5.0. Additionally, novel studies addressing cybersecurity threats (Vajda et al., 2024) and the pursuit of sustainable industrial transformation (Ghobakhloo & Iranmanesh, 2023) offer valuable perspectives on the obstacles and prospects linked to this evolving landscape. The body of literature highlights several pivotal themes: Human-Centric Manufacturing: Industry 5.0 prioritizes a workplace dynamic where artificial intelligence enhances human abilities without substituting them. Sustainability and Circular Economy: Innovative approaches aim to minimize industrial waste, boost energy efficiency, and promote the use of renewable resources. Ethical AI and Regulation: There is a growing recognition of the necessity for the formulation of AI systems that are transparent, accountable, and devoid of bias (Martini et al., 2024; Sarkar et al., 2024; Vajda et al., 2024; Ghobakhloo & Iranmanesh, 2023).

A human-centered approach is one of the five Industry 5.0 principles. Participants in industrial systems shall be engaged in shaping them in such a way that it aims at improving human life. Human cognitive power and collective intelligence may play a key role in Industry 5.0; if the previous revolutions have allowed a reduction of hard tasks for the workforce, thus transforming mankind into supervisory agents, Industry 5.0 aims at using collective intelligence to re-launch competitiveness. The concept of manufactories has been developed recently in order to express the material form of Industry 5.0. It should not only focus on the environment and standards but also include the development of social capital, including trust and socially shared behaviors in their everyday operation to increase competitiveness and contribute to delivering safe and excellent products to humankind worldwide (Ramírez-Gordillo et al., 2023).

Human participation is achieved through these other principles of Education 5.0, securitization 5.0, circularity 5.0, and Region 5.0. Industry 5.0 is human-centric, focuses not only on competitiveness but also on people and the common good, and it uses enabling technology. Such technology is at the service of these three small sub-strategies and not the main goal. Industry 5.0's main focus is people and the common good; Industry 5.0 is human-centric; Industry 5.0 is not necessarily anti-competitive and does not necessarily exclude people from the production of goods or services; Industry 5.0 triggers the current century's big debate concerning innovation and standards; Industry 5.0 is a sub-strategy of Industry 4.0. These principles should not be understood individually; they are a sub-part of a general design (Adel & Alani, 2024; Lu et al., 2022).

3.1. Human-Centric Design

One important feature of the industry 5.0 narrative is the importance of human-centric design. At its core, human-centric design is about the holistic design of systems that consider the human experience. Often, this is from usability and an interface point of view, but it invariably reflects back to the physical ergonomics of the system as well. A well-designed product will both increase productivity and job satisfaction. Consideration of these will undeniably also change the employee value proposition. In turn, considering job satisfaction and ergonomics of the operator opens your company to a diverse and protected talent pool. It is clear that the focus on humans is driving economic and business impacts. Improved usability has been shown to reduce training costs and insurance premiums for deployment and use of machinery. Effectively, good interface design reduces the price of change (Lu et al., 2022; Grosse et al., 2023).

The reason for the notable and recent explosion of human interface devices can be traced back to the increased significance of the human element throughout the entire value chain. Alongside various non-technological changes that have emerged, there have also been considerable transformations in how humans can be incorporated into the cycles of design. The approach of designing with a focus on humans, while considering the specific tasks that individuals need to accomplish, has established a clear and explicit user feedback loop. This feedback loop is essential, as it ensures that the design not only meets current needs but evolves alongside the changing demands of the users. Given that user feedback generally transpires in timescales that are swifter than those of consumer demand, integrating this feedback explicitly into the design process guarantees that market fit remains strong and relevant. Moreover, this feedback loop is inherently self-reinforcing, which implies that a design that is adaptable and flexible will effectively respond to the ensuing set of user requirements as products inevitably evolve over time.

Interdisciplinary research into human-centric design illustrates the growing acknowledgment within academia of the value that lies in concentrating on the human dimensions within the system. At a socio-technological level, this focus is fundamentally concerned with minimizing risks posed to human life in tasks that individuals are not optimally suited to perform. When highlighting the worker, it becomes apparent that changes to workplaces are increasingly directed at enhancing overall well-being. This shift is imperative because the relationship between productivity and workers' well-being is being recognized as more feasible and beneficial, especially considering that the individuals who inhabit these workplaces are also consumers of various products and services. In essence, if the goal is to empower your workers with the financial means to spend on your business's offerings, it is crucial that they have the opportunity to work flexibly, engage in a meaningful role, and experience happiness in their work environment. The culmination of these factors will naturally feed back into product design, ensuring that products are not only designed for functionality but are also aligned with the well-being and needs of the workers who contribute to the success of the enterprise (Ystgaard & De Moor, 2023; Perikangas et al., 2022).

4. TECHNOLOGIES DRIVING INDUSTRY 5.0

Technological innovation is the fuel driving Industry 5.0. A set of new and cutting-edge technologies is taking over world markets: artificial intelligence, Internet of Things, cloud computing, virtual reality, robotics, block-chain, big data, and Industry 5.0 itself, among others. These new technologies are characterized by three factors: they are digital; they are platforms that entangle other technologies within them; and they are usually transparent, so they can help in decision-making. When integrated, these technologies allow industries to augment human decision-making, productivity, and efficiency. Besides automation, a panel discusses that one major characteristic of the industry 5.0 landscape is that these technologies go hand in hand with human activity. The centralized characteristic of Industry 5.0 is trust in 4.0 technologies, which are transparent and possibly regenerative. They believe that transparency mitigates risks, which is the main obstacle to taking the other route for decision-making (Adel, 2023).

The road to achieving that ideal is not straightforward. New technologies are continuously developed and deployed, and as they are being put into industries, they have to exemplify four prerequisites: cyber security; price in competition; adaptability to new scenarios; and following established norms, among others. Currently we are already in Industry 5.0 technologies, albeit at low levels of proportion, argues a respondent in the panel. Industry 5.0 automation solutions are ready; they just need to be adapted for nation-states and corporations. One of the main traits of Industry 5.0 digital solutions is that trust netted from 4.0 solutions is needed as a major input, the discussion goes on to say. Therefore, Industry 5.0 differs from 4.0 in that technology is replaced by smart, traceable inhabitants and transparent digital solutions (Zizic et al., 2022; Kasinathan et al., 2022).

4.1. Internet of Things (IoT)

The Internet of Things (IoT) serves as one of the foundational and pivotal core technologies that are vital for enabling the transformative vision of Industry 5.0. At its very essence, IoT extends the interconnectivity of a vast array of devices, which significantly enhances both the quality and functionality of industrial processes. Firstly, the IoT landscape promises to create an ecosystem of better-connected devices and sophisticated product systems that are capable of sharing increasingly large and complex amounts of data with each other over the internet on a continuous basis. This remarkable advancement means that, for the dedicated factory worker, an industrial device such as a cutting-edge robot or a complex machine equipped with these advanced IoT capabilities will be able to communicate seamlessly and adapt to rapidly changing conditions much more swiftly-indeed, in real time-in direct response to the worker's presence, actions, or specific requirements. Ultimately, this dynamic interaction results in significantly increased flexibility and enhanced overall productivity on the factory floor. Additionally, these smarter, interconnected devices and highly integrated product systems also enable improved system maintenance and extended longevity of machinery. With advanced insights derived from extensive historical knowledge or sophisticated predictive models, manufacturers can strategically deploy machines in ways that aim to minimize wear and prolong the overall life expectancy of these critical assets, ultimately leading to more efficient operations and optimized resource utilization (Zong et al., 2021; Chander et al., 2022).

This vision of increased connectivity, resulting in improved decision making and business operations through data sharing between devices, leads to capabilities often associated with smart systems. In industrial settings, an IoT induction heating process in the 'smart factory' can, for example, automatically re-tune its parameters based on a component or user associated with necessary or desired changes in the finished product, or predict maintenance needs by evaluating conductivity and thermal risks in the manufacturing platform based on its material and historical data, effectively improving both granularity and timing of maintenance schedules in the process. In both examples, regardless of the details, it is evident that the user and the system are fundamentally co-adaptive to each other (Shaer & Shami, 2023; Vajda et al., 2024).

5. APPLICATIONS OF INDUSTRY 5.0

The technologies and practices proposed over the last few decades in research are guiding the evolution of various industries-often in new directions that their proposers had not envisaged. Below, we present a few examples of such applications across various sectors. All of these examples have one thing in common: they demonstrate the true value, scalability, and opportunities opened up when human-centric innovations and technologies are combined, designed to ensure a deeper human, institutional, and socio-technical impact while leveraging technology. The idea for these examples is to provide relatively simple yet significantly useful global solutions, translating the more theoretical concepts into thematic applications (Castagnoli et al., 2024; Olaitan & Elshennawy, 2024).

The first essential principle of Industry 5.0 is human-centric design. Applications use technologies to develop socially motivated solutions for different purposes. Cooperation based on genuinely aligned interests is challenging for different stakeholders, as well as for broad-scale integration. Additionally, each socio-technical system application must be adapted given different cultural, social, institutional, regulatory, educational, and historical assets and qualifiers. Using frameworks in a more generic way, we can see what kind of partnerships, professional teams, educational advancements, etc. we need to invest in and start working on (Alves et al., 2023; Longo et al., 2020).

Industry 5.0 influences healthcare, education, and SMEs, presenting unique challenges for human-centric AI adoption. In healthcare, it fosters human-AI collaboration for personalized medicine, with tools like IBM Watson improving disease detection but raising concerns about data privacy and access, particularly in developing areas. Public policies need to ensure ethical AI use and equitable access. Education is transformed through AI tutoring and AR/ VR tools, enhancing personalized learning, but digital inequality remains a barrier. Investment in EdTech, teacher training, and cybersecurity is essential to safeguard student data. SMEs can leverage AI and cloud automation but encounter barriers like limited skilled labor and finances. Policymakers should provide support through subsidies and training to promote digital transformation. Without addressing these barriers, socio-economic inequalities may deepen, especially in rural and developing areas, where the digital divide persists. Governments must ensure universal digital access and collaborate to narrow the skills gap. Social inclusion is vital, focusing on algorithmic bias and ethical AI practices to protect marginalized groups. Effective governance is necessary to balance innovation with societal protection, demanding comprehensive regulations for AI, workforce transition, and sustainability. Industry 5.0 offers chances to merge AI and sustainability, but tackling challenges in healthcare, education, and SMEs is crucial to avoid widening disparities. A successful transition relies on cooperation among governments, businesses, and educational systems to promote inclusive AI education and ethical practices. Holistic frameworks and investments are needed to ensure Industry 5.0 benefits everyone.

5.1. Smart Manufacturing

Smart manufacturing, which is known in Germany as Industry 4.0, stands as a prominent application of the concepts and principles found within Industry 5.0. This particular sector serves as a prime example that perfectly embodies the ideals of human-centric innovation, which is crucial for fostering a sustainable future. In the realm of smart manufacturing, the integration of advanced information and communication technologies plays a vital role. These technologies are extensively utilized to create and develop production systems that are not only highly efficient but also cost-effective and adaptable to various conditions.

The advanced ICTs allow the manufacturing systems to inherently sense their operational context, which is an essential feature of their functionality. This heightened awareness enables the systems to trigger adaptive responses to different operating conditions in real time, which is critical for maintaining optimal performance and efficiency. Additionally, these systems have the capability to collect, store, and share a vast amount of information. This information is instrumental in driving analytics-based continuous improvement initiatives and helps in the design of effective disaster recovery systems.

Furthermore, they utilize a range of analytical and simulative tools to evolve decision-making paradigms, which play a significant role in optimizing processes. Ultimately, this evolution influences the fundamental architecture of the manufacturing system itself, leading to enhanced operational dynamics and productivity levels. While automation acts as a crucial pillar in the landscape of smart manufacturing, it is important to recognize that, within this framework, automation serves more as a supportive fabric. This fabric facilitates the way humans conduct their functions, providing both effective structural and process support throughout the systems.

Consequently, it is clear that technology in smart manufacturing does not serve the purpose of replacing human workers. Instead, it aligns with the true essence of robotics, which is to augment and enhance the capabilities of humans. The harmony between human intelligence and technological advancements is what ultimately drives innovation and efficiency in this evolving domain of smart manufacturing (Lu et al., 2022; Yang et al., 2024).

Smart manufacturing has significant advantages. By reducing the complexity caused by some of the existing best practices, it enables more radical improvements in aspects such as operational resilience through reconfigurability and scalability. It allows production processes to inherently adapt to product demands, minimizes waste, optimizes resources, and ensures the consistency and quality of the output. At the macroeconomic level, there is a string of successful case studies of smarter production systems across industry sectors that have led to the employment of thousands of employees in forward-looking companies, proving not just profit and growth for industry owners and shareholders but for society at large. Data analytics, and especially deep learning, is often the driver and enabler of further system innovation and improvement (Sajjad et al., 2021).

6. IMPACT ON SUSTAINABILITY

Industry 5.0 leverages human-centric innovation for dramatic results. Imagine for a moment fully optimized operations that consume only the immediate and exactly necessary resources, reducing waste to zero. Still more striking is the possibility that such dramatic 'right-sizing' of operations could lead to entirely new and highly desired capabilities, such as rapid process reconfiguration, on-the-fly property optimization, or even resilient and resource-right production strategies. All of these resulting strategies are based on the intuitive, but for operations, profoundly different principles of Industry 5.0 (Adel, 2023; Saikia, 2023).

Principles of Industry 5.0 emphasize focusing on balancing trade-offs across longer-term and more connected ecological boundaries than currently considered in strategic and tactical decision making. The impact of this shift is to 'right-size' operations to maximize utility, and not just profit, while continuously improving on waste. Through resource availability and waste management, capital becomes more efficiently allocated, reducing environmental impact, cost, and uncertainty. Ultimately, the transition to Industry 5.0 and industrial sustainability represents the figurative and literal 'price of admission' as economic trade-offs move from pure finance to include often competing principles of human well-being, ecology, technology, governance, and human agency. Populating these transitions are potential breakthrough strategies such as collaborative manufacturing, zero waste operations, leveraging the circular economy, industrial synergy, and many collaborative production strategies that can lead to significant resource-right and resilience-right operational advantages. Moreover, the reshaping of consumption technologies and industrial techniques to achieve this balance leverages approaches like design for environment and energy-efficient designs in its focus on resource leverage and closure (Ghobakhloo et al., 2024; Costa, 2024; Rame et al., 2024).

What is significantly altered through the Industry 5.0 and industrial sustainability transition is the notion of collaboration and stakeholder interests. Although creating partnerships with suppliers, environmental activists, and the local community remain building blocks of Industry 5.0, a system-of-systems view on productions can lead to uncommon pairings among those typically isolated in operational considerations. Throughout, compatibility and conflict among stakeholder interests will remain the central components of collaboration in achieving progress. Still, successful negotiations on these interests can and do yield significant operational advantages throughout an enterprise, moving a discussion of interests to that of systems behavior (Wang et al., 2023; Dwivedi et al., 2023; Ghobakhloo & Iranmanesh, 2023).

6.1. Resource Efficiency

Resource efficiency is likely the standout element in any truly sustainable and efficient move toward Industry 5.0. As such, resource efficiency is traditionally described as a measure of the quantity of resources required to produce three units of output, hence reducing the number of resources required because of factors such as improved processes and the reduction of waste. In our future vision, we adopt a broader, more contemporary, and systems-based concept of resource efficiency. With resources encompassing the energy required for ongoing operations, materials, water usage, financial capital, and more, resource efficiency should be thought of as crossing organizational domains to embed sustainability through the multiplicative efficiencies across the enterprise (Shehzad et al., 2024). Extending from the preceding discussion, a primary motivation for enhancing resource efficiencies is the reduction in the utilization of the associated resources. Energy, water, and materials are process inputs and inherently represent a cost to replenish. Outputs, such as waste or effluent, represent a further cost to be discharged. Furthermore, there are numerous techniques and technologies available to enhance resource efficiency in business, with many more being established during a current push towards increased efficiencies. Investment in these areas is likely to enhance business resilience and contribute to sustainable future performance (Faeni, 2024).

Creating a business environment that both values and manages resource efficiency through an inclusive workforce will yield socioeconomic and ecological benefits. The aim is for practitioners and business leaders to place more focus on the engagement of people to identify waste within their respective value chains. The human-centric approach places value in the contributions from workers on the shop floor to those at the hunt-and-peck era of technology. The multi-tool, human-centric approach exhibits versatility, as it can be adapted to a multitude of environments, such that the "environment" it operates within is irrelevant. The focus is on resource efficiency in the hope that political, business, or policymakers can see that greater resource efficiency has long-term benefits. What we hope to propose is that individual process resource efficiency could contribute to a new emerging sustainable paradigm-Industry 5.0, or what could be referred to as a human-centric innovation system (Khan & Johl, 2021). That is, practitioners can improve the collaborative pool through greater engagement with workers, resulting in a culture of continuous and transparent improvement. Despite the countless benefits interwoven into increasing resource efficiencies, we acknowledge that achieving these benefits has its challenges and interventions to materialize change. There are many barriers' organizations encounter when trying to increase their resource efficiencies. Local factors-such as a lack of collaboration and understanding of the need for action-are inherent in this innovative space. As such, what could be recommended could be suggested by those in each organization responsible for operations (Popo-Olaniyan et al., 2022; Malhotra et al., 2020).

7. CHALLENGES AND BARRIERS TO ADOPTION

Transitioning to Industry 5.0 presents several key challenges, particularly concerning the need for revised regulatory and policy frameworks. It is crucial for governments to create policies that promote collaboration between humans and AI while safeguarding against monopolistic practices in automation technologies. The establishment of ethical AI guidelines is vital to ensure that decision-making processes remain transparent, fair, and accountable. Furthermore, labor laws require modification to protect employees adapting to AI-enhanced positions, thus ensuring job security and equitable compensation.

Figure 3. Challenges and solutions in Industry 5.0

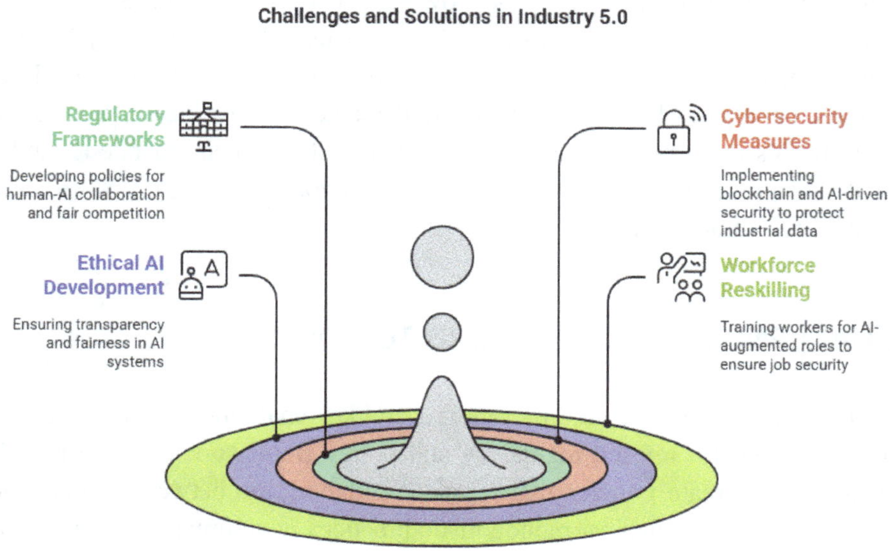

Strengthening environmental regulations is also necessary to foster sustainable manufacturing practices, which in turn promote eco-friendly industrial operations and the responsible use of resources. Additionally, cybersecurity threats pose a significant risk in the context of Industry 5.0, especially with the extensive integration of AI and IoT within industrial systems. The increased connectivity of smart factories heightens vulnerability to cyber threats, such as substantial data breaches that can jeopardize sensitive operational information. Hacking attempts that manipulate AI systems can lead to biased outcomes and failures in automation, while security weaknesses in IoT devices can expose systems to further risks.

To counter these challenges, it is essential to enhance cybersecurity measures through strategies like blockchain-based authentication, AI-driven threat detection, and robust encryption techniques, ensuring secure industrial operations. The ethical and social implications linked to Industry 5.0 are equally important. While AI integration can boost workforce productivity, it is necessary to address issues such as algorithmic bias and the potential for job displacement. AI systems must be developed with ethical principles in mind to avoid discriminatory results and promote inclusivity.

Providing AI ethics training for developers can support responsible AI development and deployment. Moreover, encouraging interdisciplinary teamwork among engineers, sociologists, and policymakers can lead to the creation of equitable and socially beneficial AI systems. Lastly, implementing re-skilling initiatives for workers transitioning from manual labor to AI-assisted roles is critical for facilitating workforce adaptation, minimizing job displacement, and fostering inclusive economic growth.

There exist many factors that may inhibit the adoption of truly human-centric systems and advanced technologies. Habit and tradition in any culture mean there is resistance to change. In addition, the inertia created by powerful existing industrial systems, especially concerning oil, gas, and petrochemical production, must be accounted for. This is a major challenge for a meaningful transition towards Industry 5.0 because petroleum is used as a primary material today not only for fuel but also for a variety of other products such as electrical components, paint, canvas, makeup, household chemicals, pesticides, repellents, additives in food, drugs, and supplements, toothpaste, and many more. The petrochemical industry is regulated by two directly affected industries and others indirectly affected by higher commodity prices (Syracuse & Blanco, 2020).

Undoubtedly, the transition to Industry 5.0 is not without risks and complexities. This new era of an ever-changing world needs a competent workforce with continuous knowledge and skills development. For instance, one study showed that Building Information Modeling is still not a panacea for the construction industry; part of the problem is related to limited availability and access to software as well as the knowledge and skilled workers required using it. Investment outlays to adopt new manufacturing digital tools and services, energy and process simulation software, 3D printing in metals, partial implementation of additive manufacturing, and industrial robotics manual assembly-low complexity fixed type are also some examples of policies and initiatives that can undermine the transition towards a more deliberate and informed process for Industry 5.0 in businesses, particularly small and medium enterprises. Regulatory, ethical, and moral issues, privacy, consumer protection, and transparency to the user, along with other concerns, are important in the development of new products, systems, and services (Suciu et al., 2023; Orlova, 2021).

Additional barriers pertain to cyber security concerns, such as possible increased vulnerabilities of contested systems to system failures, excessive damage, and exploitation. Privacy breaches, for example, through excessively large-scale deployment of sensors and recordings of social spaces, might also challenge human-centric automation unless done in explicit cooperation with the people that would be affected by such actions. It is recognized that the inclusiveness of human-centric digital systems also has a profound potential to selectively exclude some less physically advantaged and some physically disadvantaged citizens. Overall, the interdisciplinary and human-centered nature of designing for Industry 5.0 underscores the need for close interdisciplinary working. Interdisciplinary investigations into the societal context for Industry 5.0 will reveal challenges that need to be addressed (Seidl, 2022; George, 2024; Kamtam, 2023).

8. CASE STUDIES AND BEST PRACTICES

In this section, evidence-based examples of management approaches that enable a more human-centered design and application of advanced technologies are presented. Each case study showcases examples of transformations from different organizations and highlights their approach, achievements, and outstanding benefits over the long term. Quantitative and qualitative information is provided, and the outcomes achieved are discussed. Insights or lessons drawn from the practices adopted by these organizations are also provided.

The case studies reflect excellence in all four critical dimensions of Industry 5.0 transformation, which are (1) purpose, vision, and leadership, (2) mission and management, (3) design, production, and service systems, and (4) change processes and the reduction of risks. The majority of the transformations that are showcased also took a stakeholder-inclusive approach, demonstrating the integration of multiple perspectives and cooperative networks across a wide range of stakeholders. Combined, these organizational factors act as a catalyst for advanced technological advancements and revolution that manifest in tangible and impactful everyday business functions and organizational management and operations. The latest insights and advancements from the cases shared in this section are summarized (Sarkar et al., 2024).

There are multiple offerings from this section that inform Industry 5.0. Some offer practical advice or guidelines and inform the value of shared experience from real-life scenarios, life science and technologies, forefront, complexity, advanced quality, innovation and design, and business. The process and the methodology of such an exercise charted the successful tailoring of this approach. Insights offer a variety of applications including, however not limited to, the potential to inform policy or decision-making for alternative investments within an organization to drive future excellence; providing a case for adopting Industry 5.0 in different industries and uses; and providing a platform for organizations to start a conversation with their stakeholders around ethical dilemmas. Each organization and case was underpinned by literature and conversations, giving them a concrete basis in subsequent academic research. The successful practice can be drawn to align with the content (Matheus et al., 2020; Sahoo & Goswami, 2023; Sánchez-Franco & Rey-Tienda, 2024).

9. INTEGRATING CRITICAL INTERPRETATION, CASE STUDIES, AND ORGANIZATIONAL IMPLICATIONS INTO INDUSTRY 5.0

While Industry 5.0 has garnered significant attention, analysis uncovers differing views on its effects and implementation. Some scholars focus on its ethical, human-centric elements, promoting improved work environments and productivity through human-machine collaboration. In contrast, others point out technological and security issues, noting automation's efficiency gains come with risks like job loss, cybersecurity threats, and AI bias. Furthermore, the transition from Industry 4.0 to 5.0 is not as seamless as often suggested, with practical challenges such as cybersecurity risks, unclear regulations, and workforce adaptation issues. Despite presenting an appealing future vision, the practical application of Industry 5.0 differs greatly across sectors and regions. A significant gap exists in literature regarding empirical studies on Industry 5.0's sector-specific adoption. Many academics propose theoretical models, but only a few investigate real-world implementations showcasing how these concepts are applied. Case studies are crucial for understanding the application of Industry 5.0 principles. For instance, Siemens has successfully implemented human-AI collaboration with collaborative robots (cobots) in manufacturing, improving worker safety and operational flexibility while reducing downtime. Tesla employs smart manufacturing aligned with Industry 5.0 through real-time AI-driven decision-making and sustainable practices using solar-powered facilities. In healthcare, AI-assisted diagnostics, such as those at Mayo Clinic, enhance patient care by facilitating accurate disease detection and ethical medical decision-making through doctor-AI collaboration. These examples emphasize that Industry 5.0 focuses on enhancing human capabilities with technology rather than replacing human roles.

For effective transition, businesses must prioritize workforce reskilling, ethical AI oversight, and sustainable business models. Unlike the automation emphasis of Industry 4.0, Industry 5.0 highlights upskilling for AI-integrated environments. Organizations should invest in AI literacy, human-centered work models, and continuous learning to foster long-term adaptability. Furthermore, establishing transparent AI governance frameworks ensures ethical, unbiased decision-making while complying with emerging regulations. Industry 5.0 also underscores sustainability, urging businesses to adopt circular economy practices, optimize energy usage, and collaborate with green-tech startups for innovative solutions. The move from Industry 4.0 to 5.0 hinges on a holistic approach, merging technological advancements with human factors and ethical concerns. The actualization of Industry 5.0's vision relies on the ability of businesses, policymakers, and researchers to connect theoretical frameworks with practical execution. By addressing current literature gaps, utilizing industry case studies, and enhancing organizational preparedness, Industry

5.0 can transform from theoretical notions into actionable guidance for the future. By concentrating on human-centric innovation, accountable AI development, and sustainable practices, Industry 5.0 has the potential to foster an industrial ecosystem that balances technological advancement with human welfare and ecological responsibility.

10. FUTURE TRENDS AND FORECASTS

The sweeping pendulum swing from Industry 3.0 (centered on technology) to Industry 4.0 (driven by digital), and onwards to Industry 5.0 (anchored in human-centric collaboration) has serious implications for levels and types of industrial innovation. Numerous discussions have begun to address the trajectory of innovative practices that will support, drive, and result from Industry 5.0. Some jump directly from Industry 4.0 to Industry 5.0 in appraisals of industry futures as an area ripe for research, while others base predictive assessments of future business trends on investigations of new and emerging technology. In the complementary areas of human resources and consumer science, forecasts indicate a future characterized by a significant consumer preference for companies and products that are effective at integrating humanity and technology. There are also projections for a market ripe for services and products that work to restore humanity whenever technological advancement has sidelined it. The potential to advocate for and forecast the future importance of these services is so great that simply indicating the market potential for them warrants its own discussion (Calzavara et al., 2023).

But the motivations behind these trends, the potential social technologies that might support them, and the likely areas and levels of industry practice they are likely to affect directly remain under-researched and are routinely pointed to as agenda areas that must be engaged with in the years to come. The aim of this final chapter is to operate at this strategic level, with a focus on potential rather than present or near-future practices or tools. It is, in part, a speculative piece. A roadmap for the future of Industry 5.0 by 2030 is offered to those who want to adapt to and anticipate incoming trends and changes using technologies that are still developing. Such foresight will be particularly valuable for governments and legal systems, educational institutions, corporations of all sizes, industrial workers and leaders, and in commercial literature. With diverse horizons flagged, readers are encouraged to seek out the range of other scholarship that seeks to shape an organic movement industry-wide rather than suggesting the paths or leaders who will do so (Atiku et al., 2024; Maljugić et al., 2024; Behera et al., 2024).

To ensure a truly successful and effective shift toward Industry 5.0, a collaborative effort among various stakeholders is highly encouraged to adopt specific and well-defined strategies. Governments should prioritize the establishment of flexible regulatory frameworks that maintain a careful balance between fostering innovation and addressing crucial social implications that may arise. Additionally, industries ought to invest substantially in comprehensive training programs that promote seamless collaboration between humans and AI, as well as the implementation of sustainable production practices that benefit the environment. Academic institutions are particularly tasked with performing in-depth interdisciplinary studies to thoroughly explore the socio-economic effects and potential impacts of Industry 5.0 on society. Furthermore, cybersecurity professionals must take proactive measures to create advanced AI-based models specifically designed for effective threat detection, thereby ensuring the protection of vital digital infrastructure against evolving cyber threats.

11. CONCLUSION

In this chapter, we have described the key concepts and principles behind Industry 5.0 and, more broadly, behind the strategy of human-centered innovation. At the heart of this vision is the principle that companies and policymakers should focus on human welfare-rather than innovation for innovation's sake. For Industry 5.0, this principle means that companies should open up more opportunities for co-workers to interact with technology, while actively considering their workforce and, in a wider sense, society. We also observed that the aims of technology are closely connected to societal well-being, and this closeness is intensified by the principles-such as co-creation, trust, and sustainability-which are essential for Industry 5.0. In consequence, the framework suggested breaks down barriers between technical and non-technical sectors. This convergence in findings underscores the importance of combining the natural and social sciences to support an interdisciplinary vision for the future of technology.

Several risks, challenges, and barriers have been identified throughout the essay. As might be expected, our analysis suggests that the main barriers will be social-particularly inertia and resistance to change. Negative unintended consequences of adopting policies that are incompatible with the spirit of Industry 5.0 were considered. However, we also identified potential long-term social benefits and opportunities emerging through the limits imposed by finite resources-such as new markets for remanufactured or reconditioned goods. Consequently, we see considerable scope for the way that Industry 5.0 could continue to be explored or adapted within this and other contexts, engaging with individuals, communities, firms, and governmental departments to co-create and align strong visions for the future of society. As such, the research agenda is to better understand those implications and how they can be leveraged to materialize the Industry of the Future.

Industry 5.0 embodies a remarkable chance to forge an industrial environment that is not only technologically advanced but also firmly centered around the diverse needs of human beings. This new phase in industry recognizes the importance of human-centric approaches in relation to technological advancements. However, significant obstacles related to regulation, cybersecurity threats, and the adaptation of the workforce to new tools and methodologies continue to exist and pose challenges. By engaging in thoughtful, inclusive policy-making and cultivating ethical AI development practices, we can facilitate a smooth and successful transition into this exciting new era. Promoting active cooperation among policymakers, businesses, and academic institutions from various fields will enable us to create a sustainable, inclusive future, where technological advancements can progress in harmony with the well-being of individuals and communities alike, ensuring that the benefits of innovation are widely shared and accessible.

REFERENCES

Adel, A. (2023). *Unlocking the future: Fostering human–machine collaboration and driving intelligent automation through Industry 5.0 in smart cities*. Smart Cities.

Adel, A., & Alani, N. H. S. (2024). *Human-centric collaboration and Industry 5.0 framework in smart cities and communities: Fostering sustainable development goals 3, 4, 9, and 11 in Society 5.0*. Smart Cities.

Akundi, A., Euresti, D., Luna, S., & Ankobiah, W. (2022). *State of Industry 5.0-Analysis and identification of current research trends*. Applied System. MDPI.

lves, J., Lima, T. M., & Gaspar, P. D. (2023). Is industry 5.0 a human-centred approach? A systematic review. Processes. Retrieved from mdpi.com

Atiku, S. O., Jeremiah, A., Semente, E., & Boateng, F. (2024). *Eco-innovation and sustainable development in Industry 5.0*. Retrieved from. [HTML]

Behera, B., Panda, R. K., & Tiwari, B. (2024). *Understanding the drivers of innovative work behaviour among millennial employees in India's IT sector: Some exploratory research findings. Journal of Asia Business*. Retrieved from. [HTML]

Calzavara, M., Faccio, M., & Granata, I. (2023). Multi-objective task allocation for collaborative robot systems with an Industry 5.0 human-centered perspective. The International Journal of Advanced Manufacturing Technology. Retrieved from springer.com

Castagnoli, R., Cugno, M., & Maroncelli, S. (2024). A new research agenda for human-centric manufacturing: A systematic literature review. IEEE Transactions on... Retrieved from ieee.org

Chander, B., Pal, S., De, D., & Buyya, R. (2022). *Artificial intelligence-based internet of things for Industry 5.0*. ResearchGate.

Costa, E. (2024). Industry 5.0 and SDG 9: A symbiotic dance towards sustainable transformation. Sustainable Earth Reviews. Retrieved from springer.com

Dwivedi, A., Agrawal, D., & Jha, A. (2023). Studying the interactions among Industry 5.0 and circular supply chain: Towards attaining sustainable development. Computers & Industrial, Elsevier. Retrieved from [HTML]

Faeni, D. P. (2024). Green practices and employees' performance: The mediating roles of green human resources management policies and knowledge development. Journal of Infrastructure, Policy, and... Retrieved from enpress-publisher.com

George, A. S. (2024). Bridging the digital divide: Understanding the human impacts of digital transformation. Retrieved from researchgate.net

Ghobakhloo, M., & Iranmanesh, M. (2023). Actions and approaches for enabling Industry 5.0-driven sustainable industrial transformation: A strategy roadmap. Corporate Social Responsibility and Environmental Management. Retrieved from wiley.com

Ghobakhloo, M., & Iranmanesh, M. (2023). *Actions and approaches for enabling Industry 5.0-driven sustainable industrial transformation: A strategy roadmap. Corporate Social Responsibility and Environmental Management*. Wiley.

Ghobakhloo, M., Iranmanesh, M., & Fathi, M. (2024). Beyond Industry 4.0: A systematic review of Industry 5.0 technologies and implications for social, environmental, and economic sustainability. Asia-Pacific Journal of... Retrieved from emerald.com

Grosse, E. H., Sgarbossa, F., & Berlin, C. (2023). Human-centric production and logistics system design and management: Transitioning from Industry 4.0 to Industry 5.0. *International Journal of Production Research.*

Kamtam, P. (2023). Exploring the design of people-centred inclusive smart cities using integrated inclusion approaches and citizen engagement strategies. Retrieved from herts.ac.uk

Kasinathan, P., Pugazhendhi, R., & Elavarasan, R. M. (2022). *Realization of sustainable development goals with disruptive technologies by integrating Industry 5.0, Society 5.0, smart cities, and villages*. Sustainability. MDPI.

Khan, P. A., & Johl, S. K. (2021). Does adoption of ISO 56002-2019 and green innovation reporting enhance the firm sustainable development goal performance? An emerging paradigm. Business Strategy and the Environment. Retrieved from researchgate.net

Krichevsky, S. (2020). *Creation of a "cosmic" human: Ideas, technologies, projects, experience, risks, limitations, and prospects*. Future Human Image.

Kumar, S. (n.d.). *Industry 5.0 and emerging technologies: A pathway to human-centric innovation in manufacturing*. ResearchGate.

Leng, J., Sha, W., Wang, B., Zheng, P., & Zhuang, C. (2022). *Industry 5.0: Prospect and retrospect. Journal of Manufacturing*. Elsevier.

Longo, F., Padovano, A., & Umbrello, S. (2020). Value-oriented and ethical technology engineering in industry 5.0: A human-centric perspective for the design of the factory of the future. Applied Sciences. Retrieved from mdpi.com

Lu, Y., Zheng, H., Chand, S., Xia, W., Liu, Z., & Xu, X. (2022). Outlook on human-centric manufacturing towards Industry 5.0. Journal of Manufacturing.

Maddikunta, P. K. R., Pham, Q. V., & Prabadevi, B. (2022). *Industry 5.0: A survey on enabling technologies and potential applications. Journal of Industrial.* Elsevier.

Malhotra, A., Majchrzak, A., & Bonfield, W. (2020). Engaging customer care employees in internal collaborative crowd sourcing: Managing the inherent tensions and associated challenges. Human Resource. Retrieved from researchgate.net

Maljugić, B., Ćoćkalo, D., Bakator, M., & Stanisavljev, S. (2024). The role of the quality management process within Society 5.0. Societies. Retrieved from mdpi.com

Martini, B., Bellisario, D., & Coletti, P. (2024). *Human-centered and sustainable artificial intelligence in Industry 5.0: Challenges and perspectives.* Sustainability. MDPI.

Martini, B., Bellisario, D., & Coletti, P. (2024). *Human-centered and sustainable artificial intelligence in Industry 5.0: Challenges and perspectives. Sustainability.* MDPI.

Matheus, R., Janssen, M., & Maheshwari, D. (2020). Data science empowering the public: Data-driven dashboards for transparent and accountable decision-making in smart cities. Government Information Quarterly. Retrieved from sciencedirect.com

Olaitan, J., & Elshennawy, A. (2024). Quality 5.0 architecting: A techno-human-centric integrated framework. IEOM Society. Retrieved from ieomsociety.org

Orlova, E. V. (2021). Design of personal trajectories for employees' professional development in the knowledge society under Industry 5.0. Social Sciences. Retrieved from mdpi.com

Perikangas, S., Kostilainen, H., & Paananen, R. (2022). *A human-centric co-creation platform for solving wicked social challenges.* Social Innovation.

Popo-Olaniyan, O., James, O. O., & Udeh, C. A. (2022). Review of advancing US innovation through collaborative HR ecosystems: A sector-wide perspective. International Journal of... Retrieved from fepbl.com

Rame, R., Purwanto, P., & Sudarno, S. (2024). Industry 5.0 and sustainability: An overview of emerging trends and challenges for a green future. Innovation and Green Development. Retrieved from sciencedirect.com

Ramírez-Gordillo, T., Mora, H., & Pujol-Lopez, F. A. (2023). *Industry 5.0: Towards human-centered design in human-machine interaction. International Research.* Springer.

Sahoo, S. K., & Goswami, S. S. (2023). A comprehensive review of multiple criteria decision-making (MCDM) methods: Advancements, applications, and future directions. Decision Making Advances. Retrieved from dma-journal.org

Saikia, B. (2023). Industry 5.0–Its role toward human society: Obstacles, opportunities, and providing human-centered solutions. In Sustainable Businesses in Emerging Economies: The... Retrieved from [HTML]

Sajjad, A., Ahmad, W., Hussain, S., & Mehmood, R. M. (2021). Development of innovative operational flexibility measurement model for smart systems in Industry 4.0 paradigm. IEEE Access. Retrieved from ieee.org

Sánchez-Franco, M. J., & Rey-Tienda, S. (2024). The role of user-generated content in tourism decision-making: An exemplary study of Andalusia, Spain. Management Decision. Retrieved from emerald.com

Sarkar, B. D., Shardeo, V., Dwivedi, A., & Pamucar, D. (2024). Digital transition from Industry 4.0 to Industry 5.0 in smart manufacturing: A framework for a sustainable future. *Technology in Society*.

Sarkar, B. D., Shardeo, V., Dwivedi, A., & Pamucar, D. (2024). Digital transition from Industry 4.0 to Industry 5.0 in smart manufacturing: A framework for a sustainable future. *Technology in Society*.

Seidl, M. (2022). Corporate digital responsibility: Stimulating human-centric innovation and building trust in the digital world. In *Liquid Legal–Humanization and the Law*. Retrieved from. [HTML]

Shaer, I., & Shami, A. (2023). Data-driven methods for the reduction of energy consumption in warehouses: Use-case driven analysis. *Internet of Things : Engineering Cyber Physical Human Systems*.

Shehzad, N., Ramtiyal, B., & Jabeen, F. (2024). *Metaverse adoption as a cornerstone for sustainable healthcare firms in the industry 5.0 epoch. Journal of Enterprise*. Retrieved from. [HTML]

Suciu, M. C., Plesea, D. A., Petre, A., Simion, A., & Mituca, M. O. (2023). Core competence-as a key factor for a sustainable, innovative, and resilient development model based on Industry 5.0. Sustainability. Retrieved from mdpi.com

Syracuse, V., & Blanco, I. (2020). Bio-polypropylene (Bio-PP) and Bio-poly (ethylene terephthalate) (Bio-PET): Recent developments in bio-based polymers analogous to petroleum-derived ones. Polymers. Retrieved from mdpi.com

Vajda, D. L., Do, T. V., Bérczes, T., & Farkas, K. (2024). Machine learning-based real-time anomaly detection using data pre-processing in the telemetry of server farms. Scientific Reports. Retrieved from nature.com

Vajda, D. L., Do, T. V., Bérczes, T., & Farkas, K. (2024). *Machine learning-based real-time anomaly detection using data pre-processing in the telemetry of server farms*. Scientific Reports, Nature.

Wang, Z. J., Chen, Z. S., Xiao, L., Su, Q., & Govindan, K. (2023). Blockchain adoption in sustainable supply chains for Industry 5.0: A multi-stakeholder perspective. Journal of Innovation &. Retrieved from sciencedirect.com

Xu, X., Lu, Y., Vogel-Heuser, B., & Wang, L. (2021). *Industry 4.0 and Industry 5.0-Inception, conception and perception. Journal of Manufacturing Systems*. ScienceDirect.

Yang, J., Liu, Y., & Morgan, P. L. (2024). Human-machine interaction towards Industry 5.0: Human-centric smart manufacturing. Digital Engineering. Retrieved from sciencedirect.com

Ystgaard, K. F., & De Moor, K. (2023). Envisioning the future: A multi-disciplinary approach to human-centered intelligent environments. *Quality and User Experience*.

Zizic, M. C., Mladineo, M., Gjeldum, N., & Celent, L. (2022). *From Industry 4.0 towards Industry 5.0: A review and analysis of paradigm shift for the people, organization, and technology*. Energies. MDPI.

Zong, L., Memon, F. H., Li, X., & Wang, H. (2021). End-to-end transmission control for cross-regional industrial Internet of Things in Industry 5.0. *IEEE Transactions on Industrial Informatics*.

Chapter 8
Transformation to Digital Economy in the Era of Industry 5.0:
AI Adoption With Technology, Organization, and People (TOP) Framework

Syed Mudasser Abbas
https://orcid.org/0000-0002-6088-2231
Kohat University of Science and Technology, Pakistan

Muhammad Irshad
https://orcid.org/0000-0002-9782-9581
University of Chitral, Pakistan

ABSTRACT

The rise of Industry 5.0 observes a major shift toward the integration of cutting-edge technologies such as Artificial intelligence with the global economic landscape. The purpose of this chapter is to explore the importance of AI adoption in promoting digital economies, illuminating the connectivity of technology, firm strategies, and human resources. Besides, it also highlights transformative potential and the challenges associated with organizational change by addressing the complexities and implications of AI adoption. Essential components of this research are the Technology, Organization and People (TOP) framework, in which an organizational perspective is a comprehensive approach to understanding and improving AI adoption. The findings of this study will contribute to bridging gaps in present knowledge by clarifying key factors in influencing AI integration and providing visions to lead

DOI: 10.4018/979-8-3373-0159-4.ch008

strategies in the transforming digital economy.

INTRODUCTION

The present era of digital economy supported by advanced technology such as AI is changing digital economy by providing both challenges and opportunity at the same time (Bukht & Heeks, 2017). The study of past literature revealed that the concept of digital economy varies across regions. In south Asian countries and beyond, this transformation plays important role in enhancing productivity, developing socio economic. On the other hand, such digitization is packed with challenges like job displacement and privacy concerns. In context of its implication for organizational strategies and employee dynamics, there is a need of comprehensive understanding pertaining to the adoption of AI and complementary complexities. Moreover, optimization and alignment of technological readiness and human factors requires a more strategical approach for better integration of AI into organizational processes (Gloor et al., 2022). Building upon Technology, Organization, and Environment (TOE) framework, the Technology, Organization, and People (TOP) framework is a comprehensive model that incorporates the human-centric perspectives critical for successful adoption of artificial intelligence.

Background

Digital Economy

The digital economy has emerged as a rapidly advancing sector in recent years. Its evolution can be traced from the earlier concept of the information economy to the broader and more integrated framework of the digital economy. A significant milestone occurred in the 1940s with breakthroughs in microelectronics. Later, during the 1980s and 1990s, the convergence of digital and information network technologies spurred the growth of the digital economy, transforming traditional IT structures and business models. This shift laid the groundwork for the rapid advancement of digital technologies such as cloud computing and big data. The term "digital economy" was first introduced by American scholar Don Tapscott in 1996 and was further explored in a landmark study by the U.S. Department of Commerce. In recent years, China has seen a surge in research and literature on the digital economy, including works such as *Introduction to the Digital Economy: Theory, Practice, and Strategy* (2022) by the China Academy of Information and

Communications Technology, and *Theory and Governance of the Digital Economy* (2021) by Dong Yang and Xinyu Xu.

Although researchers and scholars have made significant scholarly contributions to the field of digital economy, especially in developing countries, limited understanding of the concept and definition has so far been developed. The digital economy, in broad sense, is based on business model that utilizes high-end technologies for providing good and services to its customers (Bukht & Heeks, 2017). Furthermore, it includes a broad range of activities that are directly or indirectly using data to achieve resources proficiently and productively (X. Li et al., 2023). The term digital economy is widely used in 21st century for describing the role of telecommunication infrastructure in dynamic global economic growth (Oloyede et al., 2023).

In the last decade, in both private and public sector of south Asian countries, digital economy has gained considerable attention considering its insightful impact on transforming regional economies. Conversely, the traditional economic growth has decreased, advanced version technologies such as mobile internet, cloud computing, artificial intelligence (AI) and big data analytics have boosted digital economies (Fourcade & Kluttz, 2020). As globalization quickens digitalization and IT integration, the world is concentrating on innovation, technology is progressing across borders, making the digital economy key driven behind economic growth (Li et al., 2020). Beyond its advantages, such as creating career opportunities, advancing the economy, strengthening public services, alleviating labor shortage, and scaling up efficiency and productivity etc. However, it also has some disadvantages such as redundancy due to digitalization, the digital divide, privacy concerns and security issues. Although on south Asian countries economy numerous researchers investigated AI influence, however few have examined the complex relationship between AI and digital economy.

Artificial Intelligence

Artificial intelligence (AI) is becoming a vital part of digital transformation. Some view it as sophisticated technology that is designed to imitate intelligence of human (Bohr & Memarzadeh, 2020) while others define it as a set of algorithms or digital and data science methods used to process, analyze and visualize complex information, particularly in areas like human resource management (Tursunbayeva et al., 2021). Recent progress in AI has concentrated on digital data attainment, machine learning and computing infrastructure. Consequently, AI applications that were exclusively managed by human experts are now entering groundbreaking domain. As a result, AI tools are utilized by management and human resource HR as decision support system (Ben-Ga, 2019). Organizational behavior can be affected by AI based HR systems. For instance, the intuition generated by AI and decision support systems can support employees and managers to enhance their performance and change their perceptions by revealing patterns that would otherwise go unnoticed (Gloor et al., 2022).

Organizational factors must be considered to ensure effective adoption and seamless incorporation of artificial intelligence. The alteration to a digital economy often leads to major changes in work processes, tasks, roles and responsibilities (Tursunbayeva et al., 2021). Therefore, effective AI adoption strategies need to be developed by organizations to address employee resistance and ensure a smooth transition to the digital economy (Agrawal et al., 2021). Hence, the successful adoption of AI for transforming the digital economy is only possible when considering the human factor.

Technology, Organization and People (TOP) Nexus

The technology, organization and people (TOP) framework is introduced by Steven (1989) and emerged from socio technical perspective, it highlights the significance of approaching technological, organizational and people related aspects to fully adopt AI inside organizations. The widely known framework TOE by Depietro et al (1990) concentrated on technology, the organization and environment. The TOP framework broadens the research by building focus on individual level and acknowledging the key role of human factor in adopting AI (Gupta et al., 2022). Within the organization, AI adoption for digital transformation requires coordination across the different departments and functions. Building cross functional teams and encouraging collaboration helps sharing knowledge, expertise and specific skills, empowering a more extensive and coordinated approach to digital transformation. People's motivation to accomplish skill task effectively is being affected by the adoption of AI technologies (Uren & Edwards, 2023). This human centered approach acknowledges that technology such as AI independently is not enough to ensure a successful transition to digital economies (Tursunbayeva & Chalutz-Ben Gal, 2024). In conclusion, a connection between technology, organization and people needs to be established for reshaping the digital economy. Therefore, we addressed the necessary gap of exploring the factors that influence the AI adoption at organization and employee level.

The fifth stage of industrial development, so-called Industry 5.0, has become a central element in the economic strategies of many nations. Coined in 2015, the concept of Industry 5.0 is frequently linked to advanced automation, the Internet of Things (IoT), and smart manufacturing systems. According to Özdemir and Hekim (2018), a core aim of Industry 5.0 is the democratization of knowledge production through big data analytics and symmetrical innovation. Similarly, Nahavandi (2019) highlights a critical challenge: boosting productivity without displacing human workers from the production process. Unlike previous industrial revolutions, Industry 5.0 seeks to foster collaboration—not competition—between humans and machines. Doyle-Kent and Kopacek (2019) argue that this paradigm marks a transformative shift in industrial development, comparable to the Fourth Industrial Revolution. In contrast, Rada (2018) and Babkin et al. (2022b) assert that Industry 5.0 should not be viewed as a separate revolution but rather as an evolutionary extension of Industry 4.0, designed to enhance human-robot interaction. Fedorov et al. (2021a; 2021b) frame Industry 5.0 as a foundational requirement for developing neuro-digital ecosystems. Furthermore, Breque et al. (2021) emphasize its role in promoting a sustainable, human-centric, and resilient industrial future.

Organizational-level Factors for AI Adoption

The analysis of the literature revealed that adoption of artificial intelligence for digital economy is strongly influenced by the organizational culture. A company having a culture of working in traditional workflow system finds organizational inertia in adoption of AI in the company. The introduction and implementation of such a culture requires an innovative approach at a firm level which is mostly resisted to maintain the status quo. The introduction of innovative culture requires top management support.

1. Leadership and Management Support

Leadership plays a pivotal role in shaping organizational readiness for AI adoption. The trust of the employees in AI system, critical in the pre-adoption stage, can be significantly increased through the development of trustworthy leadership (Xu et al., 2024). Strong managerial capabilities are also linked to improved organizational culture and communication, which are vital for fostering an environment conducive to innovation (Mikalef & Gupta, 2021). Moreover, active support from top management is identified as a critical factor that can drive AI adoption by ensuring that the necessary resources and strategic vision are in place (Zhang et al., 2024). Therefore, effective leadership is fundamental to navigating the complexities of AI integration.

2. Attitude of Employee Towards AI

The attitudes of employees towards artificial intelligence (AI) are critical for its successful adoption within organizations. Positive employee attitudes can facilitate the integration of AI technologies, as individuals are more likely to embrace innovations they perceive as beneficial. A study highlights that employees' behavioral intentions to use AI are significantly influenced by their affective attitudes towards these technologies (Akyazı, 2023). Furthermore, a collectivistic organizational culture can enhance these attitudes, fostering a supportive environment for AI adoption (Xu et al., 2024). Thus, cultivating a positive perception of AI among employees is essential for organizations aiming to implement AI solutions effectively.

3. Technological Readiness

Technological readiness encompasses the existing infrastructure and resources necessary for AI adoption. Organizations must assess their technological capabilities, including data quality and IT infrastructure, to ensure they can support AI initiatives (Udayanan et al., 2024). The availability of skilled personnel who can manage and implement AI technologies is also a critical factor (Bobitan et al., 2024). Furthermore, organizations need to evaluate their readiness to integrate AI into existing processes, as this can significantly impact the success of AI initiatives (Olutimehin et al., 2024). Therefore, a thorough understanding of technological readiness is essential for organizations aiming to leverage AI effectively. Adapting to strategic transition to Industry 5.0 necessitates the implementation of new digital solutions and tools for the digital strategizing of industrial systems. Consequently, the development of digital strategies has become a prominent focus in contemporary scientific research. Notably, studies by Zhuravlev and Glukhov (2021), Koroleva and Kuratova (2020), Albukhitan (2020), Hess et al. (2016), and Matt et al. (2015) explore the digital transformation strategies within economic systems. In parallel, broader approaches to the digitalization of various processes are examined by Sasev (2021), Ludwig and Stegmann (2021), and García-Esteban et al. (2021). Moreover, specific digital tools and technologies relevant to strategizing—such as digital twins and artificial intelligence—are investigated in the works of Surovitskaya (2021) and Simchenko et al. (2021). Researchers who are actively engaged in the field of digital strategizing include Morton et al. (2022), Glukhov et al. (2022), Babkin et al. (2022a), Kalinin (2021), Morton et al. (2020), Ruel et al. (2020), and Chanias et al. (2019).

4. Organizational Culture

Organizational culture is a significant determinant of AI adoption, as it influences how employees perceive and interact with new technologies. A culture that promotes innovation and adaptability can enhance the likelihood of successful AI implementation (Oyekunle & Boohene, 2024). Studies indicate that a supportive organizational culture, characterized by openness to change and collaboration, can facilitate the acceptance of AI technologies (Wael et al., 2024). Additionally, the mediating role of organizational culture in the relationship between managerial support and AI adoption further underscores its importance (Al-Shanti et al., 2024).

Thus, fostering a culture that embraces technological advancements is crucial for organizations seeking to adopt AI.

5. Skills and Training

The integration of AI into organizational processes necessitates a workforce equipped with the requisite skills. As AI technologies evolve, employees must undergo continuous training to adapt to new tools and methodologies (Bobitan et al., 2024). Organizations should invest in upskilling and reskilling initiatives to prepare their workforce for the demands of an AI-driven environment (Zirar et al., 2023). The necessity for strong interpersonal and cognitive skills, alongside technical expertise, is emphasized as essential for effectively collaborating with AI systems (Bobitan et al., 2024). Therefore, commitment to employee development is vital for successful AI adoption.

6. Regulatory and Ethical Considerations

Regulatory frameworks and ethical considerations play a crucial role in AI adoption. Organizations must navigate various legal and ethical challenges associated with AI, including data privacy and bias mitigation (Olutimehin et al., 2024). The presence of supportive regulatory environments can facilitate AI adoption by providing clear guidelines and frameworks for implementation (Wael et al., 2024). Additionally, ethical integration of AI into organizational practices is essential to maintain employee trust and ensure that AI technologies are used responsibly (Bar-Gil et al., 2024). Thus, organizations must prioritize regulatory compliance and ethical considerations to foster a sustainable AI adoption process.

7. Perceived Benefits and Usefulness

The perceived benefits and usefulness of AI technologies are crucial factors influencing adoption decisions. Employees and management must recognize the potential advantages of AI, such as improved decision-making and enhanced productivity, to foster acceptance (Alasmri & Basahe, 2022). Studies indicate that perceived usefulness directly correlates with the intention to adopt AI technologies (Wael et al., 2024). Therefore, organizations should communicate the tangible benefits of AI to encourage buy-in from stakeholders and facilitate a smoother adoption process.

8. Resource Availability

The availability of resources, including financial, technological, and human capital, significantly influences AI adoption. Organizations must allocate sufficient resources to support AI initiatives, including investments in technology and training (Oyekunle & Boohene, 2024). The ability to reallocate resources strategically can enhance an organization's capacity to integrate AI effectively (D. Chen et al., 2022). Moreover, organizations that demonstrate a commitment to resource availability are more likely to experience successful AI adoption and implementation (Olutimehin et al., 2024). Thus, ensuring adequate resource allocation is critical for organizations pursuing AI integration.

9. Change Management Strategies

Effective change management strategies are essential for facilitating AI adoption within organizations. The transition to AI-integrated processes can be met with resistance from employees; therefore, organizations must implement comprehensive change management practices to address concerns and foster acceptance (Dabbous et al., 2022). This includes clear communication, stakeholder engagement, and support systems to assist employees during the transition (Olutimehin et al., 2024). By prioritizing change management, organizations can enhance the likelihood of successful AI adoption and integration.

10. Environmental Dynamics

External environmental factors, including market competition and technological trends, can significantly impact AI adoption. Organizations must remain attuned to changes in the external environment that may necessitate the adoption of AI technologies to maintain competitiveness (H. Chen et al., 2021). Additionally, the influence of customer demands and industry standards can drive organizations to integrate AI into their operations (Oyekunle & Boohene, 2024). Thus, understanding and responding to environmental dynamics is essential for organizations looking to adopt AI effectively.

Employee Level Factors for AI Adoption

1. Knowledge and Awareness of AI

The level of knowledge and awareness employees possess regarding AI technologies plays a crucial role in their adoption. Employees who understand how AI works and its potential applications are more likely to embrace these technologies (Hornung & Smolnik, 2022). Studies have shown that a lack of understanding can lead to resistance and apprehension towards AI, as employees may fear the unknown implications of these technologies on their roles (He et al., 2024). Therefore, organizations should prioritize educational initiatives that enhance employees' knowledge about AI, thereby reducing anxiety and fostering a more accepting environment for AI adoption.

2. Skills and Competencies

The skills and competencies of employees are vital for the successful integration of AI within organizations. Employees must possess not only technical skills to operate AI systems but also soft skills such as adaptability and critical thinking to work alongside AI technologies effectively (Indrasari & Pamuji, 2024). Research suggests that organizations should focus on upskilling and reskilling their workforce to prepare them for the demands of an AI-driven environment (Panda et al., 2024). By investing in employee development, organizations can enhance their workforce's capabilities, facilitating smoother AI adoption and integration.

3. Perceived Job Security

Perceived job security is a significant factor influencing employee acceptance of AI technologies. Employees who feel threatened by the potential for AI to replace their jobs may exhibit resistance to its adoption (Liu et al., 2025). Studies indicate that organizations must address these concerns by communicating the complementary role of AI in enhancing job performance rather than replacing human workers (Wijayati et al., 2022). By fostering a sense of job security and emphasizing the value of human contributions alongside AI, organizations can mitigate resistance and promote a more positive outlook towards AI adoption.

4. Organizational Identification

The degree to which employees identify with their organization can impact their acceptance of AI technologies. Employees with a strong organizational identification are more likely to embrace changes, including the adoption of AI, as they feel a sense of belonging and commitment to their organization (Liu et al., 2025). Research highlights that enhancing organizational identification can help mitigate the negative impacts of AI on employee morale and engagement (Iram et al., 2024). Therefore, organizations should cultivate a strong sense of identity and community among employees to facilitate smoother AI integration.

5. Change Management and Support

Effective change management practices are essential for guiding employees through the transition to AI integration. Employees often experience uncertainty and stress during periods of change, making it crucial for organizations to provide adequate support (Jeong et al., 2024). Studies suggest that organizations should implement comprehensive change management strategies that include clear communication, training, and resources to assist employees in adapting to new AI technologies (Dabbous et al., 2022). By prioritizing change management, organizations can foster a supportive environment that encourages employee acceptance of AI.

6. Trust in AI Systems

Trust in AI systems is a critical factor influencing employee adoption. Employees must have confidence in the reliability and fairness of AI technologies to engage with them effectively (Panda et al., 2024). Research indicates that transparency in AI decision-making processes and the establishment of ethical guidelines can enhance trust among employees (Qamar et al., 2021). Organizations should prioritize building trust by ensuring that AI systems are designed with fairness and accountability in mind, thereby promoting greater acceptance and utilization of these technologies.

7. Work Environment and Culture

The work environment and organizational culture significantly impact employee attitudes towards AI adoption. A culture that promotes innovation, collaboration, and open communication can enhance employee engagement with AI technologies (Rožman & Tominc, 2024). Studies suggest that organizations should foster a positive work environment that encourages experimentation and supports employees in navigating the challenges associated with AI integration (Fousiani et al., 2024).

By cultivating a culture that values technological advancement, organizations can facilitate a more favorable atmosphere for AI adoption.

8. Emotional and Psychological Factors

Emotional and psychological factors, including stress and anxiety related to AI adoption, can influence employee acceptance. Employees may experience fear of obsolescence or concerns about their ability to adapt to new technologies (He et al., 2024). Research indicates that organizations should address these emotional factors by providing support systems, such as counseling and training, to help employees manage their concerns (Jeong et al., 2024). By acknowledging and addressing the psychological impacts of AI adoption, organizations can promote a more positive employee experience and facilitate smoother integration.

9. Employee Engagement and Involvement

Employee engagement and involvement in the AI adoption process can significantly enhance acceptance. When employees are actively involved in decision-making and implementation processes, they are more likely to feel a sense of ownership and commitment to the changes (Wijayati et al., 2022). Research suggests that organizations should encourage employee participation in AI initiatives, allowing them to voice their concerns and contribute to the development of AI strategies (Hughes et al., 2019). By fostering engagement, organizations can create a more inclusive environment that supports successful AI adoption.

Figure 1. Organizational and employee-level factors of AI adoption

DISCUSSION

The adoption of artificial intelligence (AI) within organizations is a multifaceted process influenced by various factors at the technology, organization, and people (TOP) levels. At the technology level, the characteristics of AI systems, such as their complexity and perceived usefulness, play a crucial role in shaping employee attitudes and intentions towards adoption. Research indicates that the perceived ease of use and the ability of AI systems to enhance job performance significantly influence employees' willingness to engage with these technologies (Kim et al., 2024). Moreover, the integration of AI into existing workflows must be seamless to minimize disruption and resistance from employees, as highlighted by studies emphasizing the importance of understanding how AI tools fit into organizational processes (Owoyemi et al., 2024). Thus, organizations must carefully evaluate the technological attributes of AI systems to ensure they align with employee needs and organizational goals. The development of digital strategies has become a prominent focus in contemporary scientific research. Notably, studies by Zhuravlev and Glukhov (2021), Koroleva and Kuratova (2020), Albukhitan (2020), Hess et al. (2016), and Matt et al. (2015) explore the digital transformation strategies within economic systems. In parallel, broader approaches to the digitalization of various processes are examined by Sasev (2021), Ludwig and Stegmann (2021), and García-Esteban et al. (2021). Moreover, specific digital tools and technologies relevant to strategizing—such as digital twins and artificial intelligence—are investigated in the works of Surovitskaya (2021) and Simchenko et al. (2021). Researchers who are actively engaged in the field of digital strategizing include Morton et al. (2022), Glukhov et al. (2022), Babkin et al. (2022a), Kalinin (2021), Morton et al. (2020), Ruel et al. (2020), and Chanias et al. (2019).

At the organizational level, factors such as leadership support, organizational culture, and resource availability are critical for fostering an environment conducive to AI adoption. Leadership plays a pivotal role in establishing a vision for AI integration and providing the necessary resources and training to employees (Chatterjee et al., 2020). A supportive organizational culture that encourages innovation and collaboration can enhance employee engagement with AI technologies, as employees are more likely to embrace change when they feel valued and supported (Udayanan et al., 2024). Furthermore, organizations must ensure that they have the necessary infrastructure and resources to facilitate AI adoption, as inadequate support can lead to frustration and resistance among employees (Indrasari & Pamuji, 2024). Therefore, a holistic approach that encompasses both technological and organizational considerations is essential for successful AI integration.

Finally, at the people level, individual employee factors such as attitudes, skills, and perceived job security significantly impact the adoption of AI technologies. Employees' attitudes towards AI, shaped by their experiences and organizational support, can either facilitate or hinder adoption (Kim et al., 2024). Additionally, the skills and competencies of employees are vital for effectively leveraging AI technologies; organizations must invest in training and development to equip their workforce with the necessary skills (Wang, 2023). Perceived job security also plays a crucial role, as employees who feel threatened by AI's potential to automate their roles may resist its adoption. Therefore, organizations must prioritize employee engagement and support, addressing concerns related to job security and fostering a positive attitude towards AI to ensure successful adoption.

Practical Contributions: A Way Forward for Tech Leaders

For technology leaders navigating the complexities of AI adoption in the digital economy, a strategic and human-centric approach is essential. The Technology, Organization, and People (TOP) framework provide a practical roadmap to ensure AI implementation aligns with organizational objectives while fostering employee engagement and technological readiness. First, tech leaders must prioritize AI literacy and workforce development by investing in reskilling and upskilling programs that equip employees with the necessary digital competencies. AI adoption should not be seen as merely a technological shift but as an organizational transformation that requires continuous learning and adaptation. Establishing cross-functional AI task forces can further drive collaboration between technical teams, HR, and business leaders, ensuring that AI solutions are seamlessly integrated into workflows without disrupting productivity. To embrace Industry 5.0, the leadership must be optimistic. This new phase blending human creativity with advanced technologies like AI, robotics, and IoT—offered tremendous potential. But beneath the surface of innovation, a quiet but powerful resistance began to grow among the employees. For many, the memories of automation and job insecurity from Industry 4.0 still lingered. Some feared being replace by robots, others were overwhelmed by the thought of upskilling. The challenge to bring people along in the journey without losing their trust or engagement is to establish a transparent communication. Instead of corporate jargon, leaders used real-life examples. They explained how Industry 5.0 was not about replacing humans but partnering technology with human insight enhancing creativity, personalization, and well-being.

Moreover, leadership commitment and cultural transformation are pivotal for sustaining AI adoption. Tech leaders must actively champion AI initiatives, promoting an innovation-driven culture that minimizes resistance and encourages experimentation. Transparent communication about AI's role in augmenting rather than replacing human jobs can alleviate fears related to job security, fostering trust and acceptance among employees. Additionally, ethical AI governance frameworks must be implemented to ensure responsible AI deployment, addressing concerns about bias, privacy, and data security. By embedding AI ethics into corporate policies and aligning AI strategies with business objectives, tech leaders can enhance organizational agility and long-term competitiveness. Ultimately, organizations that strike a balance between technological advancements and human-centric strategies will be better positioned to harness AI's full potential, driving innovation, efficiency, and sustainable growth in the digital economy.

CONCLUSION

The integration of artificial intelligence (AI) into the digital economy presents both opportunities and challenges, particularly within the context of South Asian economies. As AI continues to drive digital transformation, its adoption must be carefully managed through a strategic approach that considers technological readiness, organizational culture, and human factors. The Technology, Organization, and People (TOP) framework provide a comprehensive model for understanding AI adoption, emphasizing the interplay between technological infrastructure, leadership support, and workforce adaptability. While AI offers benefits such as enhanced productivity, economic growth, and innovation, its successful implementation depends on overcoming barriers such as employee resistance, ethical concerns, and the digital divide. Addressing these challenges requires strong leadership, investment in training and skill development, and fostering a culture that embraces technological change.

At the organizational level, AI adoption is significantly influenced by leadership vision, resource allocation, and change management strategies. Employee attitudes, trust in AI systems, and perceived job security are equally critical in determining AI acceptance and usage. Organizations must implement inclusive strategies that engage employees, provide transparent communication, and ensure that AI enhances rather than threatens job roles. Moreover, regulatory and ethical considerations must be carefully navigated to maintain trust and fairness in AI deployment. As AI continues to shape the digital economy, organizations that effectively balance technological capabilities with human-centric strategies will be better positioned to drive sustainable growth, innovation, and competitive advantage in the evolving economic landscape.

REFERENCES

Agrawal, A. K., Gans, J. S., & Goldfarb, A. (2021). *AI Adoption and System-Wide Change* (No. 28811).

Akyazı, T. E. (2023). A Study on the Relationship between Employees' Attitude towards Artificial Intelligence and Organizational Culture. *Asian Journal of Economics. Business and Accounting*, *23*(20), 207–219.

Al-Shanti, A., Jebreel, M., Qabajeh, M., Nassoura, A., & Airout, R. (2024). The role of organizational antecedents in fostering accounting intelligence adoption: The mediating influence of organizational culture. *Human Systems Management*, *43*(4), 495–511.

Al Wael, H., Abdallah, W., Ghura, H., & Buallay, A. (2024). Factors influencing artificial intelligence adoption in the accounting profession: The case of public sector in Kuwait. *Competitiveness Review*, *34*(1), 3–27.

Alasmri, N., & Basahe, S. (2022). Linking Artificial Intelligence Use to Improved Decision-Making, Individual and Organizational Outcomes. *International Business Research*, *15*(10), 1–15.

Bar-Gil, O., Ron, T., & Czerniak, O. (2024). AI for the people? Embedding AI ethics in HR and people analytics projects. *Technology in Society*, *77*, 102527. https://doi.org/https://doi.org/10.1016/j.techsoc.2024.102527

Ben-Ga, H. C. (2019). An ROI-based review of HR analytics: Practical implementation tools. *Personnel Review*, *48*(6), 1429–1448.

Bobitan, N., Dumitrescu, D., Popa, A. F., Sahlian, D. N., & Turlea, I. C. (2024). Shaping Tomorrow: Anticipating Skills Requirements Based on the Integration of Artificial Intelligence in Business Organizations—A Foresight Analysis Using the Scenario Method. *Electronics (Basel)*, *13*(11), 2198.

Bohr, A., & Memarzadeh, K. (2020). The rise of artificial intelligence in healthcare applications. In *Artificial Intelligence in Healthcare* (pp. 25–60). Academic Press.

Bukht, R., & Heeks, R. (2017). *Defining, conceptualising and measuring the digital economy*.

Chatterjee, S., Nguyen, B., Ghosh, S. K., Bhattacharjee, K. K., & Chaudhuri, S. (2020). Adoption of artificial intelligence integrated CRM system: An empirical study of Indian organizations. *The Bottom Line (New York, N.Y.)*, *33*(4), 359–375. https://doi.org/https://doi.org/10.1108/BL-08-2020-0057

Chen, D., ESPERANÇA, J., & Wang, S. (2022). The impact of artificial intelligence on firm performance: An application of the resource-based view to e-commerce firms. *Frontiers in Psychology*, *13*, 884830. PMID: 35465474

Chen, H., Li, L., & Chen, Y. (2021). Explore success factors that impact artificial intelligence adoption on telecom industry in China. *Journal of Management Analytics*, *8*(1), 36–68.

Dabbous, A., Barakat, K. A., & Sayegh, M. M. (2022). Enabling organizational use of artificial intelligence: An employee perspective. *Journal of Asia Business Studies*, *16*(2), 245–266.

Depietro, R., Wiarda, E., & Fleischer, M. (1990). *The processes of technological innovation*. Lexington Books.

Fourcade, M., & Kluttz, D. N. (2020). A Maussian bargain: Accumulation by gift in the digital economy. *Big Data & Society*, *7*(1).

Fousiani, K., Michelakis, G., Minnigh, P. A., & De Jonge, K. M. M. (2024). Competitive organizational climate and artificial intelligence (AI) acceptance: The moderating role of leaders' power construal. *Frontiers in Psychology*, *15*, 1359164. PMID: 38596327

Gloor, P., Colladon, A. F., & Grippa, F. (2022). Measuring ethical behavior with AI and natural language processing to assess business success. *Scientific Reports*, *12*(1), 10228. PMID: 35715458

Gupta, S., Leszkiewicz, A., & Potapov, D. (2022). Digital Analytics: Modeling for Insights and New Methods. *Journal of Interactive Marketing*, *51*(1), 26–43.

He, C., Teng, R., & Song, J. (2024). Linking employees' challenge-hindrance appraisals toward AI to service performance: The influences of job crafting, job insecurity and AI knowledge. *International Journal of Contemporary Hospitality Management*, *36*(3), 975–994.

Hornung, O., & Smolnik, S. (2022). AI invading the workplace: Negative emotions towards the organizational use of personal virtual assistants. *Electronic Markets*, *32*(1), 123–138.

Hughes, C., Robert, L., Frady, K., & Arroyos, A. (2019). *Artificial Intelligence*. Employee Engagement, Fairness, and Job Outcomes.

Indrasari, M., & Pamuji, E. (2024). Enhancing Employee Performance through Strategic Initiatives. *Journal of Business Management and Economic Development*, *2*(1), 383–396.

Iram, T., Bilal, A. R., Khan, R., Mehmood, S., & Kumar, H. (2024). From awareness to action: unraveling the interplay of employee AI awareness and change leadership in fostering knowledge hiding. *Kybernetes, ahead-of-p*(ahead-of-print).

Jeong, J., Kim, B.-J., & Lee, J. (2024). Navigating AI transitions: How coaching leadership buffers against job stress and protects employee physical health. *Frontiers in Public Health*, *12*, 1343932. PMID: 38601504

Kim, Y., Blazquez, V., & Oh, T. (2024). Determinants of Generative AI System Adoption and Usage Behavior in Korean Companies: Applying the UTAUT Model. *Behavioral Sciences (Basel, Switzerland)*, *14*(11), 1035. PMID: 39594336

Li, K., Kim, D. J., Lang, K. R., Kauffman, R. J., & Naldi, M. (2020). How should we understand the digital economy in Asia? Critical assessment and research agenda. *Electronic Commerce Research and Applications*, *44*, 101004. PMID: 32922241

Li, X., Wang, H., & Yang, C. (2023). Driving mechanism of digital economy based on regulation algorithm for development of low-carbon industries. *Sustainable Energy Technologies and Assessments*, *55*, 102909.

Liu, P., Yuan, L., & Jiang, Z. (2025). The dark side of algorithmic management: Investigating how and when algorithmic management relates to employee knowledge hiding? *Journal of Knowledge Management*, *29*(2), 342–371.

Mikalef, P., & Gupta, M. (2021). Artificial intelligence capability: Conceptualization, measurement calibration, and empirical study on its impact on organizational creativity and firm performance. *Information & Management*, *58*(3), 103434. https://doi.org/https://doi.org/10.1016/j.im.2021.103434

Oloyede, A. A., Faruk, N., Noma, N., Tebepah, E., & Nwaulune, A. K. (2023). Measuring the impact of the digital economy in developing countries: A systematic review and meta- analysis. *Heliyon*, •••, 9. PMID: 37501966

Olutimehin, D. O., Ofodile, O. C., Ejibe, I., Odunaiya, O. G., & Soyombo, O. T. (2024). Implementing Ai in Business Models: Strategies for Efficiency and Innovation. *International Journal of Management & Entrepreneurship Research*, *6*(3), 863–877.

Owoyemi, A., Okpara, E., Salwei, M., & Boyd, A. (2024). End user experience of a widely used artificial intelligence based sepsis system. *JAMIA Open*, *7*(4), ooae096. PMID: 39386065

Oyekunle, D., & Boohene, D. (2024). Digital Transformation Potential: The Role of Artificial Intelligence in Business. *International Journal of Professional Business Review*, *9*(3), 1.

Panda, G., Dash, M. K., Samadhiya, A., Kumar, A., & Mulat-weldemeskel, E. (2024). Artificial intelligence as an enabler for achieving human resource resiliency: Past literature, present debate and future research directions. *International Journal of Industrial Engineering and Operations Management*, *6*(4), 326–347.

Qamar, Y., Agrawal, R. K., Samad, T. A., & Jabbour, C. J. C. (2021). When technology meets people: The interplay of artificial intelligence and human resource management. *Journal of Enterprise Information Management*, *34*(5), 1339–1370.

Rožman, M., & Tominc, P. (2024). Navigating Gender Nuances: Assessing the Impact of AI on Employee Engagement in Slovenian Entrepreneurship. *Systems*, *12*(5), 145.

Tursunbayeva, A., & Chalutz-Ben Gal, H. (2024). Adoption of artificial intelligence: A TOP framework-based checklist for digital leaders. *Business Horizons*. Advance online publication. DOI: 10.1016/j.bushor.2024.04.006

Tursunbayeva, A., Pagliari, C., Di Lauro, S., & Antonelli, G. (2021). The ethics of people analytics: Risks, opportunities and recommendations. *Personnel Review*, *51*(3), 900–921.

Udayanan, Rooshma, A., Bargavi, D. N., Awasthi, D. S., Deshmukh, D. S. V., & Jadhav, D. D. Y. (2024). Determinants Influencing the Adoption of Artificial Intelligence in Driving Effective Human Resource Management. *Journal of Informatics Education and Research*, *4*(2).

Uren, V., & Edwards, J. S. (2023). Technology readiness and the organizational journey towards AI adoption: An empirical study. *International Journal of Information Management*, *68*, 102588.

Wang, Q. (2023). The Impact of AI on Organizational Employees: A Literature Review. *Journal of Education. Humanities and Social Sciences*, *19*, 45–53.

Wijayati, D. T., Rahman, Z., Fahrullah, A., Rahman, M. F. W., Arifah, I. D. C., & Kautsar, A. (2022). A study of artificial intelligence on employee performance and work engagement: The moderating role of change leadership. *International Journal of Manpower*, *43*(2), 486–512.

Xu, Y., Huang, Y., Wang, J., & Zhou, D. (2024). How do employees form initial trust in artificial intelligence: Hard to explain but leaders help. *Asia Pacific Journal of Human Resources*, *62*(3), e12402.

Zhang, X., Antwi-Afari, M. F., Zhang, Y., & Xing, X. (2024). The Impact of Artificial Intelligence on Organizational Justice and Project Performance: A Systematic Literature and Science Mapping Review. *Buildings (Basel, Switzerland)*, *14*(1), 259.

Zirar, A., Ali, S. I., & Islam, N. (2023). Worker and workplace Artificial Intelligence (AI) coexistence: Emerging themes and research agenda. *Technovation*, *124*, 102747.

KEY TERMS AND DEFINITION

Digital Economy: Digital economy is a segment of economy that relies on digital technology and depends on business models arranged by digital goods and services.

Artificial Intelligence (AI): Artificial intelligence is a set of algorithms or digital and data science methods used to process, analyze and visualize complex information, particularly in areas like human resource management.

Technology, Organization and People (TOP) Framework: The technology, organization and people (TOP) framework, emerging from socio technical perspective, highlights the significance of approaching technological, organizational and people related aspects to fully adopt AI inside organizations.

Industry 5.0: Industry 5.0 is a vision for the future of industry building upon Industry 4.0, advocating human-machine augmentation, resilience, and sustainability, with the aim of well-being of employees.

Technological Readiness: Technological readiness includes the existing infrastructural support and resources essential for the adoption of AI.

Organizational Identification: Organizational identification is the degree to which an employee perceives a sense of belonging to their company, defining themselves in terms of their membership and values.

Employee Engagement: Employee engagement refers to the level of commitment and enthusiasm an employee experience in their workplace, resulting in higher productivity and performance.

Compilation of References

Abhinav, K.. (2020). Blue economy: Opportunities and challenges. *International Journal of Management, 11*(7), 1348–1357.

Abimbola, C., Eden, C. A., Chisom, O. N., & Adeniyi, I. S. (2024). Integrating AI in education: Opportunities, challenges, and ethical considerations. *Magna Scientia Advanced Research and Reviews, 10*(2), 6–13. DOI: 10.30574/msarr.2024.10.2.0039

Adams, R. (2024). *The new empire of AI: the future of global inequality*. John Wiley & Sons.

Adel, A. (2023). *Unlocking the future: Fostering human–machine collaboration and driving intelligent automation through Industry 5.0 in smart cities*. Smart Cities.

Adel, A., & Alani, N. H. S. (2024). *Human-centric collaboration and Industry 5.0 framework in smart cities and communities: Fostering sustainable development goals 3, 4, 9, and 11 in Society 5.0*. Smart Cities.

Adler, P. A., & Adler, P. (2020). The Role of Ethnography in Understanding the Global Community of Digital Nomads. *Journal of Global Mobility, 8*(3), 267–282.

Agrawal, A. K., Gans, J. S., & Goldfarb, A. (2021). *AI Adoption and System-Wide Change* (No. 28811).

Ahmad, Z., Ammar, M., Siby, N., Bhadra, J., Sellami, A., & Al-Thani, N. J. (2023). Do research experience programs promote capacity building in Qatar: Investigating the trend and participation differences. *Heliyon*. https://www.cell.com/heliyon/fulltext/S2405-8440(23)09279-4

Ahmed, F. M. (2020). *The adoption of artificial intelligence in the UAE education sector* [Master's thesis, The British University in Dubai]. https://bspace.buid.ac.ae

Akundi, A., Euresti, D., Luna, S., & Ankobiah, W. (2022). *State of Industry 5.0-Analysis and identification of current research trends*. Applied System. MDPI.

Akyazı, T. E. (2023). A Study on the Relationship between Employees' Attitude towards Artificial Intelligence and Organizational Culture. *Asian Journal of Economics. Business and Accounting*, *23*(20), 207–219.

Al Wael, H., Abdallah, W., Ghura, H., & Buallay, A. (2024). Factors influencing artificial intelligence adoption in the accounting profession: The case of public sector in Kuwait. *Competitiveness Review*, *34*(1), 3–27.

Alach, P. (2020). Digital Nomad Visas: A Comparative Analysis of National Policies and Programs. *Journal of International Mobility*, *3*(1), 45–63.

Alasmri, N., & Basahe, S. (2022). Linking Artificial Intelligence Use to Improved Decision-Making, Individual and Organizational Outcomes. *International Business Research*, *15*(10), 1–15.

Aldawsari, F. I. (2023). *Understanding policy enactment of technology in Saudi Arabia: Three case studies in intermediate schools pursuing the Future Gate Project* (Doctoral dissertation, Flinders University). https://flex.flinders.edu.au/file/62afc95c-6b89-4134-813c-cedb8f7bdde1/1/AldawsariThesis2023.pdf

Alfaraz, C., & Tully, C. (2024). Mobilizing social transformation with technology. The shaping of social processes since the development of industrial society and beyond: Innovation input and social processes. *Innovation (Abingdon)*, •••, 1–17.

Allal-Chérif, O., Guijarro-García, M., Ballester-Miquel, J. C., & Carrilero-Castillo, A. (2021). Being an ethical leader during the apocalypse: Lessons from The Walking Dead to face the COVID-19 crisis. *Journal of Business Research*, *133*, 354–364. PMID: 36540061

AlNuaimi, B. K., Singh, S. K., Ren, S., Budhwar, P., & Vorobyev, D. (2022). Mastering digital transformation: The nexus between leadership, agility, and digital strategy. *Journal of Business Research*, *145*, 636–648. DOI: 10.1016/j.jbusres.2022.03.067

Aloisi, A., & De Stefano, V. (2022). *Your boss is an algorithm: artificial intelligence, platform work and labour*. Bloomsbury Publishing.

Al-Shanti, A., Jebreel, M., Qabajeh, M., Nassoura, A., & Airout, R. (2024). The role of organizational antecedents in fostering accounting intelligence adoption: The mediating influence of organizational culture. *Human Systems Management*, *43*(4), 495–511.

Alswedani, S., Mehmood, R., & Katib, I. (2022). Sustainable participatory governance: Data-driven discovery of parameters for planning online and in-class Education in Saudi Arabia during COVID-19. *Frontiers in Sustainable Cities*, 871171. https://www.frontiersin.org/articles/10.3389/frsc.2022.871171

Alswedani, S., Mehmood, R., & Katib, I. (2022). Sustainable participatory governance: Data-driven discovery of parameters for planning online and in-class education in Saudi Arabia during COVID-19. *Frontiers in Sustainable Cities, 871171*. https://www.frontiersin.org/journals/sustainable-cities/articles/10.3389/frsc.2022.871171/full

Alswedani, S., Mehmood, R., & Katib, I. (2022). Sustainable participatory governance: Data-driven discovery of parameters for planning online and in-class education in Saudi Arabia during COVID-19. *Frontiers in Sustainable Cities*. https://doi.org/ DOI: 10.3389/frsc.2022.871171

Alyammahi, A. H. (2019). The impact of Alef Platform on students' performance at Al Asayel School in Abu Dhabi, UAE. Retrieved from https://bspace.buid.ac.ae/buid_server/api/core/bitstreams/e8fc67ed-8575-406a-a1bc-baa383844f3c/content

Amazon. (2021). Amazon Upskilling Report 2021. Retrieved from https://assets.aboutamazon.com/80/a2/7e01e544475aaf15b4f8d5067cc6/amazon-upskilling-report-final.pdf

Ambarita, A. A.. (2024). Digital twin development towards integration into blue economy: A bibliometric analysis. *Sustainability*, *16*(18), 8072.

Ambarita, E. E., Karlsen, A., Scibilia, F., & Hasan, A. (2024). Industrial digital twins in offshore wind farms. *Energy Informatics*, *7*, 5. Advance online publication. DOI: 10.1186/s42162-024-00005-4

Ambrozi, A. (2023). 11 Challenges Of Adopting AI In Business (And How To Address Them Head-On). Forbes. Retrieved from https://www.forbes.com/councils/forbesbusinesscouncil/2023/10/24/11-challenges-of-adopting-ai-in-business-and-how-to-address-them-head-on/

Amin, S. M., El-Gazar, H. E., Zoromba, M. A., El-Sayed, M. M., & Atta, M. H. R. (2025). Sentiment of nurses towards artificial intelligence and resistance to change in healthcare organisations: A mixed-method study. *Journal of Advanced Nursing*, *81*(4), 2087–2098. PMID: 39235193

Antonopoulou, H., Halkiopoulos, C., Barlou, O., & Beligiannis, G. N. (2021). Associations between traditional and digital leadership in academic environments during the COVID-19 pandemic. *Emerging Science Journal*, *5*. Advance online publication. DOI: 10.28991/esj-2021-01286

Ariganello, J. (2024). *Council Post: AI and the C-Suite: Crafting Compelling Narratives for Executive Buy-In*. Forbes. https://www.forbes.com/councils/forbescommunicationscouncil/2024/10/29/ai-and-the-c-suite-crafting-compelling-narratives-for-executive-buy-in/

Aroles, J., Granter, E., & de Vaujany, F. X. (2020). 'Becoming mainstream': The professionalisation and corporatisation of digital nomadism. *New Technology, Work and Employment*, *35*(1), 114–129.

Arvind Mallik, D. M. (2024). Promoting Green Innovation in India's Industry 4.0: Paving the Way to a Net-Zero Economy. In Singh, R., Khan, S., Kumar, A., Luthra, S., & Chokshi, H. (Eds.), *Net Zero Economy, Corporate Social Responsibility and Sustainable Value Creation. CSR, Sustainability, Ethics & Governance*. Springer., DOI: 10.1007/978-3-031-55779-8_13

Atiku, S. O., Jeremiah, A., Semente, E., & Boateng, F. (2024). *Eco-innovation and sustainable development in Industry 5.0.* Retrieved from. [HTML]

Autor, D. H. (2015). Why are there still so many jobs? The history and future of workplace automation. *The Journal of Economic Perspectives*, *29*(3), 3–30. DOI: 10.1257/jep.29.3.3

Autsadee, Y., Jeevan, J., Mohd Salleh, N. H. B., & Othman, M. R. B. (2023). Digital tools and challenges in human resource development and its potential within the maritime sector through bibliometric analysis. *Journal of International Maritime Safety, Environmental Affairs, and Shipping*, *7*(4), 2286409. DOI: 10.1080/25725084.2023.2286409

Ayeni, O. O., Al Hamad, N. M., Chisom, O. N., Osawaru, B., & Adewusi, O. E. (2024). AI in education: A review of personalized learning and educational technology. *GSC Advanced Research and Reviews*, *18*(2), 261–271.

Azam, M. S., & Ponnam, A. (2023). Disparity in Agri-Marketing Challenges in India: Organic vs. Conventional Food Producers. *Journal of International Food & Agribusiness Marketing*, •••, 1–29. DOI: 10.1080/08974438.2023.2228783

Badawy, H. R. I., Alkaabi, A. M., Qablan, A. M., Ndlela, N. P., & Associates. (2024). *Nurturing future innovators: Integrating computational thinking, AI, and STEM in early education.* In *Empowering early education with computational thinking, AI, and STEM* (Chapter 4). IGI Global. https://doi.org/DOI: 10.4018/979-8-3693-6210-5.ch004

Baggio, A., Digentiki, E., & Varma, R. (2019). Organizations do not change. People change! McKinsey & Company. Retrieved from from https://www.mckinsey.com/capabilities/people-and-organizational-performance/our-insights/the-organization-blog/organizations-do-not-change-people-change

Bajpai, R., & Ghosh, A. (2021). Digital Nomads: The Impact of Visa Programs on Tourism. *Journal of Tourism Research*, *12*(3), 345–362.

Baker, J. (2023). The impact of digital nomads on local economies: Strategies for engagement and growth. *Journal of Economic Development*, *45*(1), 45–58.

Baker, R. S., Wang, Y., & Aleven, V. (2022). *Educational data mining and learning analytics: Improving education through big data*. Springer.

Baker, S., & Wall, A. (2021). The impact of digital nomadism on local economies: A case study approach. *Journal of Tourism and Cultural Change*, *19*(2), 142–158. DOI: 10.1080/14766825.2021.1949533

Baldry, C. (2021). Work and technology: The impact of remote work on global employment. *Journal of International Employment Studies*, *5*(3), 211–234.

Balnojan, S. (2024). How Unlearning Helps To Build $7B Data & AI Companies. There Data Point Thrusday. Retrieved from https://www.thdpth.com/p/how-unlearning-helps-to-build-7b

Bankins, S., Jooss, S., Restubog, S. L. D., Marrone, M., Ocampo, A. C., & Shoss, M. (2024). Navigating career stages in the age of artificial intelligence: A systematic interdisciplinary review and agenda for future research. *Journal of Vocational Behavior*, •••, 104011.

Bar-Gil, O., Ron, T., & Czerniak, O. (2024). AI for the people? Embedding AI ethics in HR and people analytics projects. *Technology in Society*, *77*, 102527. https://doi.org/https://doi.org/10.1016/j.techsoc.2024.102527

Baričević, M., & Tadić, M. (2022). Economic impact of digital nomads on local tourism: A case study from Croatia. *Tourism Economics*, *28*(4), 943–959. DOI: 10.1177/13548166221104790

Behera, B., Panda, R. K., & Tiwari, B. (2024). *Understanding the drivers of innovative work behaviour among millennial employees in India's IT sector: Some exploratory research findings. Journal of Asia Business*. Retrieved from. [HTML]

Bellamy, R. K. E., Dey, K., Hind, M., Hoffman, S. C., Houde, S., Kannan, K., Lohia, P., Martino, J., Mehta, S., Mojsilovic, A., Nagar, S., Ramamurthy, K. N., Richards, J., Saha, D., Sattigeri, P., Singh, M., Varshney, K. R., & Zhang, Y. (2019). AI Fairness 360: An extensible toolkit for detecting and mitigating algorithmic bias. *IBM Journal of Research and Development, 63*(4/5), 4:1-4:15. https://doi.org/DOI: 10.1147/jrd.2019.2942287

Bénassy-Quéré, A., & Coulibaly, S. (2021). The rise of digital nomad visas: New opportunities for mobility. *European Economic Review*, *130*, 103579. DOI: 10.1016/j.euroecorev.2021.103579

Ben-Ga, H. C. (2019). An ROI-based review of HR analytics: Practical implementation tools. *Personnel Review*, *48*(6), 1429–1448.

Benson, A. (2021). Exploring the benefits of digital nomad visas for host countries. *International Journal of Hospitality Management*, *95*, 102927. DOI: 10.1016/j.ijhm.2021.102927

Bergan, T. L., Gorman-Murray, A., & Power, E. R. (2021). Coliving housing: Home cultures of precarity for the new creative class. *Social & Cultural Geography*, *22*(9), 1204–1222.

Bernovskis, A., Sceulovs, D., & Stibe, A. (2024). Society 5.0: Shaping the future of e-commerce. *Journal of Open Innovation*, *10*(4), 100391.

Bérubé, M., Giannelia, T., & Vial, G. (2021). Barriers to the Implementation of AI in Organizations: Findings from a Delphi Study. *Proceedings of the 54th Hawaii International Conference on System Sciences*, 6702-6711.

Binns, R., Van Kleek, M., Veale, M., Lyngs, U., Zhao, J., & Shadbolt, N. (2018). 'It's Reducing a Human Being to a Percentage' Perceptions of Justice in Algorithmic Decisions. In *Proceedings of the 2018 Chi conference on human factors in computing systems* (pp. 1-14).

Bishop, R. (2022). Digital Nomads and Their Safety Concerns: A Qualitative Study of Experiences Abroad. *Journal of Travel Research*, *61*(4), 789–802.

Bobitan, N., Dumitrescu, D., Popa, A. F., Sahlian, D. N., & Turlea, I. C. (2024). Shaping Tomorrow: Anticipating Skills Requirements Based on the Integration of Artificial Intelligence in Business Organizations—A Foresight Analysis Using the Scenario Method. *Electronics (Basel)*, *13*(11), 2198.

Böcker, L., & Meisner, L. (2019). The Digital Nomad: Lifestyle and Work-Travel Balance. *Tourism Management Perspectives*, *31*, 100–109. DOI: 10.1016/j.tmp.2019.05.001

Bohr, A., & Memarzadeh, K. (2020). The rise of artificial intelligence in healthcare applications. In *Artificial Intelligence in Healthcare* (pp. 25–60). Academic Press.

Booyse, D., & Scheepers, C. B. (2024). Barriers to adopting automated organisational decision-making through the use of artificial intelligence. *Management Research Review*, *47*(1), 64–85.

Bostrom, N., & Yudkowsky, E. (2011). The ethics of artificial intelligence. Cambridge Handbook of Artificial Intelligence, 1–20. Retrieved from https://nickbostrom.com/ethics/artificial-intelligence.pdf

Bradford, N. (2025). How Organizational Culture Shapes AI Adoption and Success: Q&A with Jessica Kriegel of Culture Partners. *SHRM*. https://www.shrm.org/topics-tools/flagships/ai-hi/how-organizational-culture-shapes-ai-adoption-success

Bronsdon, C. (2024). Metrics for Measuring and Improving AI Agent Performance. Galileo. Retrieved from https://www.galileo.ai/blog/ai-agent-metrics

Brynjolfsson, E., & McAfee, A. (2017). *The Second Machine Age: Work, Progress, and Prosperity in a Time of Brilliant Technologies*. W.W. Norton & Company.

Buckley, R., & Bexton, R. (2021). Digital nomads: A new paradigm for tourism and work. *Tourism Management Perspectives*, *38*, 100834. DOI: 10.1016/j.tmp.2021.100834

Bukht, R., & Heeks, R. (2017). *Defining, conceptualising and measuring the digital economy*.

Butcher, T. (2021). *Book review: Rachael A. Woldoff and Robert C. Litchfield, Digital Nomads: In Search of Meaningful Work in the New Economy*. https://doi.org/DOI: 10.1177/09500170211043056

Butcher, T. (2021). Digital nomadism and global labor: Neo-colonial dynamics in remote education and entrepreneurship. *Journal of Global Mobility*, *9*(2), 205–222.

Cabinet, U. A. E. (2021). *The UAE Cabinet: Projects of the 50*. https://uaecabinet.ae/en/the-50-s-projects/second-set-of-projects-of-the-50-nafis

Cacá, A., & Matias, J. C. (2022). The economic impact of digital nomads on local economies: Evidence from emerging destinations. *Journal of Economic Geography*, *22*(3), 501–525. DOI: 10.1093/jeg/lbab029

Calzavara, M., Faccio, M., & Granata, I. (2023). Multi-objective task allocation for collaborative robot systems with an Industry 5.0 human-centered perspective. The International Journal of Advanced Manufacturing Technology. Retrieved from springer.com

Cardona, M., Kretschmer, T., & Strobel, T. (2013). ICT and productivity: Conclusions from the empirical literature. *Information Economics and Policy*, *25*, 109–125. DOI: 10.1016/j.infoecopol.2012.12.002

Castagnoli, R., Cugno, M., & Maroncelli, S. (2024). A new research agenda for human-centric manufacturing: A systematic literature review. IEEE Transactions on... Retrieved from ieee.org

Cathrine Williams. (2024). How Web3 Technology Reinvents Supply Chain Management in 2024? *Published in Coinmonks.* https://medium.com/coinmonks/how-web3-technology-reinvents-supply-chain-management-in-2024-e5af5f275e07 (Accessed on 20th July).

Cathrine, C. (2024). *Blockchain Technology as a Catalyst for Sustainable Development: Exploring Economic.* Social, and Environmental Synergies.

Certified, M. Azure AI Fundamentals. (2024). Microsoft Learn. Retrieved from https://learn.microsoft.com/en-us/credentials/certifications/azure-ai-fundamentals/?practice-assessment-type=certification

Chakravorti, B., & Chaturvedi, R. S. (2017). Digital planet.

Chander, B., Pal, S., De, D., & Buyya, R. (2022). *Artificial intelligence-based internet of things for Industry 5.0.* ResearchGate.

Chatterjee, S., Nguyen, B., Ghosh, S. K., Bhattacharjee, K. K., & Chaudhuri, S. (2020). Adoption of artificial intelligence integrated CRM system: An empirical study of Indian organizations. *The Bottom Line (New York, N.Y.), 33*(4), 359–375. https://doi.org/https://doi.org/10.1108/BL-08-2020-0057

Chauhan, R., & Thangavelu, C. (2024). *Transforming leadership for the digital era: Embracing collaboration and technological proficiency.* Educational Administration: Theory and Practice. https://doi.org/DOI: 10.53555/kuey.v30i6.6033

Chen, D. (2023). Remote work and the digital nomad phenomenon: An analysis of global work trends. *International Journal of Remote Work, 15*(2), 104–125.

Chen, D., ESPERANÇA, J., & Wang, S. (2022). The impact of artificial intelligence on firm performance: An application of the resource-based view to e-commerce firms. *Frontiers in Psychology, 13*, 884830. PMID: 35465474

Chen, H., Li, L., & Chen, Y. (2021). Explore success factors that impact artificial intelligence adoption on telecom industry in China. *Journal of Management Analytics, 8*(1), 36–68.

Chen, L., Chen, P., & Lin, Z. (2020). Artificial intelligence in education: A review. *IEEE Access : Practical Innovations, Open Solutions, 8*, 75264–75278. DOI: 10.1109/ACCESS.2020.2988510

Chen, P., & Pun, N. (2024). 'Re-coupling site'of social media and the workplace in digital nomadism: Chinese female workers' self-produced vlogs with class and gender connotations. *Information Communication and Society*, •••, 1–17.

Chen, W., Huang, X., Liu, Y., Luan, X., & Song, Y. (2019). The impact of high-tech industry agglomeration on green economy efficiency—Evidence from the Yangtze river economic belt. *Sustainability*, *11*(19), 5189.

Chen, W., Wang, S., & Lin, Z. (2020). The role of AI in advancing leadership in education. *AI in Education Journal*, *15*(4), 256–271. DOI: 10.1016/j.aiedu.2020.06.001

Chen, Y., Xiao, H., & Zhang, N. (2019). A bibliometric analysis of research on green economy. *International Journal of Environmental Science and Technology*, *16*(12), 7815–7830.

Choudhary, B., Dhar, V., & Pawase, A. S. (2024). Blue carbon and the role of mangroves in carbon sequestration: Its mechanisms, estimation, human impacts and conservation strategies for economic incentives. *Journal of Sea Research*, *199*, 102504. DOI: 10.1016/j.seares.2024.102504

Choudhury, P. (2022). Geographic mobility, immobility, and geographic flexibility: A review and agenda for research on the changing geography of work. *The Academy of Management Annals*, *16*(1), 258–296.

Cinite, I., Duxbury, L. E., & Higgins, C. (2009). Measurement of perceived organizational readiness for change in the public sector. *British Journal of Management*, *20*(2), 265–277.

Connell, J. (2020). Digital nomads and the changing landscape of work: A global perspective. *Global Networks*, *20*(3), 349–368. DOI: 10.1111/glob.12308

Cook, D. (2023). What is a digital nomad? Definition and taxonomy in the era of mainstream remote work. *World Leisure Journal*, *65*(2), 256–275.

Cook, J. (2022). Digital nomads: The rise of location-independent work. *Journal of Global Mobility*, *10*(2), 157–174. DOI: 10.1108/JGM-12-2021-0062

Costa, E. (2024). Industry 5.0 and SDG 9: A symbiotic dance towards sustainable transformation. Sustainable Earth Reviews. Retrieved from springer.com

Costa, T. (2024). Discover the power of Microsoft Certifications for your career. TechCommunity, Microsoft. Retrieved from https://techcommunity.microsoft.com/t5/microsoft-learn-blog/discover-the-power-of-microsoft-certifications-for-your-career/ba-p/4090763

Coyle, M. (2021). Skills today for tomorrow's jobs. Amazon. Retrieved from https://www.aboutamazon.com/news/workplace/skills-today-for-tomorrows-jobs

Crist, C. (2024a). Ikea embarks on companywide AI literacy initiative. Retail Dive. Retrieved from https://www.retaildive.com/news/ikea-companywide-ai-literacy-initiative/713863/

Crist, C. (2024b). Salesforce offers free hands-on AI courses for everyone through 2025. HR Dive. Retrieved from https://www.hrdive.com

Curtis, S. (2019). Digital transformation—The silver bullet to public service improvement? *Journal Public Money & Management*, *39*(5), 322–324.

Dabbous, A., Barakat, K. A., & Sayegh, M. M. (2022). Enabling organizational use of artificial intelligence: An employee perspective. *Journal of Asia Business Studies*, *16*(2), 245–266.

Dagli, K. (2022). 10 companies with Exceptional Employee Development Programs: Together mentoring software. RSS. Retrieved from https://www.togetherplatform.com/blog/best-training-and-development-programs

Dahiya, V. K., Dahiya, R., Dev, R., Sharma, A., Sharma, A., Kiran, P. B. N., . . . Yadav, S. (2024, October 24). Exploring the role of artificial intelligence in predictive analytics for financial markets. 2024 International Conference on Computing, Sciences and Communications (ICCSC), 1–5. Presented at the 2024 International Conference on Computing, Sciences and Communications (ICCSC), Ghaziabad, India. doi:DOI: 10.1109/iccsc62048.2024.10830442

Dahiya, S., Yadav, M., & Dahiya, S. (2024). Exploring the Use of Virtual Reality to Support Environmentally Sustainable Behavior Change. *Sustainability*, *16*(3), 1096.

Danfernandezmsft, S. Supernova-eng, & Dend. (2020). Microsoft Learn Overview and tour. Microsoft Learn. Retrieved from https://learn.microsoft.com/en-us/teamblog/microsoft-learn-tour

Davenport, T. H., & Ronanki, R. (2018). Artificial intelligence for the real world. *HBR'S 10 MUST*, 67.

Davey, K. (2024). AI-Powered LMS Platform: How to Improve Learning with AI. Docebo. Retrieved from https://www.docebo.com/learning-network/blog/ai-lms/

Davis, F. D. (1987). User acceptance of information systems: the technology acceptance model (TAM). Working Paper. https://deepblue.lib.umich.edu/handle/2027.42/35547

De Cremer, D. (2025, March). *Employees Won't Trust AI If They Don't Trust Their Leaders*. Harvard Business Review. https://hbr.org/2025/03/employees-wont-trust-ai-if-they-dont-trust-their-leaders#

De Freitas, J. (2025). *Why people resist embracing AI.* Harvard Business Review. https://hbr.org/2025/01/why-people-resist-embracing-ai

De Sousa, B. V., Bastida, M., & Vieira, E. (2025). Unraveling digital nomadism: A comprehensive bibliometric review of emerging research and trends. *Journal of Global Mobility: The Home of Expatriate Management Research.* https://doi.org/ DOI: 10.1108/jgm-04-2024-0029

Deloitte Development LLC. (2024). *AI Readiness & Management Framework (AIRMF).* https://www2.deloitte.com/content/dam/Deloitte/us/Documents/public-sector/ai-readiness-and-management-framework.pdf

Dempsey, M., Geitner, L., Brennan, A., & McAvoy, J. (2021). A review of the success and failure factors for change management. *IEEE Engineering Management Review, 50*(1), 85–93.

Depietro, R., Wiarda, E., & Fleischer, M. (1990). *The processes of technological innovation.* Lexington Books.

Deri, M. N., Singh, A., Zaazie, P., & Anandene, D. (2024). Leveraging artificial intelligence in higher educational institutions: A comprehensive overview. *Revista de Educación y Derecho.* Retrieved from https://revistes.ub.edu/index.php/RED/article/view/45777

Durlik, I., Miller, T., Cembrowska-Lech, D., Krzemińska, A., Złoczowska, E., & Nowak, A. (2023). Navigating the Sea of Data: A Comprehensive Review on Data Analysis in Maritime IoT Applications. *Applied Sciences (Basel, Switzerland), 13*(17), 9742.

Durlik, I., Miller, T., Cembrowska-Lech, D., Krzemińska, A., Złoczowska, E., & Nowak, A. (2023). Navigating the sea of data: A comprehensive review on data analysis in maritime IoT applications. *Applied Sciences (Basel, Switzerland), 13*(17), 9742. DOI: 10.3390/app13179742

Du, X., Alghowinem, S., Taylor, M., Darling, K., & Breazeal, C. (2023). *Innovating AI leadership education. In 2023 IEEE Frontiers in Education Conference.* FIE., DOI: 10.1109/FIE56618.2023.10343238

Dwivedi, A., Agrawal, D., & Jha, A. (2023). Studying the interactions among Industry 5.0 and circular supply chain: Towards attaining sustainable development. Computers & Industrial, Elsevier. Retrieved from [HTML]

Eager, B., Maritz, A., & Millemann, J. (2022). The silver economy on wheels: A narrative review of the mature-aged, hypermobile gig worker phenomena. *Small Enterprise Research, 29*(1), 68–85.

Edmondson, A. (1999). Psychological safety and learning behavior in work teams. *Administrative Science Quarterly*, *44*(2), 350–383.

Edmondson, A., & Moingeon, B. (1998). From organizational learning to the learning organization. *Management Learning*, *29*(1), 5–20.

Education Middle East. (2023, March 4). UAE to introduce policy on generative AI technology in education. https://educationmiddleeast.com/news/uae-to-introduce-policy-on-generative-ai-technology-in-education/

Ellis, R. A. (2024). *The education leadership challenges for universities in a postdigital age*. Postdigital Science and Education., DOI: 10.1007/s42438-024-00461-9

Emara, N., Ali, N., & Abu Khurma, O. (2023). Adaptive learning framework (Alef) in UAE public schools from the parents' perspective. *Social Sciences*, *297*, •••. https://www.mdpi.com/2076-0760/12/5/297

Erhan, T., Uzunbacak, H. H., & Aydin, E. (2022). From conventional to digital leadership: Exploring digitalization of leadership and innovative work behavior. *Management Research Review*, *45*(11), 1524–1543. DOI: 10.1108/mrr-05-2021-0338

Ericsson Transforms Workforce Learning with Degreed (n.d.) Degreed. https://explore.degreed.com/success-stories/ericsson/

European Commission. (2020). *Responsible Research and Innovation: Europe's Approach to Science and Innovation*. Publications Office of the European Union. https://op.europa.eu/en/publication-detail/-/publication

European Commission. (2021). Proposal for a regulation laying down harmonized rules on artificial intelligence (Artificial Intelligence Act). Retrieved from https://ec.europa.eu

Fadlelmula, F. K., & Qadhi, S. M. (2024). A systematic review of research on artificial intelligence in higher education: Practice, gaps, and future directions in the GCC. *Journal of University Teaching & Learning Practice*, *21*(6). Advance online publication. DOI: 10.53761/pswgbw82

Faeni, D. P. (2024). Green practices and employees' performance: The mediating roles of green human resources management policies and knowledge development. Journal of Infrastructure, Policy, and... Retrieved from enpress-publisher.com

Fang, X., Zhang, Y., Yang, J., & Zhan, G. (2024). An evaluation of marine economy sustainable development and the ramifications of digital technologies in China coastal regions. *Economic Analysis and Policy*, *82*, 554–570.

Fauscette, M. (2024). Generative AI and Personalized Education: Adapting Learning Materials to Individual Needs. Arion Research LLC. Retrieved from https://www.arionresearch.com/blog/generative-ai-and-personalized-education-adapting-learning-materials-to-individual-needs

Favour Oluwadamilare Usman, F., Adeleke, A., & Bello, B. (2024). AI-driven entrepreneurship in the digital age: Innovation, scalability, and workforce strategies. *Journal of Digital Business Innovation*, *11*(1), 65–82.

Fernandez, A. A., & Shaw, G. P. (2020). Academic leadership in a time of crisis: The coronavirus and COVID-19. *Journal of Leadership Studies*, *14*(1), 39–45. DOI: 10.1002/jls.21684

Ferrara, E. (2023). Fairness and bias in artificial intelligence: A brief survey of sources, impacts, and mitigation strategies. *Sci*, *6*(1), 3.

Fidalgo, P., & Thormann, J. (2024). The Future of Lifelong Learning: The Role of Artificial Intelligence and Distance Education.

Finley, A. P. (2023). The Career-Ready Graduate: What Employers Say about the Difference College Makes. American Association of Colleges and Universities. Retrieved from https://dgmg81phhvh63.cloudfront.net/content/user-photos/Research/PDFs/AACU-2023-Employer-Report.pdf

Fong, J., Etter, B., & Sullberg, D. (2023). The Effect of Employer Understanding and Engagement on Non-Degree Credentials. University Professional and Continuing Education Association, Collegis Education. Retrieved from https://collegiseducation.com/wp-content/uploads/2023/02/UPCEA-Collegis-Employers-and-Microcredentials-Report.pdf

Fourcade, M., & Kluttz, D. N. (2020). A Maussian bargain: Accumulation by gift in the digital economy. *Big Data & Society*, *7*(1).

Fousiani, K., Michelakis, G., Minnigh, P. A., & De Jonge, K. M. M. (2024). Competitive organizational climate and artificial intelligence (AI) acceptance: The moderating role of leaders' power construal. *Frontiers in Psychology*, *15*, 1359164. PMID: 38596327

Fox, A. (2024). Mayo Clinic taps AI start-up to unlock data. Healthcare IT News. Retrieved from https://www.healthcareitnews.com/news/mayo-clinic-taps-ai-start-unlock-data

Frazier, M. L., Fainshmidt, S., Klinger, R. L., Pezeshkan, A., & Vracheva, V. (2017). Psychological safety: A meta-analytic review and extension. *Personnel Psychology*, *70*(1), 113–165.

Friedman, S. (2020). The rise of remote work: How digital nomad visas are shaping the future of travel. *Tourism Management Perspectives*, *35*, 100724. DOI: 10.1016/j.tmp.2020.100724

Fuchs, C. (2022). Digital nomadism: Community and cultural exchange in a globalized world. *International Journal of Cultural Studies*, *25*(2), 120–136.

Fügener, A., Grahl, J., Gupta, A., & Ketter, W. (2021). Cognitive Challenges in Human–Artificial Intelligence Collaboration: Investigating the Path Toward Productive Delegation. *Information Systems Research*, *33*(2), 678–696.

Fullan, M., Azorín, C., Harris, A., & Jones, M. (2023). Artificial intelligence and school leadership: Challenges, opportunities and implications. *School Leadership & Management*, *44*(4), 339–346. DOI: 10.1080/13632434.2023.2246856

Gallacher, G., & Hossain, I. (2020). Remote work and employment dynamics under COVID-19: Evidence from Canada. *Canadian Public Policy*, *46*(S1), S44–S54. PMID: 38629973

Gallagher, S. (2019). How the value of educational credentials is and isn't changing. *Harvard Business Review*. Retrieved from https://hbr.org/2019/09/how-the-value-of-educational-credentials-is-and-isnt-changing

Gamage, D., & Vithanage, K. (2023). AI-based curriculum design in inclusive education. *Journal of Educational Technology Research*, *39*(1), 91–112. DOI: 10.1109/JETR.2023.0101

George, A. S. (2024). Bridging the digital divide: Understanding the human impacts of digital transformation. Retrieved from researchgate.net

Ghai, N. (2024). NTT DATA launches AI upskilling programme for all employees. The Economic Times. Retrieved from https://economictimes.indiatimes.com/news/company/corporate-trends/ntt-data-launches-ai-upskilling-programme-for-all-employees/articleshow/114547254.cms?from=mdr

Ghamrawi, N., Shal, T., & Ghamrawi, N. A. (2023). Exploring the impact of AI on teacher leadership: Regressing or expanding? *Education and Information Technologies*, *29*(7), 8415–8433. DOI: 10.1007/s10639-023-12174-w

Ghamrawi, N., & Tamim, R. M. (2022). A typology for digital leadership in higher education: The case of a large-scale mobile technology initiative (using tablets). *Education and Information Technologies*, *28*, 7089–7110. DOI: 10.1007/s10639-022-11483-w PMID: 36465422

Ghobakhloo, M., & Iranmanesh, M. (2023). Actions and approaches for enabling Industry 5.0-driven sustainable industrial transformation: A strategy roadmap. Corporate Social Responsibility and Environmental Management. Retrieved from wiley.com

Ghobakhloo, M., Iranmanesh, M., & Fathi, M. (2024). Beyond Industry 4.0: A systematic review of Industry 5.0 technologies and implications for social, environmental, and economic sustainability. Asia-Pacific Journal of... Retrieved from emerald.com

Ghobakhloo, M., & Iranmanesh, M. (2023). *Actions and approaches for enabling Industry 5.0-driven sustainable industrial transformation: A strategy roadmap. Corporate Social Responsibility and Environmental Management*. Wiley.

Global Opportunity Forum. (2022). Five companies investing in upskilling the workforce. Retrieved from https://goi.mit.edu/2022/04/21/five-companies-investing-in-upskilling-the-workforce/

Gloor, P., Colladon, A. F., & Grippa, F. (2022). Measuring ethical behavior with AI and natural language processing to assess business success. *Scientific Reports*, *12*(1), 10228. PMID: 35715458

Goel, A., & Polepeddi, L. (2016). *Jill Watson: A virtual teaching assistant for online education*. Georgia Institute of Technology Research Papers.

Golgeci, I., Ritala, P., Arslan, A., McKenna, B., & Ali, I. (2025). Confronting and alleviating AI resistance in the workplace: An integrative review and a process framework. *Human Resource Management Review*, *35*(2), 101075.

González, M. E., & Eguizábal, A. (2022). Digital Nomad Visas and Their Economic Impacts on Local Communities. *Tourism Economics*, *28*(6), 1323–1340. DOI: 10.1177/13548166211035939

Gössling, S., Scott, D., & Hall, C. M. (2020). Global Trends in Sustainable Tourism: A Review of the Literature. *Journal of Sustainable Tourism*, *28*(12), 1749–1765.

Government, U. A. E. (2024). *Artificial intelligence in government policies*. https://ai.gov.ae

Government, U. A. E. (2024). *Artificial intelligence in government policies*. https://u.ae/en/about-the-uae/digital-uae/digital-technology/artificial-intelligence/artificial-intelligence-in-government-policies

Grace, R., Vidhyavathi, R., & Malathi, D. (2023). Ethical AI for education: Frameworks and governance models. *Journal of Educational Innovation*.

Grace, E. G., Vidhyavathi, P., & Malathi, P. (2023). AI in education: Opportunities and challenges for personalized learning. *Industrial Engineering Journal*, *52*(5), 750–759. DOI: 10.36893/iej.2023.v52i05.750-759

Graceffo, E. (2024). Live at build: Microsoft Learn releases new AI skill-building resources. TechCommunity, Microsoft. Retrieved from https://techcommunity.microsoft.com/t5/microsoft-learn-blog/live-at-build-microsoft-learn-releases-new-ai-skill-building/ba-p/4137354

Grosse, E. H., Sgarbossa, F., & Berlin, C. (2023). Human-centric production and logistics system design and management: Transitioning from Industry 4.0 to Industry 5.0. *International Journal of Production Research*.

Grubaugh, S., & Levitt, G. (2023). Artificial intelligence and the paradigm shift: Reshaping education to equip students for future careers. *International Journal of Social Sciences and Humanities Invention*, *10*(6), 7931–7941. DOI: 10.18535/ijsshi/v10i06.02

Gupta, S., Jaiswal, R., & Gupta, S. K. (2024). Digital nomads: a systematic literature review and future research agenda. *Tourism Review*.MBO Partners. (2023). The State of Independence in America 2023. MBO Partners. Retrieved from https://www.mbopartners.com

Gupta, S., Leszkiewicz, A., & Potapov, D. (2022). Digital Analytics: Modeling for Insights and New Methods. *Journal of Interactive Marketing*, *51*(1), 26–43.

Gyanamurthy, V., & Radhanath, S. (2023). Leading change in the AI era: Strategies for transformational leadership. *International Journal of Advanced Engineering Technologies and Innovations*, 164–184. https://scholar.google.com/scholar_lookup?q=Leadership+Challenges+and+Strategies+in+the+Era+of+AI+Transformation

Gyanamurthy, V., & Radhanath, S. (2023). *Leading Change in the AI Era: Strategies for Transformational Leadership*. International Journal of Advanced Engineering Technologies and Innovations.

Hamilton, D. (2025). *The rise of AI resentment at work: Why employees are pushing back*. Forbes. https://www.forbes.com/sites/dianehamilton/2025/02/03/the-rise-of-ai-resentment-at-work-why-employees-are-pushing-back/

Hannonen, O. (2020). In search of a digital nomad: Defining the phenomenon. *Information Technology & Tourism*, *22*(3), 335–353. DOI: 10.1007/s40558-019-00177-z

Hannonen, O. (2023). Emergent geographies of digital nomadism: Conceptual framing, insights and implications for tourism. *Tourism Geographies*, •••, 1–11.

Haque, M., Akhtar, M. W., Bala, R., & Azam, M. S. (2023). Impact of Green Marketing on Market Performance in Rural India. *Academy of Marketing Studies Journal, 27*(2), 01-11.

Hashemi-Pour, C., Kirvan, P., & Brush, K. (2024). What is a learning management system (LMS)? TechTargetNetwork. Retrieved from https://www.techtarget.com/searchcio/definition/learning-management-system

Hassan, S. (2022). Building a digital nomad-friendly infrastructure: Key considerations for governments. *Journal of Urban Planning, 34*(4), 210–226.

Hat, R. (2024). *Evaluating frameworks to define an AI corporate strategy*. Harvard Business Review. https://hbr.org/sponsored/2024/03/evaluating-frameworks-to-define-an-ai-corporate-strategy

Hayden, C. (2022). Remote workers and economic resilience in tourism economies. *Journal of Travel Research, 61*(5), 1158–1175. DOI: 10.1177/00472875221103714

He, C., Teng, R., & Song, J. (2024). Linking employees' challenge-hindrance appraisals toward AI to service performance: The influences of job crafting, job insecurity and AI knowledge. *International Journal of Contemporary Hospitality Management, 36*(3), 975–994.

Hensellek, S., & Puchala, N. (2021). The emergence of the digital nomad: A review and analysis of the opportunities and risks of digital nomadism. In *Human Resource Management* (pp. 195–214). Springer., DOI: 10.1007/978-3-030-62167-4_11

Holleran, M., & Notting, M. (2023). Mobility guilt: Digital nomads and COVID-19. *Tourism Geographies, 25*(5), 1341–1358.

Holmes, W., Bialik, M., & Fadel, C. (2021). *Artificial Intelligence in Education: Promises and Implications for Teaching and Learning*. Center for Curriculum Redesign.

Hong, R. (2023). Road warriors to digital nomads: Portable computers, habitats, and remote work. *Cultural Studies, 37*(3), 508–535.

Hornung, O., & Smolnik, S. (2022). AI invading the workplace: Negative emotions towards the organizational use of personal virtual assistants. *Electronic Markets, 32*(1), 123–138.

Howard, C. (2025). The Top CIO Challenges, According to 12k+ of Your CIO Peers. *Gartner*. https://www.gartner.com/en/articles/cio-challenges#:~:text=Sixty%2Dnine%20percent%20of%20CIOs,evolve%20the%20cybersecurity%20operating%20model

Huang, L. (2021). The rise of digital nomad visas: Implications for global work and travel. *Journal of International Business Studies*, *52*(3), 345–362.

Hughes, C., Robert, L., Frady, K., & Arroyos, A. (2019). *Artificial Intelligence*. Employee Engagement, Fairness, and Job Outcomes.

Hutson, J., & Rains, T. J. (2024). *Charting the AI Transition in Education and Business Environments: Navigating the Generative Inflection Point for Industry 4.0 Success*. Taylor & Francis.

Hwang, J., & Lee, J. (2021). Community building among digital nomads: The role of social media. *Journal of Business Research*, *126*, 494–502. DOI: 10.1016/j.jbusres.2020.12.051

Indrasari, M., & Pamuji, E. (2024). Enhancing Employee Performance through Strategic Initiatives. *Journal of Business Management and Economic Development*, *2*(1), 383–396.

Ingka Group. (2024). Ikea retail unleashes AI Revolution: Empowering Thousands to master the future of tech. Retrieved from https://www.ingka.com/newsroom/ikea-retail-unleashes-ai-revolution-empowering-thousands-to-master-the-future-of-tech/

Insights, D. (2020). Talent and workforce effects in the age of AI. Retrieved from https://www2.deloitte.com/content/dam/insights/us/articles/6546_talent-and-workforce-effects-in-the-age-of-ai/DI_Talent-and-workforce-effects-in-the-age-of-AI.pdf

Iram, T., Bilal, A. R., Khan, R., Mehmood, S., & Kumar, H. (2024). From awareness to action: unraveling the interplay of employee AI awareness and change leadership in fostering knowledge hiding. *Kybernetes, ahead-of-p*(ahead-of-print).

Isaac, A., Mascarenhas, R., & Kamble, S. S. (2023). An interpretive model to assess the barriers to ocean energy toward blue economic development in India. *Renewable Energy*, *211*, 822–830.

Ismail, S., Reza, H., Salameh, K., Zadeh, H. K., & Vasefi, F. (2023). Toward an intelligent blockchain IoT-enabled fish supply chain: A review and conceptual framework. *Sensors (Basel)*, *23*(11), 5136. DOI: 10.3390/s23115136 PMID: 37299864

Jaiswal, R., Gupta, S., & Gupta, S. K. (2024). The impending disruption of digital nomadism: Opportunities, challenges, and research agenda. *World Leisure Journal*, •••, 1–31.

Jaworski, B. K., Webb Hooper, M., Aklin, W. M., Jean-Francois, B., Elwood, W. N., Belis, D., & Hunter, C. M. (2022). Advancing digital health equity: Directions for behavioral and social science research. *Translational Behavioral Medicine*, *13*(3), 132–139. DOI: 10.1093/tbm/ibac088 PMID: 36318232

Jayasekara, D., & Hansson, F. (2024). The Digital Economy Takes Over. In *THE CITY REBOOTED* (pp. 65–104). Networks, Connectivity and Place Identities in Singapore.

Jeong, J., Kim, B.-J., & Lee, J. (2024). Navigating AI transitions: How coaching leadership buffers against job stress and protects employee physical health. *Frontiers in Public Health*, *12*, 1343932. PMID: 38601504

Joffe, J. (2024). Training the AI muscle: PwC's approach to bridging AI theory and everyday use. Ragan Communications. Retrieved from https://www.ragan.com/pwc-bridging-ai-theory-and-everyday-use/

Jöhnk, J., Weißert, M., & Wyrtki, K. (2021). Ready or not, AI comes—An interview study of organizational AI readiness factors. *Business & Information Systems Engineering*, *63*(1), 5–20.

Johnson, K., & Pereira, L. (2021). Digital nomad visas: Redefining the boundaries of work and travel. *Journal of Global Mobility*, *9*(2), 134–149. DOI: 10.1108/JGM-05-2021-0029

Jones, L., & Kennedy, E. (2023). *Effective technology tools for school leadership: Understanding digital and data-driven strategies*. Routledge.

Kamtam, P. (2023). Exploring the design of people-centred inclusive smart cities using integrated inclusion approaches and citizen engagement strategies. Retrieved from herts.ac.uk

Karakose, T., & Tülübaş, T. (2023). Digital leadership and sustainable school improvement—A conceptual analysis and implications for future research. *Educational Process International Journal*, *12*(1), 7–18. DOI: 10.22521/edupij.2023.121.1

Karakose, T., Yirci, R., & Papadakis, S. (2022). Exploring the emerging field of digital leadership: A bibliometric analysis. *Sustainability*, *14*(15), 9003. DOI: 10.3390/su14159003

Kashif, M., David, A., Azam, M. S., & Kumar, S. (2024). Utilization of Robo-Advisory Tools in Decision Support Systems. In *Robo-Advisors in Management* (pp. 76–89). IGI Global., DOI: 10.4018/979-8-3693-2849-1.ch005

Kasinathan, P., Pugazhendhi, R., & Elavarasan, R. M. (2022). *Realization of sustainable development goals with disruptive technologies by integrating Industry 5.0, Society 5.0, smart cities, and villages*. Sustainability. MDPI.

Katiyar, N., Awasthi, M. V. K., Pratap, R., Mishra, M. K., Shukla, M. N., & Tiwari, M. (2024). AI-driven personalized learning systems: Enhancing educational effectiveness. *Educational Administration: Theory and Practice*, *30*(5), 11514–11524. DOI: 10.53555/kuey.v30i5.4961

Kavita, S., & Gupta, M. (2022). Social and Cultural Impacts of Remote Work Migration: Insights from Digital Nomads. *The Global Studies Journal*, *14*(2), 134–148.

Khalid, M. (2024). Smart grids and renewable energy systems: Perspectives and grid integration challenges. *Energy Strategy Reviews*, *51*, 101299.

Khalid, M. A. (2024). *Deciphering the Dynamics of Human-Environment Interaction in China: Insights into Renewable Energy*. Sustainable Consumption Patterns, and Carbon Emissions.

Khan, P. A., & Johl, S. K. (2021). Does adoption of ISO 56002-2019 and green innovation reporting enhance the firm sustainable development goal performance? An emerging paradigm. Business Strategy and the Environment. Retrieved from researchgate.net

Kim, S. (2024). How AI Supports Knowledge Transfer in A&D Manufacturing. iBase-t. Retrieved from https://www.ibaset.com/how-ai-is-solving-knowledge-transfer-challenges/

Kim, Y., Blazquez, V., & Oh, T. (2024). Determinants of Generative AI System Adoption and Usage Behavior in Korean Companies: Applying the UTAUT Model. *Behavioral Sciences (Basel, Switzerland)*, *14*(11), 1035. PMID: 39594336

Kinsella, K. (2021). The sustainability of digital nomad lifestyles: An environmental perspective. *Sustainability*, *13*(14), 7592. DOI: 10.3390/su13147592

Kong, L. (2021). The economic impact of digital nomad visas on small nations. *Economic Development Quarterly*, *35*(2), 124–138.

Korpela, K. M. (2021). Digital nomadism and local economic development: Opportunities and challenges. *Urban Studies (Edinburgh, Scotland)*, *58*(6), 1125–1141. DOI: 10.1177/0042098020970789

Koskela, K., & Beckers, P. (2024). Typologizing Digital Nomad Visas: Comparing Policy Rationales from Tourism to Wealth Accumulation to Immigration. *Journal of Comparative Policy Analysis*, *26*(5), 407–425. DOI: 10.1080/13876988.2024.2343696

Krichevsky, S. (2020). *Creation of a "cosmic" human: Ideas, technologies, projects, experience, risks, limitations, and prospects*. Future Human Image.

Kumar, A. (2024). Top 15 Challenges of Artificial Intelligence in 2025. Simplilearn.com. Retrieved from https://www.simplilearn.com/challenges-of-artificial-intelligence-article

Kumar, S. (n.d.). *Industry 5.0 and emerging technologies: A pathway to human-centric innovation in manufacturing*. ResearchGate.

Kumar, S., Verma, A. K., & Mirza, A. (2024). Digital Transformation. *AI & Society*. PMID: 39302202

Lake, K. (2024). Leveraging AI For Effective L&D Measurement. eLearning Industry. Retrieved from https://elearningindustry.com/leveraging-ai-for-effective-ld-measurement

Lakshmi, A. J., Kumar, A., Kumar, M. S., Patel, S. I., Naik, S. L., & Ramesh, J. V. N. (2023). Artificial intelligence in steering the digital transformation of collaborative technical education. *The Journal of High Technology Management Research*, *34*(2), 100467. DOI: 10.1016/j.hitech.2023.100467

Lanier, J. (2017). *Dawn of the New Everything: Encounters with Reality and Virtual Reality*. Henry Holt and Company.

Latupeirissa, J. J. P., Dewi, N. L. Y., Prayana, I. K. R., Srikandi, M. B., Ramadiansyah, S. A., & Pramana, I. B. G. A. Y. (2024). Transforming public service delivery: A comprehensive review of digitization initiatives. *Sustainability*, *16*(7), 2818. DOI: 10.3390/su16072818

Learning Ecosystem Case Study | Visa University | Watershed. (n.d.). https://www.watershedlrs.com/case-studies/financial-services/visa/?utm_source=chatgpt.com

Learning Ecosystem Case Study: Danone | Watershed. (n.d.). https://www.watershedlrs.com/case-studies/food-and-beverage/danone/

Legislation, U. A. E. (n.d.). UAE's international stance on artificial intelligence policy. https://uaelegislation.gov.ae

Leng, J., Sha, W., Wang, B., Zheng, P., & Zhuang, C. (2022). *Industry 5.0: Prospect and retrospect. Journal of Manufacturing*. Elsevier.

Lennerfors, T. T., Fors, P., & Rooijen, V. J. (2015). ICT and environmental sustainability in a changing society: The view of ecological World Systems Theory. *Information Technology & People*, *28*, 758–774. DOI: 10.1108/ITP-09-2014-0219

Leung, D., Weiler, B., & Kim, H. (2019). Cultural Identity and Interaction: A Study of Digital Nomads in Southeast Asia. *Annals of Tourism Research, 78*, 102738.

Li, B., & Wang, R. (2022). Marine renewable energy development in China: Status, challenges and policy recommendations. *Renewable & Sustainable Energy Reviews, 167*, 112747.

Li, H. S., Tian, Y. X., & Li, W. J. (2014). Internet thinking and traditional enterprise reengineering. *China Ind. Econ., 10*, 135–146. DOI: 10.19581/j.cnki.ciejournal.2014.10.011

Li, J., Zhou, W., & Cai, Z. (2014). The impact of environmental regulation on firm's green innovation and financial performance: Evidence from China's listed companies. *Journal of Cleaner Production, 112*, 1569–1577.

Li, K., Kim, D. J., Lang, K. R., Kauffman, R. J., & Naldi, M. (2020). How should we understand the digital economy in Asia? Critical assessment and research agenda. *Electronic Commerce Research and Applications, 44*, 101004. PMID: 32922241

Li, L., Fengchao, Y., & Zhang, E. (2024). A systematic review of learning task design for K-12 AI education: Trends, challenges, and opportunities. *Computers and Education: Artificial Intelligence, 100217*. Advance online publication. DOI: 10.26855/jhass.2024.04.039

Li, L., Fengchao, Y., & Zhang, E. (2024). Bridging the digital divide in AI-enhanced learning environments: Policy and practice recommendations. *Computers and Education: Artificial Intelligence, 5*, 100217.

Lin, X., & Tao, N. (2025). Audiobooks in the Cultural Metaverse: Reimagining New Quality Productive Forces and the Future of the Audio Culture Industry. In *International Conference on Metaverse* (pp. 124-133). Springer, Cham.

Lipniewicz, R. (2024). Digital Nomads and International Taxation of Income from Employment. *Krytyka Prawa, 16*(2), 268–285.

Liu, P., Yuan, L., & Jiang, Z. (2025). The dark side of algorithmic management: Investigating how and when algorithmic management relates to employee knowledge hiding? *Journal of Knowledge Management, 29*(2), 342–371.

Li, X., Wang, H., & Yang, C. (2023). Driving mechanism of digital economy based on regulation algorithm for development of low-carbon industries. *Sustainable Energy Technologies and Assessments, 55*, 102909.

Li, Y., & Li, X.-Z. (2024). Utilizing unmanned aerial vehicle technology for environmental monitoring: Future trends, methods, and applications. *Internet Technology Letters*. Advance online publication. DOI: 10.1002/itl2.526

Li, Z. G., & Wang, J. (2022). The dynamic impact of digital economy on carbon emission reduction: Evidence city-level empirical data in China. *Journal of Cleaner Production*, *351*, 131570. DOI: 10.1016/j.jcleprc.2022.131570

Li, Z., & Li, L. (2024). Remote sensing of coastal litter based on constrained energy minimization detector. *Frontiers in Marine Science*, *11*, 1336030.

Longo, F., Padovano, A., & Umbrello, S. (2020). Value-oriented and ethical technology engineering in industry 5.0: A human-centric perspective for the design of the factory of the future. Applied Sciences. Retrieved from mdpi.com

López, A., Jiménez, J., & Schmidt, M. (2022). The economic impact of digital nomadism: A case study of Portugal's digital nomad visa. *Journal of Economic Development*, *42*(3), 112–136.

Lu, Y., Zheng, H., Chand, S., Xia, W., Liu, Z., & Xu, X. (2022). Outlook on human-centric manufacturing towards Industry 5.0. Journal of Manufacturing.

Lukan, E. (2024). 9 Impactful Uses of AI in Learning and Development in 2024. Synthesia. Retrieved from https://www.synthesia.io/learn/ai-applications/learning-and-development

lves, J., Lima, T. M., & Gaspar, P. D. (2023). Is industry 5.0 a human-centred approach? A systematic review. Processes. Retrieved from mdpi.com

Madanchian, M., Taherdoost, H., Vincenti, M., & Mohamed, N. (2024). Transforming leadership practices through artificial intelligence. *Procedia Computer Science*, *235*, 2101–2111. DOI: 10.1016/j.procs.2024.04.199

Maddikunta, P. K. R., Pham, Q. V., & Prabadevi. B. (2022). *Industry 5.0: A survey on enabling technologies and potential applications. Journal of Industrial*. Elsevier.

Madsen, S. R., Miller, D., & John, C. R. (2005). Readiness for organizational change: Do organizational commitment and social relationships in the workplace make a difference? *Human Resource Development Quarterly*, *16*(2), 213–234.

Makimoto, T., & Manners, D. (1997). The Digital Nomad. Wileyand sons.

Makimoto, T., & Manners, D. (2021). *Digital nomadism and the transformation of the workplace*. Routledge.

Malhotra, A., Majchrzak, A., & Bonfield, W. (2020). Engaging customer care employees in internal collaborative crowd sourcing: Managing the inherent tensions and associated challenges. Human Resource. Retrieved from researchgate.net

Maljugić, B., Ćoćkalo, D., Bakator, M., & Stanisavljev, S. (2024). The role of the quality management process within Society 5.0. Societies. Retrieved from mdpi.com

Mallisetty, M. S. (2023). *Digital transformation: advancements in business*. Book Saga Publications.

Mancinelli, S. (2022). Digital nomad visas: A comparative study of their role in post-pandemic recovery and global mobility. *Journal of Tourism & Hospitality (Los Angeles, Calif.)*, *12*(1), 67–83.

Marr, B. (2020). How Estonia became the first country to offer a digital nomad visa. *Forbes*. Retrieved from https://www.forbes.com

Marr, B. (2024). *Examples that illustrate why transparency is crucial in AI*. Forbes. https://www.forbes.com/sites/bernardmarr/2024/05/17/examples-that-illustrate-why-transparency-is-crucial-in-ai/

Martin, C. (2024). *Research: More than half of large businesses are increasing investments in AI, big data*. AI Business. https://aibusiness.com/data/research-more-than-half-of-large-businesses-are-increasing-investments-in-ai-big-data

Martin, K. (2024). 9 Common Challenges to AI Adoption and How to Avoid Them. Naviant. Retrieved from https://naviant.com/blog/ai-challenges-solved/

Martini, B., Bellisario, D., & Coletti, P. (2024). *Human-centered and sustainable artificial intelligence in Industry 5.0: Challenges and perspectives*. Sustainability. MDPI.

Masera, M. L. (2024). Redefining Tomorrow: A Comprehensive Analysis of AI's Impact on Employment and Identity.

Masood, A. (2025). The Agentic Imperative Series Part 5— Return on Investment of Agentic AI: A business leader's Perspective. *Medium*. https://medium.com/@adnanmasood/the-agentic-imperative-series-part-5-return-on-investment-of-agentic-ai-a-business-leaders-8e4f9784c4b0#:~:text=Recent%20studies%20indicate%20that%20this,Opportunity%20Value%20of%20Agentic%20AI)

Matheus, R., Janssen, M., & Maheshwari, D. (2020). Data science empowering the public: Data-driven dashboards for transparent and accountable decision-making in smart cities. Government Information Quarterly. Retrieved from sciencedirect.com

Matsushita, K. (2023). How the Japanese workcation embraces digital nomadic work style employees. *World Leisure Journal*, *65*(2), 218–235.

Maurer, R. (2024). Study highlights worker attitudes toward AI adoption. *SHRM*. https://www.shrm.org/topics-tools/news/technology/study-highlights-worker-attitudes-toward-ai-adoption

Mayer, H., Yee, L., Chui, M., & Roberts, R. (2025). *Superagency in the workplace: Empowering people to unlock AI's full potential*. McKinsey & Company. https://www.mckinsey.com/capabilities/mckinsey-digital/our-insights/superagency-in-the-workplace-empowering-people-to-unlock-ais-full-potential-at-work#/

Mayer, J., & Flynn, T. (2023). Economic impacts of digital nomadism on local economies: A case study. *Economic Development Quarterly*, *37*(1), 27–42. DOI: 10.1177/0891242422110583

McGregor, J. (2023). The Future Of Work 50 2023. *Forbes*. Retrieved from https://www.forbes.com/sites/jenamcgregor/2023/11/08/the-future-of-work-50-2023/?

Mckenzie, S. (2025). *Transparent AI: How Advanced Reasoning is Reshaping Trust in Machine Intelligence*. World Certification Institute. https://www.worldcertification.org/how-advanced-reasoning-is-reshaping-trust-in-machine-intelligence/

McLuhan, M. (1994). *Understanding media: The extensions of man. MIT press. Noble, S. U. (2018). Algorithms of Oppression: How Search Engines Reinforce Racism*. NYU Press.

Merhi, M. I. (2023). An evaluation of the critical success factors impacting artificial intelligence implementation. *International Journal of Information Management*, *69*, 102545.

Messenger, J. C., & Gschwind, L. (2016). Three generations of telework: New ICTs and the (r)evolution from home office to virtual office. *New Technology, Work and Employment*, *31*(3), 195–208. DOI: 10.1111/ntwe.12073

Miake-Lye, I. M., Delevan, D. M., Ganz, D. A., Mittman, B. S., & Finley, E. P. (2020). Unpacking organizational readiness for change: An updated systematic review and content analysis of assessments. *BMC Health Services Research*, *20*, 1–13. PMID: 32046708

Mikalef, P., Conboy, K., Lundström, J. E., & Popovič, A. (2022). Thinking responsibly about responsible AI and 'the dark side'of AI. *European Journal of Information Systems*, *31*(3), 257–268.

Mikalef, P., & Gupta, M. (2021). Artificial intelligence capability: Conceptualization, measurement calibration, and empirical study on its impact on organizational creativity and firm performance. *Information & Management*, *58*(3), 103434. https://doi.org/https://doi.org/10.1016/j.im.2021.103434

Milton, J., & Al-Busaidi, A. (2023). New role of leadership in AI era: Educational sector. *SHS Web of Conferences, 156*, 09005.

Mishra, V., & Singh Kaurav, R. P. (2024). Leveraging Disruptive Technologies and Strategies for Competitive Advantage. In *Review of Technologies and Disruptive Business Strategies* (pp. 1–16). Emerald Publishing Limited.

Mitchell, R. (2022). How to launch—and scale—a successful AI pilot project. CIO. Retrieved from https://www.cio.com/article/410642/how-to-launch-and-scale-a-successful-ai-pilot-project.html

Mohn, T. (2021). The Rise of the Digital Nomad: How Remote Work is Transform

Muhammad, F., & Orji, C. M. (2024). Revolutionizing education in the digital era: The role of AI in promoting inclusivity, equality, and ethical innovation. *The American Journal of Social Science and Education Innovations*, *6*(09), 151–157.

Nandwani, P., & Bhatnagar, D. (2023). Comprehensive and Psychological Review and its Impact on Technology Driven Applications on Business Development and Diversities of Tourism and Hospitality Industry during Pandemic in Indian Prospective. *Journal for ReAttach Therapy and Developmental Diversities*, *6*(8s), 405–418.

Nawaz, W., Koç, M., Nawaz, W., & Koç, M. (2020). *Case Study: Qatar.* In *Industry, University and Government Partnerships for the Sustainable Development of Knowledge-Based Society* (pp. 71–106). Springer.

Nawaz, W., Koç, M., Nawaz, W., & Koç, M. (2020). Case Study: Qatar. In *Industry, University and Government Partnerships for the Sustainable Development of Knowledge-Based Society: Drivers, Models and Examples in US, Norway, Singapore and Qatar* (pp. 71–106). Springer. https://link.springer.com/section/10.1007/978-3-030-26799-5_5

Nembe, J. K., & Idemudia, C. (2024). Designing effective policies to address the challenges of global digital tax reforms. *World Journal of Advanced Research and Reviews*, *22*(3), 1171–1183.

Newsfile Corp. (2024). EveryAnswer Launches AI Expert Platform for Enterprise Knowledge Management and customer Service. Retrieved from https://finance.yahoo.com/news/everyanswer-launches-ai-expert-platform-152200456.html?guccounter=1&guce_referrer=aHR0cHM6Ly93d3cucGVycGxleGl0eS5haS8&guce_referrer_sig=AQAAANMCO-LGmukIJzoIml2Ij9r-qw-bBxK3W7sOjcarQq4FZIwZeX2Cq6JZXExEJT28wZOigbfZ74TrL41AeMAgVenfqQkI9jKSRip0liY_bIpqMPf8s h4xrp1ZUXx7pZRBV7Qll_lC2CflKFcjIO1mnb8BVQXDB9Y3hb-O-qEvBque

Nguyen, A., Ngo, H. N., Hong, Y., Dang, B., & Nguyen, B.-P. T. (2022). Ethical principles for artificial intelligence in education. *Education and Information Technologies*, *28*(4), 4221–4241. DOI: 10.1007/s10639-022-11316-w PMID: 36254344

Nham, N. T. H., Hoa, T. T. M., & Ha, L. T. (2023). Influences of digitalization on sustaining marine minerals: A path toward sustainable blue economy. *Ocean and Coastal Management*, *239*, 106589.

Nham, T. H., Hoa, H. V., & Ha, D. T. (2023). Factors Influencing Blue Economy Investment Decisions: Evidence From Egypt. *Journal of Risk and Financial Management*, *16*(11), 484.

Nordell Westling, A. (n.d.). Sana Learning Platform. MIT SOLVE. Retrieved from https://solve.mit.edu/challenges/good-jobs-and-inclusive-entrepreneurship/solutions/30709

NTT DATA Establishes Generative AI Talent Development Framework. (2024). NTT DATA. Retrieved from https://us.nttdata.com/en/news/press-release/2024/october/ntt-data-establishes-generative-ai-talent-development-framework

Oakes, T. (2024). Toward a critical geopolitics of smart tourism. *Tourism Geographies*, •••, 1–12.

OECD. (2019). OECD principles on artificial intelligence. https://www.oecd.org/going-digital/ai/principles/

OECD. (2023). *Artificial intelligence in education: Global policy perspectives*. OECD Publishing. https://www.oecd.org/

Olaitan, J., & Elshennawy, A. (2024). Quality 5.0 architecting: A techno-human-centric integrated framework. IEOM Society. Retrieved from ieomsociety.org

Oloyede, A. A., Faruk, N., Noma, N., Tebepah, E., & Nwaulune, A. K. (2023). Measuring the impact of the digital economy in developing countries: A systematic review and meta- analysis. *Heliyon*, •••, 9. PMID: 37501966

Oltean, O., & Taylor, A. (2023). Back to the Future: How the Convergence of Globalization and Technology is Changing Labour and Mobility. *Social Change Review*, *20*(1), 19–44.

Olutimehin, D. O., Ofodile, O. C., Ejibe, I., Odunaiya, O. G., & Soyombo, O. T. (2024). Implementing Ai in Business Models: Strategies for Efficiency and Innovation. *International Journal of Management & Entrepreneurship Research*, *6*(3), 863–877.

Orel, M. (2023). Wanderlust workforce: A journey into understanding digital nomadism. *World Leisure Journal*, *65*(2), 143–149.

Organisation for Economic Co-operation and Development (OECD). (2019). *OECD Principles on Artificial Intelligence*. https://www.oecd.org/going-digital/ai/principles/

Organisation for Economic Co-operation and Development (OECD). (2023). *Artificial intelligence in education: Global policy perspectives*. OECD Publishing. https://www.oecd.org/

Orlova, E. V. (2021). Design of personal trajectories for employees' professional development in the knowledge society under Industry 5.0. Social Sciences. Retrieved from mdpi.com

Örtenblad, A. (2018). What does "learning organization" mean? *The Learning Organization*, *25*(3), 150–158. DOI: 10.1108/TLO-02-2018-0016

Owoyemi, A., Okpara, E., Salwei, M., & Boyd, A. (2024). End user experience of a widely used artificial intelligence based sepsis system. *JAMIA Open*, *7*(4), ooae096. PMID: 39386065

Oyekunle, D., & Boohene, D. (2024). Digital Transformation Potential: The Role of Artificial Intelligence in Business. *International Journal of Professional Business Review*, *9*(3), 1.

Pace, L. A., Borch, K., & Deidun, A. (2023). Bridging Knowledge Gaps towards 2030: The Use of Foresight for the Strategic Management of a Sustainable Blue Economy. *Sustainability*, *15*(13), 10026.

Pace, L. A., Saritas, O., & Deidun, A. (2023). Exploring future research and innovation directions for a sustainable blue economy. *Marine Policy*, *148*, 105433.

Pacheco, C., & Azevedo, A. (2023). Mapping the journey of the CoLiving experience of digital nomads, using verbal and visual narratives. *World Leisure Journal*, *65*(2), 192–217.

Pago, L. M. (2024). Artificial intelligence empowerment in leadership: A systematic review of positive impacts and applications. *International Journal of Multidisciplinary Research and Analysis*, *7*, 4118–4125. DOI: 10.47191/ijmra/v7-i08-57

Pallardy, R. (2024). The AI Skills Gap and How to Address It. Information Week. Retrieved from https://www.informationweek.com/it-leadership/the-ai-skills-gap-and-how-to-address-it

Panda, G., Dash, M. K., Samadhiya, A., Kumar, A., & Mulat-weldemeskel, E. (2024). Artificial intelligence as an enabler for achieving human resource resiliency: Past literature, present debate and future research directions. *International Journal of Industrial Engineering and Operations Management*, *6*(4), 326–347.

Pandey, M., Yadav, P. S., & Pothireddy, R. R. (2024). Role of gamification in influencer marketing. In Marketing and Gamification (pp. 157–169). doi:DOI: 10.4324/9781032694238-13

Pandey, M., & Yadav, P. S. (2023). Understanding the role of individual concerns, attitude, and perceived value in green apparel purchase intention; the mediating effect of consumer involvement and moderating role of generation Z&Y. *Cleaner and Responsible Consumption*, *9*(100120), 100120. DOI: 10.1016/j.clrc.2023.100120

Panetta, K. (2019). The CIO's Guide to Artificial Intelligence. *Gartner*. https://www.gartner.com/smarterwithgartner/the-cios-guide-to-artificial-intelligence

Papanikolaou, V., Roussakis, Y., & Tzionas, P. (2023). Knowledge nomads: An educational cultural fusion of the local with the global to promote democratic cooperation. *Globalisation, Societies and Education*, •••, 1–21. DOI: 10.1080/14767724.2023.2166464

Pardo, S. B. (2024). Tech workers could earn up to 35% more by switching to an AI / ML role, data reveals. *The Accountant*. https://www.theaccountant-online.com/news/tech-workers-could-earn-up-to-35-more-by-switching-to-an-ai-ml-role-data-reveals/?cf-view

Partners, M. B. O. (2022). Digital nomad report. MBO Partners. Retrieved from https://www.mbopartners.com

Perikangas, S., Kostilainen, H., & Paananen, R. (2022). *A human-centric co-creation platform for solving wicked social challenges*. Social Innovation.

Phelps, K. C. (2014). "So much technology, so little talent"? Skills for harnessing technology for leadership outcomes. *Journal of Leadership Studies*, *8*(2), 51–56. DOI: 10.1002/jls.21331

Pinski, M., Haas, M. J., & Benlian, A. (2024). Building metaknowledge in ai literacy–the effect of gamified vs. text-based learning on ai literacy metaknowledge.

PiSit. N. (2024). Remote Work and Its Implications on Personal Financial Planning Beyond Covid-19. *Available at* SSRN *4845642*.

Popo-Olaniyan, O., James, O. O., & Udeh, C. A. (2022). Review of advancing US innovation through collaborative HR ecosystems: A sector-wide perspective. International Journal of... Retrieved from fepbl.com

Pourak, K. (2024). Navigating AI Integration In Manufacturing: Challenges, Benefits And Strategies. Forbes. Retrieved from https://www.forbes.com/councils/forbestechcouncil/2024/05/31/navigating-ai-integration-in-manufacturing-challenges-benefits-and-strategies/

Qamar, Y., Agrawal, R. K., Samad, T. A., & Jabbour, C. J. C. (2021). When technology meets people: The interplay of artificial intelligence and human resource management. *Journal of Enterprise Information Management*, *34*(5), 1339–1370.

Quaquebeke, N. V., & Gerpott, F. H. (2023). The now, new, and next of digital leadership: How artificial intelligence (AI) will take over and change leadership as we know it. *Journal of Leadership & Organizational Studies*, *30*(3), 265–275. DOI: 10.1177/15480518231181731

Rai, A., Constantinides, P., & Sarker, S. (2019). Next Generation Digital Platforms: Toward Human-AI Hybrids. *Management Information Systems Quarterly*, *43*(1), iii–ix.

Rame, R., Purwanto, P., & Sudarno, S. (2024). Industry 5.0 and sustainability: An overview of emerging trends and challenges for a green future. Innovation and Green Development. Retrieved from sciencedirect.com

Ramírez-Gordillo, T., Mora, H., & Pujol-Lopez, F. A. (2023). *Industry 5.0: Towards human-centered design in human-machine interaction. International Research*. Springer.

Ransbotham, S., Kiron, D., Khodabandeh, S., Chu, M., & Zhukhov, L. (2024). *Learning to Manage Uncertainty, With AI*. MIT Sloan Management Review and Boston Consulting Group.

Reichenberger, I. (2018). Digital nomads–a quest for holistic freedom in work and leisure. Annals of Leisure Research, 21(3), 364-380.Schor, J. B. (2020). After the Gig: How the Sharing Economy Got Hijacked and How to Win It Back. University of California Press.

Robinson, L., & Reisdorf, B. (2024). The double digital divide: Technology, marginalized populations, and inclusive education. *Digital Inclusion Studies Quarterly*, *3*(1), 1–19.

Robinson, L., & Reisdorf, B. C. (2024). Digital equity in education: Navigating remote learning and access in post-pandemic institutions. *Educational Policy Futures*, *14*(1), 48–64.

Robinson, L., & Reisdorf, B. C. (2024). Digital inclusion and equity: Lessons from post-pandemic education. *Journal of Digital Equity and Leadership*, *3*(1), 45–67.

Robinson, L., & Reisdorf, B. C. (2024). Prejudice, impression management, and digital communications: Leadership challenges in marginalized remote communities. *Journal of Communication and Social Change*, *12*(1), 29–46.

Robinson, L., & Reisdorf, B. C. (2024). Remote education and inclusion: Impacts of digital access and autonomy. *Education and Information Technologies*, *29*(2), 189–204.

Rogers, E. M. (2003). *Diffusion of innovations* (5th ed.). Free Press.

Rosen, J., & Alvarez León, L. F. (2024). Signaling hinterlands and the spatial networks of digital capitalism. *Annals of the Association of American Geographers*, *114*(8), 1841–1853.

Roshanaei, M., Olivares, H., & Lopez, R. R. (2023). Harnessing AI to foster equity in education: Opportunities, challenges, and emerging strategies. *Journal of Intelligent Learning Systems and Applications*, *15*(4), 123–143. DOI: 10.4236/jilsa.2023.154009

Rožman, M., & Tominc, P. (2024). Navigating Gender Nuances: Assessing the Impact of AI on Employee Engagement in Slovenian Entrepreneurship. *Systems*, *12*(5), 145.

Sahoo, S. K., & Goswami, S. S. (2023). A comprehensive review of multiple criteria decision-making (MCDM) methods: Advancements, applications, and future directions. Decision Making Advances. Retrieved from dma-journal.org

Saikia, B. (2023). Industry 5.0–Its role toward human society: Obstacles, opportunities, and providing human-centered solutions. In Sustainable Businesses in Emerging Economies: The... Retrieved from [HTML]

Sajjad, A., Ahmad, W., Hussain, S., & Mehmood, R. M. (2021). Development of innovative operational flexibility measurement model for smart systems in Industry 4.0 paradigm. IEEE Access. Retrieved from ieee.org

Salesforce. (2024). *85% of IT leaders see AI boosting productivity, but data integration and overwhelmed teams hinder success.* https://www.salesforce.com/news/stories/connectivity-report-announcement-2024/#:~:text=Adding%20to%20these%20concerns%2C%2098,overly%20dependent%20on%20one%20another

Sánchez-Franco, M. J., & Rey-Tienda, S. (2024). The role of user-generated content in tourism decision-making: An exemplary study of Andalusia, Spain. Management Decision. Retrieved from emerald.com

Sánchez-Vergara, J. I., Orel, M., & Capdevila, I. (2023). "Home office is the here and now." Digital nomad visa systems and remote work-focused leisure policies. *World Leisure Journal, 65*(2), 236–255.

Sarkar, B. D., Shardeo, V., Dwivedi, A., & Pamucar, D. (2024). Digital transition from Industry 4.0 to Industry 5.0 in smart manufacturing: A framework for a sustainable future. *Technology in Society.*

Satya, R., & Mohammed, L. A. (2024). Interdisciplinary insights: The convergence of AI and educational leadership. *International Journal of Research and Innovation in Social Science, 8*(4), 1872–1887. DOI: 10.47772/ijriss.2024.804131

Schatten, J., & Aires, T. (2025). *AI Will Take Your Job, and It's for the Best.* Emerald Publishing.

Segal, M. (2021). Amazon Commits $1.2 Billion to Provide Access to Education and Skills Training for Workforce. ESG Today. Retrieved from https://www.esgtoday.com/amazon-commits-1-2-billion-to-provide-access-to-education-and-skills-training-for-workforce/

Seidl, M. (2022). Corporate digital responsibility: Stimulating human-centric innovation and building trust in the digital world. In *Liquid Legal–Humanization and the Law*. Retrieved from. [HTML]

Senge, P. (1990). The Leader's New Work: Building Learning Organizations. Sloan Management Review reprint series; reprint 3211.

Serrat, O. (2017). *Knowledge solutions: Tools, methods, and approaches to drive organizational performance.* Springer Nature.

Shaer, S., O'Neil, A., Salem, F., Akrout, Z., & Shibl, E. (2023). Advancing Artificial Intelligence Impact in Dubai: Future Directors Towards Strengthening the Digital Economy. *Future of Government Series.*

Shaer, I., & Shami, A. (2023). Data-driven methods for the reduction of energy consumption in warehouses: Use-case driven analysis. *Internet of Things : Engineering Cyber Physical Human Systems.*

Sharma, R. (2025). *Why transparency is key to unlocking AI's full potential.* World Economic Forum. https://www.weforum.org/stories/2025/01/why-transparency-key-to-unlocking-ai-full-potential/

Shawkat, S., Rozan, M. Z. A., Salim, N. B., & Shehzad, H. M. F. (2021). Digital nomads: A systematic literature review. *IEEE*, 1–6. https://doi.org/DOI: 10.1109/icriis53035.2021.9617008

Shehzad, N., Ramtiyal, B., & Jabeen, F. (2024). *Metaverse adoption as a cornerstone for sustainable healthcare firms in the industry 5.0 epoch. Journal of Enterprise.* Retrieved from. [HTML]

Shuja, J., Ahmad, R. W., Gani, A., Ahmed, A. I. A., Siddiqa, A., Nisar, K., Khan, S. U., & Zomaya, A. Y. (2017). Greening emerging IT technologies: Techniques and practices. *Journal of Internet Services and Applications*, *8*, 9. Advance online publication. DOI: 10.1186/s13174-017-0059-2

Shuja, J., Alam, M. M., & Khan, F. H. (2017). Greening emerging IT technologies, techniques, and practices: A survey. *Journal of Internet Services and Applications*, *8*(1), 1–11.

Singh, S. (2023). Leadership challenges and strategies in the era of AI transformation. In *2023 International Conference on Computational Science and Computational Intelligence (CSCI)*, 119–124. https://ieeexplore.ieee.org/abstract/document/10590476/

Singh, J., Kumar, A., & Singh, S. (2025). Digital platforms for sustainable waste management in a circular economy: A review. *Environmental Science and Pollution Research International*, *32*(1), 1–17. PMID: 39663305

Singh, M., Michael, R. A., Saheb, S. S., Yadav, P. S., Kiran, P. B. N., & Malhi, A. (2025). A study on digital intelligence and influencer marketing for sustainable diversification of India's retail economy. In *Advances in Logistics* (pp. 1–22). Operations, and Management Science., DOI: 10.4018/979-8-3693-8492-3.ch001

Singh, M., Syed, S. M., Saheb, S. S., Yadav, P. S., & Kiran, P. B. N. (2025). Role of influencer marketing in the Indian retail business sector. In *Advances in Marketing* (pp. 105–130). Customer Relationship Management, and E-Services., DOI: 10.4018/979-8-3693-8542-5.ch005

Skills Report, A. I. (2024). Pluralsight. Retrieved from https://www.pluralsight.com/resource-center/ai-skills-report-2024

Sood, D., & Juneja, M. (2024). Bleisure Travel: The Rise of Flexible Work and Its Impact on Tourism. In *Bleisure Tourism and the Impact of Technology* (pp. 22-45). IGI Global.

Spalding, M. J. (2016). The new blue economy: The future of sustainability. *Journal of Ocean and Coastal Economics, 2*(2). *Article, 8*, 1–21.

Sposato, M. (2024). *AI leadership for education 4.0: Strategic perspectives*. Springer.

Sposato, M. (2024). Leadership training and development in the age of artificial intelligence. *Development and Learning in Organizations, 38*(4), 4–7. DOI: 10.1108/dlo-12-2023-0256

Staff, A. (2024). 9 free skills training programs for Amazon employees. Amazon. Retrieved from https://www.aboutamazon.com/news/workplace/our-upskilling-2025-programs

Stiepan, D. (2022). Using AI in radiology clinical practice. Mayo Clinic. Retrieved from https://newsnetwork.mayoclinic.org/discussion/using-ai-in-radiology-clinical-practice/

Stokes, E. (2024). NTT DATA introduces Generative AI Talent Development Framework for global workforce — EdTech Innovation Hub. EdTech Innovation Hub. Retrieved from https://www.edtechinnovationhub.com/news/ntt-data-gen-ai-talent-development-framework

Strich, F., Mayer, A. S., & Fiedler, M. (2021). What do I do in a world of artificial intelligence? Investigating the impact of substitutive decision-making AI systems on employees' professional role identity. *Journal of the Association for Information Systems, 22*(2), 9.

Stryker, C. (2024). Artificial Intelligence Implementation: 8 Steps for Success. IBM. Retrieved from https://www.ibm.com/think/insights/artificial-intelligence-implementation

Suciu, M. C., Plesea, D. A., Petre, A., Simion, A., & Mituca, M. O. (2023). Core competence-as a key factor for a sustainable, innovative, and resilient development model based on Industry 5.0. Sustainability. Retrieved from mdpi.com

Suntharalingam, H. (2024). Enhancing digital learning outcomes through the application of artificial intelligence: A comprehensive review. *International Journal of Innovative Science and Research Technology, 9*(4), 718–727. DOI: 10.38124/ijisrt/ijisrt24apr530

Susskind, R. (2020). *The Future of the Professions: How Technology Will Transform the Work of Human Experts*. Oxford University Press.

Syracuse, V., & Blanco, I. (2020). Bio-polypropylene (Bio-PP) and Bio-poly (ethylene terephthalate) (Bio-PET): Recent developments in bio-based polymers analogous to petroleum-derived ones. Polymers. Retrieved from mdpi.com

Taha, S., Abulibdeh, E., Qunais, J., Skaik, H., Alghazo, E. M., Daoud, S., & Bouzenoun, A. (2023). Exploring the utilization of augmented reality in higher education: Perceptions of media and communication students. *Emerging Science Journal*, *7*, 204–216. DOI: 10.28991/esj-2023-sied2-016

Tapscott, D., & Tapscott, A. (2016). *Blockchain Revolution: How the Technology Behind Bitcoin Is Changing Money, Business, and the World*. Portfolio Penguin.

Tariq, M. U. (2024). Generative AI in Curriculum Development in Higher Education. In Fields, Z. (Ed.), *Impacts of Generative AI on Creativity in Higher Education* (pp. 227–258). IGI Global., DOI: 10.4018/979-8-3693-2418-9.ch009

Tariq, M. U. (2024). Smart Transportation Systems: Paving the Way for Sustainable Urban Mobility. In Munuhwa, S. (Ed.), *Contemporary Solutions for Sustainable Transportation Practices* (pp. 254–283). IGI Global., DOI: 10.4018/979-8-3693-3755-4.ch010

Tariq, M. U. (2025). *AI-Driven Learning and Engagement in Higher Education*. IGI Global., DOI: 10.4018/979-8-3693-4074-5

Tariq, M. U. (2025). Navigating Bias and Fairness in Digital AI Systems. In Bhattacharya, P., Hassan, A., Liu, H., & Bhushan, B. (Eds.), *Ethical Dimensions of AI Development* (pp. 127–156). IGI Global., DOI: 10.4018/979-8-3693-4147-6.ch006

Tariq, M. U., & Sergio, R. P. (2025). Ethical Considerations and Social Impact of AI and Computational Intelligence in Society 5.0. In Pandey, R., Srivastava, N., Prasad, R., Prasad, J., & Garcia, M. (Eds.), *Open AI and Computational Intelligence for Society 5.0* (pp. 225–248). IGI Global Scientific Publishing., DOI: 10.4018/979-8-3693-4326-5.ch010

Tarisayi, K. S. (2024). Strategic leadership for responsible artificial intelligence adoption in Higher Education. *CTE Workshop Proceedings, 4–14*. https://acnsci.org/journal/index.php/cte/article/view/616

Tello, J., & Subramanian, L. (2022). The magic behind turning data into profit. Deloitte Development LLC. Retrieved from https://www2.deloitte.com/content/dam/Deloitte/us/Documents/deloitte-analytics/us-ai-institute-challenges-of-using-artificial-intelligence-final.pdf

Topol, E. (2019). *Deep Medicine: How Artificial Intelligence Can Make Healthcare Human Again.* Basic Books.

Tremblay, R. (2024). What is Learning Analytics & How It's Used in L&D. Docebo. Retrieved from https://www.docebo.com/learning-network/blog/learning-analytics/

Tursunbayeva, A., & Chalutz-Ben Gal, H. (2024). Adoption of artificial intelligence: A TOP framework-based checklist for digital leaders. *Business Horizons.* Advance online publication. DOI: 10.1016/j.bushor.2024.04.006

Tursunbayeva, A., Pagliari, C., Di Lauro, S., & Antonelli, G. (2021). The ethics of people analytics: Risks, opportunities and recommendations. *Personnel Review, 51*(3), 900–921.

UAE Ministry of Education. (2023). *AI implementation in education: Progress report.* https://www.moe.gov.ae

Udayanan, Rooshma, A., Bargavi, D. N., Awasthi, D. S., Deshmukh, D. S. V., & Jadhav, D. D. Y. (2024). Determinants Influencing the Adoption of Artificial Intelligence in Driving Effective Human Resource Management. *Journal of Informatics Education and Research, 4*(2).

UNESCO. (2022). *AI and the futures of learning: Ensuring inclusion and equity.* UNESCO. https://unesdoc.unesco.org

UNESCO. (2022). *Recommendation on the Ethics of Artificial Intelligence.* https://unesdoc.unesco.org

Uren, V., & Edwards, J. S. (2023). Technology readiness and the organizational journey towards AI adoption: An empirical study. *International Journal of Information Management, 68*, 102588.

Vajda, D. L., Do, T. V., Bérczes, T., & Farkas, K. (2024). Machine learning-based real-time anomaly detection using data pre-processing in the telemetry of server farms. Scientific Reports. Retrieved from nature.com

Vajda, D. L., Do, T. V., Bérczes, T., & Farkas, K. (2024). *Machine learning-based real-time anomaly detection using data pre-processing in the telemetry of server farms.* Scientific Reports, Nature.

Van Hoof, L. (2019). *Blue growth: opportunities and challenges for the EU.* European Parliament.

Van Hoof, L., Fabib, G., Johansen, V., Steenbergen, J., Irigoien, X., Smith, S., Lisbjergg, D., & Kraush, G. (2019). Food from the ocean; towards a research agenda for sustainable use of our oceans' natural resources. [REMOVED BIBLIOGRAPHY FIELD]. *Marine Policy*, *105*, 44–51.

Vargas, J. (2022). What employers want: The battle between skills and degrees. The EvoLLLution. Retrieved from https://evolllution.com/programming/credentials/what-employers-want-the-battle-between-skills-and-degrees

Vashishth, T. K., Sharma, V., Sharma, K. K., Kumar, B., Chaudhary, S., & Panwar, R. (2024). Security and Privacy Challenges in Blockchain-Based Supply Chain Management: A Comprehensive Analysis. In Khan, M., Khan, N., & Ghouri, A. (Eds.), *Achieving Secure and Transparent Supply Chains With Blockchain Technology* (pp. 70–91). IGI Global Scientific Publishing., DOI: 10.4018/979-8-3693-0482-2.ch005

Venkatesh, N., Morris, N., Davis, N., & Davis, N. (2003). User acceptance of information Technology: Toward a unified view. *Management Information Systems Quarterly*, *27*(3), 425. DOI: 10.2307/30036540

Venkatesh, V., & Davis, F. D. (2000). A theoretical extension of the technology acceptance model: Four longitudinal field studies. *Management Science*, *46*(2), 186–204. DOI: 10.1287/mnsc.46.2.186.11926

Vogl, T., & Micek, G. (2023). Work-leisure concepts and tourism: Studying the relationship between hybrid coworking spaces and the accommodation industry in peripheral areas of Germany. *World Leisure Journal*, *65*(2), 276–298.

Vo, T. T. E., Ko, H., Huh, J.-H., & Kim, Y. (2021). Overview of smart aquaculture system: Focusing on applications of machine learning and computer vision. *Electronics (Basel)*, *10*(22), 2882. DOI: 10.3390/electronics10222882

Wallerstein, I. (2004). *World-Systems Analysis: An Introduction*. Duke University Press.

WAM. (2024, January 12). Hamdan bin Mohammed launches initiative to expand teacher AI training. *Emirates News Agency*. https://www.wam.ae/en/article/b3mmuob-hamdan-bin-mohammed-launches-initiative-expand

WAM. (2024, January 17). Minister of Education highlights AI's role in revolutionising education at Davos 2024. Retrieved from https://www.wam.ae/en/article/13pwt81-minister-education-highlights-ai%E2%80%99s-role

Wang, Y. (2021). Data privacy challenges in AI-based education systems. *Journal of Information Privacy and Security*.

Wang, Z. J., Chen, Z. S., Xiao, L., Su, Q., & Govindan, K. (2023). Blockchain adoption in sustainable supply chains for Industry 5.0: A multi-stakeholder perspective. Journal of Innovation &. Retrieved from sciencedirect.com

Wang, J. (2021). Nomadic work and the isolation paradox: A cultural critique. *Cultural Studies in Work, 19*(3), 45–59.

Wang, Q. (2023). The Impact of AI on Organizational Employees: A Literature Review. *Journal of Education. Humanities and Social Sciences*, *19*, 45–53.

Wang, Y. (2021). Artificial intelligence in educational leadership: A symbiotic role of human-artificial intelligence decision-making. *Journal of Educational Administration*, *59*(3), 256–270. DOI: 10.1108/JEA-10-2020-0216

Wang, Y. (2021). When artificial intelligence meets educational leaders' data-informed decision-making: A cautionary tale. *Studies in Educational Evaluation*, *69*, 100872. DOI: 10.1016/j.stueduc.2020.100872

We Built this Citi on Learning & Skills (n.d.). https://explore.degreed.com/wp-content/uploads/2024/01/Citi-Degreed-Success-Story-1.pdf

WEF. (2025). *Future of Jobs Report 2025*. World Economic Forum. https://reports.weforum.org/docs/WEF_Future_of_Jobs_Report_2025.pdf

WEF. (2025). *Future of Jobs Report 2025*. World Economic Forum. https://www.weforum.org

WEF. (2025). *Schools of the future: Defining new models of education for the Fourth Industrial Revolution*. World Economic Forum. https://www.weforum.org

Welding, L. (2024). The Rise and Future of Microcredentials in Higher Education. BestColleges.com. Retrieved from https://www.bestcolleges.com/research/microcredentials-rise-in-higher-education/#fn-4

West, S. M., Whittaker, M., & Crawford, K. (2019). *Discriminating systems: Gender, race, and power in AI.* AI Now Institute. https://ainowinstitute.org/discriminatingsystems.html

Whig, P. S., Ahmad, S., & Mishra, S. (2024). The Legal Implications of Data Privacy Laws, Cybersecurity Regulations, and AI Ethics in a Digital Society.

Whig, P., Sharma, P., Aneja, N., Elngar, A. A., & Silva, N. (Eds.). (2024). *Artificial Intelligence and Machine Learning for Sustainable Development: Innovations, Challenges, and Applications* (1st ed.). CRC Press., DOI: 10.1201/9781003497189

Wijayati, D. T., Rahman, Z., Fahrullah, A., Rahman, M. F. W., Arifah, I. D. C., & Kautsar, A. (2022). A study of artificial intelligence on employee performance and work engagement: The moderating role of change leadership. *International Journal of Manpower*, *43*(2), 486–512.

Wiley. (2023). How MBA programs are changing with the market. AACSB. Retrieved from https://www.aacsb.edu/insights/articles/2023/03/how-mba-programs-are-changing-with-the-market

Wilkinson, L. (2024). Legacy tech upgrades cost the average business nearly $3M last year. *CIO Dive*. https://www.ciodive.com/news/legacy-technology-technical-debt-costs-enterprise-data-AI/721885/#:~:text=Dive%20Brief:%20*%20Legacy%20tech%20upgrades%20cost,systems%2C%20according%20to%20the%20report%20published%20Thursday

Winstead, A. (2023). Fostering a Culture of Continuous Learning in the Workplace. Intellum. Retrieved from https://www.intellum.com/resources/blog/continuous-learning-in-the-workplace

Wirtz, B. W., Weyerer, J. C., & Sturm, B. J. (2020). The dark sides of artificial intelligence: An integrated AI governance framework for public administration. *International Journal of Public Administration*, *43*(9), 818–829.

World Economic Forum. (2025). *Schools of the Future: Defining New Models of Education for the Fourth Industrial Revolution*. https://www.weforum.org/

Xiao, J., Shen, Y., Wang, Y., Yuan, W., Zhang, Y., & Wu, S. (2023). Large discrepancies in quantifying mountain vegetation growth dynamics using multiple remote sensing indices. *Ecological Indicators*, *154*, 110697.

Xiao, Y., Wu, S., Liu, Z. Q., & Lin, H. J. (2023). Digital economy and green development: Empirical evidence from China's cities. *Frontiers in Environmental Science*, *11*. Advance online publication. DOI: 10.3389/fenvs.2023.1124680

Xu, X., Lu, Y., Vogel-Heuser, B., & Wang, L. (2021). *Industry 4.0 and Industry 5.0-Inception, conception and perception. Journal of Manufacturing Systems*. ScienceDirect.

Xu, Y., Huang, Y., Wang, J., & Zhou, D. (2024). How do employees form initial trust in artificial intelligence: Hard to explain but leaders help. *Asia Pacific Journal of Human Resources*, *62*(3), e12402.

Yadav, P. S., Kiran, P. B. N., Vemula, R., Kumari, P., Wazir, R., & Sharma, A. (2025). A deep understanding of virtual reality's role in human resource management, with a specific focus on recruitment. In The Future of HRM in a World of Persistent Virtual Reality (pp. 87–107). doi:DOI: 10.1108/978-1-83662-110-220251004

Yadav, M., & Dahiya, S. (2025). Can green finance and innovations promote environmental sustainability: Empirical evidence from India. *Social Responsibility Journal*, *21*(1), 167–184.

Yadav, P. S., & Pandey, M. (2021). Influencer Marketing: Social-media-Influencer On Shopper stress Deviation and Purchase Intention. *Turkish Online Journal of Qualitative Inquiry*, *12*(8), 6926–6947.

Yang, J., Liu, Y., & Morgan, P. L. (2024). Human-machine interaction towards Industry 5.0: Human-centric smart manufacturing. Digital Engineering. Retrieved from sciencedirect.com

Yang, H., He, S., Feng, Q., Xia, S., Zhou, Q., Wu, Z., & Zhang, Y. (2024). Navigating the depths of seafood authentication: Technologies, regulations, and future prospects. *Measurement Food*, *14*, 100165. DOI: 10.1016/j.meafoo.2024.100165

YEC. (2023). 10 Hurdles Companies Are Facing When Implementing AI (And How To Overcome Them). Forbes. Retrieved from https://www.forbes.com/councils/theyec/2023/10/25/10-hurdles-companies-are-facing-when-implementing-ai-and-how-to-overcome-them/

Yi, M., Liu, Y. F., Sheng, M. S., & Wen, L. (2022). Effects of digital economy on carbon emission reduction: New evidence from China. *Energy Policy*, *171*, 113271. DOI: 10.1016/j.enpol.2022.113271

Ystgaard, K. F., & De Moor, K. (2023). Envisioning the future: A multi-disciplinary approach to human-centered intelligent environments. *Quality and User Experience*.

Yue, S., & Berrios, D. (2024). Introducing WMDP: Measuring and Mitigating Catastrophic Risk Potential from LLMs. Scale. Retrieved from https://scale.com/blog/measuring-mitigating-risk-wmdp

Yu, K., Zhang, J., & Hannam, K. (2024). Welcome to 'Dalifornia': Chinese digital nomads as mobile entrepreneurs. *Current Issues in Tourism*, •••, 1–15.

Yusriadi, Y., Rusnaedi, R., Siregar, N., Megawati, S., & Sakkir, G. (2023). Implementation of artificial intelligence in Indonesia. *International Journal of Data and Network Science*, *7*(1), 283–294.

Zhang, X., Antwi-Afari, M. F., Zhang, Y., & Xing, X. (2024). The Impact of Artificial Intelligence on Organizational Justice and Project Performance: A Systematic Literature and Science Mapping Review. *Buildings (Basel, Switzerland)*, *14*(1), 259.

Zhang, Y., Fang, Y., Wei, K. K., & Chen, H. (2010). Exploring the role of psychological safety in promoting the intention to continue sharing knowledge in virtual communities. *International Journal of Information Management*, *30*(5), 425–436.

Zhou, Z., Li, L., & Huang, X. (2021). Personalized learning with Squirrel AI: Opportunities and challenges. *Chinese Journal of Education Technology*.

Zirar, A., Ali, S. I., & Islam, N. (2023). Worker and workplace Artificial Intelligence (AI) coexistence: Emerging themes and research agenda. *Technovation*, *124*, 102747.

Zizic, M. C., Mladineo, M., Gjeldum, N., & Celent, L. (2022). *From Industry 4.0 towards Industry 5.0: A review and analysis of paradigm shift for the people, organization, and technology*. Energies. MDPI.

Zong, L., Memon, F. H., Li, X., & Wang, H. (2021). End-to-end transmission control for cross-regional industrial Internet of Things in Industry 5.0. *IEEE Transactions on Industrial Informatics*.

Zuboff, S. (2019). *The Age of Surveillance Capitalism: The Fight for a Human Future at the New Frontier of Power*. PublicAffairs.

About the Contributors

Patricia Ordóñez de Pablos is a professor in the Department of Business Administration in the Faculty of Business and Economics at The University of Oviedo, Spain. She completed her education in The London School of Economics, UK. Her teaching and research interests focus on the areas of strategic management, knowledge management, organizational learning, intellectual capital and information technologies, with special interest in Asia (Bhutan, China, Laos, Myanmar). She is Editor-in-Chief of the International Journal of Learning and Intellectual Capital (IJLIC) and International Journal of Asian Business and Information Management (IJABIM), respectively. She has edited books for IGI Global, Elsevier, Routledge, and Springer. In 2021, 2022 and 2023, she earned placement on Stanford University's "Ranking of the World Scientists: World's Top 2% Scientists" list. Additionally she is listed in World Top Scientists of Research.com in the Areas of Social Science and Humanities in Spain and Engineering and Technology in Spain.

Xi Zhang is the professor and department head of Information Management and Management Science, College of Management and Economics, Tianjin University, China. His research interests are knowledge management systems, digital transformation, and people analytics. He has published several papers in international journals such as Journal of Knowledge Management, Journal of MIS, CHB, IEEE TEM, IEEE TKDE, etc. He also served as editorial board of IJABIM, IJSWIS, JMSE and JSTPM.

Muhammad Anshari has been named on the Stanford University List of Top 2% World Researchers in 2022 for the categories of ICT, Business & Management. He has published many peer reviewed journal papers, book chapters, and edited books. He is a Senior Assistant Professor at the Universiti Brunei Darussalam School of Business and Economics (UBDSBE) and currently serves as Deputy Director for the Institute of Policy Studies. His professional experience started when he was IT Business Analyst at Astra International. After completion of his PhD, he worked as research fellow at National Taiwan University. Before that he pursued research fellowship at King Saud University - the Kingdom of Saudi Arabia 2009. His research interests are Business Information Systems, E-government, Health Information Systems, Digital Business and Social Computing.

Mohammad Nabil Almunawar is currently a full professor at the School of Business and Economics, Universiti of Brunei Darussalam (UBDSBE), Brunei Darussalam. He was the former dean of UBDSBE. He received his bachelor's degree in 1983 from Bogor Agricultural University, Indonesia, master's degree (MSc) from the Department of Computer Science, University of Western Ontario, London, Canada in 1991, and PhD in Computer Science/Information Systems from the University of New South Wales in 1998. Dr. Almunawar has published more than 250 papers in referred journals, books, book chapters, and encyclopedias. He has more than 30 years of teaching experience in the area of information systems and e-business/e-commerce. His overall research interests include applications of IT in management, e-business/commerce, digital marketplace/platform, digital business ecosystem, health informatics, information security, and cloud computing. Currently, he focuses his research on digital transformation, digital marketplace platforms, and digital business ecosystems.

***

Syed Mudasser Abbas is working as a full-time faculty member at Institute of Business Studies, Kohat University of Science and Technology, Kohat Pakistan. His research interests include AI adoption, HRM and innovation management

Aggala Chiranjeevi is a distinguished academician and industry expert with over 14 years of rich experience across academia and industry. Currently serving as the Dean of Placements at Ramachandra College of Engineering (Autonomous), he plays a pivotal role in bridging the gap between education and employment through strategic placement initiatives and robust industry collaborations. With a Doctorate in Computer Science Engineering from Shri Jagdish Prasad Jhabarmal Tibrewala University, Rajasthan, Dr. Chiranjeevi has made significant contributions to student career readiness and institutional growth. He is a member of MIIET (Membership No: IIET-M-CSE-062023-53) and a lifetime member of the Andhra Pradesh Training and Placement Officers (AP TPOs) Association. His exceptional efforts in placement facilitation have been recognized by Atos Global in 2022 and BlackBucks in 2023. Further, he was honored with the Bharat Education Excellence Award by Andhra University in April 2024 for his exemplary contributions to the research and education sectors.

Teresa Aires is an Organizational Psychologist and PhD candidate in Management at Nova School of Business and Economics. Her research focuses on Artificial Intelligence, negotiations, and well-being. Teresa's recent work examines appraisal processes in AI use within organizations. She has collaborated with companies to restructure business processes and improve employee well-being. Teresa aims to leverage AI to develop data-driven strategies for optimizing organizational dynamics in the evolving work landscape.

Sumayya Robbin Andi is a distinguished educator, strategist, and leader with over 20 years of experience in educational reform, strategic advising, and capacity building. Currently pursuing a PhD in Educational Leadership and Policy Studies at UAEU, Sumayya also holds a Master's degree in Educational Leadership from Zayed University and a Bachelor's degree in Applied Mathematics. Her career is marked by pioneering achievements in education, organizational transformation, and stakeholder collaboration. Sumayya's contributions span a diverse range of roles, including serving as an Advisor to the Chairperson at ADEK and DGE, CEO of Al Mariah United Group, and leadership positions in both public and private sectors. She has spearheaded initiatives such as Abu Dhabi's first gifted education center, the Future Scientist Program, and high-impact partnerships with organizations like Mubadala and the Crown Prince Court. Her expertise in aligning STEAM education with the UAE's innovation goals has led to transformative projects and lifelong learning frameworks. Her international experience includes leading educational quality assurance efforts with the Tribal Group in Riyadh and directing Sharjah's SPEA school reviews. Sumayya is a seasoned advocate of high-performance learning methodologies and the integration of technology in education, working extensively to align local education systems with global standards. In addition to her professional accomplishments, Sumayya is dedicated to fostering leadership, innovation, and ethical governance. She has actively contributed to the development of vocational education pathways, strategic school revamps, and early childhood initiatives. A passionate mentor, Sumayya continues to inspire future educators and leaders while shaping policies to advance educational excellence and societal impact.

Hosam Badawy holds a Ph.D. candidacy in Leadership and Policy Studies in Education from the United Arab Emirates University (UAEU) and a Master's in Educational Leadership. He is also TESOL and TEFL certified. In his current role at Al Soqoor Cycle 2 School, he has successfully led educational transformations, integrating modern technology and state-of-the-art teaching strategies to foster a dynamic learning environment. His professional achievements include publishing research on innovation in educational leadership, STEM, and inclusive education, and presenting at national and international conferences. Hosam has been recognized for his contributions to education, particularly for his work with students of determination and gifted students. His leadership skills are further exemplified by his role in delivering professional development sessions and his involvement with the school leadership team in developing and implementing STEM education. Hosam's dedication to education is driven by his belief in the transformational approach, achieved through collaboration and the integration of modern technologies. His career objective is to continue developing as an innovative leader, supporting and inspiring students and educators to reach their full potential.

Tiago Jordão Cardoso is a Specialized Technical Officer at the General Secretariat of the Environment in Portugal, where he focuses on the integration of artificial intelligence and chatbots within public administration. Currently completing a master's in public administration, his research centers on technological acceptance, particularly in the public sector's use of AI to enhance sustainability and resilience. With strong involvement in climate change initiatives, Tiago explores the intersection of AI-driven innovation and sustainable practices, co-authoring articles on these topics and preparing additional proposals on AI's role in environmental resilience.

Muhammad Irshad is working as an Assistant Professor at Department of Management Science, University of Chitral, Pakistan. He holds a PhD in Human Resource Management. His research interest HRM, knowledge management and talent management.

Vikas Kumar is an Assistant Professor at the Mittal School of Business, Lovely Professional University (LPU), Jalandhar. He holds a Ph.D. in Management from Kurukshetra University and is UGC-NET qualified in both Commerce and Management. His research interests include Behavioral Economics, International Business, Digital Marketing, and the application of Artificial Intelligence in market analysis. Dr. Kumar's work examines the psychological aspects of market behavior and consumer decision-making, with a particular focus on integrating AI technologies to address real-world business challenges.

M. Ruben Anto, a seasoned academician, holds a Ph.D. in Commerce and International Business, specializing in the impact of GDP and international trade on pollution. He had done his Master's in Business Administration specializing in Marketing. With over a decade of teaching experience, he currently serves as an Program Coordinator & Assistant Professor at School of Business and Management, CHRIST University. Dr. Anto's expertise spans subjects like Marketing, Export Import, Services Marketing, and Global Maritime Business. His research contributions include over 22 publications, covering diverse topics from environmental studies to corporate governance. Additionally, he actively mentors' students, organizes conferences, and volunteers as the Youth Red Cross Volunteer. Dr. Anto's dedication to academia and social service underscores his invaluable contributions to education.

Raffi Mohammed, Founder of IIET - The Institute for Innovations in Engineering and Technology and IIETRAFI FOUNDATION, is a renowned Professor of Mechanical Engineering at Ramachandra College of Engineering, Andhra Pradesh. With 77 publications in refereed journals, 8 authored books, four copyrights, and multiple patents, he is an expert in materials science and hybrid composites. Awarded Best Young Researcher (2018), he inspires innovation in engineering education and research.

P. Thirumoorthi, currently working as Professor in Management Studies. Having specialized in Operations and Systems Management. Current research works are related to Technology Management and Supply Chain Economics. He has authored more than 50 journal articles and 5 books. He has also produced 15 Ph.D scholars and 21 M.Phil scholars. He has completed 3 funded projects sponsored by various funding agencies.

Subramanya Sarma S is a Professor of ELECTRICAL AND ELECTRONICS ENGINEERING has been a full-time faculty member since 2008. He is currently holding the position of Dean Academics at RAMACHANDRA COLLEGE OF ENGINEERING (AUTONOMOUS), ELURU and is also a member of the Board of Governance of RCE. He is a unique amalgam of academics and research. He has professional experience of close to two decades. He is pursuing his Post-Doctoral Fellowship at CCU, South Africa. He has published 32 research articles in national and international journals of repute, In relation to his research areas. His research interests include distributed generation, reliability, renewable energy sources, Internet of Things (IoT), artificial intelligence, electric vehicles and optimization techniques.

Jagan Mohan Rao S. is an author of numerous publications alongside holding an Instrumentation Engineering PhD and a degree in Electronics Engineering. He also has over three decades of experience in electronics, automation, and control systems, making him a highly creditable academic. Now, as a senior professor at Ramachandra College of Engineering located in Eluru, Andhra Pradesh, he is an expert on hardware design, IoT, adaptive control systems, as well as agile software development. Dr. Jagan Mohan's research and profundity in the fields parallel his inventive methods, making him a highly regarded mentor for students and working professionals interested in electronics engineering. Innovations in power sector automation have been possible largely due to his senior role. He helped design state of the art automation equipment like the Programmable Logic Controllers (PLCs) and underscored Digital Distributed Control Systems (DCS) to optimize industrial processes. His contribution has enhanced the global performance and credibility of manufacturing and electrical power automation. Apart from his educational and industrial activities, Dr. Jagan Mohan Rao is also a very active researcher and academician, with numerous publications in top-class journals and conferences. His technical papers are very useful reading material for young engineers and professionals alike, covering a vast area of topics from embedded systems to industrial automation. Committed to the development of the science of electronics engineering, Dr. Jagan Mohan continues to be engaged in inspiring and guiding the next generation of engineers with innovation and technological excellence in solutions.

Jeff Schatten is an Associate Professor of Business Administration at Washington and Lee University, specializing in artificial intelligence and organizational behavior. With a Ph.D. in Managerial Sciences from Georgia State University, Jeff has conducted extensive research on the transformative impact of AI on business and society. His interdisciplinary approach, combining philosophy and business, offers unique insights into how AI is reshaping the future of work and organizational dynamics.

Muhammad Usman Tariq has more than 16+ year's experience in industry and academia. He has authored more than 200+ research articles, 110+ case studies, 115+ book chapters and several books other than 4 patents. He is founder and CEO of The Case HQ, a unique repository for courses, narrative and video case studies. He has been working as a consultant and trainer for industries representing six sigma, quality, health and safety, environmental systems, project management, and information security standards. His work has encompassed sectors in aviation, manufacturing, food, hospitality, education, finance, research, software and transportation. He has diverse and significant experience working with accreditation agencies of ABET, ACBSP, AACSB, WASC, CAA, EFQM and NCEAC. Additionally, Dr. Tariq has operational experience in incubators, research labs, government research projects, private sector startups, program creation and management at various industrial and academic levels. He is Certified Higher Education Teacher from Harvard University, USA, Certified Online Educator from HMBSU, Certified Six Sigma Master Black Belt and has been awarded PFHEA, SFSEDA, SMIEEE, and CMBE.

Rajesh Vemula is a distinguished academic with over 14 years of experience in teaching and research in marketing. He completed his Ph.D. in Marketing from GITAM University in 2022, focusing on advanced marketing theories and practices. Dr. Vemula's expertise spans consumer behavior, retail marketing, and digital marketing, which is evident in his innovative teaching methods and substantial research contributions. His career is marked by a commitment to understanding consumer behavior, optimizing retail strategies, and applying digital marketing techniques to enhance business performance. Dr. Rajesh Vemula actively participates in research projects, conferences, and publications, enriching the academic and professional discourse in marketing. His dedication to bridging theory with practice highlights his role as a respected educator and researcher in the field.

Pinnika Syam Yadav is a distinguished researcher and academician, Whose Expertise and dedication have significantly advanced the field of business and Marketing analytics. Withholding a PhD and over two years of teaching experience at Mittal School of Business, Lovely Professional University, He has made notable contributions to Academia with his work. Currently working as an Assistant Professor at Christ University, School of Business and Management, Dr. Yadav, PS. He continues to excel in research and education, demonstrating a profound commitment to his field area by guiding and awarding 2 PhD Scholars under his guidance. His Innovative approach and extensive knowledge have earned him recognition as a leading figure in his field, inspiring young research scholars to follow in his footsteps

Index

A

C

D

E

F

G

H

I

K

L

N

O

R

S

T